WITH THE KAISER'S ARMY IN 1914

A NEUTRAL OBSERVER IN BELGIUM & FRANCE

BY

SVEN HEDIN

AUTHORISED TRANSLATION FROM THE SWEDISH BY
H.G. DE WALTERSTORFF

EDITED AND INTRODUCED BY
BOB CARRUTHERS

Pen & Sword
MILITARY

This edition published in 2014 by

Pen & Sword Military
An imprint of
Pen & Sword Books Ltd
47 Church Street
Barnsley
South Yorkshire
S70 2AS

This book was first published as 'With the German Armies in the West'
by John Lane, London, & John Lane Co., New York,1915.

Copyright © Coda Books Ltd.
Published under licence by Pen & Sword Books Ltd.

ISBN: 9781783463183

A CIP catalogue record for this book is available from the British Library

Printed and bound in England
By CPI Group (UK) Ltd, Croydon, CR0 4YY

Pen & Sword Books Ltd incorporates the imprints of Pen & Sword Aviation, Pen & Sword
Family History, Pen & Sword Maritime, Pen & Sword Military, Pen & Sword Discovery, Pen
& Sword Politics, Pen & Sword Atlas, Pen & Sword Archaeology, Wharncliffe Local History,
Wharncliffe True Crime, Wharncliffe Transport, Pen & Sword Select, Pen & Sword Military
Classics, Leo Cooper, The Praetorian Press, Claymore Press, Remember When, Seaforth
Publishing and Frontline Publishing

For a complete list of Pen & Sword titles please contact

PEN & SWORD BOOKS LIMITED
47 Church Street, Barnsley, South Yorkshire, S70 2AS, England
E-mail: enquiries@pen-and-sword.co.uk
Website: www.pen-and-sword.co.uk

FOR THE HOSPITALITY, THE CONFIDENCE
AND THE COMRADESHIP WHICH HAVE BEEN
SHOWN TO ME IN THE GERMAN ARMIES AT
THE WESTERN FRONT, I TENDER MY MOST
HEARTFELT THANKS.

SVEN HEDIN
STOCKHOLM
27TH JANUARY, 1915

CONTENTS

AUTHOR'S PREFACE 9

INTRODUCTION 12

CHAPTER I
ON THE WAY TO THE FRONT 14

CHAPTER II
THE EMPEROR WILLIAM 56

CHAPTER III
ON THE WAY TO THE FIFTH ARMY 68

CHAPTER IV
A DAY AT ECLISFONTAINE 94

CHAPTER V
A DAY AT DUN 119

CHAPTER VI
BACK AT MAIN HEADQUARTERS 135

CHAPTER VII
TO SÉDAN 143

CHAPTER VIII
IN THE REAR OF THE FOURTH ARMY 167

CHAPTER IX
WITH THE FOURTH ARMY 195

CHAPTER X
QUIET DAYS 235

CHAPTER XI
TO BELGIUM 252

CHAPTER XII
ANTWERP THE DAY AFTER ITS FALL................279

CHAPTER XIII
MORE DAYS IN ANTWERP................303

CHAPTER XIV
STILL IN ANTWERP................326

CHAPTER XV
VIA GHENT AND BRUGES TO OSTEND................346

CHAPTER XVI
OSTEND BOMBARDED................361

CHAPTER XVII
TWO MORE DAYS ON THE CHANNEL COAST......373

CHAPTER XVIII
TO BAPAUME................392

CHAPTER XIX
AN EXCURSION TO THE FRONT AT LILLE................406

CHAPTER XX
TRENCH LIFE................422

CHAPTER XXI
SUNDAY THE FIRST OF NOVEMBER................440

CHAPTER XXII
ENGLISH PRISONERS FROM YPRES................460

CHAPTER XXIII
FAREWELL TO BAPAUME................482

CHAPTER XXIV
A FINAL DAY ON THE WESTERN FRONT................497

CHAPTER XXV
HOME TO TRÄLLEBORG................506

AUTHOR'S PREFACE TO THE ENGLISH EDITION

L ONG BEFORE MY book dealing with my personal recollections from the war theatres of France and Belgium had been translated into English, it was made the subject of a criticism in the "Daily Telegraph" of February 15th.

The author, Mr. William Archer, complained that I have not once introduced into my narrative any harsh and condemnatory utterances regarding Germany's conduct of the war. The fact is that I have had no occasion for such utterances. My self-imposed task was, as I have repeatedly made clear, merely to describe what I saw with my own eyes and as much as possible to refrain from citing the experience of others. During the two months that I spent on the German western front, I did not see a *single instance* of cruelty to prisoners or wounded, let alone ill-treatment of the civil population and its goods and chattels. The Germans maintained the same incorruptibly severe and just discipline that existed, according to the testimony of history, in the Swedish armies which Gustavus Adolphus and Charles XII. led to victory during the epic period of my own country.

But even in peace time not a day passes but that crime is committed even in the most civilised countries. How, then, can one expect that it shall disappear in a war? I therefore by no means deny that there have been isolated instances of offences and cruelty in an army of several million men. But I have not *seen* them and need not therefore embark upon the subject. I have a shrewd suspicion that criminal statistics generally will testify in favour of the Germanic peoples - as compared, for instance, with the Slavs and the Latins.

Mr. William Archer has something to say about my "outspoken contempt for England." Here he is mistaken. I have no feeling of hatred towards England and have never entertained any feelings of ill-

Sven Hedin.

will towards its great and admirable[1] people. It is only the part which England has played and plays in this world-wide crisis that I abhor and deplore. The earth is large enough to hold both England and Germany, and England would have gained more by keeping neutral in this war. The hatred of England which pervades Germany is new - it began on the 4th August, 1914. Prior to that date it did not exist. Whether England's policy has gained the sympathy and approval of the neutral countries is not for me to judge. One can respect and admire a nation for its splendid qualities and for its colossal contribution to the advancement

1. The more literal translation would be "excellent and admirable," or "capital and admirable"; the term is difficult to render to a nicety. - Translator.

of the world, and yet not admire its policy at a given juncture. This is the nature of the feelings I now entertain for England, and I deeply regret that her guiding statesmen were not able to avert a situation which must inevitably bring misfortune upon their country. Did the English *people itself* desire this war? That question will be answered in the early future.

Mr. William Archer is surprised that I do not speak about the Battle of the Marne. Here I will remind him once more of what I say in the introduction to the book, to wit, that it was not my intention to write the history of the war. I have simply described the happenings at which I myself was present.

In conclusion Mr. William Archer says: "It would be curious to know whether Dr. Hedin now feels so confident of Germany's triumph as he did in the golden prime..." As to that, after the events which have occurred *since* "the golden prime," especially on the eastern front, my faith in Germany's victory is more unshakable than ever.

It is very kind of Mr. William Archer to say that German culture is not in danger. I really think that he is right. The Germans have shown that they are men, capable of defending their culture against I might almost say the whole world, and I pity those who thought that by their united forces they would be able to reduce Germany to a second or third rate power.

SVEN HEDIN
STOCKHOLM, 25TH FEBRUARY, 1915

INTRODUCTION

SWEDISH PROFESSOR, WRITER, illustrator and adventurer Sven Hedin was a renowned Germano-phile. His works were widely published and were particularly well received in Germany where Hedin frequently gave lectures which attracted a glittering audience including Kaiser Wilhelm himself. On the outbreak of the Great War he requested, and was given, complete unrestricted access to visit the German armies fighting in France and Belgium. As a trusted neutral with a strong academic reputation he spent a remarkable amount of time with the German leadership including most of the Corps commanders in the field and was even granted an audience with Kaiser Wilhem II.

Hedin was so well trusted and respected he was provide with a car and escort and then given a comprehensive tour of the German Armies of the West in September and October of 1914. Stops included Berlin, then on to France, Belgium and Luxembourg, at every point Hedin was given unfettered free access to German armies and leadership. The resulting book 'With The German Armies In The West' was quickly finished and published, originally in Swedish in 1914, then swiftly translated and printed and published in early 1915 by John Lane of The Bodley Head Press , London at a time while the events described in the book were still fresh.

During his battle-front tour, Hedin took the opportunity to roam around the Army's rear areas with a couple trips to the rearmost of the front-line trench network. He was an artist of great skill and was allowed to sketch many scenes, usually depicting German troops and logistics on the march, but also their artillery batteries as well. He conducted many interviews, ranging from German privates to British and French POWs. He also documented the condition of post-August 1914 Belgium and described the situation in a very different light to the febrile tones of most neutral sources.

Hedin was a sympathiser who gave an enormous amount of support to the German war effort. He believed in Germany's superiority in the conflict, but was also anxious to present the unvarnished account and was very honest in his depiction of the German Army and offers a surprisingly intimate viewpoint. This invaluable study of the German Army in the First World War is a great addition to the literature of the Great war providing a rare glimpse into the German Army of 1914.

BOB CARRUTHERS
GRAND CAYMAN ISLAND

CHAPTER I
ON THE WAY TO THE FRONT

THE TOCSIN BELL has ceased to ring. Swedish men are no longer being called to arms. Quiet has once more descended upon Stockholm, and it is only occasionally that one encounters a detachment of Landsturm men marching through the streets to join their units or on their way home. People go about their business in the old familiar way. It would be hard to believe that the great world-war was raging outside, did not the newspapers with their great black headlines and their fateful contents form a sinister reminder.

But the individual who under these conditions started out from the Stockholm Central terminus with Berlin as his immediate objective, was only too well aware that it was not an ordinary trip on the Continent on which he was embarking. He travelled from the quiet of the North to the storm in the South - to the great capital where history was being made, the heart of the great empire which was at war with seven states, of which four were great powers. When Stockholm's thousand lights faded into the distance, he felt that peace faded away with them, and that each passing day would bring him nearer to war. He was committed to a journey the spell of which would each day grow stronger, and he was a prey to a tension which was only to give way before the excitement and the thrill of action.

The train clanged through the pitch-black night, and the rain wove its delicate tracery on the window-panes. On Trelleborg quay only a couple of baggage and mail wagons were brought on board the ferry, which bears King Gustafs name. No Swedish passenger coaches are allowed on the German system in war-time, and similarly Germany does not permit hers to enter Sweden.

The sun has broken through the clouds, but the mist has wiped Trelleborg and the Swedish coast from the horizon. A fresh breeze is blowing from the south-west, the Baltic is coated with swirling white-capped waves, and the ferry cuts through the foam on its way to the German coast. There is not a ship in sight, no cruisers, no destroyers or torpedo boats, none of the greyhounds of the sea to track and hold up doubtful shipping. These are peaceful waters. None of the hot winds of war are yet blowing over this sea, only the cool autumnal breezes caress the wave crests. But no doubt grim times are in store even here, so it is as well to make the most of the fleeting hour.

At Sassnitz we set foot on German soil which formerly belonged to us. Everything is as usual, the traveller's excitement has been groundless. Nothing - unless it be a solitary Landsturm soldier with shouldered rifle - to remind one of war. On landing, our passports are vised and our hand luggage is examined at the Custom House. Everything is done in a quiet and orderly manner. The German railway and customs officials are most polite, and look very well in their new ornamental uniforms.

The train swings across Rügen to Altefähr and boards the ferry for the mainland. Here the time-worn churches rear their spires over our old possession Stralsund, where we stop a while at the station. Everything is as it used to be, no hurry or bustle; people go about their business as in times of piping peace. But just as the train is about to steam out, a squad of Landwehr soldiers with their kits under their arms rush on to the platform and take their seats in the last carriage. They are not bound for the front as yet, for they alight at Greifswald. A blurred mass of red-tiled roofs framed in the luxuriant foliage of late summer, and a number of churches pointing their spires aloft - that is all we see of the old university town. But there is nothing unusual to be seen, everything runs its normal course, "Papers!" "Beer!" cry the boys on the platform, and, anxious for news, one buys a paper from one and, to quench one's thirst, a glass of good, dark beer of the other. A light meal is provided by a woman, who at 30 pfg. each sells small bags of waffles, plums and grapes.

From some belated fields the corn is still being brought in, and black and brindled cattle, and here and there a flock of sheep, is seen grazing in the meadows. Summer and prosperity seem to reign everywhere in Germany, and there is meat and bread in abundance. Is it possible that it is six weeks since this country has been involved in the greatest war in history? Everything betokens peace on earth, even the sky is cloudless and the sun sheds its golden rays over Pomerania. Among the trees by the roadside some women are walking with little children in their arms. They are engaged in earnest conversation and walk with bowed heads. No doubt their menfolk are at the war, and perhaps one of them knows already that she is a widow. A conscientious observer might notice that there are fewer adult men than usual. But the difference is so slight that one would not think of it unless one knew that there was war. Old men, women and children seem a little more in evidence than in peace time: that is all.

At Anklam station, not far from where the Peene flows into the Baltic, another body of soldiers board the train. Their uniforms are dark blue with very bright red collars. They are Landsturm men in the prime of life, and have probably been called up for service within Germany; for at the front hardly anything is seen but field-grey uniforms, a protective colouring which blends with the appearance of the soil and is very hard to distinguish.

Prenzlau - so now we are in Brandenburg. Fresh bodies of Landsturm men clamber into the train, which is to carry them away from their homes to an unknown fate. They come running and singing across the platform, as if they long to get away. Their blue tunics with red collars and shoulder-straps, and the red cap-bands, form a bright contrast to the dress of the civilians. They are strong and powerful specimens of the Teutonic type, but too stout for perfect symmetry. One does not see amongst them any ideal specimens bearing the distinguishing characteristics of the Caucasian race, no broad shouldered, deep-chested, strapping fellows such as one meets with in the mountains of Georgia; but they are a blonde, sound, calm and yet cheery set of men, all animated by one single thought - to conquer or to die. Their women, children and other relations have followed them to the train to say good-bye. All are cheerful, they chat and laugh. There is no weeping and complaining, it is the great day of joy, when every able-bodied man goes to do his duty for the welfare of his country.

My carriage is filled with officers. They are engaged in very animated conversation; they do not care what is going on around them; they don't look out of the window and don't allow themselves to be disturbed by the bustle and crush in the corridor. They talk about the affairs of their units and regiments, about the equipment of the troops and the departure for foreign parts. They discuss Hindenburg's victories and give vent to their admiration for him. The cares and solemnity of war do not rest heavily on these men; they are animated by a glad longing and sure feeling of victory, and without knowing them one realises that they have staked their lives and their existence on one single goal. About the result they have no doubt. They *must* win, otherwise their country is lost.

But the hours speed away, dusk settles down over Brandenburg, and soon the earth is wrapped in darkness. The carriages are not lighted - I don't know why. As we approach Berlin it is dark within, but outside there are rows of electric lamps lighting up the interior of the carriage in a fantastic manner.

The train stops at *Stettiner Bahnhof.* On the platform there is the same busy hum and bustle as in peace time. A whole crowd of *Gepäckträger* hurry to the window to receive the passengers' luggage - one notices no lack of men. A policeman hands out numbered cab-discs, the heavy luggage is got out in a twinkling, and up one jumps into one of the numberless taxicabs ranged outside and drives off to one's hotel.

I am an old customer at the Kaiserhof, but this time I was told that I ought to stay in Unter den Linden in order to be able to study at my leisure from a balcony the endless processions of patriots, who, especially at night, file down the road with proud bearing, singing patriotic songs. I therefore chose the Hotel Bristol. Its name has been removed from the large illuminated sign facing the street. Bristol - this name reminded one too much of England's faithlessness towards her Teutonic kinsmen! Only the first letter remained, to be interpreted as one might wish.

The hotel was only half full. Most of the visitors were Scandinavians and Americans. It was just as well that there were not too many, as the staff had also been reduced by half - the other half was at the front. The quiet which reigned in the big building was reflected by the atmosphere of the famous avenue outside. To-day there were no closely packed crowds, no singing processions. Only those people who had business to attend to or who wanted to glean the latest news were seen on the pavements - the others kept indoors. The traffic was, if anything, less lively than in peace time, and an amazing calm had descended upon the great city.

I went out in the evening to see the people and listen to their conversation. The talk was almost entirely about the war. I walked through Friedrichstrasse, Leipzigerstrasse and the other familiar streets. Everything is just as usual. Berlin is wrapped in absolute peace. Innumerable shop-windows still shed their light upon the pavements. In some of them large maps are shown, small flags indicating the positions of the armies. On one such map the flags were waving and fluttering, as if a storm were ravaging the plains of Europe. Outside, in the street, little groups formed to talk about the war and to express the hope that the German flags would soon be shifted further into the steppes in the east and towards the sea in the west.

"Why are the streets so silent?" I ask somebody. "I understood that Berlin was in such high spirits."

"It is so long since we heard of any great victories," is the answer.

"Patience," I retort, "you must not expect a Tannenberg every week."

Here comes a woman hurrying along with a bundle of newspapers. It is the latest edition with fresh telegrams from the front. She is hustling as much as possible in order to impress on the public that they must look sharp and get the news as fresh as possible. On the opposite pavement runs a boy with the same newspaper, calling out his ware in a loud voice. At a street corner stands an old man with his bundle of papers. He is too tired to run, and his cracked voice cannot even be heard above the subdued hubbub of street-life and the quick flow of talk of the people. It is all the same news, and it deals chiefly with the gigantic battle of Lemberg.

The restaurants are well filled, in fact they are all overcrowded with customers. Through the big windows one can see the honest bourgeois seated at his little table, where sausage and *wienerschnitzel*, *dunkles* or *helles* may be had in abundance. I entered and sat down at a table, overhearing scraps of talk from all sides - all about the war, about brothers and sons who are fighting, one hardly knows where, as the field post has brought no news for a long time. But perhaps the next day will bring a greeting from the front. Maybe a son who has been reported in the papers as missing, has turned up again. But nevertheless the personal sorrow and anxiety is thrust into the background. Every sacrifice must be gladly made, and the loved ones may lie dead on the field of battle so long as Germany wins her fight against almost the whole of Europe.

On the 13th September the lingering summer came to an end, and autumn suddenly asserted itself. It poured with rain, it was dark, windy, cold and raw. Shallow puddles covered the asphalt in Unter den Linden, which resembled an enormous river bed still drenched with the flow, and from which the tide had just ebbed. The great avenue now looks desolate with a vengeance. From my balcony I can only see a few solitary individuals sheltered under more or less elegant umbrellas, Berlin's inhabitants prefer to keep in their comfortable homes, and not even the longing for war news can tempt them out in such weather.

The rain falls thick and heavy and patters down on the dripping limes outside my balcony. Berlin is dull and miserable in the autumn when the rain sweeps its long, monotonously straight streets with their heavy, dark houses. Not even the trooping of the colours and the march past at midday raise the drooping spirits, and only a few pedestrians with open umbrellas join the band and march in step with the soldiers. The motor-cars buzz past over the asphalt, flinging up a spray of water as they rush along. They are plainly far less numerous than usual. No calls are made, no visits paid, for the whole of the aristocracy is in mourning for lost relatives and everybody's thoughts are centred on the war. Nobody feels inclined for the futile pleasures of ordinary times when the newspapers speak of a father who has lost four sons at the front, or of a mother whose three sons have each died a hero's death for Emperor and country. But no complaints are heard, no tears seen. In the streets one seldom sees signs of mourning. There is perhaps a tacit convention not to express in black and white the sorrow which is felt at the bottom of the heart, but to make the grief subservient to the proud consciousness that the beloved one has fallen for his country, never to return!

Already in Berlin I was greatly impressed by the worldwide influence of German thought. Here is a nation which for long years back has known how to read the inexorable message of time, which has not rested on the laurels gained in its last war, which has needed no warnings, and whose watchmen never closed their eyes and never dallied with an inevitable fate. Here is a nation which during the decades of peace has armed itself to the teeth and which now, when the hour has struck, stands ready to meet four great powers in fierce combat and to contend with one of them for the mastery of the seas. It is true that the German people have been divided into parties, as the democratic spirit of our age demands, but the political factions have nevertheless realised the necessity of a strong defence of their common country. And now that the war is raging in all directions, the parties have disappeared completely. Germany at the present time is inhabited by a people which is at one with itself. Here we have but one party - that of the soldiers. Here everyone has but one goal, and there is no one who does not realise that this is a fight of life and death for Germany; all have the same thoughts, all hold the same hopes and offer up the same prayers, from the Emperor who stands first and foremost in war as in peace, to the street urchin who flattens his nose against the shop window and studies the positions of the tiny flags.

But the rain keeps on falling and beats against the windowpanes. I hurry downstairs, jump into a taxi and in a few minutes I am sitting in an elegant drawing-room at the dainty new residence of the Swedish Minister, at the corner of Friedrich Wilhelmstrasse and Tiergartenstrasse, chatting with old friends - needless to say, about the war. When I last met Count Taube in Berlin, I had just returned from a long journey in the Far East. Now I stood on the threshold of a new journey, which might be infinitely longer than the last! Later in the day I visited another nobleman. Prince von Wedel, whom I had met in Vienna when he was ambassador there, and in Strassburg when he was Governor. We had much to talk about, but what is there to discuss in these days but the great and bloody drama which occupies everyone's thoughts -the War!

My most important visit in Berlin was to the Foreign Office. But before narrating what took place there I must say a few words about the reasons which led up to my journey. It was desirable that no one in a responsible position in Sweden should have an inkling of my journey to the front. Our country belonged to the neutral states, and thus no authority must entertain the slightest shadow of a suspicion that I was travelling on any sort of secret mission. No, - the reason was a very simple one. Only a few days' journey away the greatest war of all time was being waged. It was clear that the outcome of this struggle would decide the political development for the next fifty or hundred years, or perhaps longer. In any case its shadows must envelop the remainder of the lives of the present generation.

The war of 1870-71 became the starting-point of a new era in Germany's development. Now Germany is once again at war, and the new political problems which may be expected to come up for discussion in the immediate future will doubtless be rooted in the great Germanic war. If the two contending groups of powers were to come out of the struggle only with depleted forces, the war of 1914 would, in its dying embers, carry the seed of a new world conflagration, even more devastating perhaps than the last. But if Germany were to win at all points, the map of the world would undergo sweeping changes, and Germany would then, in the great triumph of her power, discountenance and forbid fresh wars. If Russia were to win, the fate of Sweden and Norway would be sealed. Whatever happens, great and memorable events will arise out of this struggle. How instructive would it be, then, to study the War on the very scene of the momentous conflict, and to visit the ravaged regions where the German soldiers carried the fate of Germany and of the whole Germanic world on the point of their bayonets! No one who has not seen with his own eyes how the Germans fight, can fully and clearly grasp what the struggle means to Germany. But his presence there will enable him to comprehend more plainly what the future holds in store for us, and the happenings which in due course will be unfolded before our vision.

Thus I look upon my journey to the front first and foremost as a political study.

But there were also other reasons and other thoughts that made me long to get out to the theatre of war. I wanted to see with my own eyes and become familiar with war as it really is, and I wanted to gain the personal experience which would enable me to describe to others the dark as well as the bright sides of war. Its dark sides are the hate, the desire for vengeance, the destruction, the gutted homesteads, the ruined crops, the wounded, the maimed, the graves, the grief and privation, but war is bright when it is fought by a united nation, determined to live and to retain its independence.

The unity, self-sacrifice and confidence in victory of the German nation is one of the bright sides of this war, which otherwise reveals an abyss of human misery. I thought it would be instructive to see for myself how far civilisation, Christianity and pacificism had advanced nineteen hundred and fourteen years after the birth of Christ.

During the first phase of the war the British press accused the Germans of barbaric cruelty to their prisoners and to wounded opponents. Not for one moment did I believe these reports, but for the sake of the Teutonic race I wanted to uproot this calumny and to bring to light the truth. If one cannot ask anything else of a people which stands on the pinnacle of culture, one may at least expect it not to accuse its opponents of crimes which were never committed. German protests against the accusations of foreign newspapers were of course of no avail. Perhaps I shall be believed if I protest before God that I will not write a single line which is not true and will describe nothing but what I have seen with my own eyes.

Finally, it was my wish to study the psychology of war, I mean the *Geist* and the fighting spirit with which armies went into battle, the mood in which they returned therefrom, the thoughts and feelings of the wounded, the spirit with which the soldiers entered the fray for the second time after having been slightly wounded, tended and healed. In the last phase of the Manchurian campaign there was a noticeable weakening of purpose which led to slackened efforts on both sides and caused the war to die, so to speak, of inanition. Was a like form of mental fatigue, an exhaustion of soul and body under the stupendous hardships in the field to leave its mark on the Germans too? Or would their conviction, that the war meant to them the life or death of Germany, endow them with a buoyancy and tenacity enabling them to fight through to victory? It might be of interest to us, Teutons of the north, to gain some insight into this problem. Such knowledge might be useful, should we at some future time be confronted with a situation comparable with that of Germany at the present moment. The outcome of a campaign does not merely depend upon preparations, war matérial and training. The fighting spirit and general mental attitude of the soldier also plays a most important part. The soldier must know *why* he is fighting and *what* he is fighting for. The psychological factor is therefore of the utmost importance. The officer leading his men to the front and into the firing line has neither the attitude of mind nor the time for such studies. His whole attention is and must be concentrated on the fighting itself; he only thinks of utilising the striking power of his men with the utmost effect at the right moment and in the right place. He is therefore - and quite rightly- blind to everything else. A layman on the other hand, whose attention is not distracted by considerations of conduct of war, has better opportunities of studying the psychology of the soldiers.

Once this war is over, whole libraries of books will be written about it. I do not think it an exaggeration to say that on the western front alone upwards of a million and a half diaries are being kept at the present moment. In all directions, in all fighting units down to the company, the platoon and the battery, official war journals are being kept and accounts of the fighting are being prepared from the bedrock furnished on the one hand by the draft of outgoing reports and on the other by incoming papers, orders, reports and communications. The soldiers record their own personal experiences, the officers their military observations. Many a note-book has no doubt protected a heart or checked the death-dealing bullet. Thus the sections of the German General Staff, whose task it will be in due course to prepare the matérials, will be occupied for many years to come with this monumental labour.

When I went out to the front, it was clearly established in my mind that my narrative would be quite different from the military accounts. I was not going to devote any attention to matters of purely military science, which could only be dealt with by experts. Even Sweden has from the very beginning had its military attaché. Major Adlercreutz, of the Scanian Dragoons, and later on Lieut.-Col. Bouveng received permission to accompany the German forces. Strategical and tactical observations would thus be absent from my narrative. It would no doubt have been interesting and instructive to familiarise myself in some measure with these subjects. But it was evident to me from the beginning that I should always have to observe the utmost tact and discretion, and even avoid obtaining knowledge of military matters which ought to remain secret until the end of the campaign. This veto comprised the distribution of German forces, army corps, divisions, regiments and other units, as well as any regrouping of forces which might be effected during my presence at the front. I was destined often to hear of such details, but made up my mind to take no notes in that connection.

Neither did I propose to embody in my narrative any account of the events that led up to the war or of the Notes despatched hither and thither across Europe during the days preceding its outbreak. All this had been fully dealt with before. My book was only to constitute a conscientious account of what I myself had seen and experienced whilst I was the guest of the German Army in the field. Towards this army and towards the German people I thus incurred a certain responsibility - my sketch, in order to possess any value, must therefore be a true and faithful one. Towards Germany's enemies I also had a duty, not to be unfair to them, I further felt a certain responsibility towards Swedish officers as a body, for although it might have been my wish that my observations should be of use to them, it was more than doubtful whether I should succeed in my object. As regards the public, whatever I might witness, I had to guard against the temptation to satisfy its craving after sensation.

Besides, it was evident to me that in a modern war there was very little to be left to the imagination, and that the reality would in most cases render it unnecessary to strive after effect. I wanted to describe life and death on the battlefield, that was all.

Such were my thoughts and plans at the beginning of September. They had arisen and matured in my own mind without the shadow of any incentive from German or Swedish quarters. When I had made up my mind, all that remained for me to do was to obtain permission to go to the front and to spend some time with the German Army. With this object I applied to the German Minister in Stockholm, His Excellency von Reichenau, who with the greatest kindness undertook to transmit my request to the competent authority in Germany. After waiting a week I received a very courteous reply saying that I was very welcome to visit the front. The following day, September 11th, I set out on my fateful journey, and at the present moment - when I broke the thread of my narrative - I am standing on the doorstep and ringing the bell at the Foreign Office at 76 Wilhelmstrasse, Berlin.

The Under Secretary of State, Herr von Zimmermann, who is acting Foreign Minister in Berlin whilst His Excellency von Jagow is at the Main Headquarters, received me with open arms and said that all he knew was that I was to proceed straightway to the said Headquarters.

"But where are the Main Headquarters?" I asked.

"That is a secret," Herr von Zimmermann answered, with a smile.

"Good, but how am I to get there?"

"Oh, the Chief of the Great General Staff, Colonel-General von Moltke, has given instructions that a car is to be kept at your disposal. You may decide yourself when you would like to start. An officer and an orderly will accompany you, and if you like you can travel to the Main Headquarters day and night without stopping, or you can choose your own road and time. In fact, you are at liberty to do as you like."

"And afterwards?"

"After that your fate will rest in the hands of His Excellency von Moltke. No doubt he will map out a plan for your journey. The only thing you have to think about now is to get to him."

"And where shall I find the car?"

"This paper will tell you."

Herr von Zimmermann handed me a permit from the Great General Staff which read as follows: "The bearer of this permit is entitled to use the relays of the Imperial Volunteer Automobile Corps to the Main Headquarters. Everything that can in any way expedite his journey is to be placed at his disposal."

In conclusion I was told that the offices of the Volunteer Automobile Corps were at 243 Friedrichstrasse, and that the Acting Chief was a Dr. Arnoldi.

After heartily thanking Herr von Zimmermann and receiving his good wishes for the impending journey, I went off to look for Arnoldi and his office. I found him in a large room full of maps, piles of papers, telegrams, officers and orderlies, and my reception was as usual most cordial - in future I shall not have to repeat this pleasing fact, for everyone has been equally courteous and friendly. To begin with, I was shown a map of the great relay road, but for obvious reasons I must not tell anything about it.

Then came the question:

"Do you wish to travel independently of all regulations or by relays, that is to say, 700 kilometres in 16 hours - 44 kilometres an hour on end?"

I thought a moment, then chose to be independent, for if I had done the journey in sixteen hours, I should have been obliged to travel over the most interesting part of the road by night when there is nothing to be seen, and, after all, I had come to see as much as possible. The trip from Berlin to Headquarters ought to mean a continuous crescendo. I ought to know what it felt like to leave peace behind and gradually to approach the scorching firing lines. I thought in my innocence that the roads in Western Germany would be more or less encumbered with soldiers and vehicles. Not a bit of it! It was a long time before we had to drive slowly on account of the congestion, for within Germany all transports were effected by rail.

"Who is going to be my chauffeur?"

"An officer, accompanied by an orderly. Both are on duty with the Volunteer Automobile Corps."

"Who appoints the officer?"

"I do; and I am just thinking that Rittmeister von Krum, of Württemberg, will be the right man."

Dr. Arnoldi touched a button. An orderly entered and was asked whether Captain von Krum was at hand.

"Yes, the Rittmeister is here." "Ask him to come in." And an officer in field-grey uniform, of the most attractive appearance and charming manners, enters the room. Dr. Arnoldi tells him what his duties are, namely, to take me to the mysterious region in the west, and I wonder in my own mind whether it will bore him to jog along with me on the road through more than half of Germany. I even ask him how he feels about it, and he replies that it will be a great pleasure to him to take *me*, of all people, to the theatre of war. I assure Captain von Krum that it pleases me greatly to have *him*, of all people, as my travelling companion, chauffeur and guide.

My Rittmeister had retired from active service, but on the outbreak of war he had rallied to the colours and placed his car at the disposal of the Crown in accordance with the mobilisation decree. He drives it himself in the service of the Army and the orderly who is to accompany us is, in peace time, his own chauffeur. I was told that the Volunteer Automobile Corps now mustered 350 cars. The owner of a car reports himself and is paid for his vehicle, and he may at the end of the war buy back his car from the Crown. It is reckoned that the serviceable life of a car is five years. If the owner paid ten thousand marks for his car and has used it for four years, he only gets paid at the last year's valuation, i.e. two thousand marks, whilst if the car is quite new he receives the full amount.

Three hundred and fifty cars - it doesn't sound much, but these cars merely form the Volunteer Corps, and I suppose you will feel more at ease when I tell you that at the western front alone there are altogether fifty thousand cars in use, whilst forty thousand are left in Germany. That means fifty thousand chauffeurs. When one considers that each car usually has a crew of two, it will be seen that the equivalent of over two army corps are attached to the Automobile Service. There are plenty of men in Germany, plenty for every purpose. On the eastern front I was told that cars are useless outside the German boundaries, owing to the shocking state of Russian and Polish roads. There one has to ride or requisition ordinary vehicles. But in the west the cars play a part the importance of which had only remotely been guessed at, as may be gathered from the course of this narrative.

Finally, von Krum was told to collect all maps (scale 1:100,000) that we should require from Berlin to Main Headquarters. I myself received the pleasing news that I need only give ten minutes' notice before starting, as car, Rittmeister and orderly were always ready, likewise Dr. Arnoldi's wolfskin coat, which he advised me to take with me.

I had thus every reason to be satisfied with my day's work. The trip to Main Headquarters was evidently only the first step. What was to follow? Probably a trip along the line of German lines of communication to the fighting zone, and possibly to the firing line itself. Perhaps it would be my good fortune to catch at least a glimpse of a modem fight. After such a beginning the rest was sure to go well. My excitement on starting had now changed to longing, and I felt that I was about to be carried with lightning speed along magnificent roads towards a spectacle which I would never forget: the German Army in all its overpowering strength drawn up for the greatest contest in the world's history. The German Army! These words convey nowadays far more than formerly, and the same may be said of the French Army. In these days it is not armies of mercenaries that meet one another in the field, it is entire nations that range up for battle. The difference is only that the Gennan Army is one homogeneous whole and pure in race, whilst the French Army is reinforced with Englishmen and a whole colour-scheme of imported heathens.

The next day I was out with my friend the Rittmeister and got fitted out from head to foot with motor cap, boots and puttees, a sporting suit of suitable warmth, leather coat and vest, rain-coat, a warm muffler and a pair of motor goggles, which I never used.

I ended my day at a reception at the house of the Countess Wilamovitz, née Fock, whose husband, Captain of one of the Reserve Regiments of the Uhlans of the Guard, is fighting at the front. The sole topic of conversation among the guests was the War and the final victory.

The 15th of September we started out. I turned up in good time at the offices of the Imperial Volunteer Automobile Corps, where the car was waiting. But as usual it takes a long time to get away; von Krum has several papers to sign and maps to arrange and Dr. Arnoldi conveys to me very hearty greetings from Lieut. -Colonel Gross, the great airship expert and inventor, who is commanding the Field Telegraph Battalion. Before I left he insisted on my going out to inspect his magnificent establishment. So we drove out to see him and were received at the gate by the Colonel himself, an energetic, virile, distinguished little man surrounded by several officers. The establishment is truly imposing, a whole row of barracks, workshops, depots, stores and stables surrounding an enormous yard, where masts for wireless telegraphy tower aloft. The station is thus in communication with the whole of Germany, and the aerial news operator was just engaged in reading out for the general edification some atrocity stories received that moment from English sources. The telegraph battalion with equipment, men and horses, is, of course, in the field with its Army Corps. But, nevertheless, depots, barracks and stables are replete with a completely new set of everything. In the stables every stall was occupied by recently requisitioned farm horses, fat and sleek and contented in their new unaccustomed surroundings. As regards the men, they were all volunteers, who had offered themselves in far greater numbers than were needed. Just as we were walking across the yard a detachment drove in at full speed with its loads of masts and wire. It had been out practising, and the precision and resolution which distinguished the work of the men was astonishing, seeing that they had only had four weeks' training. One of them, by the scars on his cheeks, showed himself to be an old University student, and was now headmaster in a school. When addressed by the Colonel he came to attention and saluted with a smartness which made us suspect that he preferred the driver's seat on a field telegraph lorry to the schoolmaster's desk. We also visited the immense sheds containing the wagons with their substantial provision for batteries, telegraph and telephone apparatus, insulators, tools, wires and the innumerable objects required for field telegraph lines. The wagons, which are motor-driven, resemble enormous but well-built and graceful boxes. They are of immense weight and can only be used on paved or macadamised roads. On the Polish roads, soaked by the autumn rains, they would not get far. But on the western front it is sufficient if they keep to the main roads, where they are stationed at suitable points as depots from which supplies are conveyed in lighter vehicles to the spot where they are wanted. One store shed contained perfect mountains of gigantic wire coils. The wire seemed to me somewhat thin, but I was told that it fully answers its purpose. The Colonel showed me the lances by means of which experienced and expert riders throw up the telegraph and telephone wires among the branches of an avenue of trees. When I saw all these heavy lumbering vehicles and appliances and all these thousands of miles of wire, the idea crossed my mind that it was all very well when it was all ranged up before one as at an exhibition in Berlin, but how would it all work out in war? Was it possible that everything would turn out as calculated? Would the wagons arrive in time and would there not be endless bother with all these wires in trees and on the ground? I was soon to learn how wonderfully everything panned out and with what meticulous care every detail was superintended by trained soldiers.

But time flies, we rush back to Berlin, cross Unter den Linden and pass out through the Brandenburger Tor. The war cars always create a good deal of interest. The Rittmeister sits at the wheel himself and steers his car with wonderful assurance. He threads his way with the most daring turns and twists in between and past other cars and carriages in the Tiergartenstrasse, and by pressing a little bulb on the wheel he produces a piercing, twittering noise which during the day caused an officer to shout after us: "That's a nice little canary you've got hold of!"

By the side of von Krum sits the chauffeur, the excellent Deffner, also from Württemberg, an enormous chap. His rifle is lashed to the front of the car. I myself occupy the back seat, where I have the map of the General Staff at hand, making hasty notes now and again. At the bottom of the car is my luggage, two bags no larger than can be carried by myself if necessary. In the field one should not carry more baggage than one can cope with personally. Our first halt is at Potsdam, 28.9 kilometres. We fly along at a rattling pace on the magnificent road lined by avenues of trees, parks and long rows of large new houses. Here we have the Wannsee with its innumerable sailing boats at anchor, its leafy nooks, its villas and inns. There are very few people about and we seldom meet another vehicle. But when we sight one down the road, the shrill sound of the canary rends the atmosphere, and Deffner conjures forth a melodious note out of his hooter.

We are not far from Beelitz when a report is heard under the car - it is not a shell, merely a burst tyre which compels us to stop and change it. A horseshoe nail has worked its way through the cover, but Deffner is a handy man and it is put right in no time. There is a fresh breeze blowing, and it murmurs through the pines by the roadside - it is the last breath of summer complaining that autumn is so near. One finds it rather windy travelling in an open car at sixty kilometres an hour with a head wind, but it is delightful and exhilarating to travel fast, to fly along the road regardless of everything and to approach the scene of events which are now daily filling the pages of the world's history. All unpleasant thoughts are blown away, all fuss and pettiness which one otherwise has to endure are left behind, one simply runs away from it all and is filled with a feeling of buoyant joy and freedom as one rushes past the fields, the homely villages, the farms, the copses, the endless, straight avenues of ash, oak, maple and elm - everything flits past and disappears, whilst the hand of the indicator marks seventy kilometres an hour. There is nothing to indicate that Germany is in the throes of her greatest war. Huge cartloads of scented hay are being brought in from the meadows - not all Germany's horses are busy pulling guns and ammunition. The sails of the windmills travel round busily with several reefs taken in, grinding the corn which is to be made into bread for millions of soldiers and their families at home. At Treuenbrietzen we encounter groups of merry school children who shout and wave, and in the fields outside women, young and old, are busy gathering potatoes and beet. They greet us with a flutter of aprons and handkerchiefs. Why on earth are they waving to us, I say to myself, but the answer is obvious - the uniforms and the streamer denote a war car, and they realise that we are on the way to the front; whether they know us or not does not matter, but perhaps they think we shall meet their own dear ones who are fighting out there for hearth and home!

Now the country opens up more and stretches out in undulating vistas before us. Presently we reach the top of a rise and see the tower and roof of Wittenberg church in a hollow before us - the Elbe valley. Here is the Schlosskirche, and I see in my mind's eye the wonder-struck crowds gathering before the portals where the monk Luther nailed up his ninety-five theses. But disturb not the peace which reigns within the church, where the great reformer rests before the pulpit! Outside in the street a body of volunteers are marching; they look cheerful, they march well with a rhythmical firm step and sing a lively and inspiriting war song. At the next street corner we meet another detachment on the way to or from its drill ground. They are strapping young fellows of martial bearing, and one can see how they are longing to get out to fight. They do not sing, they whistle a pleasing tune which sounds quaint among the venerable houses of Wittenberg. They are Teutons, they were not born to be conquered by Slavs and Latins. Their forefathers were described by Tacitus, and they fought and conquered in the Teutoburger Wald. Now it is the descendants of the old Teutons who are gathered under the German eagles to struggle for freedom between the Rhine and the Vistula, and far beyond the valleys of the great rivers. It is a dangerous game to trifle with the eagle, for he may leave his nest and spread his wings for flight. But Germany's fateful hour has now struck, and the moment has come for the Teutons to assert themselves and to lay the foundation for an assured future. Listen to the echo of their ringing stride in the streets of Wittenberg - the same echo is heard in all German cities where the volunteers rally round the flag! It is a migration the like of which the world has never seen, and the country is filled with the spirit of resolution and enthusiasm which does not know what fear is or doubt, an understanding which asks no questions. They march off to unknown fates, glorious and horrible alike. Very soon they will say their evening prayers to the accompaniment of the thunder of guns and the shrieking of shells. It is not for German liberty alone that they are fighting, it is for the independent existence of the other Germanic nations as well that they fearlessly face death on the battlefield. So no wonder that my eye follows them until they disappear round the next street corner - the sound of their music still ringing in my soul.

Zum König von Preussen, Zum Goldenen Anker - they show wonderful fertility of mind in hitting upon attractive names to lure the customers into their inns! Many a *Bierkneipe* in these parts has venerable associations, and inns are still to be found where it is known that Luther sat and quaffed his good old beer.

But Wittenberg also has Swedish memories. Many a Swedish soldier has marched over the Elbe bridge since the memorable 3rd September, 1631, when Gustavus Adolphus came over for the first time to rescue Protestantism and the liberty of thought on earth - up to the October day, 1813, when our old regiments for the last time trod the road to Leipzig to take part in the struggle against Napoleon. How different was the conduct of war on these two occasions, but how alike were the will and spirit of the people!

It was with a mixture of pride and melancholy that I sat thinking of those good old times, as we skimmed the surface with lightning speed.

With the car as a pair of compasses we measure out the distances on the full-scale map of Germany itself. The Elbe valley has disappeared behind us, and we now pick up and leave one village after the other. Sometimes the village streets are paved with cobbles, and our speed slackens considerably. In other places rattling carts drawn by powerful dogs in complete harness come jogging along at a brisk pace. It is a pleasure to look at them. Truly they are examples of faithfulness and conscientiousness. With panting mouths and dripping tongues, and with all muscles and sinews of their bodies strained to the utmost, they tug so fiercely that their paws and chests might be expected to be a mass of sores. The man at the cart does not urge them and has no whip in his hand. He seems, on the contrary, to wish to hold them back when they struggle along too fast. If anyone seems to approach too close to their master's barrow, they set up a ferocious bark. They long to be in harness as soon as the sun gets up, just like Jack London's pals in Alaska. It is touching to see their sense of duty and honour. And yet they are but dogs. I felt I would like to follow them on the road and study them. But the car goes on inexorably, and in a twinkling they are far, far behind.

Gräfenhainischen - what a delightful little monosyllable! One must never be in a hurry when one lives at Gräfenhainischen. As long, nay, longer than the name is the narrow street that leads through the village and finally loses itself in the fiat country beyond.

Mulde with its bridge and Bitterfeld, where the market is in full swing, are the next landmarks in our journey. The stalls with the busy market life around them look very picturesque. Full of colour, but at the same time so old fashioned and tranquil - nobody could imagine here that Germany is at war. On the road outside the town we see plenty of women driving or walking back to their rustic farmsteads after their marketing.

At the lignite mines outside Bitterfeld the little baskets on the cableways are busy carrying the coal to the factories, where it is made into briquettes.

Next we roll into Halle and are now on the most classic ground of our national history, for it was at Halle that Gustavus Adolphus rested from the loth to the 17th September, 1631, with the army which had conquered at Breitenfeld on the 7th of the same month. In passing over the bridges we cross a seemingly inextricable maze of railway lines. The bridgeheads here, as everywhere in the German Empire, are guarded by Landsturm sentries with loaded rifles. All railways and high roads, all arteries of communication on land and water, in fact everything that can pass by the name of road is of the utmost importance in war time, as they are the means of carrying the troops to the parts where the fighting is going on. But most important of all are the bridges, especially those spanning the great rivers. Any accident to one of these bridges means the severing of an artery for some time ahead. It may mean the loss of a battle. Everything must run as if it were greased, in war there must be no miscalculations, no sundering of the points which join the front with the interior. The cutting of his lines of communication is a distinct reverse to the enemy. The profession of the spy and plotter carries with it little honour and much danger. But had the allies been able to do so, they would certainly with the aid of enterprising emissaries have attempted to destroy the bridges, say across the Rhine, and thus stop or delay the German advance. Hence every important bridge throughout Germany has been guarded with sentries since the beginning of the war, and no bridge and viaduct is ever without one or two Landsturm men of middle-age, wearing dark blue uniforms, and in the evenings and at night grey overcoats; they pace faithfully up and down at their posts on the bridges or under arches with arms crossed and the rifle held vertically inside the left arm, until they are relieved by their comrades. As the car dashes past with its fluttering war streamer, they come briskly to attention with the rifle to the order.

Well, we are now at my dear old Halle on the Saale, where I once studied geography with the charming and humorous, one eyed but yet keenly wide awake Professor Kirchhoff. Halle is exactly as it used to be. In its main street there are plenty of people about, mainly children and young people, for this is the great highway to Merseburg and to the fighting West, and many military cars dashed past during the hour we halted in the town. Here also large war maps are exhibited in the booksellers' windows, and outside them interested groups of Halle folk are gathered, mostly schoolboys, who talk importantly in loud voices of the silent, significant evidence of the little flags. At Halle another horseshoe nail or maybe a bit of glass caused tyre Number 2 to burst, and as the accident happened exactly opposite Schultheiss's door, von Krum and I saw in this a direct hint from fate that we wanted a glass of beer. There we sat and chatted at the table with its many-coloured cloth and round discs of felt under the beer mugs, and wondered how far we should get before nightfall. But as we sat and talked, dusk quietly descended upon Halle and when we got outside the street lamps were being lit. Further away in the west on the horizon the sky was a flaming red - a symbol of the bloody battlefield.

After lighting our lamps, off we went from Halle southward past Merseburg on the way to Naumburg, still hugging the Saale valley. We are still on classic Swedish soil. November memories of 1632 - Pappenheim's cuirassiers, Isolani's Croatians, holding sway at Halle and Merseburg whilst Gustavus Adolphus is lying at Naumburg. Two hours before daybreak the King left this very town for Lützen. One can almost hear the Swedish cavalry bugle-calls. It was at this same Merseburg that the proud dragoons of the bodyguard under Field Marshal Count Rehnsköld were installed in 1706-7.

The bright light from our lamps shows up the road for some distance ahead. We have now slackened to 40 kilometres an hour. The leafy trees by the roadside are lit up from beneath, and we seem to travel through an endless fantastic tunnel of foliage. Far away on both sides of the road are strings of glistening lights - the windows of farms and villages where fathers and mothers, brothers and sisters, maids and children are sitting round the lamp to read for the twentieth time the letters and cards received from their soldiers at the French and Belgian front. What do these letters say? I have read several. There are millions of them. The soldier tells his people how he likes his billet, what food tastes like after the heat and stress of the day, what it feels like when the shells burst close by and comrades fall at one's side. They tell also that the enemy is done for, that he will be thrown back as soon as the commander deems fit to order them to charge. They speak with good-nature of the Frenchmen as courteous and honest soldiers, but of the English with glowing hatred And, as often as not, the soldier finishes up by saying that there can be no question of any return to the village until he is wounded or useless - which God forbid - and until victory has been gained over Germany's enemies. For the soldiers know, from the oldest veteran to the youngest drummer boy, that Germany was armed to the teeth to be ready for the war, but that Germany's Emperor and statesmen did all in their power to avert a disaster which would surely affect the whole world and cause rivers of blood and tears to flow, bring nameless misery to ravaged homes and ruined countrysides, untold nights of anguish and expectation and long years of inconsolable grief and sorrow.

But the evening is wearing on. We have left Naumburg behind us. The good people in the town have gone to bed, for the lights are mostly out and the windows dark. Tucked into their snug beds they listen to the whir of the motor-cars and the warning tooting of horns, and their thoughts no doubt run on to the fateful west whither the cars are speeding. But they will soon get left behind, the buzz dies away in the distance, and sleep carries them into the peaceful realm of dreams. I too begin to get a little sleepy. My eyelids begin to droop and my head feels heavy; it sinks down and recovers with a jerk as the car quickly takes a corner. The excellent Rittmeister seems to suspect something, for he slackens speed and says it is only a few minutes to Kösen; he asks what I think of this little watering-place as a spot for putting up for the night. Yes, I think Kösen is an ideal spot and quite agree that we ought to stop there. So we drive quietly into the little town, the two halves of which are separated from one another by the Saale, but reunited by a stone bridge. We stop at the hotel *Zum nintigen Ritter* and are soon wide awake again in its parlour, with a warming cup of steaming tea before us. The host keeps us company and tells us that all the visitors disappeared like magic when the war broke out, and that his own hotel business has dwindled to nothing at all. "But what does that matter as long as we win," he adds.

The 16th September was heralded by a cloudy sky and heavy, sleepy raindrops, which, however, soon stopped falling after obligingly laying the dust. From Kösen there was a steady rise across and along the heights which line the Saale and Ilm valleys in the north. Pretty vistas open up at the sides, where the valleys sink between the hills and where the forest, dark and heavy, silently mounts guard over its secrets. A little further on the country becomes more broken and the road winds along in big curves. On the left we leave the Apolda and its valley. On a commanding height we catch sight of a so-called Bismarck tower of granite, with the great chancellor's name hewn into the stone at the top and his portrait medallion at the bottom. These towers are often to be met with in Germany, and on certain days of national rejoicing huge bonfires are lit on their summits.

We cannot drive through Weimar without visiting the house where Goethe lived for forty years, and which stands in the square now bearing his great name. It is with a feeling of reverence that one sets foot on the steps and thresholds and in apartments where Germany's, perhaps the Avorld's, greatest poet and thinker lived his life. As far as possible the furniture has been reinstated and restored to its former state. One admires Goethe's discrimination as a collector and the quick intelligence he brought to bear on all departments of the natural sciences. These traits are evidenced by his large and magnificent geological and mineralogical collections, his zoological and botanical finds, and his physical laboratory. I stop, however, longest before the cabinets containing in large portfolios his pen-and-ink and water-colour sketches. I am touched as I look at them. Every stroke of the brush in these landscapes, portraits and groups has been made by his own hand. Their execution is masterly, and the perspective and general effect superb. Yet this was but a trifling detail in his wonderful endowment. Equally fascinating almost are the busts which render his glorious head and the oil paintings for which he sat. What wonderful eyes, full of life and energy and geniality! They reveal an intellect to which everything is as clear as crystal. With a feeling of awe and without daring to speak to the courteous Dr. Hans Kroeber, who showed us over one of the greatest national treasures of Germany, we entered Goethe's study on the ground floor with its windows looking out on to the little garden. How simple and modest everything is; it occurs to one that one of the lighter rooms upstairs would have been a good deal pleasanter to work in. Behind the study we see his little bedroom, rigidly simple, where, with the words "More light," he ended the saga of his wonderful life.

When the mind has tarried for a little while in this world of great and precious memories, and is suddenly confronted on issuing into the square with a detachment of Landsturm soldiers marching off to their shooting range, when one leaves Goethe's home behind and is once more surrounded by the modern world and thinks of Germany's gigantic struggle against half the world - then, indeed, one has to rub one's eyes and steady oneself mentally so as not to lose one's balance. And this people, which has produced Goethe, and which now with honour and splendid courage fights on half a dozen fronts, has by the press of many countries and in fact entire nations been called a people of barbarians!

But let us continue our trip along the great highway; it is now lined for a long distance with plum trees where women and girls on ladders are seen picking the great violet fruit and collecting it in baskets drawn on small barrows by dogs. On the whole we do not see many people, apart from the handful of peasants driving hay home in their carts drawn by cows, and a few women mowing the grass on banks and meadows.

Next we come to Erfurt, a town which like so many others in these parts is memorable to us Swedes. At "The Tall Lily" Gustavus Adolphus spent one night of his great life. It was the night between the 28th and 29th October, 1632, after the assembling of the Swedish Army which a few days later was to fight and conquer at Lützen. At Erfurt one also thrills with pride at the memory of Field-Marshal Johan Baner. Here, as everywhere, the Landsturm soldiers sing as they march along. We lose ourselves in the labyrinth of oldworld streets, and not even my experienced guide von Krum is able to find his way. "Which way to Gotha?" we cry at every street corner, and the answer comes quickly, *rechts, links* or *gerade aus*. At last we work our way out of the tangle and fly along towards Gotha, the city of Justus Perthes and the Almanach de Gotha. Here it is easy to find the way, and before we know where we are we find ourselves once again dashing along through avenues of tall, graceful poplars towards Eisenach.

On our left the ground rises towards the rain-shrouded, misty ridges of the Thüringer Wald, but the road itself runs through smiling villages with their picturesque houses of the timber framework type, where cackling geese and clucking turkeys sometimes do their best to get run over or at all events to hamper our progress. At every bridge we come to, we receive a smart military salute from the sentries. We spin along at a lightning pace to Eisenach, and are as quickly out of it. The road now turns sharp to the south-west and by a series of gentle curves ascends the heights of the Thüringer Wald. On both sides of the road is a fine wood of lofty pines. I could almost fancy that I had been transplanted to certain parts of my own land where the eye is accustomed to dwell on these dark green, solemn firs standing like sentinels by the roadside. It is a beautiful piece of country. The smell of damp earth and juicy pine-needles rises in the air and reminds one vividly of the country on the road from Rawalpindi to Kashmir.

From the top of the hills a vast perspective opens up towards the south-west. Once again the road runs in serpentine curves down from the Thüringer Wald. The forest here consists largely of foliaged trees rather than conifers. Marksuhl is situated in a broken piece of country, where the higher-lying parts are occupied by clusters of trees whilst the rest of the land is cultivated. At Vacha we cross the important River Werra. From this point we progress again at lightning pace. Villages, fields, meadows, farms, gardens and leafy coppices, everything seems to fly past us.

Here we have Hünfeld in Hesse. Let us stop a moment and drink a cup of tea. There is a cosy dining-room in the restaurant. At a table sits a nurse with the Red Cross badge on her arm talking to two gentlemen, evidently doctors, for they speak of the care of the wounded soldiers. A few sportsmen enter with their bags full of partridges and hares. They are dressed in brown and green, with sporting-looking felt hats with plumes, and carry their guns on the shoulder.

We jump into the car once more and proceed to the old bishopric of Fulda, which does not long engage our attention, then across bridges and streams through a series of villages, one of which with its sinuous main street is called Schlüchtern. We continue to be delayed by poultry, geese and dogs, but the children seem to have learnt to leave the roadway clear. The boys give us a military salute and shoulder their little wooden guns, whilst the little children play on steps and benches, the mothers waving to us almost affectionately as if to say, "Give him my love and God bless him and you and the whole of our country!"

Via Gelnhausen we travel on to Hanau, in which neighbourhood we come across swarms of civilian cyclists. "Who on earth are these people, are they recruits on the way to join the army?" I ask, "Bless you, no; they are workmen from the factories and workshops at Hanau returning to their villages at the end of their day." Big and majestic the Main sends its muddy waters towards the sea. It is raining a little, the roads are soaked but just as good. We can see that we are approaching a big town, the traffic on the road increases, people live closer together, and the telegraph wires combine into mighty clusters - those silent wires which yet talk and know far more than we. When I come to the Valley of the Main I seem once more to hear the good old Swedish music and to see Stalhandske's cavalry before me, and into the moaning of the tree tops I seem to read the words of Adler Salvius: "Our Finnish lads who are getting used to those wine-lands are not likely to come back to Savolaks in a hurry. In the Livland wars they often had to put up with water and coarse mouldy bread with their beer-broth; now the Finn quaffs his wine out of his helmet." Such wealth and such abundance our poor old horsemen and their retainers had never even dreamt of.

Before us through the mist and gloaming twinkled the thousand lights and electric lamps of Frankfurt. When Gustavus Adolphus first came to Frankfurt the good burghers did not want to let him in, but made excuses and put the blame on the Elector of Mayence. But the King answered that he knew of no Elector of Mayence but himself. "I do not want to be delayed. If you refuse to open the gates, I dare say I can find some keys as I have done before in places which have fallen into my hands." The city surrendered at once. During the winter of 1631-32, when Sweden's King held his court at Frankfurt, this city was the centre of Europe. It was from here that Gustavus Adolphus said to the French who asked him not to direct his armies against Alsace, which country they pretended to have claimed ever since the death of the remote Dagobert: "I have come not as a traitor to Germany, but as its protector. I will restore it, not rend it asunder."

We drive on and on. The clusters of houses in the outskirts and suburbs close up into the streets of a large town. The traffic grows, the tram bells ring, the motors hoot, vast crowds of people walk about busily under umbrellas, and after a short while we stop before the entrance of the Hotel which before the war was called *Englischer Hof,* but which has now been re-baptised the *Hessischer Hof,* owing, to the feelings of the Germans towards their Germanic kinsmen of the island kingdom.

It is wonderful how attached one gets to one's car on a long journey! It is with a feeling of boredom that one stops at the hotel where the night is to be spent, and with a sensation of delight that one rises from the breakfast table the next morning to enter the car once more. This is how we felt on the 17th of September, a fine and pleasant day, though heavy clouds raced across the sky. But we could not start at once, we had first to go to a garage to get petrol and then to an *Immobiles Kraftwagen Depot,* where absolutely everything that may be wanted for repairing war cars is to be had. Here we took five spare tyres, which we lashed to the right side and to the back of our car. Of course, we do not pay a single *pfennig* - for we are travelling on Government service.

At last we are off again and follow the long streets of Frankfurt, leaving the city by the western outskirts with their large working-class population. Perhaps it might be thought that these workmen are opposed to the war which Germany is now conducting for the sake of her future? It certainly does not look like it . The social democratic workmen have equipped their little sons with helmets and wooden swords to fight out real battles in the backyards, and you hear them call each other Kluck and Hindenburg.

Once more we get out into the open country, and follow the great road which runs in a direct line to Wiesbaden. The avenue skirting it consists chiefly of apple and pear trees, weighed down with fruit. Farther on we meet with poplars, standing like sentries along the roadside. We do not stop at all in the graceful and elegant Wiesbaden, but fly past its parks and gardens, which are quieter and emptier than usual.

Soon we begin to ascend the Taunus heights via the Eiserne Hand. The rise is gradual and the curves numerous. A trim and straight-stemmed pine wood skirts the road on both sides. One seldom meets a vehicle or a pedestrian. From an eminence a vast panorama is suddenly spread out before us, but the weather has got foggy again and one cannot see far. At Langen Schwalbach the elegant hotels form a striking contrast to the solemn Red Cross flags and the wounded soldiers, now convalescent, who are sitting on balconies and in gardens, taking the air. The road now winds upwards once more, and we breathe a crisper atmosphere, but the view across to smiling dells and wooded hills is limited through fog. Up we go and down again over the gentle undulations of the country, where the ploughed fields merge together in a colour scheme of green, yellow and brown.

Next the road descends steeply to Nassau on the River Lahn. The country is gloriously pretty, its roads magnificent, its forests regal in their dark, silent splendour. On the brow of a hill stands an old ruined castle. The people in Nassau are friendly and greet and wave to us, and a stylish-looking young girl throws a red rose into our car - not for us, forsooth, but as a greeting to her lover, who no doubt is fighting in the war.

A moment later we skim the pretty riverside road to Ems along the Lahn, line up the car in a side street and walk back to the pavement to greet with bared head and a salute a funeral procession which is going through. The dead man was a major who had succumbed to his wounds. First comes a band playing a slow and melancholy march, then two banners which precede the black-caped coffin on its carriage, and behind it the *Kampfgenossen*, members of the Ems *Kriegerverein*, all in tall hats, frock-coats and black ties; the procession is closed by a number of wounded convalescent soldiers housed in the Kursaal. The solemn cortege moves slowly up the street to the railway station, for the dead major's body is to be sent to his own home. After a while the band returns accompanied by the convalescent soldiers. But now it plays a spirited and lively march. I was told that this was customary after military funerals - first the grief and the sorrow at the parting, the duty towards the honoured dead, then the joy of the survivors returning to the things of life.

The Kurhaus, a fine and roomy building, now contains eighty patients, and more are expected. Most of the badly wounded are in bed, but those who can get up are sitting about on balconies and enjoying the fresh air, and from what they said to me they all long to be back at the front.

I was told here that a young French lieutenant who had been badly wounded in the war had found an asylum in the Kurhaus, and recollecting the reports of the horrible cruelty with which the Germans, according to the English press, treat their French prisoners, I could not resist the temptation to enquire what the French lieutenant had to say about it. His room, which he occupied alone, was certainly not a matter for complaint; it was immediately above one of the six small rooms in which King William I. spent a short time each year from 1867 to 1887, and the view over Ems and the Lahn valley was the same as the King had enjoyed all those years. The wounded man was tended by a German doctor, who entertained good hopes of his recovery, and by two sisters of mercy, one of whom spoke French. But I hasten to add that Lieutenant Verrier, on my asking whether he was satisfied with the treatment he received in Germany, at once answered "yes" with warmth and conviction, and I suppose that wherever his fate will direct his steps he will always remember with gratitude the time he spent over William I.'s apartments in Ems, where the doctor did all in his power to save his leg and the sisters all they could to alleviate his suffering and dispel in a measure his loneliness and homesickness. I am sure that he will be the first to acknowledge that I am right.

I went up to his room and was at once admitted. He lay in a large bed with clean white sheets. His face was little less pale than these, but he looked very handsome with his hair brushed from his forehead, his finely shaped nose and well-kept moustache over a firm mouth, and his black French eyes bespoke a *joie de vivre* and a bright intelligence. He told me that he had come home from New Guinea in June and that he was just about to be married when the war came and took him away from his bride and parents. He received his wound in the scrap at Rossignol in Belgium. It was a terrible day, spent in the midst of bursting shells and fire from rifles and machine guns. His bullet had struck him obliquely through the knee and calf. He fell and remained lying all night on the field of battle. The following morning he was picked up and taken to a German Field Hospital and subsequently by easy stages to Ems. At the end of August Emperor William visited the town and when he heard that there was a wounded Frenchman there he went to see him. Lieutenant Verrier told me that the Emperor had enquired in excellent French about his adventures in the war and how he felt. I said that I should in all probability soon be meeting the Emperor, and would then tell his Majesty of the impression the gracious visit had made on the invalid. When later I carried out my self-imposed task, the Emperor remembered the French lieutenant very well and was gratified to hear of the hopes entertained for his recovery.

In conclusion I asked Lieutenant Verrier whether there was anything I could do for him within the limits permitted by the German regulations. He seemed almost to have longed for this question, for he had the answer quite ready. Day and night he had been tormented by one single thought: "How are my parents and my fiancee to learn that I am still alive and doing well? I am now in enemy country and have no means of writing." I asked him for his address, and he wrote in my diary, "Monsieur Verrier Cachet, Horticulteur, 52, rue du Quinconce, Angers, Marne et Loire." A minute later I was seated at a desk and wrote on postcards in German the adventures of the young Frenchman and sent them to my family in Stockholm, who, with the assistance of the French Minister, would forward the news to the above address. I know that it reached its destination and caused great joy, for later on I received very hearty greetings and thanks from Verrier's home.

I have often since wandered with a heavy and lingering step through the "field" and war hospitals, especially the wards containing wounded Frenchmen, British and Belgians who lay there counting the slowly passing hours. How easy would it not have been for me, who had both liberty and health, to send off a postcard here and there which would have reached distant homes with a message of release from the wearing anguish of anxiety! There is nothing so trying and so difficult to bear as the uncertainty of the fate of those we love. When the name of a son, a brother, or a husband appears in the list of missing after a battle, the sickening anguish is almost greater to those at home than if they knew that he had fallen. Their mental vision pictures him as wounded, bleeding to death, alone and abandoned to the horrors of darkness, cold and thirst. But I had really no grounds for such qualms of conscience, for in the first place I had no business to interfere with the regulations of the German military authorities regarding the communication between wounded prisoners and their homes, and in the second place there were far too many of them, and by the evening I realised that the task of acting as a good Samaritan was an altogether hopeless one.[1]

Meanwhile I took a hearty farewell of Verrier and wished him a speedy recovery and a happy reunion with his people at home at Angers.

Before leaving, we looked at the memorial stone commemorating the fateful and firm reply given on the 13th of July, 1870, at 9.30 A.M." by King William to the French Ambassador Benedetti, which gave the signal for the FrancoGerman war. And now, after a lapse of forty-four years, we were back again at the same point. Now it seemed that the thought of revenge for Alsace-Lorraine had ripened into action - unless it be indeed that other evil powers had exploited France's longing for revenge, or revived it when, as some say, it was dead, to benefit themselves thereby and stop the advance of German prosperity. The near future will be the judge.

After dinner we mounted our car once more and the canary began to sing so that the good people of Ems might get out of our way. We proceeded along the right bank of the Lahn, following its bends in noble curves. The country round here is exceedingly pretty. It is almost a pity that we have to travel so fast; one hardly has time to visualise the beauty of a perspective before the picture disappears and is replaced by another, if possible even finer. Suddenly, beyond a steep spur jutting from the mountain on our right, the majestic Rhine is revealed to our vision, whilst on the crest of a hill on our left towers a romantic old castle. We dash under another railway bridge faithfully guarded by the worthy Landsturm men. Suddenly we enter a street so narrow that its entire width is taken up by a Red Cross flag of more than ample dimensions. Following this street as far as it goes, we suddenly come to the bank

1. After the beginning of October all prisoners, even wounded Frenchmen in German hospitals, had permission to correspond with their homes. This was given after the French Government had granted the same privilege to German prisoners and wounded.

of the enormous river whose German waters silently flow between its prosperous and well-populated banks to deliver their burden through neutral Holland into the mighty bosom of the sea.

Once more the river is hidden by narrow streets, but soon it greets us again in all its wonderful splendour as we cross its dancing wavelets by a long pontoon bridge guarded more zealously than any we have yet passed. Next we are in Coblenz, where, at the point where the Moselle empties itself into the Rhine, stands a gigantic statue of old Emperor William on a charger. The plinth of this monument bears the following memorable inscription: *Ninimer wird das Reich zerstöret wenn Ihr einig seid und treu.*[2] The truth of these significant words is now indeed brought home to Germany and to the world.

The road next takes us up along the right bank of the Moselle, where a stone bridge with beautiful arches takes us across and past a couple of Moselle steamers which are lying moored, carrying the Red Cross flag. The narrow, winding streets are filled with tramcars, cabs, vans, men and women, and last but not least soldiers in German army uniforms. We breathe more freely as we come out again on to the open road and speed along the bank of the great Rhine tributary. There is plenty for the eye to feast on. Now and again we catch sight of a Uttle steamer or tug gliding on the river; on the steep left bank stone buttresses support the vineyards. The landscape itself is indescribably beautiful round these endless bends, as one village after another comes into view, the grey houses with their black slate roofs and the beautiful churches showing up strikingly against the luxuriant background of foliage. Still bowling along at lightning speed, we soon reach Treis, where a curious-looking ferry, reminding me of those of the Siberian rivers, is ready to take us and our car across to the left bank. We drive down on to the other end of its deck so that another car which has just arrived can be taken on board. The principle upon which the ferry is worked is as follows: A stout cable is stretched across the river and made fast on the left bank to the rock and on the right bank to a securely imbedded pile. From a ring on this

2. "Never shall the Empire be destroyed if ye united are and faithful."

cable runs a line, the other end of which is made fast to the bows of the punt-shaped ferry. A long steering-oar projects into the water astern. The rest is done by the current. By reversing the action and the steering-oar, the ferry runs back to the opposite bank.

On the left bank we continue our swift, winding journey. Here and there we pass a military convoy or meet an ambulance train, the first two carriages of which contain wounded Frenchmen, the others Germans. The Frenchmen are no better or worse off than the Germans; all lie on straw and are covered with blankets. The sliding doors of these goods wagons, fitted up specially for the transport of wounded, stood open in order to admit fresh air to the wounded.

At the village of Eller we stop for a moment at an inn, where the host, Herr Meinze, entertains us with what he knows about the war. His young daughter runs off to fetch a letter just received from the son of the family, twenty-two years old, an Uhlan of the Guard from Potsdam. The letter bears the somewhat vague postal address of La Ferté, and the writer complains that he has not had a word from home for a month. He mentions that he was present on an occasion when a French airman dropped a bomb over a gun team, killing three men and wounding twenty. Of his British opponents he speaks very disrespectfully. But he forgets that the English mercenaries, whatever their faults, show great personal courage and fight with bravery and contempt of death. He ends his letter with the hope that Germany will soon have made mincemeat of all her enemies. The chief trait which pervades all these field postcards is the bright and cheery spirit of the soldiers and their blind faith in the unconquerable might of the German Army and final victory. That *I* may fall is of no account. That *I* may not be one of the triumphant army which will march in through the Brandenburger Tor cannot be helped, but Germany must win, if not before, then after the spring flowers have begun to sprout and blossom round my grave.

At Alf, where a white paddle-steamer flying the Red Cross flag lies at her moorings, we leave the Moselle and follow the laconic advice of a signpost pointing up towards the hills which mark the nearest way to Treves. It pours with rain. We put up the awning and the rain patters loudly on the taut canvas. Owing to the great speed we get one drenching after another. The water in the puddles spurts up around the wheels as before the bows of a swift steamer. The road is only half as wide as the great main road eastward. But on the other hand the traffic is insignificant. "Way to Wittlich?" von Krum asks in a village, when uncertain of the road. "To Paris!" comes the retort of a couple of joyous maidens who point in the direction we are to go. In due course we get to Wittlich and struggle through its horribly narrow streets, which, to make matters worse, are encumbered with all sorts of vehicles. The houses both of villages and towns in this part of the country are almost entirely of stone, and the streets are very narrow - sometimes one almost gets the impression that they were originally built with a view to protection against foreign invasion.

Off we go again down to the banks of the Moselle and to its beautifully situated villages, and when at length we stop at the *Trierischer Hof* at Treves, it is pitch-dark and raining pitilessly. We were drenched to the skin, and had intended to proceed to Luxemburg after a moment's rest to dry our clothes. But as the deluge grew worse instead of better, and as we were told that there were no rooms to be had at Luxemburg for love or money, we decided to stop where we were. Soon we were sitting in the restaurant at our belated dinner. The place teemed with officers, and in the streets the soldiers splashed about in the wet in their grey overcoats. We asked everybody where the Main Headquarters were, but nobody knew anything about it. Some said that the General Staff was at Luxemburg, others that it had moved to Belgium. "Well, we shall get there in time," we said to ourselves.

The *Trierischer Hof* actually had a couple of modest rooms, where we made ourselves at home. My excellent friend von Krum told me that officers were entitled in war time to billet where they liked. Room with breakfast must always be placed at their disposal free of charge. Dinner and other meals they have to pay for. The officer has only to fill in a printed receipt which he hands to the host on leaving in place of currency. On producing this receipt before the competent military authority, the host receives his money, but not at the same rate as in peace time, for values are set at a lower figure than under normal conditions. The same applies to horses, carts, motor-cars and much else that is needed in war. Everything is valued by special committees and then paid for with a receipt. At Treves it was impossible to get a car or even a horse-cab, as there were no horses left. When therefore our host received a telegram saying that his son, who had probably been slightly wounded at the front, was expected at 3 A.M., there was no means whatever of getting a conveyance to meet him and take him home in. He asked if he might borrow our car, but unfortunately we were not allowed to leave it in civilian hands. In the end he managed to borrow a doctor's car and found his son in pretty good condition.

Luckily the trams were running, and in the evening we took one to the Horn Barracks, usually occupied by Infantry Regiment No. 29 *von Horn* (3rd Rhenish). But now the entire regiment is in the field and the barracks have been turned into a hospital. They hold in peace time three battalions, but at the present time only 500 wounded, as the latter need more room with special accommodation for doctors and nursing staff. Premises have, in addition, been requisitioned for operating theatres, bath-rooms, store-rooms, etc. Just now there is plenty of room, as only 220 beds are occupied, of which 150 by Frenchmen. Six doctors and one head surgeon, assisted by a great number of Red Cross sisters, were in charge of the wounded soldiers. In due course we arrived at the barracks, were passed by the sentry at the gate, entered a corridor and knocked at a door which was duly opened, and a moment later we had become the bosom friends of a couple of young doctors sitting at supper before a steaming bowl of soup which had just been brought in. I asked them, whatever they did, not to interrupt their meal, as we could sit and chat with them in the meantime. But no, that would not do at all, the soup could wait, and guided by a little oil lamp we marched out through the long corridor and began at once by inspecting a couple of the operating theatres, which had been rigged up hurriedly on the outbreak of war and equipped as far as possible on thoroughly modem lines. The operating tables were in the middle of the room. Water-pipes, vessels, appliances and a number of surgical instruments - everything was in superb condition. The walls and floor of these rooms had been painted over in oil and an average of fifteen operations took place in them daily. Several other barracks at Treves have been fitted up as hospitals in a like manner.

Thereupon we went into a large ward filled with wounded German soldiers, and chatted with several of them. All were very satisfied and cheerful, they all felt thoroughly at home and could not conceive it possible to receive better and kindlier treatment than they got at the hospital. Nevertheless time hung heavily on their hands, and they could not help thinking of their comrades in the field. They longed to be back at the war and hoped soon to be about again - that is to say, those who knew that they would not be crippled for life.

We left them with a "*Gute Nacht, gute Besserung,*" and proceeded to a ward higher up, where French soldiers were being tended. Here we also spoke with some of the patients. They were all polite and communicative, but lacked the cheery disposition of the Germans, which was really not to be wondered at, as they were in enemy country and cut off from all communication with their own people. One of them had been wounded at Rossignol like Lieutenant Verrier, but did not know him. He had been shot through the left hand and the left leg, which the surgeon had been obliged to amputate. When he got his bullet wounds, he had strength and presence of mind enough to creep into a ditch for protection against the weather and the firing. He had torn off strips of cloth from his greatcoat and wound them round his wounds. Next day the German ambulance men had found him, applied a proper "first field dressing" and carried him to the nearest field hospital, from which not long ago he had been conveyed by rail to Treves.

Another soldier had been left lying on the field for two nights and had suffered maddening torture from thirst. The thirst had if possible caused him greater suffering than his wounds. Twice the Germans had in passing given him water and chocolate. Finally the ambulance people had found him and taken him to a field hospital. Like his comrade, he expressed his gratitude for the treatment he had met with here at Treves, and several assenting voices were heard from the neighbouring beds.

The two German doctors who took us round told us that the French wounded usually did not want to leave the hospital, as they knew that as soon as they recovered they would be treated as ordinary prisoners. This view of the matter is quite natural and is most certainly shared by all wounded, no matter to what nation they belong. For it is pleasanter to lie in one's comfortable bed and be coddled in every way, than to live in a barracks or a concentration camp with crowds of other prisoners, including Senegalese negroes, Moroccans and Indians.

Finally our guide took us to the door of a room containing three French officers. One of them, who had been shot through the lung, slept well and did not permit himself to be disturbed by our talk. Another had a more dangerous lung wound and was continually troubled by a nasty cough which, whenever it attacked him, threw his head backwards and forwards with great violence. His condition was considered very critical, and even if one had known the address of his people it would have been no relief to them to learn his condition.

The third, a big and somewhat stout Captain, had served for several years in southernmost Morocco and was accustomed to little scraps with the Tuaregs in the Sahara. But *this* was something very different. It was terrible, *terrible!* He had been called home from his African station to take part in this horrible struggle. His right foot had been smashed in a fight in Belgium by a rifle bullet, whilst another had carried away a couple of his fingers. He said he had a sort of recollection of having the wound dressed on the battlefield by German Red Cross men or doctors who had done all they could to check the flow of blood. Afterwards he had been taken to a dressing station, where his wounds had received further treatment. As he was classed amongst the comparatively slightly wounded, he had been taken to Luxemburg and now at length to Treves. He was probably aware that when discharged as convalescent he would remain a prisoner with all the privileges to which his rank entitled him, receiving, besides, half the pay he had been getting at home. There he lay, the poor Captain, with his jovial face, aquiline nose and heavy beard. He was cheerful and good-tempered, and assured us that he had absolutely nothing to grumble about - apart from the fate which denied him the honour to continue fighting for his country. But it was evident that he was a bit of a philosopher and he bore his unkind fate like a man. He lay there with a smile on his lips and was grateful for anything that was done for him and for the interest taken in him by the unknown visitors. During the long lonely hours of the night he often heard his comrades struggling and wrestling with death, whilst his own thoughts wandered to the palm trees on the desert fringe, and he seemed to hear the dromedaries' swishing steps over the sand and the desert winds calling "come home, come home!"

The young doctors who accompanied us told us that the German soldiers always and without exception longed to be back at the front, unless their condition was such that they had not strength enough to desire anything. Among the French the feeling was different: "Whatever you like, anything but the fire at the front." But this is, on psychological grounds, quite natural and cannot well be otherwise. There is nothing that depresses and demoralises the soldier as much as being a prisoner. He feels that he is playing the part of the weaker, that he is entirely at the mercy of others, that his strength is gone, his initiative taken from him and his fighting spirit rendered unavailing. In such a situation, to gain personal advantages and to make the best of a bad job, he will say much that he would never have dreamt of uttering on his own side of the fighting line. It is therefore unfair to judge the fighting value of an army by the remarks of prisoners detached from it.

Herein we have perhaps the explanation of the fact observed at the Treves hospitals, or, at all events, at the Horn barracks, that the mortality amongst the Frenchmen was incomparably greater than amongst the Germans. It would be futile to try to explain it by the suggestion that the doctors and nurses involuntarily felt greater compassion for their own countrymen, for when it is considered that 35,000 wounded have been transported through Treves *Westbahnhof* - latterly 1500 a day - it will be realised that the doctors available must be so overwhelmed with work as to have no time for sentiment. To them the case is everything, and it is a point of honour with them to save as many as possible. The whole care of the wounded becomes a professional, almost mechanical, matter, and one cannot wonder at it when one sees the stream of wounded passing through. I was told that the wounds of the Germans heal better and quicker than those of the Frenchmen, whatever the reason may be. But plainly the psychological factor has something to do with this also.

To this must be added another point of view - the wounds of the Frenchmen are usually more malignant than those of the Germans. Whilst the former are all too frequently hit in the lungs, stomach or abdomen, the Germans in the great majority of cases are wounded in the shoulders, arms and legs. It becomes obvious that the Germans must keep closer to the ground and are more skilled in using cover. It would be interesting to know exactly in what measure this point is affected by the French army uniform, the dark blue tunic and the bright red trousers, exactly the same as worn in 1870-71. This dress obviously presents a most excellent target, whilst the Germans with their grey field uniforms and grey headgear merge into their environment.

We were talking in this strain as we were leaving the hospital, and the young doctors were inexhaustible in their stories of what they had experienced during their work at Treves. It was not only the barracks that had been converted into hospitals - churches and schools had also been requisitioned. "But how do the children get on with their schooling if the schools are turned into hospitals?" "Well, it is this way. Since the younger professors and masters were called to the war, older teachers, both men and women, have turned up from almost everywhere and carry on the work to the best of their ability. Thus they earn a little money which they badly need in these hard war times,"

We also spoke, of course, about the unceasing stream of wounded who are being brought into Germany. The seriously wounded and those not expected to recover are kept near the front, as they cannot stand being moved. But the lightly wounded, or at all events those who can stand the journey, are sent home. Soldiers who have had a bullet through the hand or a flesh wound in the arm, may, if they wish it, go straight home to their people. In such cases, on leaving the army, they are provided with the receipt which entitles them to free medical care at home. They must then attend daily at a certain hour at the doctor's for examination; when fully recovered they return to their own regiment. Soon I suppose there will not be a single village in Germany without its war hero and its Iron Cross. One can imagine the pride and joy with which a son is received on returning home after his deeds of valour, and the heartfelt good wishes which accompany him when for the second time he leaves for the front!

I was told that a fresh train-load of wounded was expected at Treves at half-past twelve the same night. The doctors were holding themselves in readiness to receive another avalanche of exhausted and maimed heroes. Our doctors told us that when the train stopped they used to go through all the carriages to examine the patients. Those who were too bad to go any further were carried on hammock-stretchers to the hospitals. The others were allowed to go on after having their wounds redressed. This is another phase of the struggle between life and death - the doctor on the side of life struggling to snatch back those whom death has vainly sought to capture on the battlefield.

To wind up our visit, we had a peep into a store-room, the floor of which was encumbered with entire bales of cotton, gauze dressings, oil cloth, sticking-plaster and bandages of all kinds. Entire railway trains full of dressings and bandages, surgical instruments and drugs, are constantly running east and west from the heart of Germany. Our hospital at Treves was also permeated with a strong scent of carbolic, ether and chloroform. When one sees the pale faces and red scars of the wounded and the mountains of dressings, and when one inhales this penetrating hospital odour, one almost seems to hear the ping of the rifle bullets and the fierce shrieking of the shells. At such moments the deep and horrible solemnity of war seems to draw closer, and one realises indeed its sinister reality. Late in the evening, as we wandered back in the wet to the *Trierischer Hof*, I felt that we were, indeed, not far away from those parts of Europe where entire nations are grappling in a life-and-death struggle.

CHAPTER II
THE EMPEROR WILLIAM

STILL AS IGNORANT regarding the whereabouts of the Main Headquarters as when we left Berlin, we set out from Treves in the morning of the 18th September, recrossed the Moselle, and cast a glance up at the heights from which on August 4th Frenchmen in mufti were heliographing to the airships, who wanted to know how the German mobilisation was getting on. At the flying station we stopped a moment to have a look at the *Taubes* in their canvas sheds.

The gentle undulations of the country give it a picturesque aspect. At Igel stands the sandstone tower, 2000 years old and twenty-three metres in height, called the *Igeler Säule*, and considered to be the finest relic left by the Romans north of the Alps. To this very day an inscription can be seen, testifying that this monument was raised by Secundinius Aventinus and Secundinius Securus in memory of their parents and kinsmen. How different from the frail wooden crosses we were to see by the roadside, and which will disappear when the spring sun draws the frost out of the ground and the plough cuts fresh furrows in the soil!

But we must now take leave of the Moselle. On the left we have already behind us the roads to Metz and Saarbrücken, and not far to the south is the boundary of Lorraine. Along a road passing through an orchard we reach Wasserbillig, cross the Sauer stream and enter the Grand Duchy of Luxemburg, the entire population of which does not nearly approach that of Stockholm. On the way to Grevenmacher we passed by numberless nurseries and gardens given up to the cultivation of roses. But there are also woods in Luxemburg, and our road takes us by frequent copses of larch and beech, and further on of pine and beech.

At a railway crossing we are stopped by an empty train of enormous length, going to Germany to bring out fresh soldiers. The natives of

Luxemburg regard us with indifference. The greetings and friendly wavings of handkerchiefs are a thing of the past, here no one greets and no one betrays his thoughts, which is as well perhaps, as they cannot be particularly friendly. The apple trees are succeeded by an avenue of chestnut, ash and plane trees. The bedrock consists of the same variety of limestone of which the houses in the villages are usually built.

At length our road winds down into a pleasant valley, and at its bottom lies a part of the pretty and trim little town of Luxemburg, where the equally pretty and trim Grand Duchess has her residence. But the more fashionable part of the town lies on the height above the valley, reached by a very steep street presenting somewhat peculiar views, as, for instance, when one suddenly finds oneself on a level with a church spire.

Now we begin to look about. Yes, it is obvious that the Main Headquarters are still at Luxemburg. Sentries at the entrances to all hotels, soldiers everywhere, officers rushing past in motor-cars. In a market-place large tents have been put up for horses, and round them walk the sentries smoking their pipes; in another open space there are rows of motorcars laden with petrol and oil in cylinders.

We must observe becoming military precision in our search and consequently make at once for the house where the great General Staff has taken up its quarters, and which in ordinary times is a Luxemburg school. Von Krum gets down and soon returns with the intimation that we must report ourselves to a Lieutenant-Colonel Hahnke. He sent us off to the Chief of the General Staff, His Excellency von Moltke, who with his charming Swedish Countess has just sat down to dinner at the *Kölnischer Hof*, where they reside. The Countess was on a short visit to Luxemburg in the service of the Red Cross. Here I felt almost as if I were at home, for I had many times been a guest in their hospitable home in Berlin. As calm as if he had been on manoeuvres, the Chief lit his cigar and made detailed enquiries about my plans and wishes. I said I wanted to go to the front and see as much as I might be allowed to, mentioning that it was my intention subsequently to describe what I had seen of the war with my own eyes. If possible I wanted to get an impression of a modern battle, and hoped also to get an opportunity of visiting the occupied parts of Belgium.

The Chief thought for a moment. Permission to visit the front had already been granted to me by the Emperor, and it only remained to decide which would be the best place for me to begin my observations. The army of the German Crown Prince was the nearest, only a couple of hours away. The Chief would arrange everything for my journey, and I was shortly to receive details of the programme. "Of course, there can be no question of safety in the fighting zone," he said, "it is not far away. If you listen you can hear the thunder of guns from Verdun."

Later in the day I was the possessor of a so-called *Ausweis* or permit signed by the Chief of the General Staff, and intimating that I had "permission to witness the course of events at the different sections of the army" and requesting "all authorities in command to meet my wishes as far as they possibly could," and to assist me with word and deed. This document was to me an "open sesame." It gave me almost unlimited liberty of movement. Once I had begun I could go practically where I liked. But it did not take me long to realise that I had been wrong in thinking that a couple of weeks would suffice for a layman to get an insight into the complicated apparatus of a field army; a couple of months would be nearer the mark. I hasten to add that the time I spent at the front was far from sufficient. For every step one takes, for every hour that passes, one is overwhelmed with fresh impressions which there is no time to assimilate, and when the first month is gone one retains but a very superficial conception of this enormously complicated piece of machinery, which nevertheless under the firm hand of the master runs as smoothly and noiselessly as clockwork.

Then we spoke of other things. I learnt that a troop train passes through Luxemburg station every half-hour, and that the only pause is at midday to prevent congestion. It is the pulse which beats in the arteries of the German railway system. One wave of human energy after another thus sweeps out towards the battlefields and flings itself against the enemy's fire; the spirit of gaiety resounds from the overfilled wagons, accompanied by the glorious songs of *Deutschland, Deutschland über Alles* and *Die Wacht am Rhein*. There is no trace of fear, not a sign of despondency anywhere. All are willing and cheerful. What would life be worth as long as the dear fatherland was not free and great and powerful! One wonders if these soldiers have any conception of the dangers and struggles that await them. Of course they read about it daily in the newspapers, but the more difficult it looks the more eager they become. The Bavarians are the most warlike. They are in their element with bayonets lowered for the charge. Superhuman power is required to withstand them, once they have decided to "go ahead." Here at Headquarters everyone also speaks with the greatest respect of the Frenchmen as opponents, and no one denies the bravery of the British soldiers." They go straight into perdition without flinching and fall, but do not yield, before the fire of machine guns." Of the prisoners, it was said that there was a great difference between the British and the French. The former would stand with their hands in their pockets and a pipe in their mouth when spoken to by an officer, and a salute was only elicited by a reprimand. The Frenchmen, on the other hand, always salute the German officers without being told, and this is probably due to their inherited military spirit and to the trait of inborn courtesy which pervades the whole nation.

When speaking of the troop trains, the Countess Moltke suggested a visit to the railway station, and we accordingly proceeded there, accompanied by von Krum. We were just in time to see an ambulance train - that is to say, not a properly equipped hospital train - roll into the station. Immediately some doctors began their round of the carriages, where the wounded lay on a thick layer of straw and were covered with blankets. A goods wagon in a troop train holds forty men or eight horses, but only thirty-six wounded at the most. The seriously wounded are sorted out and carried out on stretchers to large ambulance motor-cars, which take them to the hospitals in the town. The remainder, who are to be taken into Germany, receive new dressings if necessary. All are fed whilst the train is standing in the station with soup, sausages, bread and coffee in ample quantities. The Red Cross sisters have installed a kitchen at the station, in which cooking is in full swing day and night.

Temporary nurses and servants do the waiting and go from carriage to carriage with large buckets filled with steaming and fragrant soup or coffee. A kindly old gentleman accompanied by a porter slowly goes the round of the carriages and distributes newspapers and entire armfuls of cigars. Two carriages were occupied by Frenchmen only. They were treated otherwise in exactly the same way as the Germans, but the old gentleman devoted himself only to his countrymen. The latter, who were clearly on the road to recovery, were singing cheery soldiers' ditties and delighted in recounting their experiences to anyone who would listen. One of them had had three horses shot under him on a critical occasion, but at last got hold of a mule which enabled him to carry on his duties. "You need not believe him if you don't want to," said one of his comrades laughingly, but he went on nevertheless with his tales and declared that he slept like a child whilst the shells were falling thick around him.

From the railway we drove to a private hospital, of which there are several, supported by private contributions. This small house had over sixty beds, of which fifty-three were now occupied by soldiers. Forty Catholic sisters tended them. A sister of refined and distinguished appearance took us round from bed to bed, and Countess Moltke spoke in a friendly and interested manner with all the wounded. Here lay men with bullets through arms and legs, through a foot or a hand, or through the lung. One had lost his right hand. Another felt his lung wound only at the point where the bullet had passed out through the back. A couple of French officers were lodged in a separate room. All, and not least the Frenchmen, were very satisfied with the treatment they received. Most of them had been wounded at the battles of Vitry and Longwy.

It would take too long to describe all the interesting acquaintances I made in Luxemburg and to introduce to the reader all the eminent men with whom I spoke during the two days I spent in this little town. Suffice it to mention the Imperial Chancellor von Bethmann Hollweg, the Foreign Minister von Jagow, the War Minister Lieutenant-General von Falkenhayn, and the Chief of the Imperial Volunteer Automobile Corps the young Prince Waldemar, son of Prince Henry.

The Main Headquarters are the head or rather the brain of the army in the field, where all plans are made and from which all orders are issued. It is an incredibly complicated apparatus with an organisation of which every detail has been prepared in advance. When an apparatus of this kind is installed in a small town like Luxemburg, all hotels, schools, barracks, Government offices, as well as a number of private houses, have to be requisitioned for billets. The invaded country has no alternative but to resign itself to its fate. But nothing is taken promiscuously, everything will be made good after the war. The War Ministry is housed in an hotel, the General Staff - as already mentioned - in a school, the offices of the Automobile Corps in a private house, and so on. The Commander-in-Chief, von Moltke, resided at the *Kölnischer Hof,* the Imperial Chancellor and the Foreign Minister in an exceptionally elegant private house, whilst the Emperor's personal staff and suite were stopping at the *Hotel Staar,* where a room was also placed at my disposal.

But although for several obvious reasons I could not remain long at the Main Headquarters, I must nevertheless say a few words about a man whom I met there and whom I regard as one of the most remarkable figures of the world's history, the most powerful and most impressive ruler of our time, and, moreover, one of the most genial and most fascinating men one could wish to meet.

When in June, 1913, William II. celebrated his twenty-five years' jubilee as German Emperor, I wrote about him in the *Magdeburgische Zeitung* the following words, which in a large measure have already been borne out by events: "By his strong and powerful personality William II. stamps his impress on the era to which he belongs. Hitherto this has only been in the sphere of peace. What the future carries with it no one knows. But this much we know, that no foreign State will unchastised dare to challenge Germany's honour and security. Even if an unkind fate should sometime draw letters of blood across his firmament, the Emperor, with the same energy and impulsive force which distinguished him in times of peace, will lead his legions into the fire, and the golden eagle on his helmet will point the way to fresh victories."

History will bear out as an indisputable fact that Emperor William throughout a quarter of a century has done all in his power to keep the thunders of war from the confines of the German Empire and from Europe. On more than one occasion peace hung by a hair. All who know the facts agree that it has been the Emperor's personal intervention which averted a catastrophe. Once, not long ago, the war was nearer than people thought, and here again it was the Emperor's love of peace that became the deciding factor. Many blamed him for this, and called his attitude irresolute and yielding. But here also the judgment of history will be in his favour. In the meantime Germany armed herself for the sanguinary conflict as to the coming of which no far-sighted man could doubt. In the end the struggle for the maintenance of peace became hopeless. This was realised by no one better than by the Emperor himself, and for this reason he has throughout his reign striven to strengthen the Empire's fighting resources on land and water. At the present moment the fleet is riding on the seas like a gigantic monument to the wise and clear eyed foresight of its creator. For it is the Emperor himself who, in co-operation with his peerless Grand Admiral von Tirpitz, created the floating fortresses without which Germany's position would have been precarious when England came along with her declaration of war.

When the spark of war was kindled, Emperor William was spending his usual summer vacation off the coast of Norway. He went home at once - with the same haste that brought President Poincaré from Stockholm, where he was spending a day after his doubtless very important visit to Petrograd. Since then events have succeeded one another rapidly. The little spark at Serajevo has become a conflagration which has spread over the entire earth like a devastating prairie fire. It was a fortunate thing for Germany and her Germanic neighbours that she was armed to the teeth and possessed a ruler who knew what he wanted, who wanted what was right and beneficial to his country, and who fully realised the grave responsibility which rested on his shoulders.

But let us return to the Great Headquarters.

Directly I arrived in Luxemburg, I was honoured with an invitation to dine with the Emperor William the following day at one o'clock. Most of the guests were stopping at the *Hotel Staar*, and the cars were to leave there in good time. I went with Adjutant -General, Lieutenant General von Gontard, Acting General a la suite. The street close to the Imperial residence was railed off, the barriers being withdrawn by the soldiers to let our car pass. The Emperor lived in the house of the German Minister and had his private apartments on the first floor. On the ground floor was the chancellerie, where enormous maps of the theatres of war were mounted on easels, and next to it was the dining-room, quite a small apartment.

The guests, all in field uniform, without any display, forgathered in the chancellerie. I myself was dressed in the most flagrant everyday clothes - in the field nothing is carried for show. Among the Emperor's suite I recognised a couple of old acquaintances, the Headquarters Commandant, Adjutant General, Colonel-General von Plessen, and the President of the Navy Council, Admiral von Müller, of Swedish descent, who spoke Swedish as fluently as German, The others were his Excellency von Treutler and Lieutenant-General Baron Marschall, Colonel von Mutius, acting aide-de-camp, the Princes Pless and Arnim and the Emperor's body-physician. Dr. Ilberg. We were thus ten all told.

At the stroke of one the door from the vestibule was opened and Emperor William entered with a firm, quiet step. All glances were fixed on the strongly built, well-knit figure. The room became as quiet as the grave. One realised that one was in the presence of a great personality. The little room, otherwise so humble, now had a deeper significance. Here was the axis, the pivot round which the world's happenings turned. Here was the centre from which the war was directed. Germany is to be crushed, so say its enemies. *"Magst ruhig sein,"*[3] says the German army to its Fatherland. And here in our midst stands its supreme war-lord, a picture of manliness, resolution and honourable frankness. Around him flit the thoughts and passions of the whole world. He is the object of love, blind confidence and admiration, but also of fear, hate and calumny. Round him, who loves peace, rages the greatest war

3. From the line *"Lieb Vaterland magst ruhig sein"* (Be undismayed, dear Fatherland"), in *Die Wacht am Rhein.*

of all times, and his name is ringed with strife. A man who, in a nation sprung from the same race, can arouse such fierce hatred and call forth such outrageous indictments, must indeed possess a very remarkable personality. For otherwise his detractors would leave him in peace and empty the vials of their wrath on someone else, more formidable still. But all that calumny, meanness and craven fear can inspire has been poured on his head. His intentions are distorted, his words are misconstrued and his actions are turned into crimes. But in the whole of Germany, throughout the German army, his praises are sung. In the field services, in all the churches of Germany, everywhere fervent prayer's for his safety are offered up. *"Magst ruhig sein,"* the soldiers may well say to their Emperor, and they on their part know that he will never fail in his duty and that he will never withdraw a single soldier from the fighting line until Germany's future is assured.

It is not a Charlemagne or an Imperator who enters the chancellerie. It is merely an officer in the simplest uniform imaginable, a greyish blue tunic with a double row of buttons, dark-coloured breeches and brown top-boots. Not even the little black and white ribbon of the Iron Cross adorns his breast. But it is nevertheless a fascinating and compelling personality, an urbane and courteous man of the world, that we see entering the room. It is a man whose quick intuition and superb powers of description reveal the observer and the artist, whose wise speech betrays the statesman, whose kindly manner betokens humility and sympathy and whose military, commanding voice indicates the master, accustomed to be obeyed. Happy is the people which especially in troubled times possesses such a leader, a chieftain round whom all gather in confidence and whose ability no one doubts.

But it is also his eyes that possess a singular magnetic power, and which fascinate all when the Emperor enters. It is as if the whole room suddenly became lighter, when one meets the glance of the Emperor's calm, blue eyes. They are wonderfully expressive. They bespeak first and foremost an iron will and unconquerable energy. They betray a certain melancholy at the thought that all may not understand that he is actuated absolutely by the will to do what is pleasing unto God and beneficial to his people. They also betray a sparkling wit, an intellect to which nothing human is foreign and a spirit of humour which is irresistible. They betoken honour, love of truth and a steadfast sincerity, firm and indomitable, the spirit of which penetrates to one's very marrow as one meets his glance.

Any feeling of timidity one may have had whilst waiting for the most powerful and most remarkable man in the world vanished completely once the Emperor, after a more than hearty handshake and a cheery welcome, began to speak. His voice is manly and military, he speaks extraordinarily plainly without slurring over a single syllable, he is never at a loss for a word, but always strikes the nail on the head - often in exceedingly forceful terms. He punctuates his sentences with quick and expressive gestures. His speech flows smoothly, is always terse and interesting and is often suddenly interrupted by questions delivered with lightning precision, which one must endeavour to answer equally quickly and clearly. A good answer never fails to elicit the Emperor's approval. He is exceedingly impulsive and his conversation is a mixture of earnest and jest . A ready repartee or an amusing tale causes him to laugh so heartily that his shoulders shake with it.

At the Emperor's bidding we passed into the dining-room. Admiral von Müller sat on the left, I on the right of our august host, and opposite him was Adjutant-General von Gontard. The table was simply laid. The only luxury that could be discovered was a bell of gold placed in front of the Emperor's cover, and which he rang when a new course was to be brought in. The dinner was equally plain, consisting of soup, meat with vegetables, a sweet dish and fruit with claret. I have seldom been as hungry as when I rose from this table: not on account of the dishes, but because there had not been a moment's silence up to the time when the bell rang for the last time and bade the uniformed servants withdraw our chairs as we rose. The Emperor talked to me all the time. He began by reminding me of my last lecture in Berlin, at which he was present, and he conjectured that Tibet, where I had passed through such stirring times, would probably soon be the only country in the world where peace reigned. Then we spoke of the political position and of the storms that are sweeping over Europe. It pleased me especially to hear with what respect and sympathy the Emperor referred to France. He regretted the necessity which, contrary to his wish, compelled him to lead his army against the French, and he hoped that the time would come when Germans and Frenchmen might live on amicable and neighbourly terms with one another. For this goal he had striven for twenty-five years and he hoped that quite a new order of things would arise out of the present war. An understanding between Germany and France would of necessity lay the solid foundation for future peace. But first there must be victory over the innumerable legions which four great powers had hurled against Germany's frontiers and the German possessions in other continents, then an honourable and assured peace in all directions, and finally the great and abiding world-peace. First and foremost the Emperor placed his faith in God, but he also relied implicitly on the German people, on this great and noble army which had now for six weeks asserted itself so gloriously, and on his powerful fleet, longing to fight out its battle on the waves of the Atlantic. He relied on his soldiers' superb bravery and contempt of death and on the officers who led them on land and water.

If the French had any idea of the Emperor's real feelings towards them, they would judge him very differently. Surely no one thinks that I would take the responsibility of attributing to the Emperor opinions other than those which had fallen from his lips and which I myself had heard! It would be an ill reward for the hospitality I met with in the German Army.

The conversation turned besides on many other topics. The Emperor said many strong and manly things. He spoke like Gustavus Adolphus, when he first landed in Germany with his Swedish Army to bring succour to the Protestant princes and to fight for the liberty of thought and religion on this earth. When the German Emperor talks thus - then I have truly no time to eat beef and vegetables - then I prefer to listen and to order sandwiches afterwards, when back in my room at the hotel.

On a table in the chancellerie were cigars and cigarettes round a lighted candle. Here the conversation was continued with zest and vigour, and jest and earnest, horrors of war and funny stories were all jumbled together; finally the Emperor took his leave, wishing me a successful and instructive trip, and went up to his apartments, where no doubt piles of papers and letters, reports and telegrams awaited him.

The talk of the Emperor having aged during the war, and of the war with all its labours and anxieties having sapped his strength and health, is all nonsense. His hair is no more pronouncedly iron grey than before the war, his face has colour, and far from being worn and thin, he is plump and strong, bursting with energy and rude health. A man of Emperor William's stamp is in his element when, through the force of circumstances, he is compelled to stake all he possesses and above all himself for the good and glory of his country. But his greatest quality is that he is a human being and that with all his fulminant force he is humble before God.

CHAPTER III
ON THE WAY TO THE FIFTH ARMY

I HAD HARDLY returned to the hotel when my excellent friend and travelling companion Captain von Krum came and knocked at my door to give me the bad news that he had received orders from the office of the Imperial Volunteer Automobile Corps to proceed to the twelfth Army Corps on a special mission. He comforted me with the assurance that I should get another car and another officer for the trip to the German Crown Prince's Army, probably one whose duties took him in that direction. There was nothing to be done in the matter - we took a hearty farewell of one another and arranged to meet again, if not before, then after the end of the war.

When I had lost von Krum, the cold, rainy, windy weather seemed worse than ever. It needed an hour in the friendly and delightful company of His Excellency and Countess von Moltke to dissipate the gloom. We talked about the German soldiers, their good-nature, their humane conduct and kindly camaraderie towards prisoners and wounded opponents. It is probably to lessen neutral countries' sympathy towards Germany and to egg on their own troops that the newspapers of the Entente Powers have on repeated occasions accused the German soldiers of inhuman cruelty. Such tales are entirely without foundation and are in themselves highly improbable, for it is not and never has been part of the Teutonic character to show cruelty to vanquished, defenceless enemies. In this respect the Latins and the Slavs have much to learn from the Teutons. The wave of vandalism which passed over a part of Louvain was let loose by the inhabitants themselves. The anger felt by the German soldiers at the treachery of the civil population is justified. The treacherous firing of *franctireurs* from behind bushes and windows, in the dusk and dark, is bound in the end to bring about reprisals, for the soldier reasons something like this: "The war must be conducted between *soldiers*, and when either party is defeated and the conqueror marches into the vanquished town, the civilians must not fire from windows on the troops entering. And if the nuisance cannot be checked in any other way, then the town must be punished." Such was the case with Louvain, which is an unfortified town and where not a single window-pane would have been broken, had not the *franctireurs* themselves brought about the destruction. Things actually went to such lengths that German soldiers who tried to extinguish the fire in the burning houses next to the Townhall, in order to save this valuable building, were shot down during their work by *franctireurs*. The German conduct of the war is severe, but it is not cruel.

During the first stage of the war, when the troops had entered a town and burnt or demolished those houses from which civilians had been shooting, solitary houses were often to be seen which remained untouched in the midst of the desolation. The doors of such remaining houses often bore, written in chalk and in a soldier's hand, some such inscription as: "Here lives an aged couple," or: "Here lives an invalid who must be spared," or: "There has been no firing from this house"; or again: "The inhabitants of this house are friendly people." Such houses are then spared by the troops who come after. In the course of my narrative I shall have frequent occasion to mention traits of kindliness on the part of the German soldiers towards the local population. On the other hand, I have never either seen or heard of a single act of cruelty.

After one more visit to the railway station and taking a look at troops from Lunéville on the way to Belgium, likewise several infantry trains from Metz, I returned to the *Hotel Staar* just in time to meet the young lieutenant who had been instructed by General Moltke to take me to the Headquarters of the Crown Prince's Army. His name was Hans von Gwinner and he is the son of the great banker and Bagdad Railway magnate in Berlin. He was a wide-awake and capable young fellow and drove his car himself. I sat down beside him, whilst the orderly accompanying us took his seat inside.

It poured with rain as we left the town. The road was slippery, but we had studded tyres and the lieutenant drove at terrific speed. We had started off rather late and we wanted to get in before dark. It is better thus, otherwise one is not entirely safe from the attentions of *franctireurs*. A whole lot of them had recently been caught by the Fifth Army and shot without hesitation.

Our road took us westward. In the south we left behind an area of rich ore deposits, and at Rödingen we passed the frontier of French Lorraine. "Load carbine!" came quickly from the lieutenant to the orderly, and I looked round involuntarily, but without noticing anything out of the common. It was just a precaution apparently, but the order sounded strange when heard for the first time. Longlaville is the first place we come to in France. Here we find numerous traces of German shells, but the factories and their lofty chimneys have been spared. In the middle of the road and at its sides are numerous pits where shells have burst, and here and there a tree has been cut clean off by a "bull's-eye." Of some houses there is hardly anything left but the walls, whilst others have only had the roof carried away, evidently by projectiles striking them at a tangent. The tramway laid at the edge of the road has been roughly dealt with. Here and there its rails have been twisted as if made of wire. High up in the church towers one notices that the slates have been removed to make room for machine-guns and to provide posts of observation for the officers watching the German artillery positions and the effect of the French fire.

"Où est la route four Longwy?" enquires von Gwinner, and the answer comes, *"Tout droit, monsieur."* The people always answer politely, whatever they may feel at heart. We leave one of Longwy's two detached forts on the right and presently we enter the busy little manufacturing town, which is situated in a hollow, surrounded on all sides by hills. On one of them stands Longwy fortress, which was easily taken by the Germans right at the beginning of the war after an exceedingly violent bombardment. A couple of thousand prisoners then fell into the hands of the conquerors. In the previous war - January, 1871 - Longwy also capitulated. We had no time to visit the fortress on this occasion, and

drove straight through the town. It certainly looks anything but cheerful. But what can one expect of a town which has quite recently been ravaged by war and has been cut off from its country, its Government and administration? Nor did the rain and mud help to lessen the gloom. Nevertheless, the town looked by no means dead and deserted, for a large proportion of its inhabitants had returned after the heavy hand of war had moved further westward, and life had begun to settle down again in its old groove.

Outside the town stand the naked walls of a house ravaged by fire. The German troops had been fired upon from its windows and in accordance with the custom of war it had been set fire to. We are travelling a little too fast to gather more than a hasty impression, but wherever I look I see the devastating effects of battle, I think to myself as we go along that the sooner I get accustomed to such sights the better. On both sides of the roads, in fields and ditches, French knapsacks and tattered fragments of uniforms are lying about. An upturned motor-car lies by the roadside, evidently flung aside so as not to be in the way of the traffic, and a little further on is a motor-lorry in the same position. Here we see broken bits of rifles and ammunition wagons, or the crescent-shaped shield of a field-gun. A grave with a wooden cross strikes the eye, then another and yet another, a whole row of graves - here is the resting-place of soldiers who have fallen in the fighting. In the middle of the road are a couple of shell holes filled with rain water - these are dangerous, for one is apt in the hurry to take them for shallow puddles. But von Gwinner has travelled this way several times and knows the road.

To the right and left of the road are deep, narrow trenches with shallow parapets; but the soldiers have gone away by now and the plain is silent - silent where not a month ago 300,000 soldiers were fighting for their lives. In many fields the harvest has been brought in by German troops to supply their own needs. By the side of ditches, in woods and copses, small, low huts are still standing, built of branches and boughs, in which the French soldiers had sought protection from rain and cold. The German infantry, on the other hand, is equipped with shelter tents. Each man carries with his equipment a part of the brown tarpaulin, which, joined together, forms a temporary shelter for a certain number of soldiers.

We now pass through a stretch of wooded country. The French are very clever in maintaining their positions on wooded ground. They often succeed in contriving concealed positions for machine-guns in the leafy tops of trees. Ravines with streams at the bottom or woods are considered by the Germans to present greater obstacles to attack than the more open ground met with in central and southern France.

Our road takes us through Longuyon and follows its main street. It has a desolate appearance. Over a long stretch there is not a single house standing. Everything is in ruins, the road is lined with piles of wreckage, swept aside so as not to impede the traffic, and naked walls with yawning window gaps meet the eye. The bridges are guarded by German sentries; otherwise no human beings are to be seen. How miserable the inhabitants must feel when they return and vainly look for their homes and belongings!

We emerge into the open country where armies have been marching through. Small blackened holes in the earth are all that is left of the bivouac fires and cooking-pits. Here the transport columns have rested for the night. The village of Noërs is burned and its church steeple has been shot away, the music of a maxim gun having been traced to the spot from which at other times the church bells call to evensong. No dead bodies are seen, no fallen soldiers, no carcasses of horses. All remains of men and horses have for sanitary reasons been interred by the Germans. They would otherwise poison the air and give rise to epidemics. Still there is quite enough left to recall the ravages of war. Here we have a row of straw shelters backed on to a hedge, there some upturned carts with which the French had endeavoured to bar the way. This is the most magnificent high road imaginable, lined everywhere with avenues of trees. Along the roadside runs a telegraph line, which had been destroyed by the defenders but repaired by the German Telegraph Corps, not by the field telegraph troops, whose sphere of activity is nearer the front.

We have now reached Marville, and the road becomes livelier. At one side a supply column has turned off into a field and lined up its wagons, which with their canvas awnings give the impression of an open-air barrack-yard. The column is resting, and the men have commenced cooking. Round the encampment sentries are posted. Precautions must be taken. Yesterday in this very neighbourhood nineteen French civilians, who had fired on an ammunition column, were arrested. They were to be tried by court-martial and shot if the offence could be brought home to them. A little further on another supply column, consisting of more primitive wagons, had halted by the roadside, for it is the rule that a transport column must not pause for any length of time on the road itself, which for the sake of the traffic must always be kept as clear as possible. It is, moreover, considered easier to supervise, and, if necessary, protect a column of wagons drawn up several deep and thus shortened in length.

We now drive past a motor-lorry with field post for the 5th Army. It makes a terrific noise as it rattles past on the hard road surface. Presently the road is encumbered by another supply column, but unlike the others, this one is on the move. We must drive more slowly in order that the horses of the mounted escort may not take fright and come into collision with the car. In passing I catch sight of the words, *"Reserve Park Kolonn 15"* on one of these wagons, each of which is marked with a number.

We next drive through Montmédy, whose little fort surrendered without bombardment. But before the garrison withdrew, they blew up the railway tunnel through the mountain. Thereupon the Germans immediately began building a new railway round the rock on which the fort was built; as we drove past, French prisoners were still engaged on this work. It was a curious sight to see these toiling soldiers in blue and red uniforms supervised by grey-clad German privates with shouldered rifles. Chauvency is a little place on the River La Chiers, whose bridge had been destroyed by the French. One of the arches had been blown up. German engineers had forthwith built a wooden bridge below the old one.

The weather cleared up towards evening, and the sun went down like a big red ball. Its last rays fell upon a convoy of French prisoners, who, under German escort, bent and footsore, made their way to Montmédy. The Frenchmen had nothing to carry, but the Germans had their rifles with fixed bayonets. In front of us lies the valley of the Meuse and the little town of Stenay. The faint outlines of heights and hills disappear in the dim blue distance. On the left bank of the river the French had at this point occupied a fortified position, which, however, was taken by storm at the beginning of the campaign. So this is the Meuse, or in German Maas, on which are situated so many towns rendered famous by this and previous wars, such as Sédan, Givet, Dinant, Namur, and Liège! To the left is the great main road which on the right river bank runs via Dun to Verdun.

We descend gradually until the Meuse is reached, meeting fresh ammunition and food columns on the way. In the latter I notice huge motor-lorries loaded with flour, bread and other foodstuffs. Now and again we come across horsemen, always in pairs. They are mounted police and are out to maintain order on the roads.

We stop outside the house in which the General in Command of the 5th Army has taken up his quarters. I was able to speak there without difficulty to one of my friends from the Main Headquarters, Landrat Baron von Maltzahn, Member of the Reichstag and a personal friend of the Crown Prince. He was able to give me the welcome news that I was expected and that I must hurry in order to be in time for supper, which was served at eight o'clock. So we drove at once up to the little French château, where His I. & R. Highness had elected to stay. Here I said good-bye to my excellent friend Lieutenant von Gwinner and thanked him for his companionship. Thus he, too, disappears from my horizon, and I stand before a new association of acquaintances and friendships.

Footmen in military uniforms at once took charge of my baggage and conducted me to my room on the first floor, next door to the Crown Prince's private apartments. A few minutes before eight the acting Lord-in-waiting, Court Marshal von Behr, knocked at my door. He was a pleasant young man of distinguished and attractive appearance, and he had come to bring me in to supper. We went out through the upper vestibule and down the stairs, from the landing of which we were fortunate enough to witness a pleasing ceremony. In the lower hall stood a number of officers in line, and opposite them some twenty soldiers formed up in the same way. Then came the Crown Prince William, tall, slim and royally straight, dressed in a dazzling white tunic and wearing the Iron Cross of the first and second class; he walked with a firm step between the lines of soldiers. An adjutant followed him, carrying in a casket a number of Iron Crosses. The Crown Prince took one and handed it to the nearest officer, whom he thanked for the services which he had rendered to his Emperor and country, and then with a hearty handshake he congratulated the hero whom he had thus honoured.

When all the officers had received their decorations, the reward for their bravery, the turn came of the soldiers, the ceremony being precisely the same as with the officers; but I found it hard to distinguish what the soldiers said in their loud, rough and nervous voices. At last I distinguished the words: *Danke untertänigst Kaiserliche Hoheit* (I humbly thank your Imperial Highness).

When the knights of the Iron Cross had taken their departure, we went down into the hall, where the Crown Prince stepped up to me and bade me heartily welcome to his Headquarters and to the seat of war. The meal, which might as well have been called dinner as supper, was attended by the following gentlemen: Lieutenant-General Schmidt von Knobelsdorff, Chief of Staff of the 5th Army, Court-Marshal von Behr, Chief of the Medical Corps, Body-Physician Professor Widenmann, Majors von der Planitz, von Müller, personal Adjutant to H.I. & R.H., and Heymann, Lieutenant von Zobeltitz and a few members of the Staff, who arrived later after the day's work in the field and took their seats at the lower end of the table.

Would you like to know what the German Crown Prince, the Crown Prince of Prussia, eats for supper? Here is the menu: cabbage soup, boiled beef with horse-radish and potatoes, wild duck with salad, fruit, wine, and coffee with cigars. And what would you say the conversation was about? It is hard to say exactly, but we travelled over almost the whole world with the ease bred by familiarity. The Crown Prince, like the Emperor, began with Tibet, and from there it was but a step across the Himalayas to the palms of the Hugh Delta, the pagodas of Benares, the silver moonlight over Taj Mahal, the tigers of the jungle and the music of the crystal waves of India beating against the rocks of Malabar point. We also spoke of old unforgettable memories and of common friends who now love as no longer - of the brave and famous Kitchener, the conqueror of Omdurman and South Africa, of the Mararajahs and their fairy-like splendour at Bikanir, Kutch Behar, Gwalior, Kashmir and Idar.

We also talked about the war and its horrors, and the terrible sacrifices it demands. "But it cannot be helped," said the Crown Prince, "our Fatherland asks us to give all we have, and *we will, we must* win, even if the whole world takes up arms against us."

"Is not the calm here wonderful! We seem to be living tonight in the most absolute peace, and yet it is but a couple of hours' drive to the firing line," observes my Imperial host after listening to a short, concise and satisfactory report made in a ringing voice by an officer who has just entered. "Yes, your Imperial Highness, I had imagined the Staff Headquarters of an army to resemble a buzzing beehive, but now that I have the reality before me, I find no trace of anxiety or nervousness, nothing but calm and assurance everywhere. But what I should like to see most of all would be a battle, for I suspect that in common with most other civilians I have formed an erroneous opinion on this subject."

The Crown Prince smiles and answers: "Yes, battle painters like Neuville and Détaille would have little use for their art in these days. Of the fighting men one sees practically nothing, for they are concealed by the ground and in the trenches, and it is rather dangerous to get too close to a bayonet charge - unless one's duty takes one there. Generally speaking, the distance between the fighting forces increases with the improvement in fire-arms. Those who have the best artillery have the best prospects of winning. To us the field-grey uniform is a great advantage, as we merge into the colouring of the ground, whilst the brilliant uniforms of the French are visible from afar. To *see* a battle is practically impossible - not even the Commander directing it sees much of it, his direction is effected by telephone and is dependent on information and reports received, which in turn are carefully sifted and weighed. For a spectator to post himself on a height in the neighbourhood is not advisable, for then he may be sure of being taken for an observer directing the artillery fire, and becomes at once the target of the enemy's shells. You shall, however, during your visit here be allowed to witness all that it is possible to see."

What life and spirit at the Crown Prince's Headquarters! Everything was gay with the freshness of youth, and devoid of restraint. No trace of the stiffness of court ceremonial. Even General Schmidt, who usually maintained the strictest discipline, was infected by the prevailing spirit of camaraderie. But owing to the terrible burden of work which rested on the shoulders of the Chief of Staff, it was not unusual for him to come in for his meals after the others. The supper, or rather the talk after it, went on till about eleven - these were the only hours when one could meet in quiet, for during the day everyone was busy with his duties, and the Crown Prince then occupied his post as commanding officer at suitable points at the front.

The château where we were staying belonged to an aristocratic French lady - if I remember rightly her name was du Vernier. When the war broke out she moved to Bordeaux. On her return after the contest she will find her château, her estates and the beautiful park in the same condition as when she went away. There was a certain aristocratic grandeur about the château, though signs of decay were already making themselves apparent. On the mantelpiece in my room stood a pendulum clock of gilt bronze of an antique mythological design, and on each side stood a couple of gorgeous candelabra. The walls were decorated with a few unassuming pictures, amongst them a portrait of an old French warrior.

I open my window, it is pitch-dark outside, and the rain falls close and heavy upon the trees and lawns outside. Tired after a somewhat ambitious day's work, I hurry to bed, the more so as I suspect the next day's programme to be no less exacting.

September 21st. I was called early to be ready for breakfast at seven, when all his entourage gathers round the Crown Prince. After breakfast H.I. & R.H. asked me to accompany him to the Staff quarters, where a "plan of campaign" for my day was to be drawn up. General Schmidt quickly made up his mind. He thought it might be of interest to me to begin by watching the artillery fire at Septsarges, and instructed three officers to take charge of me. Major Matthiasz was the leader of the party, and a soldier came as chauffeur. The two other officers were Liebrecht of a battalion of Chasseurs, and Schmidt of the Volunteer Automobile Corps.

Whilst the car was got ready I was being coached on a large map in the grouping of the 5th Army and of the artillery positions which we were to visit. The General Staff of the Chief Command of the Army was housed in an *École de Garçons*, which still contained relics of its former state, such as natural history pictures and maps, and a couple of school benches with the master's desk, above which could still be seen in black and white the golden rules: *Ne vous vantez pas*, and *Liberie, Égalité, Fraternité*. How hollow and foolish did they not seem before the brutal reality now presiding over the world!

The car is ready. We step in. I am dressed in furs and have a mackintosh. I also bring a pair of field-glasses and a sketch-book. It is no longer raining, but the sky is overcast and the weather chilly and autumnal after all the suffocating heat which the soldiers had to endure during the first phase of the campaign. We drive southward at breakneck speed. I cannot deny that I had to struggle against the feeling of growing excitement. It was not mere manoeuvres; it was war itself, a part of the greatest struggle that had ever been fought on earth. It was, moreover, the struggle on the western front, the fight against the French, rightly considered to be the sturdiest and best soldiers among Germany's opponents. When one approaches such a spot, and when for the first time in one's life one enters the zone of fire, it is difficult not to feel, whether one admits it or not, a certain tension, even if one has been through some wild adventures in Asia. Every minute we get nearer the firing line, and as the car slows down at the corners we hear the cannonade more plainly. The booming of the guns sounds dull and heavy, the ground quivers.

But events move all too fast. Observations and impressions follow so quickly upon one another that it is difficult to assimilate them all. I make my notes as usual, even when the car is racing along at its fastest, and my writing is far from copper-plate. We still have 32 kilometres to Septsarges, a village 21 kilometres north-west of Verdun. How often did I not wish to stop - to impress more strongly on my mind some vivid and warlike picture, but as I am stopping for two days with the 5th Army, I shall, no doubt, have an opportunity of revisiting this section. The whole road is full of supply columns moving southward, and we meet innumerable empty transport lorries on the way north, to be reloaded at some railway station. Here we also see fresh young troops, all strapping fellows, who have come direct from Germany to go straight to victory or death. All are jolly and eager; truly, they look as if the whole affair were to them but an autumn manoeuvre, and as if they felt no trace of excitement. They march along with easy bearing and sing merry soldiers' ditties under the leaden skies now darkening this unhappy bleeding France. They light their pipes and their eternal cigarettes, laugh and chat - as if they were going to a picnic in the country. In reality they are going out to fill the gaps made by the French fire in the ranks of their comrades. They are *Ersatztfuppen*, i.e. reinforcements, but I do not see a single face which betrays the slightest feeling that death is near. They hear the thunder of the guns better than we do, for the humming of the car drowns all other sounds. But they seem to delight in the dull music, and yet their place is far in advance of the artillery positions. *Ersatztruppen!* it means that their duty is to *replace* the fallen, and that the same fate awaits themselves. Yet they are gay and happy. *"Dulce et decorum est pro patria mori."*

The soldiers' helmets are provided with covers of the same shade of grey as the uniforms. On their backs they carry knapsacks containing their most indispensable kit, their share of the tent, and a couple of bowls with spoon, knife and fork. At the side they carry the bayonet and the "portable tool," spade or axe. To the waist-belt are fastened the filled cartridge pouches, the whole outfit weighing about 56 English lbs. It is a fairly substantial weight and, although figuratively speaking the soldiers march into battle with a light step, their steps are in reality pretty heavy, especially on country roads softened by rain. Anyhow, their marching capacity is nothing short of wonderful - I for my part should not get far with such a load. Practice makes perfect, as the whole German nation knows. That is why the Germans do not refuse to spend enormous sums on their defence. And that is why they conquer, even though attacked by four great powers whose soldiers have not received the same thorough scientific training in times of peace.

We fly through Dun. One can hardly speak of more than one street in this prettily situated little village on the banks of the Meuse. Yet this street has indeed been hardly dealt with. It is a melancholy comfort to know that its comely houses have been destroyed by the French Army's own artillery, so as to make the stay at Dun as disagreeable as possible for the Germans. It is now a "line of communication" base depot with Depot *Kommandantur* , a "line of communication" hospital and store depot, and also has large supplies of arms and ammunition. The railway, now under Prussian management, is being worked up to this point, where the transfer takes place from the supply trains to the great columns of the Army Service Corps.

The population, which fled on the approach of the Germans, has already begun to return. The two bridges over the Meuse have been blown up, but one of them, the one of stone, over which the main road passes, has been repaired by the Engineers. The little village of Liny, on our right, has been more fortunate. Here the pretty little white houses with their red-tiled roofs are almost untouched.

We now begin to notice that we are approaching the firing line. The whole road is encumbered with troops. Here comes a detachment of wounded on foot, with bandages round heads and hands, or with the arm in a sling. We meet an empty ammunition column, an endless string of rattling wagons. We always keep to the right of course. Woe to him who breaks this rule and causes a stoppage on the road.[4] If it is not broad enough, it becomes rather awkward at times to get along. And how often does it not happen that two transport columns meet

4. In Sweden (as in England) one always keeps to the left.

on the same bit of road, one empty going northward and the other fully laden travelling south! Suddenly we find ourselves in the narrow passage between two such moving walls. If into the bargain another car with field post comes along - every corps has its own post - a temporary congestion is not infrequently the result, but thanks to the smartness of the drivers and chauffeurs the trouble is soon overcome.

The artillery ammunition column which we are just now passing is an impressive sight. The noise of these vehicles, dull and heavy, is quite different from that of the empty wagons on our left, but then they are loaded to the top with heavy ammunition, shells for 21-cm. mortars at Septsarges and neighbouring villages. Every ammunition wagon - consisting of limber and wagon body - with its team of six horses requires the services of six men. Three of them - drivers - ride on the off-side[5] horses, two are seated on the limber, and one facing the rear on the wagon body. They are armed with Mauser pistols fastened on the left side of the belt, but the swords of the drivers are securely strapped on to the left side of the saddle.

The horses are fat and sleek, and pull without exerting themselves unduly. They move at a walking pace - anything else would be impossible on this road. It is a far finer sight to see one of these columns trundling along at full speed with the horses moving at a sharp trot or gallop. Even at the pace at which they are now travelling these endless columns are an impressive and attractive sight. What does it matter if the helmets, in order not to glitter and attract attention, are concealed by a cover which even hides the spike surmounting them; what does it matter if the mens' uniforms are of the same dirty grey as the clay and mud of the soil? The whole team looks picturesque enough with its massive, solid wagon, its pole, its leather fittings and its harness.

Tramp, tramp go the horses' hoofs, and behind them comes the rattling of the heavy wagons. One rider sings, another whistles and a third is shouting at a refractory horse. Behind sit a couple of men rolling cigarettes, which by the way is more difficult than it sounds

5. i.e. The left-hand horse. As Germans drive to the right this is their "off" side.

when a wagon is jolting up and down. This column also has a mounted escort. The train is wound up by a field kitchen with a couple of store wagons on which a few bundles of firewood are also lying. Without ceasing, this eternal tramp, tramp, keeps dinning into our ears as the columns slowly travel southward, a never-ending stream of warriors, horses, ammunition and provisions. "Germany must have inexhaustible supplies of everything," I remark to Major Matthiasz.

He smiles and replies: "Here on the western front we must have quite fifty roads such as this, all equally crowded with men, horses and matérials."

"It must cost a tidy bit of money."

"Yes, it is best not to think of it, but then it means everything to us."

We have now reached the front of the great column. At its head ride a couple of officers, the commander and his adjutant. They salute us. We have hardly left them behind before we drive past the tail-end of an infantry ammunition column, the wagons of which are manned by three men and drawn by four horses with only one driver, mounted on the off leader.

By the side of the road are numberless great pits where shells have struck. Here the fire has been heavy with a vengeance. This fact is brought home to us still more as we re-descend to the Meuse at the point where the village of Vilosnes received such a pounding, and where a permanent bridge was blown up, only to be replaced in a twinkling by a temporary structure by the German Engineers. The ground round the village reminds one almost of a cake of Swedish ryebread pitted all over with holes. The blankness of desolation is most curiously contrasted by the busy military life around. Almost every inch of ground is occupied by the transport columns with their endless streams of wagons, drafts of reinforcements who had elected to halt here - the men resting on the wet ground round their piled rifles - military police in their green uniforms and crescent-shaped metal badges, and countless horses to replace those which have fallen, for Vilosnes has now been made into a horse depot.

The thunder of the guns has now become louder and we have not far to go to reach the German batteries. As yet there is no danger.

The countless shell-pits have not been formed in the present fighting. Since these shells fell, the Germans have made an advance. But we are, nevertheless, immediately behind the firing line, and that is why all these supplies are required to feed men, horses, guns and rifles. A little way from the village an ammunition column has halted; its wheels look awful, coated with thick layers of mud and clay up to the axles. The men are like moving clay statues. In the midst of the mire, in fields and meadows, are ammunition parks and field hospitals, although it would be impossible to find a single dry patch on which to rest one's tired body for the night. Presumably the men sleep in the wagons as far as space allows. They are hardy and brave, these men, always singing, never complaining.

We come a step nearer the fire when we drive up to the village of Dannevoux, which is crowded with *Ersatztruppen*. Here we can study the reinforcement organisation more closely still. Here fresh soldiers stand ready to move up into the firing line to replace the killed and wounded, whilst the work of provisioning and bringing up fresh ammunition is in full swing, so that no fatal break need occur in the firing. Dannevoux church has been turned into a field hospital, where Germans and Frenchmen are tended without discrimination.

In a modest little house in Dannevoux a Divisional Commander has taken up his quarters, and here we pay a short visit to General von Gossler, who is in the act of examining some fifty French prisoners drawn up in two files, who had just been captured. They reply calmly and politely to all questions and say that their regiment has been almost wiped out. They are from the south of France, most of them from Marseilles - that is to say they belong to the 15th Army Corps. Here we also meet Colonel von Rath, whose acquaintance I had made in Breslau.

Dannevoux had been horribly knocked about by shells, and was still far from safe. The next day we heard that General von Gossler had miraculously escaped being hit by a shell which had dropped hardly twenty metres from the spot where he was standing.

We mount the car once more to travel the six kilometres which separate us from the little village of Septsarges, in a south-westerly direction. On our left, hardly a kilometre distant, was a little coppice which had been bombarded that very morning. The day before yesterday the French had learnt from spies amongst the civil population or through one of their aviators that this was an important *Beobachtungstand*, or observation station, and yesterday a thousand shells were rained upon it, but by that time the observers had already withdrawn and only left a picket behind, who found the necessary shelter in a bomb-proof cave.

The road we take is within the range of the French batteries, and now and again a shell drops by the roadside. The ground is pitted with the marks of shell fire, but we manage to steer clear. We are as yet concealed by a slight rise in the ground south of the road. It was lucky that a little accident that happened to the car compelled us to stop just at this point. A little further on we should have been in sight of the French observation posts, and should no doubt have drawn their fire. The French artillery is exceedingly vigilant and considers it can afford to waste ammunition even on single individuals.

I am worried by an inquisitive wasp buzzing round me and contrast it vaguely in my mind with the somewhat larger winged creatures issuing from the muzzles of the guns. Once more the car is ready to start. "Drive quickly over the high ground," orders Major Matthiasz, but it is easier said than done; this by-road is narrow and has been converted into a perfect quagmire with enormous ruts by all the heavy traffic it has had to bear. We have to be content with such speed as we can manage, and trust that the French observers will not notice us or that their directions will not be obeyed until we are over the hill. On the left, towards the south, are two French captive balloons. It is a little unpleasant to know that they are in telephonic communication with the batteries beneath. Neither is it very encouraging to see a row of wooden crosses surmounting fresh graves by the roadside. In the ditch lies a dead horse which had not been able to struggle on any further. The shell craters are now so frequent that we do not pay them the slightest attention.

Here by the roadside stands a transport convoy which ha brought oats for the horses of a mortar section. We have not far to go to the first batteries, each consisting of four of these gigantic "growlers." We drive up between two battery positions whilst they are firing. "Load!" calls the head of the battery, a Captain. *"Fertig zum Feuer!"*[6] - and directly after, *"Feuer"*[7] and all four guns are discharged simultaneously. Immediately a spout of fire issues from the gun-muzzle, accompanied by a report which rends the air and causes the ground to shake for some distance around. Then is heard that peculiar, horrible whistle through the air, as the projectile sweeps the space which separates us from the French positions. Each mortar has a shield, and by the side of the guns the gunners have dug a trench for *"Deckung"* or protection in case the French fire should press the battery too hard.

Presently we reach Septsarges, where all alleys, yards and open spaces are filled with soldiers. The village is situated in a shallow hollow, and the men here are fairly safe from the French fire. But a fiat -topped rise in the ground immediately south of the village is struck now and again by a shell.

Septsarges also accommodates a few field kitchens, which stand ready with their smoking chimneys. The food is prepared during the day, and as dusk sets in the vehicles are driven up in proximity to the infantry positions, hugging the dips in the ground as much as possible and sheltering behind any cover there may be. The men in the trenches know where the canteen is set up, and betake themselves thither under the shelter of the darkness to get their tin bowls filled with boiling hot broth.

We did not remain in the village longer than was necessary to get information from a couple of officers. Thereupon we continued on our way, leaving the car at a point beyond the range of artillery. Then we went up the hill towards the south, with the nearest mortar battery on the left and a field artillery position on the right. Even the field artillery gunners had dug trenches by the side of the guns, covered over with boughs, straw and leaves, thus carefully masking themselves from the French aviators.

6. Ready to fire!

7. Fire!

From the car, which we left in line with the artillery positions, we walked some 800 metres in the direction of the French fire. One has to imagine the infantry positions in two approximately parallel lines, only a few hundred metres distant from one another. Behind them come the artillery positions, also generally speaking in parallel lines. Thus we were now moving within the space situated between the German artillery positions and the German infantry lines, that is to say, the zone bombarded by the French artillery. The risk was, therefore, fairly great, and we took such precautions as the ground allowed. Our objective was an observation post located on the crest of the rise, where a couple of non-commissioned artillery officers stood immovable as if nailed to the ground, by the side of their telescope mounted on a tripod. They were observing the fire of the mortar batteries and telephoned where the shells had struck and the position of the hit in relation to the object aimed at. It is from the reports of aviators and of advanced observation posts and patrols of officers that the range is obtained and the fire is directed.

On the lowest part of the slope we were fairly safe, as at this point we were not visible from the French side. "Look out for telephone wires," warned Matthiasz, who was leading the way, as we passed the lines resting on the grass. When we had reached the middle of the slope, where we were exposed to view from several points on the French line, we descended into a long communication trench, which led to the vicinity of the post of observation. The trench was hardly more than a metre deep and we had to walk almost double in order not to be seen over its edge. The bottom was very unpleasant. Owing to the sloping ground nearly all the water had been drained off, but there was still enough to convert the trench into a greyish blue bath of slime and mire, through which we laboriously made our way with our boots sticking in the mess, and now and again sinking down to the calves, and this was not made pleasanter by some delightful relics which the soldiers had left behind.

Dressed in their greatcoats, the observation officers stand on the crest of the hill, with a very low, short parapet in front of them. As a rule one is anything but welcome when successful in sneaking up to one of these points, for one may easily attract the enemy's attention and thus place the observers in great danger. No wonder, therefore, that they saluted us rather curtly and continued, immovable as statues, to observe the French fire. We walked the last bit of the way in single file, so as to make it appear to the opposite batteries as if there were only one man, and not, by open order, to create more movement than necessary on the hill crest. Sitting on our heels, we observed the country southward in the direction of Malancourt, and took our bearings as best we could. The Major was just explaining what heights, copses, villages and roads were occupied by the Germans and where the French positions began, when a shrapnel shell exploded close by us, a little to our left. *"Deckung!"* cried Matthiasz, and threw himself down at full length behind the parapet. We had hardly time to follow his example when three other of these infernal machines spat out their contents, a little further away, however, than the first. It was now obvious that we had been seen by the French observers, and that the fire from a battery had been concentrated on us. We, therefore, thought it wise to move on to a safer place - when one has been discovered there is nothing else to do if one wishes to get away with a whole skin. To begin with we moved down to the nearest mortar battery, where we passed a few moments. Whilst they were loading for the next salvo I drew the accompanying very rough sketch. But one can hardly be expected to show the requisite presence of mind and coolness to accomplish a detailed drawing, when at any moment one may be smothered in shell fragments. In the picture the mortar barrel is lowered for loading; on the right is a projectile on a *Trage*, or little iron barrow.

By a more westerly road, and still passing endless transport columns, we next proceed northward , and ascend a height which seems to be outside the firing line, and from which with greater tranquillity we can observe the martial spectacle southward. There is really little to be seen. The only thing that we see and hear is the German batteries, and, if the weather is clear, the impact and bursting of the shells. The French batteries are, of course, equally well hidden behind mounds and masked by bushes and young trees, and one sees and hears nothing of their fire but the impact of their shells and the report. The French fire on this particular day consisted mainly of shrapnel, and it made itself known chiefly by a shrill whistling sound and by the little puffs of white smoke which denoted the bursting of the shells overhead.

The streets of the village of Cunel are full of Württemberg Landwehr and their steaming field kitchens and long trains of supply columns. The roads are swarming with infantry and Uhlans. Here also are large bodies of *Ersatztruppen* or reinforcements, ready to move up and fill the gaps. We have brought with us a whole bundle of fresh newspapers to distribute amongst the men. Nothing gives them greater pleasure than this kind of news from home. Out here the soldiers get, of course, no particulars of the war but what they can see with their own eyes. Of course, they can draw certain conclusions from the orders given out day by day. But about the general situation on the various fronts they know nothing. Their hunger and thirst are stilled at field kitchens, which are run so smartly and so thoroughly that the question of hunger or thirst really never arises. Cigars and cigarettes are also heartily welcome, and are sent to the front as *Liebesgaben* (love gifts) in entire wagon -loads, perhaps mainly to the 5th Army, thanks to the Crown Prince's spirited appeals to the generosity of the public. But on the whole the longing for news is the greatest, and I think that the soldiers would often gladly go hungry and thirsty for a while and forfeit their beloved smokes, if they could only learn how Germany's great war was going on and how their people were at home. *Lieb Vaterland, magst ruhig sein* they sing with tremendous gusto, when the news of fresh victories reaches them.

In the village of Romagne we were on the territory of a new Army Corps. The house at which we stopped is owned by a French Major who has retired from the Army and lives there with his wife in the midst of the confusion. As a consequence his house and he are quite unmolested. He is on the billet register, and sees to it that his German guests are properly looked after. At Romagne there is also a field hospital, occupying several houses. Every Army Corps has twelve such hospitals, each of which has six wagons, all flying the Red Cross flag.

The next village we pass is Bantheville, from which the population fired on the Germans from the windows when they entered. The guilty persons were seized and hanged, and a couple of houses which were fired from were burnt down. Now the village was full of troops and transport columns. Horrible-looking water-filled holes in the road and by the roadside betokened the effect of the German guns during the advance. In a field stands a whole row of wagons filled with sacks of oats. Near by is a flying station and a field bakery detachment with its engines, which look like baking ovens, and its big yellow tents where the dough is kneaded and moulded in gigantic troughs.

At length we drive back to Dun, where the traffic is if possible still livelier than in the morning. It took some time to make our way between the trains of vehicles on the bridges and in the narrow village street. *Proviant Kolonn I Wagen 23* with its team of four and drivers seemed to wish to bar our way, but the officer in charge got a terrific scolding from the Major. The noise - the shouting, the creaking of wagons, the cracking of whips, the jolting and the neighing - in this village road is indescribable. The 5th Army seems to be in need of nothing, least of all of soldiers. As we pass through, fresh regiments come marching along, singing and smoking. When at last we get clear of the village we find no diminution of traffic, but we are at least no longer helplessly blocked in the narrow streets.

A sharp shower patters down once more on the arched canvas roofs of the service wagons, and this poor land, so saturated with blood and water, receives another drenching. We ourselves come to no harm, but we cannot help thinking of the soldiers lying frozen in the firing line. The trenches are not a pleasant place to live in during these autumn rains. A German officer once told me that the water was a foot deep in many trenches, and that the men had no alternative but to stand up in it. Sometimes they were able to dig "dug-outs" above the water level so as at least to have somewhere to sit or lie, but any attempt at drying is futile. Even if it were possible to make up a fire, this is strictly forbidden, as the enemy's gun-fire would be guided by the light.

Here comes a string of vehicles with long, rough tree trunks for some bridge construction, there lies an upturned motorcar which has come to grief. If a little stretch of road is moderately clear or only encumbered by a single file of wagons, the chauffeur immediately puts on a terrific speed to gain ground.

It was still daylight when we returned to our domicile, where the Crown Prince, just back from his day's work, was resting in the doorway. A moment later I went out for a walk in the town. At the bridges over the Meuse I was stopped by the sentries, who in authoritative but invariably polite tones asked to see my *Ausweis*. That they found me suspicious-looking, ambling along as I did with a sketch-book under my arm, was not to be wondered at. Only one of them, an honest Landwehr man, declared categorically that my pass was not sufficient. "Oh," I said. "The name of the Chief of the General Staff of the Field Army, General Moltke, does not impress you?" "No, the permit must be vised by the 5th Army," he replied. A couple of his comrades saved the situation after reading the permit, and declared that General Moltke was good enough for them.

After a short visit to a field base hospital, accommodated in a French artillery barracks, I turned my steps homeward and stopped, in an inquisitive mood, at the entrance to a shop which was open and where soldier customers came and went. As I overheard a couple of privates doing their level best to make themselves understood by the women in the shop, I stepped up to offer my services as interpreter. It turned out to be a modest sort of place for women's clothing, linen, stays, lace, handkerchiefs, stockings, scent and soap and other useful toilet articles. The proprietress, Madame Desserrey, had been a widow for three years and now lived there with her three daughters and a sister and subsisted on the profits of her little business. The soldiers who were engaged in discussion inside, wanted to buy shirts and pants, and Mme. Desserrey was trying to explain that if they would come back with the matérial, she would sew the garments they wanted. With this information they seemed satisfied, bought a couple of boxes of soap and went away.

I asked Mme. Desserrey if she had not been ruined by the war, but she replied that she had not suffered any want so far. She hoped that she would get through the autumn and winter, and that the war would soon be at an end.

"Well, and what do you think of the German soldiers?" I asked.

"They haven't done me or my family the slightest harm; they are always polite and take no liberties. They have bought everything in my shop that they can make use of and paid for it like men, and if I could only get fresh goods from Luxemburg I should do excellent business. I and three others are the only ones who keep our shops open. All the others closed and fled when the Germans came."

In the shop were two knitting machines at which the eighteen-year-old Blanche Desserrey and her sister of fourteen were sitting; they were knitting socks for the Germans, whilst their brother, eleven years old, was sitting on the steps outside watching the soldiers. Mademoiselle Blanche was a sweet and pretty girl, but she did not seem very strong; she had a look of melancholy in her dark eyes and wore an anchor of hope in her brooch. I asked if she had many relations at the war. She answered yes, and she longed for her friends who had fled from the town. "How horrible this war is," she cried, "how awful for everybody." Then she enquired whether they had been fighting hard at the front that day - she had heard the booming of the guns in the early morning. Yes, I said, they were fighting hard. It was the Germans and the French who were fighting against one another, and many a brave and promising youth had died for his country. Mademoiselle Blanche, I soon found, was not merely a seamstress for the soldiers, she was also a dreamer of beautiful dreams, sensitive and high-minded, and her heart was pure and without guile. She was cheerful, amiable, and could even raise a laugh in the midst of the billeting bothers and the knitting, but it was clear that she considered gaiety one of the transient things of this earth. The German officers and soldiers who entered eyed her with interest and treated her with respect. She assured me that she had never yet had occasion to complain of their conduct. She did not quite understand how she managed to disarm even the strongest by a look from her eyes. *Soyez comme l'oiseau, penché pour un instant sur les rameaux trop frêles. Il sent plier la branche mais il chante pourtant, sachani qu'il a des ailes.* Blanche Desserrey would have made an ideal heroine of a touching romance.

But I for my part had no time for romances just then. When I came out into the street the clock in a church tower struck six in the solemn French way, and I hastened to my room to make a few notes. Then there was a knock at the door. *"Herein"* I called with the voice of a corporal. In steps the Crown Prince with a large volume under his arm, I ask my august guest to be seated on the sofa. There we sat and talked until it was time to prepare for the evening meal.

The book which the Crown Prince had brought with him, and which he asked me to accept as a memento of him, was entitled *Deutschland in Waffen* (Germany under Arms), and contained, apart from reading matter by various authors, a series of excellently executed coloured plates of different German armies in being, in manoeuvres and sham fights, as well as of German warships at sea. The work, produced by the Crown Prince with the assistance of eminent experts, was dedicated to his father the Emperor. The copy, which I treasure in memory of the giver, contained a dedication curiously historical in tone. The motto chosen by the editor of the book was the following: "The world does not rest more securely on Atlas' shoulders than does Germany upon her army and navy." The introduction is written by the Crown Prince himself and ends with the following impressive and prophetic words:

"Doubtless diplomatic skill can and will, for some time to come, defer conflicts and even dissolve them. Those called upon in the solemn hour of decision must and will surely be fully conscious of their terrible responsibility. They will feel it their duty to make it clear to themselves that once the match has been applied to the gigantic conflagration, it will be no easy and no speedy task to quench it. But, as the lightning equalises the tension between two air strata of different charge, so will the sword, until the world comes to an end, be and remain the deciding factor. And therefore everyone who loves his country and who believes in the great future of our people must gladly and readily do all in his power to guard the old soldierly spirit of our ancestors from decadence and from the sickly taint of thought. The sword itself is not enough, it needs the practised steel-clad arm to wield it. Every man amongst us must keep fit for service in our army and navy and must in heart and soul be ready for the great and solemn hour when our Emperor calls us to the colours, for the moment when we no longer belong to ourselves but to the country only with the whole of our bodily and spiritual strength - the time when all these qualities must be strained to the uttermost to attain the 'will to conquer' which in all history has never been known to fail. If thus the entire German people is resolved gladly to adventure its life blood and all that it holds dear, it matters little if the world is 'filled with the legions of darkness' armed against us, for we shall know how to stand up against it, however great be the distress of the moment. Thus we shall indeed obey the exhortation contained in the comforting verses of Emanuel Geibel, the herald of the new German Empire:

> "Und wenn uns nichts mehr übrig blieb
> So blieb uns doch ein Schwert,
> Das zorngemut mit scharfem Hieb
> Dem Trutz des Fremdlings wehrt.

> "So blieb die Schlacht als letzt Gericht
> Auf Leben und auf Tod.
> Und wenn die Not nicht Eisen bricht,
> Das Eisen bricht die Not."[8]

The world conflagration which Crown Prince William foretold is now raging before our very eyes. Will he be justified in his steadfast faith in the people over which he is destined one day to reign? The writing on the wall from Ypres to the Wartha, from Tsingtau to the Cameroons, is telling its tale. Here is a nation which cannot go under and which never will be conquered.

---

8. *And if nought else to us be left.*
   There still remains the sword
   Which boldly wielded with fierce cleft
   Defies the foemen's horde.
   Thus combat unto death we make.
   Last arbiter indeed,
   For if need will not iron break
   Then iron shall break the need.
   The last line is a play on the German proverb, *"Not bricht Eisen"*: Necessity will (teach us to) break down (obstacles strong as) iron; and if it will not, our "iron" (sword) shall break the necessity itself.

CHAPTER IV
A DAY AT ECLISFONTAINE

SEPTEMBER 22nd. LAST night the Crown Prince distributed more Iron Crosses among the heroes of the day. At the end of the meal he suggested that I should spend my morning with Major Matthiasz, whose duties with the Chief Command of the 5th Army called him to Eclisfontaine, from which point an attack was to be delivered against Varennes and neighbouring villages which the Germans had once occupied, but from which for strategical reasons they had been obliged to retire.

At half-past three I was called, lit my candle, opened the window and looked out into the night. It was pitch-dark but for a star here and there which peered out through the crowns of the trees. It was very still, and nothing could be heard but the slow, measured tread of the sentry crunching the garden gravel.

At four I was seated alone at breakfast. A soldier accompanied me with a lantern to Major Matthiasz's residence, where a young lieutenant with an orderly stood waiting. We took our seats, wrapped in comfortable furs, and drove out of the town, our powerful headlights showing the way. At this early hour they were not of much use, however. A very dense fog lay over the ground and it was dangerous to drive fast. We accordingly made our way cautiously, the more so as the road was as usual crowded with soldiers on foot and supply columns. There is no rest on the lines of communication, even at night. It is wonderful to think that this ceaseless stream of life is never for one moment interrupted! Will there ever be an end to this incessant rattle and tramping of feet? Truly Germany seems inexhaustible in vital and matérial force.

The trees loomed up through the fog like ghostly sentinels. Yet more eerie are the transport columns in this unaccustomed and picturesque half-light. The grey-clad riders, with their cloaks thrown over their shoulders, sit and dream on patient, snorting horses and seem to spring up from nowhere out of the fog as they come within the circle of our headlights. A horse takes fright at the light and the buzz, his rider starts and wakes up out of his reverie; he pulls himself together and settles down again in the saddle. The column goes on, but new riders loom up one after the other. We hear the tramping of innumerable hoofs against the road surface, and the wagon wheels make a smacking and gurgling sound as they move onward through the mire, which clings to them some little way and then drops back in shapeless clods.

By the side of the road is a reddish light which, as we approach, gains in strength and colour; it is the camp fire of a bivouac, against which the figures of the soldiers are sharply silhouetted. They appear to be preparing something over the fire, coffee no doubt, or tea. Here and there one of them has already lit his early-morning pipe. As dark and as mist-enshrouded as the night which still enfolds the earth, is the fate that awaits them with the coming day. There seems to be something fateful in the air. A new fight no doubt is impending. To the soldiers there is nothing remarkable, nothing unusual or exciting in this. To them it is all in the day's work - there is fighting at the front and their fate beckons to them under the French fire. Maybe it is their turn to-day to fall and add to the number of graves and wooden crosses by the roadside. Maybe this dismal night has been the last in their lives. But if so they have slept well for the last time, and the flames of the bivouac fire give out a friendly and agreeable warmth.

The gleam of fresh fires shows through the mist; now clear, now pale and dim, at some distance from the road. Everywhere are groups of soldiers, soldiers, soldiers. Once we stop a moment, to allow a frightened horse to pass. The hushed voices of the night then seem louder, and the creaking of wagons, rattling of arms, tramping of the horses' hoofs or the curt orders of the officers strike our ears. The troops are moving to the front. We are on one of the arteries of a fighting army.

Once more we pass through Dun, whose naked walls and ruins present a desolate sight as they are lit up by our lamps. We drive through

Romagne, which lies wrapped in fog. At the other end of the village a vast body of horsemen blocks the way; they are what we call in Sweden, Divisional Cavalry, in contrast to cavalry acting independently. The standard is furled. Sabres rattle against stirrups and harness. The horse of one of the troopers, as nervous and thoughtless as many others of the genus *equus caballus*, frightened by the lights, begins a wild dance in front of our vehicle. Instead of leaving the road free, the horse rears up on his hind legs in front of the car, which cannot stop abruptly. This ended in a tumble, which sent horse and rider spinning. The former now seemed to realise in his troubled mind that discretion is the better part of valour, took a jump across the ditch and cantered off across fields and meadows. Angry at his adventure, the unseated rider entered upon the pursuit and soon disappeared in the mist.

It is evidently quite impossible to drive fast. We wriggle along kilometre after kilometre and constantly fresh swarms of soldiers seem to rise up out of the fog. It is clearly the reserves of an army who are on the march. Now the sky seems to grow lighter in the east, and the grey coats of the soldiers appear to assume a queer, ashen-grey, colourless tone. Here is another ammunition column and a string of motor-wagons belonging to some hospital establishment; they look like gigantic boxes with an enormous red cross on a white background on their sides. There is an infantry battalion which has bivouacked for the night and is now ready to break up and take up its prearranged position in the column of march. A little further on we are stopped by an artillery detachment, accompanied by its train. Even if the road is clear of vehicles for a hundred metres or so, we pass isolated companies of soldiers on foot, orderlies on cycles, despatch riders and police.

It grows a little lighter and the fog lifts somewhat, but the columns grow ever denser. An ammunition column has halted owing to some congestion ahead. The riders have dismounted and the men on the wagons likewise. They stand in groups, talking and smoking, with their half-frozen hands in their breeches' pockets. All the time the road is packed with soldiers and we cannot drive faster than they march.

At last, at half-past six, we arrive at Eclisfontaine, a junction where several roads unite and where by-roads and paths debouch on to the main road. Cavalry, riding past at a sharp trot, with their horses' bellies caked with mire and the mud spurting up round their hoofs, is travelling in the same direction. We see at these cross-roads a few dismounted cavalry scouts. They stand there in order to show the way to oncoming detachments of the unit to which they belong or to which they have been attached. Orderlies, usually in couples, fly past at a gallop. They ask the way to Romagne and ride on directly they have received the required information. They belong to the artillery, and it seems to be their allotted duty to conduct ammunition columns to certain points where fresh ammunition has been ordered.

Daylight makes further inroads. We hear the thud of the columns which we have just passed, they come nearer and move off in different directions. The artillery fire seems less brisk than yesterday. The fog prevents accurate fire, but now and again a salvo is heard. On a by-road in the village stands a row of motor-cars, evidently belonging to superior Staff officers. We drive up and range our car behind the others.

Whilst my travelling companions go off to investigate the situation, I remain behind a moment to observe the busy life around me. I am now outside a house in which a Divisional Staff has evidently taken up its quarters; it is distinguished by a little black, white and red flag. Opposite, in a meadow, stands a group of orderlies and the escort of the Staff. The horses stand in a long row with the lances thrust into the ground; the men are standing round in little groups chatting, prepared to ride wherever they may be wanted with orders and reports. Now and again one hears the hum of a car rushing past on some errand.

A party of eight stretcher bearers hurries past towards the fighting line. The stretchers, drenched in blood, bear witness to the recent removal of seriously wounded cases to a dressing station. The Red Cross is, or should be, avoided by the fire, and its staff, therefore, carry arms for self-defence only.

A couple of French women come walking along with water in buckets. They have been to a well outside the village, where the water in these times cannot be any too good. It is wonderful how calm they look, considering that the fighting is raging round their very homes, but they are pale and have a serious look on their faces.

The remnants of the fog hang about in wisps and patches, now lighter, now denser, and do their best to challenge the rising sun. It is an important day for the Germans. They are, as I have said, to attack the enemy at and around Varennes. It is nearly eight o'clock. The infantry is said to be engaged already. The artillery is waiting to move forward to fresh positions, but in the meantime is doing its best to support the advance of the infantry from the points which it is occupying. The sound of firing increases in all directions. Close to the village stands a heavy battery, howitzers and mortars of heavy calibre. The duller and more distant reports come from the French lines. Sometimes we hear four or six reports almost simultaneously, followed by a pause before the next salvo is discharged.

Accompanied by an officer, I follow the main road through the village and peep into a little house, where all the wires of the field telephone seem to unite. Half a dozen officers are seated at a long table with receivers close to their ears and maps in front of them. All reports of the progress of the fighting at different points are brought in here, likewise any information about changes in the German and French positions and any fresh requirements and wishes entailed thereby. An officer of the General Staff seems to classify and summarise the purport of all these communications. He traces "the new position" on a map already filled with indications of the position of troops. No doubt this map is later to be submitted to the Chief of Staff. I can fancy the upshot of all this to be a telephonic order to some reserves - perhaps some of the infantry we passed at daybreak - to hurry forward to some point behind the firing line. I can almost see the impulsive thrill which passes through the ranks as the will of the High Command is made known to them. I can see in my mind's eye the column leaving the road and making its way to its post in little separate detachments. Many a queer thought occurs to the untutored layman as he looks into the smithy where the military will is forged. No superfluous words are uttered, everything is concentrated and concise. It cannot well be otherwise. When I walk away I feel that I have a clearer conception of the vital part which the telephone plays in the direction of a fight.

In the company of my friend Matthiasz I walk a little further south-westward, following the main road to the point from which the fighting proper is conducted. The ground rises gently towards this point, which has a commanding position and from which one gets an excellent view of the entire area in which the fight is raging. Here I see the General in Command, von Mudra. Here also is the almost octogenairan Field-marshal General Count von Haeseler, who, although he has no command, has not been able to resist his longing to be near his old corps, as it fights for Germany's honour and rights. All day long the two generals stand in the middle of the road, surrounded by several officers. On the fringe of the road a powerful telescope has been mounted on its tripod. A Captain is posted behind it and is closely observing the position, and reporting when the telescope reveals any changes in the situation. Now and again the Commander of the Army Corps himself walks up to the telescope.

After I had been duly introduced to the Generals and had chatted with them for a little while, I made the acquaintance of the other officers, and had the situation and the object of attack explained to me. The spot at which we were standing was not entirely without danger. A soldier standing on the road close to the telephone house was hit by a rifle bullet, but, curiously enough, without being wounded. He was knocked down by the impact or perhaps by the sudden surprise. The bullet, which had come from a great distance, had obviously spent itself. Another man was slightly wounded, likewise by a rifle bullet. Three shrapnel shells exploded fairly close to us, too high up to do any damage.

The day is long, and I find time to make numerous interesting observations. The village of Eclisfontaine and the observation station of the Generals are the terminal points of a line of about a couple of hundred metres in length along which the officers and I are moving. Here I had an opportunity of talking, now to one, now to another, whilst at off moments I sat down in the grass to make notes and observe the line of fire. From a point near the village we had an excellent view towards south-south-west in the direction of Varennes. On a stool in the middle of the road sat the Chief of Division, Lieutenant General Count von Pfeil, fat and jolly looking. When the last traces of the fog had disappeared, the dim, blue outlines of the Argonne became discernible. Three kilometres away in the direction of Varennes the ground rises to an extremely bare ridge, behind which, out of sight of the French, a couple of German field gun batteries are posted. We can see them with the naked eye. Immediately to the left of this artillery position a body of German infantry is advancing to the attack. With the aid of the field-glasses we can see the soldiers go forward bent almost double in order as long as possible to retain the shelter of the height which screens the guns. It seems likely, however, that the French have noticed the move, as shrapnel is constantly seen bursting over these lines - one little tuft of smoke after the other, and out of their midst a streak of lightning. Once we could count as many as eight such cloudlets soaring simultaneously over the German infantry, and doing their best to pour a hail of bullets over it. It must thus be at least two batteries that are concentrating their fire on this point. Besides the shrapnel, common shells also keep falling in the vicinity of the attacking lines. These shells are easily distinguishable by the dark grey columns of earth, clay and smoke thrown up on impact with the ground.

Immediately to the south of the hill in the south-west and concealed by it, a strong German infantry force lies entrenched. Here also the artillery is in position. On the near side of the batteries I notice two crescent-shaped, dark outlines on the ground, which turn out on scrutiny through my field-glasses to be bodies of infantry apparently at rest. This is the artillery cover. On their front the guns are well masked, embedded in the ground and protected by shallow parapets which resemble as closely as possible the appearance of the contiguous ground. It is only from where we are, that is to say from behind, that the guns are visible. So far no French infantry or cavalry has been observed this morning; on the enemy's side the fight is only being conducted with artillery. The Frencn artillery fire was said by the German officers to be directed very well indeed, but the projectiles often failed to burst and were therefore comparatively harmless, unless one had the bad luck to stand right in their path.

The booming of cannon is now audible all round us, even from behind, a battery of four 21-cm. mortars having been brought up from the village and unlimbered only a hundred metres away from us. They make a terrible noise and the whole ground trembles when they are discharged. I had a peculiar feeling when standing in front of these winged messengers of death, a consciousness of security mingled with respect, for are they not fighting against the enemy's positions, the duty of whose guns is to take our lives? The four reports come so close together that there is only a second or two in between. Then, for half a minute or longer, one hears a whining, singing, hissing whistle overhead, and one looks up involuntarily. The projectile is, however, only discernible if one stands right behind the mortar as nearly as possible in the extension of the line of fire. The four shells accompany one another through the air and sing the same whining song in the same high pitch. The sound arises through the air rushing to fill the vacuum behind the advancing body, and through the friction. Sometimes it seems to die away, but is heard again presently quite plainly, this being no doubt due to air currents.

Time after time the four "growlers" emptied their heavy shells over the French positions opposite, and each one was meant to cause the death of heaven knows how many human beings. Their main task was to drive the defenders out of Varennes, which is situated six kilometres south-south-west of Eclisfontaine.

After the artillery had been pounding away all day, I asked an oficer what the cost had been. He made a rapid calculation for thirty-two batteries of different types and estimated the average cost of each round at fifty marks and the number of rounds at twelve thousand, which would make an expense of six hundred thousand marks for a single day, and yet this was only for a short portion of the long German western front. Others, however, considered the estimate too high both as regards average cost and number of shots fired. In any case the artillery swallows up incredible sums in a war such as this, in which it plays a greater and more powerful part than ever before.

A little troop of soldiers without rifles come walking slowly across the fields and reach the main road between the observation station of the General in Command and the telephone house, and they must therefore march past us. It turns out to be a convoy of slightly wounded. This first lot is succeeded throughout the day by others. As a rule it is the left forearm and especially the hand that has been pierced by a bullet, the arm being carried in a sling. Here and there a man had an unimportant flesh wound in the shoulders, or his head had been grazed by a bullet. Two or three of the men looked pale, but they were all in good spirits. Their first field dressing had been applied on the field of battle. They were now on the way to a principal dressing station to be sorted out. Thence they were to proceed to a field hospital or to a collecting station for wounded, from which they would be sent to a clearing hospital and finally home.

Badly wounded soldiers are carried past us on hammock stretchers. Others are placed in ambulance wagons brought up to a halting-place in some sheltered position. Every infantry battalion has its surgeon and dressing wagon - containing medicines and dressing requisites - and staff of stretcher bearers. We saw several of these dressing wagons drive up on side-roads towards the batteries in the southwest in order to establish a *Truppenverbandsplatz* or regimental dressing station.

The "first field dressing," which is applied in the firing line by the wounded man himself or by some ambulance man, is merely temporary and intended to prevent exhaustion from loss of blood until removal can in some way or other be effected to a safer place where doctors are available. Many of these emergency dressings are saturated with blood, and by the evening the road was stained with little red spots of blood which had dripped from them. No wonder, then, that now and again I saw a pale face among the wounded.

We were busy scanning the heights opposite with our fieldglasses, when the news came that the Commanding Officer of one of the battalions deployed in front of us, Lieutenant Colonel Machenhauer, had been badly wounded and that a car was wanted at once to take him to a field hospital. Orders were immediately given that the nearest car, no matter to whom it belonged, should immediately proceed to the spot at full speed and fetch the wounded officer. It was not long before it returned with the Colonel propped up in the car between two ambulance men.

Presently Captain Bernhard of the infantry came walking along without assistance. His whole head was bandaged, but the bandages were red and the blood was dripping down his tunic and on to the road. Just as he had turned to give an order to his men, who were advancing to charge, a bullet had pierced his cheek obliquely from behind and passed out through the mouth, taking several teeth with it. It was hoped that the lower jaw and tongue had not been seriously injured, but for the moment he was disinclined to talk more than necessary. He was a plucky fellow and in excellent spirits in spite of his misfortune. The only thing that annoyed him was that the flow of blood had soiled his beautiful tunic. But one soon gets accustomed to the wounded and their injuries and ends by paying little attention to them.

It is no misfortune to bleed for one's country and one's liberty. As human beings must needs fire on one another, it is a blessing after all that so many of the wounded can be saved, even though they remain cripples for the rest of their days. But unhappiest are those who are deprived of their liberty and taken from the ranks of the defenders of their country to meet the dismal fate which awaits the prisoner of war. However kindly the treatment, a prisoner's life is after all the hardest trial that can await a soldier.

Here are some French infantrymen marching to Eclisfontaine, deprived of their arms and accoutrements but here and there carrying a knapsack. They are twenty-three in number and are escorted by two German soldiers with loaded rifles and fixed bayonets. Many, perhaps the majority, wear an indifferent expression which betrays but one thought: everything is now lost, everything is going wrong for us. Others look very distressed and one can see that they have been crying - France has been deprived of their strong right arm just as she needed them the most.

I was just talking to the Brigade Commander, Major-General Bernhard, when the Frenchmen came marching along in their tattered blue tunics and baggy red trousers narrowing towards the tops of their "jack" or high-laced boots. The uniforms were torn and soiled, which is not to be wondered at after many days' and nights' exposure in the trenches. One cannot well expect them to be neat and trim after such an experience.

General Bernhard stepped on to the road and ordered the convoy to halt. He then had the Frenchmen formed up before him in a semicircle and began to chat with some of them. One had been called out from Auxerre[9] and had on the eleventh day of mobilisation been moved via Bar-le-Duc to the neighbourhood of Varennes, where his regiment had since been stationed. Every man is carefully cross-examined. All statements are entered in the "Protocol." Valuable information about the enemy is thus gained. The uniforms alone tell one what troops one has to deal with. Nor do the German commanders in this siege warfare seem to have any difficulty in forming a pretty good idea of the grouping of the forces on the French side. General Bernhard asked how the prisoners had been fed before they were captured. The answers varied considerably. Most of them were satisfied, but a couple of soldiers said that they had only had hot food twice during the last week, which was probably due to the fact that they were posted at a point where it was impossible to bring them soup. Such inaccessible posts are by no means rare. They are also considered the most dangerous.

Finally the prisoners were asked if they had any diaries. Eight or nine men answered yes. The books were handed over to the General, who retained them. In this way one frequently gets much important information about the movement of troops on the other side, often from apparently very trivial notes, which can only be interpreted by an expert. General Bernhard afterwards read out to us an extract from one of these diaries. It was the last entry made by the prisoner on the previous day. It was as follows: "The Prussians are bombarding Varennes. They seem to aim pretty straight, for last night one of their shells hit General X—[10] just

9. Auxerre is the station of the 4th Infantry Regiment, 17th Infantry Brigade, 9th Infantry Division, 5th Army Corps.

10. I never noted his name and have forgotten it.

as he had gone to bed." At this General Pfeil exclaimed: "Good gracious, is *he* dead! I met him once." General Bernhard told me that the French prisoners always were polite and attentive, and replied carefully and truthfully to all questions. In most cases they called him *Mon Général*, showing that they knew the German insignia of rank even on the plain field-service uniform. As regards the General himself, I noticed that he spoke to the prisoners without the slightest trace of military stiffness and without that air of superiority which rank and power might otherwise tend to instill. Whilst the examination was proceeding, a French N.C.O. with a fair beard turned to me and asked: "What are they going to do with us, sir?" To which I replied: "They are going to offer you soup and bread, and if you have any wounded they are going to hand them over to the doctors." The man looked puzzled and surprised and wondered whether what I said was really true. He showed me one of his comrades whose neck had been grazed by a bullet, and whom a German lieutenant immediately placed in the hands of an ambulance man.

Thus I received close to the field of battle an immediate confirmation of what I had previously noticed at the hospitals, namely that the French prisoners in German hands are treated in a kindly and humane manner, and for the sake of truth I wish solemnly to protest before God that the allegations of certain foreign newspapers to the contrary are a mean lie and a shameless calumny. Once peace is restored and the French prisoners are allowed to return home, they will themselves be able to testify to the treatment they have received. Some of them will perhaps even remember Eclisfontaine.

Presently we see fresh groups of Frenchmen, taken prisoners in a German bayonet charge. One man told us that he was called home from Constantinople on the 5th August, another that he was a reservist and that they began to be hard up for men. They were also examined by the Field-marshal and his excellent Adjutant Rechberg, who spoke most admirable French.

One group of disarmed Frenchmen comprised a Captain. He had received a bullet through the thigh, limped badly and was supported by two soldiers. He had a frank and noble face and one could tell that he was a thorough gentleman. When his little band was to be examined, a chair was brought out for him, for he looked pale and weak.

"Is your wound causing you much pain, Captain?" a German officer asked.

"None at all, it is a mere trifle," he replied.

"Have you suffered heavy losses during the fighting?"

"Not particularly; we fill up all gaps."

"You look tired and worn, I am sure you must have had a rough time of it lately?"

"No, not by any means; I have been doing very well."

"Does it distress you to be amongst the prisoners?"

"Yes," he answered, in a low voice, without raising his head.

He was not among those who are demoralised by capture, and he was certain to retain his pride in captivity. When the examination was over he rose, saluted, and vanished round the bend of the road together with his men in blue and red.

The hours quickly pass. A kindly soul gives us some ration bread and claret. My portion was so ample that it was no charity on my part to give half of it to a French soldier, who at once proceeded to share it with three or four of his nearest neighbours.

By degrees even one uninitiated was able to notice certain changes in the situation. We see the Umbers being driven forward to the two batteries in the south-south-west with the Argonne forest as a background. The guns have been silent for a while; now they are getting ready to begin again. Gunners and drivers are hurrying to their posts and into the saddle, and the batteries roll away at a gallop in an elegant semicircle and soon disappear behind the hill. They are to accompany the infantry attack. West of the old artillery positions fresh lines are advancing in a south-south-westerly direction. We hear vividly the crackling, quivering sound of the machine-guns advancing with the infantry. The attackers have gained ground and are now entrenching themselves in new positions taken from the enemy.

I return to the observation station of the officer in command. The old Field-marshal, he who fought in 1870-1, and who ought to have been fairly tired, had actually been induced to sit down on the cane chair which had been brought for him. There the old soldier sits reviving his faded memories and cannot take his eyes off the battle-scene and the little puffs of smoke showing up where the shells have burst. His expression is solemn and severe, his face is furrowed by deep folds and wrinkles, his grey hairs hang round him like a mane. He seems to prefer to be left alone with his thoughts, but if anyone walks up to speak to him, he is full of life and vivacity.

General von Mudra, a man of fine military bearing and distinguished aristocratic features, is standing at his tripod stand telescope observing the fighting. The red collar of his light blue coat has been turned up, in his hand he holds an ordnance map of the surrounding country, and at his left side he carries a wallet for maps, note-books, pencils, compasses, etc.

A third battery of German field artillery has now advanced, and is seeking a fresh position, whilst a third wave of infantry follows the first two in the direction of Varennes. These reserves are also moving in open order so as not to offer a compact target for the enemy's fire. The men are advancing at the double, rifle in hand. They soon disappear behind the nearest rise. The rifle-fire keeps rattling away in the valley, accompanied by the crackling of the maxim guns. Presently the sound of tremendous cheering reaches our ears. It is evident that yet another position has been taken.

This little action, which is but a link in the great chain, is causing considerable liveliness in Eclisfontaine. First the ambulance wagons of the field hospitals dash forward at full speed to the point where the fight has taken place. Then comes another body of infantry reinforcements, evidently to form a nucleus round which the units scattered by the fighting may be able to assemble. Small Uhlan patrols with vertical lances seem to be riding at a gallop along the roads and paths leading to Varennes. At last come the steaming and fragrant kitchen wagons with their pleased and grinning cooks perched high aloft on the top of their paraphernalia.

But on the slopes south of us appear little groups of eight to ten men with stretchers, accompanied by collies whose duty it is to track the wounded lying lost and abandoned in ditches and ravines. When the dog discovers a wounded soldier, he stays with him and barks until the ambulance men come up with their stretchers.

The French artillery fire has now slackened, owing to their having been compelled to move further to the rear in proportion as the Germans have advanced.

Varennes, the little town where on June the 22nd, 1791, Louis XVI. was recognised, captured and taken back to Paris, is now in flames, and a brownish yellow column of smoke from its burning houses ascends into the sky. Near it Cheppy and further on Boureuilles are also burning. Cheppy church defiantly rears its spire aloft through the wreaths of smoke and sparks.

To the west of us is the broad valley of the River Aire, a tributary of the Aisne. Varennes is situated on the Aire, the eastern bank of which is lined by the famous Argonne forest. In the south, through the valley, Württemberg troops are advancing on Varennes, and a portion of their right flank is busy on the fringe of the Argonne. Their advance is plainly discernible through the tripod telescope, which now and again I was allowed to look through. But I needed no glasses to see the little white murderous wreaths of smoke which arose when the shrapnel exploded right over the heads of the Württembergers. They were answered by German spurts of fire, visible a little further away and more to the left.

An infantry ammunition column, which had found shelter behind the slight rise south of us, is now ordered to move forward. The nearest way would be to follow in a south-westerly direction the main road on which we had spent our day. But it would be too dangerous to take this route. The dusky outlines of the column would be visible from the new French positions and offer an excellent target, besides drawing the fire on to the German General Staff. The column had just begun to move down the road, when its commander was ordered to change its direction and drive behind the town where the great mortar guns were still posted. Only when dark has set in is it possible to advance right up to the troops - for the present it sufficed to go as far as the shelter afforded by the ground allowed. From the points thus reached the ammunition has to be carried up to the firing lines in daylight if a shortage becomes imminent. Such shortage of ammunition is however very rare, as an increased number of cartridges is always served out before a fight, in addition to which the cartridge belts of the dead and wounded are also carefully emptied by the men still on their legs.

A battery of light howitzers now appears north of the main road. It follows the southward course taken by the infantry. In the west-south-west we notice the bursting of six shells a couple of kilometres away, evidently intended for the advancing Württembergers. But the centre of activity is now beginning to move away from my point of vantage, and I see but an occasional ambulance man who has been left behind.

In the afternoon I made a hasty panoramic sketch of the battlefield, A young Captain provided with a map explained everything within our range of vision. In the east-south-east a battalion of reserves lay concealed in a hollow, in the southeast the French shrapnel kept on bursting, and immediately to the right of the puffs of smoke was the little wood called Bois de Cheppy. In the south-south-east the smoke from the burning village of Very rose into the sky - it had been taken in the course of the day. Immediately to the right, but further away, lay the prettily situated village of Vauquois, resembling a castle on a hill and still in the possession of the French. Immediately to the south was the burning village of Cheppy, and in the south-south-west Boureuilles and Varennes, both in flames. Yet a little further to the right, but at a greater distance, the little white cloudlets formed by the German shrapnel were sharply silhouetted against the sky. In the south-west the church tower and roofs of Montblain ville, which had just been taken by the Württembergers, showed up above the outlines of the country with the Argonne forest as background. Above the village, numerous shells kept bursting, as evidenced by the little puffs of smoke - they were intended to make the conquerors' stay in the village as unpleasant as possible. At 6 o'clock I counted eight burning villages, of which however one, west of the Argonne forest, lies within the fighting zone of the 4th Army. How many gutted homes, what appalling destruction of private property! It is pretty certain that the inhabitants have removed themselves and their portable valuables to a place of safety. But what will it look like in the thousands of homes when they return! Is it to be wondered at that one feels the deepest pity and compassion for the innocent people who are the greatest sufferers of the war? Surely it is not an unkindly thought towards France to strongly condemn the policy which has brought such nameless misfortune over the north-eastern portions of the republic. When one has seen with one's own eyes all the misery and grief, all the destruction and the ruin following in the wake of war, surely one cannot with self-respect refrain from loudly condemning the policy which alone is the cause of it all!

"But why does not the General Staff move forward, seeing that the troops have occupied positions six or seven kilometres in advance of the old ones?" I ask.

"Well," is the answer, "it is because it is impossible to extend immediately the telegraph and telephone lines and to reorganise the entire system of communications to meet the new situation."

The following day Varennes was taken, and the whole machinery was accordingly advanced a step further to the south-west.

Daylight now began to fail and the sun was sinking towards the tree tops of the Argonne forest. It had been an instructive day. I had been allowed to get a glimpse of the inner working of one of the German armies. I was deeply impressed with the sangfroid and the relentless certainty with which everything was carried out. The whole thing seemed like a game, which, subject to certain premises, it was impossible to lose. Not a single soul had the slightest doubt of the result. Whence this terrible assurance of ultimate triumph? - I need not refer to the perfected military measures which make it certain that it is beyond the power of Germany's present enemies to defeat the Empire in the field. Neither need I touch upon all that has been done to prepare for Germany's fateful hour and vital needs, or her readiness on land and sea to take up the gauntlet when it is thrown down. But there is one thing which above all needs emphasising, and that is the *inexorable will of the Gennan nation*. It cannot be broken, it lives with increasing purpose. It grows stronger every day. It does not find expression in blind and unpremeditated action, *it is conscious and disciplined.* Its voice has penetrated deep down into the bosom of every son and daughter of the German Empire. To the onlooker it finds expression in the deep and silent fixity of purpose underlying every action, but also in the dauntless courage which once animated our own Charles XII. and his men. With unshakable confidence in its leaders, this disciplined people fights with God for Empire and country. It knows that all that can be done is done, for all are animated with the immutable will to strain their resources to the uttermost, in order to attain the goal fixed by those who can discern the situation and have prepared the line of action. Trained strength has overcome the weakness of man. A reverse means nothing when met with such resolution. The skill and bravery of the opponent may sometimes thwart or delay the execution of a plan. Such things must occur. They are reckoned as part of the game. But the inherent superiority of German leadership, the superb strength of the German Army, the mutual confidence which inspires those who lead and those who execute —

We rely on one another, we on him and he on us - we march inflexibly to victory.

I witnessed that whole day in the history at Varennes, and was present at the successes won. I marvelled over the coolness with which everything was done, but on reflection I came to the conclusion that it would have been unnatural for these men, in whose midst I was, to break into expressions of triumph. What had occurred was to them merely what should and must occur. But there was another element. War is not play. Those who know it, speak of it with restraint. One does not boast when face to face with its realities. On the contrary, it inspires a feeling of humility.

Everybody still remained at the observation station or wandered up and down along the main road. *Nachrichtenoffiziere*, or intelligence officers, were still riding backwards and forwards, and orderlies were keeping up constant communication between us and the fighting line. At times the road became almost congested. On such occasions, an officer gave out the order that as many as possible should stand under the shade of the trees so as not to draw the French fire and thus disturb the direction of the fight. A car arriving from the village had been instructed to move down the hill, horsemen had been told to dismount, and a detachment of cyclists were instructed to disperse, all in order not to give the enemy any inkling of the whereabouts of the General Staff by conspicuous massing of individuals.

General von Mudra still kept to his post and old von Haeseler seemed determined to wait until the night sky was tinted red by the burning villages. At a quarter past six I took my leave. As Major Matthiasz seemed very busy, I arranged to have the company of Captain Suhlmann, who was going the same way.

Thirty kilometres and a wide, straight high road - we ought to have done it in no time. We began well at a good speed, but had not proceeded far before the car was stopped. It was four wounded soldiers who had to go to Stenay and asked for a lift. One of them was badly injured and very exhausted. He was stowed away as comfortable as possible. Then we met a string of steaming kitchen wagons carrying the conqueror's reward, his dinner, and later on several endless ammunition columns. We progressed by fits and starts. The drivers of the ammunition train, who shrewdly suspected that their dinners might be deferred, were cutting into their loaves, but turned round to gaze attentively at our wounded with their white or blood-drenched bandages. Further on the crowd becomes even denser. Fresh streams of men and wagons - a new cavalry force is moving forward. The same thing is going on throughout the immense front. Now we come to a dead stop: we must shift to the edge of the road and try to be patient An aviator is passing overhead. We hear the buzz of an aeroplane at a considerable height. The undersides of its planes are illumined by the setting sun, but it is travelling at too high an altitude to see whether it bears the mark of the Iron Cross or of the Tricolor. If the airman is a Frenchman it is unpleasant to have him right overhead, for he is certain to drop bombs. But he is probably a German, and soon he has vanished altogether.

A batch of French prisoners adds to the congestion. I speak to the one who is nearest. He says that out of his company only twenty-six men were in a position to use their arms when he was taken prisoner, that so many officers had been killed that there was hardly anybody left to command.

As we are halting by the side of our ditch, we have an opportunity of witnessing the distribution of forage by a supply column. A large fatigue party come dragging huge trusses of hay. Here is another troop of slightly wounded who are proceeding in charge of a medical service N.C.O. from a *Leichtverwundeten-Sammelplatz*, or collecting station for slightly wounded, to the nearest base. We are asked if we have room for two more men. "Yes, if you can stand on the foot-board." Yes, they were quite agreeable, and at last we get under way with our new burden. Here and there a horse has fallen during the day and lies cold and stiff by the roadside. A mortar ammunition column is proceeding in our direction. It is empty. The division stationed at Eclisfontaine has its supply for to-morrow's fighting already on the spot.

Now we are at Romagne and here we get badly stuck. There is a frightful crush in the village street. It is no use trying to force our way. We stop just in front of an emergency field hospital. The head surgeon is standing in the street and issuing his orders for the treatment and distribution of the newly arrived wounded. I am introduced to him and he declines to let me go until I have seen his organisation at work. To come to the front to study the war and not to see the field hospital at Romagne! "No, thank you, my dear Doctor, that will never do! You have spent the day watching the wounded come back from the fighting line after their first temporary field dressing. You have seen the principal dressing station at Eclisfontaine. Now you must absolutely stop for a look at the third hospital establishment, our field hospital, where all the wounded have to pass."

Thus speaking the *Herr Stabsarzt* conducts me into the beautiful and ancient little Catholic church. I seem to step into the Middle Ages as I enter this temple, where a hundred years ago Napoleon's victories had been proclaimed to rejoicing congregations. The sun is setting and twilight is descending over France. It is dusk inside, but still light enough to distinguish the precious stained-glass windows. At the altar a single lantern is burning, which seems to accentuate the darkness. The church has been turned into a hospital. It was now occupied by eighty wounded Germans. The short pews were arranged in pairs facing one another, forming with backs and seats roomy beds filled with straw. Each bed thus improvised contained a badly wounded soldier. The benches did not quite go round, and many of the wounded were lying along the walls on straw, laid out on the stone floor. Each one had been provided with a blanket, and the space between the beds was sufficient for doctors and nurses to move backwards and forwards without inconvenience. As soon as their condition permitted, the patients were sent on into Germany to make room for fresh convoys. Only the very seriously wounded, who could not stand the transport, were allowed to remain to die in peace or to recover as lifelong cripples.

Up by the altar, by the light of a lantern, several young doctors were busy round a patient who had just arrived and who was to undergo an operation. More light was brought. The head surgeon conducted me from bed to bed and was indefatigable in his information about the various cases. Quiet reigned inside the church, as its doors were kept closed, but outside the rattle of wagons and tramping of horses' hoofs continued. A wonderful, almost eerie silence reigned inside, one almost felt the struggle proceeding between life and death. One might have been in some subterranean crypt with its cold and musty atmosphere. We could hear the deep breathing of the patients, but there was no complaining. Now and again a soldier sighed, that was all. To complain would have been to show inferiority to the others and to disturb their rest. Most of them were asleep, dead-tired after the trials of the day.

We pass from one to the other and speak in whispers so as not to wake those who are asleep or disturb the solemn spirit which had descended over these eighty heroes who had this day gladly given their blood for their country. Now they are dreaming their last dreams under their Iron Crosses. Soon many of them will go to their eternal rest under the little wooden crosses in the churchyard at Romagne. Their hearts, now beating at fever-rate, will soon rest ice-cold under the soil of France.

Here lies a man who has received a bullet right through the most delicate region of the abdomen. He is as pale as his tanned and weatherbeaten skin permits and his pulse is terribly weak. But his eyes are wide open and his glance roams in unknown regions far beyond this earth. It is certainly not the trench life, which he has just left, that is reflected in his vacant gaze. What a wonderful contrast! From the turmoil out there in the fighting line he is already on the way to eternal rest. It is difficult to give a name to the heartfelt sorrow which gripped the wanderer from the north before the quiet death struggle of the nameless soldier. In the midst of all his comrades he seemed so alone and abandoned. One could not help thinking of his people at home, still full of hope but who would soon weep bitter tears. "He won't live till sunrise, I suppose?" I asked the doctor.

"No, he is growing cold already" - but the memory of the brave does not grow cold, does not die.

A school-house close to the church had also been requisitioned by the field hospital, and its rooms, usually filled with French children learning their *Liberté, Égalité, Fraternité*, are now occupied by wounded Germans. Here, too, is an atmosphere of deathly torpor and fatigue. One of the school-rooms has been turned into an operating theatre. In the field one has to do what one can to make the best of the resources at hand. A couple of young surgeons, dressed in white from top to toe, were standing by the side of the leaf of a table rigged up on high trestles, on which a handsome and fresh-looking young soldier lay stretched out. He had had both feet shot through, but was in good spirits nevertheless. "Please don't slash me about," he ordered, with some conviction. A sister of mercy, the only one so near the front - for usually the organisation in the fighting zone is purely military - now undid the emergency dressings, which, clotted with the blood, had become a shapeless mass. It hurt a bit when the clotted blood was cleaned away and the wound laid bare, but the soldier bit his lips and made no sound. The left leg was crushed above the ankle and even the uninitiated could see that it was a very nasty wound. For the moment there was nothing to be done. His feet were put in splints and a fresh bandage applied, and he thanked the doctors very heartily for having been so kind. Soon after he was carried by two attendants to an empty bed and seemed determined to go to sleep and forget all about it. "Will he keep his feet?" I asked. "Yes, as regards the one there is no danger, but the other, the one that has just been bandaged - well, we shall see in two or three days; of course, I shall do my best, but…" and he shook his head. A number of captured wounded Frenchmen had been accommodated temporarily on beds of straw in a store-room. Here they were to receive their first attention. At the moment they were busy eating bread and a nourishing hot soup of rice and vegetables. They had a fine appetite and seemed to be in good spirits; a couple of them went as far as joking and laughing at each other's remarks. To my question how they were, one replied: "Monsieur, had we always been as well off as during the last fortnight, we should never have had much cause to grumble."

Outside in the street stood a whole row of wounded, both French and German, who were anxious to get in and receive a little attention. Fighting was still proceeding and fresh lots were expected during the hours of the night. There was no rest for the doctors. The Frenchmen stood in a batch by themselves. I went up to one of them. He had his entire head enveloped in a bandage so that I could hardly see anything but eyes and nose. In reply to my question where his bullet had hit him, he pointed with his left hand to the left side of his cranium and then to the underside of his lower jaw. I asked my friend the head surgeon if it was really possible for a man to stand and walk about and see and hear with a vertical shot right through his head. He answered that the man had not yet been examined, but that all sorts of remarkable wounds occurred. The bullets take the queerest paths through the wretched human body, which is often proof against the most appalling injuries.

My experienced doctor friend said of the Frenchmen that they were wonderfully patient. They would stand for any length of time waiting for care and attention without betraying by word or gesture the slightest impatience. It may almost be said to be the rule that when a doctor' goes up to one of the Frenchmen to take charge of him, the wounded man remarks: "There are other men amongst my comrades who are in greater need of help than I am. I can wait." Or: "Sir, be good enough to attend first to that man over there - he is the father of a family and his wife is in poor circumstances." I have heard the same from other German doctors. Here is another reason why the German Medical Corps treat the French wounded with so much sympathy. I do not know how many thousands of French soldiers are lying wounded at German hospitals, but those who survive the complications of their wounds and, when peace comes, return to their homes, will be as many witnesses in the service of truth.

Thus charity, in the guise of medical science, follows in the track of cruel and relentless war. What are all these doctors, assistants, sick attendants, sisters of mercy, these endless medical trains, but guardian angels wrestling with the angel of death for the lives of the wounded? What are the ambulance wagons, the stretchers and the faithful and intrepid collies, but friends and allies of the poor wounded, bringing in their harvest on the bloody battlefields? Here is the atonement which follows war hand in hand, just as the emblem of the Red Cross combines the colour of blood with the symbol of Christian love.

"Doesn't the soldier get nervous and terrified at the sight of all these dead? I should have thought that he would realise that the danger which he runs is just as great as that of those who have already fallen?"

"No, he hardly notices the dead bodies. 'You are dead, you poor devils, but I am still alive and do not mean to die.' That is how he reflects. It is as if the sight of the fallen had steeled him in the face of the danger. And yet he may sometimes come across the bodies of friends so swollen that the buttons burst from the uniforms, and with blackened, grinning features staring up into the sun and rain."

"But surely the bodies are not left above ground?"

"No, as soon as the firing has died away on the battlefield, the civil population, or, if it has fled, our own soldiers, must inter the dead pell-mell in common pits, often without any attempt at a burial service. This can follow afterwards. The chief thing is that the dead disappear so as not to give rise to sickness and epidemics by putrefaction."

The time was now approaching when I ought to be back at Stenay. I said good-bye to the head surgeon of the Romagne field hospital and hurried with Captain Suhlmann into the car, where our seven invalids had been waiting. Our headlights had now been lit and once more we penetrated into the maze of the never ending transport columns. Does night then bring no rest at all?

At the edge of a ditch we saw two wounded soldiers sitting. They shouted and gesticulated to us to stop. We asked them what they wanted. It turned out as usual that they wanted a lift, they had not the strength to go any further. We pointed out, as they could see for themselves, that we had no room. Oh, that did not matter. They could sit on the knees of a couple of others. And they squeezed into the car. We now had a complement of twelve persons in a car made for six. One of the new arrivals was quite a character. He began by telling us that the Crown Prince had shaken hands with him that very day at Romagne and had asked him how he felt. Later on he told us that he had been in the storming party at St. André. He had even overheard his Colonel, as the day of St. André broke, say to the General in Command: "This will be a bloody day's work." And the Chief had answered: "Are you afraid?" But the Colonel was not afraid. When the time came he led the way and was immediately shot. The young soldier, on the other hand, had come through without a scratch. To-day he had been relieved of a couple of toes, a loss which did not seem to affect his good spirits in the least. He chatted away almost unconsciously, but he had quite forgotten how many of his foes had come into contact with his bayonet. The part he had not liked was when the French shot from trees. It was like shooting game.

At last we arrived home and the sentries at Madame du Vernier's iron gates looked surprised at the curious company I had brought with me. In the hall I asked a footman to let me see Herr von Behr - for I had arrived an hour late, but that could not be helped. The Crown Prince and his suite had finished supper, but remained at table to keep me company whilst between the mouthfuls I recounted my impressions of this eventful day.

CHAPTER V
A DAY AT DUN

SEPTEMBER 23rd. I had intended leaving the 5th Army that day, but at our meeting on the previous evening Crown Prince William had been kind enough to ask if I could not stay one day longer. This hospitality was the more acceptable, as I wanted to inspect the pretty, but unfortunately badly damaged little town of Dun on the Meuse.

When, therefore, the Crown Prince, called away by duty, motored that morning to Romagne, I accompanied Chamberlain von Behr in one of the Staff cars, and after an early and rapid run to Dun was ceremoniously handed over to the Commandant of the base there, Lieutenant-Colonel Betz. The latter was only just up when we entered his quarters at the Villa Saint Claude, belonging to a M. Thiébaut of Nancy. But he appeared, big, strong and pleasant, and assured me that I should be well looked after at Dun. To begin with I kept him company while he breakfasted, and he gave me an account of how Dun was taken by the Germans and how by far the greater part of the serious damage to the houses in the main street was done by French shells. But this belongs to the general history of the war, and I have pledged myself to speak of nothing but what I have seen with my own eyes.

A civilian who wanders about a recently conquered town, in which the invader's troops are quartered, looking at everything and sketching this, that and the other, is rightly regarded by sentries and patrols as a highly suspicious character. He is rigorously watched and tracked; he will notice that someone is following him like a shadow; finally he will be arrested and directed with cold military precision to accompany his captor to the proper examining authority. Little adventures of this kind might be quite amusing and exciting to me, knowing that they would always have a happy ending; but I had no time for them, and was grateful when Lieutenant-Colonel Betz told off a non-commissioned officer to escort me on my rambles through Dun.

First we crossed to the east side of the Meuse, where the high road between Montmédy and Verdun runs through a fine avenue. This road joins on to the main street of Dun, in the northern half of which the backs of the houses, wrecked by shell fire, are reflected in the river as ruins and heaps of débris. In the southern part of the same street the hospital service has requisitioned those buildings that have been spared by the shells. Here, too, we find a little garden, enclosed by a fence, which is used as a mortuary, and to which soldiers who have died in hospital are brought. Four dead men were now lying on a grass plot in the shade of the trees. They were dressed in their uniforms and had their caps on. Wrapped in blankets and with a white cloth over the face, they lay there waiting until there were enough of them to be lowered in a batch into the big grave that was kept ready in the churchyard. I went up to them and raised the cloths. The features were cold and stiff, yet infinitely calm, and bore no trace of the hard fate and severe suffering the dead had undergone. I stopped in particular before a soldier who

"seemed to be resting from a game.
His aspect as undaunted as before,
But paler far."

He was a fine-looking fellow and his face seemed carved in marble. He lay as in a deep and heavy sleep, with eyes and lips closed, oblivious alike of the cannon's roar and of ether fumes, of fatherland and songs of victory. The soil of France was receiving him in its embrace, and his relatives would never bring wreaths to his grave.

Nevertheless, as we know, the fallen do not vanish without a trace, since every soldier wears round his neck a little disc, giving his regiment and his number. All that remains to be done is to turn up the roll of his unit to find the dead man's name and home. In clearing the battlefield the discs are collected, and with their help the lists of killed are drawn up.

A steep and narrow road leads up to the crest of the hills that form the eastern boundary of the Meuse valley. On the very edge of the slope stands the handsome and noble church of Notre Dame de Bonne Garde, which dates from the time of the Emperor Charles V. It is characteristic of this part of France that the churches, even of quite insignificant places, are veritable pearls from an architectural and artistic point of view.

The porch is decorated with a little silvered statuette of Joan of Arc. On entering the nave we find on the left, behind an iron railing, a group of painted figures, three feet high, representing John the Baptist baptising Christ. Immediately opposite is a Pieta, on the altar of which helmets, knapsacks and bayonets form a sharp contrast with the ecclesiastical objects. But the floor between the railing and the altar is strewn with straw, and there soldiers have their simple beds. Notre Dame de Bonne Garde! Under her protection German sentries are now finding safe quarters.

Inside the rail under the chancel arch which separates the choir from the nave, the high altar is surrounded by camp mattresses of straw. Some wooden chairs stand about a table and on the floor arms and equipment are heaped pellmell. Where French priests formerly said mass, foreign soldiers now sit writing field postcards to their homes. On the arms of a silver candelabra stockings are hung to dry, and from niches and altarpieces saints and apostles look down with disconsolate eyes upon rifles and carbines, bayonets, belts and ammunition pouches, which lie scattered over the seats in the nave. Even the sacristy has been transformed into a bedroom. The priestly vestments of red velvet and gold brocade hang untouched in their cupboard, and on the arms of the chairs outside it hangs the soldier's modest equipment of small and well-worn objects, together with a cloak or two, tattered and worn from the life of the trenches and sooty from the flames of camp-fires. The sacred vessels are touched by nobody. In the German Army it is strictly forbidden to commit depredations on the property of the Church, the State or private persons; and so it was here at Dun.

The havoc of shells, on the other hand, is one of the privileges of war. Into the lower part of a buttress facing west a shell has penetrated the brickwork to about a third of its length. It is a *Blindgänger*, that is, one which has failed to burst on contact. It seems inadvisable to move a thing of this kind, and it will probably be allowed to stay where it is as a souvenir of the war. The shell is a French one, and its object, like that of the others that destroyed Dun, was to drive the Germans out of the place again or at least to make the first hours of their occupation as warm as possible. A projectile has badly damaged another buttress and several grave-crosses in its neighbourhood. Large blocks of masonry have crushed in their fall a flat gravestone lying close against the wall of the church. Many shrapnel holes may be seen round the clockface on the tower, and a small house beside the church has been destroyed by two shells.

We went out into the churchyard and turned our steps first to the railing at the edge of the slope. From here a magnificent view is displayed. Right under us lies Dun like a little map, and we can clearly see all the houses that have been ravaged by the French shells. We also have a bird's-eye view of the valley of the Meuse, with the almost deserted road to Verdun on the south, and on the south-west the road to Romagne and Varennes, filled as usual with whole strings of transport columns, cavalry and hooting motor-cars.

The graveyard itself offers an affecting sight. A shell has fallen in the midst of the tombstones, forming a fresh grave, which however did not expose any of the dead. But now peace reigns among these French crosses, which are often decorated with wreaths of coloured beads, expressing sorrow and loss in simple but eloquent words: *Nos Parents, Regrets, Souvenir.*

To us all these names are unknown. They are modest townsmen of Dun and peasants from the neighbourhood who are taking their long rest in the churchyard. But the gravestones are always costly and handsome, and one can see that even the poor gladly part with their savings in order to honour the memory of their dear ones in the city of the dead.

How simple, in contrast, are the memorials raised to soldiers who have died in the hospitals of Dun! Two strips of wood nailed together in the form of a cross, that is all. There one may read such epitaphs as the following: *Ein unbekannter Soldat. - Ein Landwehrmann, Kanonier. -* I. *Comp. I. R. 22.*[11] *Ein deutscher Krieger* 16/9 1914. *- Zwei Französische Krieger* 21/9. Curiously enough, *deutsch* is spelt with a small d, but *Französisch* with a big F; why, I don't know - perhaps from some kind of unconscious politeness towards foreigners. The cross signifying "dead" is carved in the glorious shape of the Iron Cross. Here, too, is the big grave prepared for those who are slumbering in the garden down below. By one of the new graves a dog howls plaintively. Perhaps he is lamenting his master - it is a very common thing for the German soldiers to adopt for the sake of company French dogs without a master, who take to them and follow them faithfully.

In a special little chapel at the side of the churchyard are buried the priests, natives of Dun, who have died there.

We descend by another way, a steep lane between ruined houses. One of them has been exposed by the fall of the outer wall, and one can see the interior of a room, the bed standing in its place with blankets and pillows, while a mirror has fallen down and been smashed to pieces. Through the dark, gaping holes in the heap of débris surrounding the house one can see into the kitchen in the basement.

One or two saw-mills and workshops driven by waterwheels had stood by the side of the river, but now nothing was to be seen but the most terrible devastation where formerly they had been. Machinery, belts and wheels lay twisted together into rubbish among charred beams. Close by were to be seen the remains of a bridge, which crossed the river in two spans, and which was blown up by the French when they had to evacuate the place. They also blew up the western span of the three-arched stone bridge over the Meuse, which carries the high road and the main street. With great skill and rapidity the German engineers have replaced the wrecked arch by a wooden bridge.

The railway to Dun has been repaired by the Germans, and the station showed a scene of animation and traffic which the little town can scarcely have witnessed before. All the storehouses and baggage-

11. No. I Company of the 22nd Regiment of Infantry. [Infanterie-Regiment Keith (1. Oberschlesisches) No. 22, quartered at Gleiwitz in peace time.]

rooms were literally packed with mountains of provisions, ready-baked loaves, tinned foods, meat, sacks of flour and oats, and even with wine. These warehouses had a smell like a grocer's shop. The supply columns are loaded at new and old platforms and then go forward to the troops. I sketched here one of these columns, consisting of requisitioned farmers' carts, drawn by horses also requisitioned at the seat of war, only two to each cart. The long lines of vehicles are brought up to their loading stations by special roads marked out by placards. Everything is done rapidly, but in silence and with unfailing accuracy. When a column is ready, you hear a shout to the horses, a crack of the whip, and the procession moves forward with creaking wheels on its way to Romagne. I noticed that - in addition to finger-posts - pickets have been posted to guide the traffic and prevent dangerous congestion at cross-roads. This is quite necessary, as column after column is constantly passing along the main road. Here was one, for instance, the wagons of which were marked "Fs. A…, III. Btl. (Mrs.) I. MK" - that is, Foot Artillery Regiment, 3rd (Mortar) Battalion, 1st ammunition column, and then the number of the wagon in the column. The stores at Dun supplied amongst others the army corps whose guest I had been the day before.

In a field quite close to the station was a base slaughterhouse and cattle depot. Here all the cattle collected from the neighbourhood were assembled in a space enclosed with posts and barbed wire. A fenced-off portion was drenched with blood from the slaughter, and here lay immense piles of ox-hides. One felt certain that these would be turned to good account. An enclosure for pigs was equally well filled. There was thus beef and pork in plenty; the troops would not go hungry. The day's requirements for 1000 men amount to 2 oxen or 6 pigs or 19 sheep, of an average weight respectively of 500, 90 and 40 kilogrammes. The depot is replenished by degrees. In most cases the troops do their own slaughtering; the animals being taken to the front by the provision columns.[12] At Dun there was also a field-bakery detachment with its attendant wagons, ovens and tents, and surrounded by a fragrant odour

12. During more mobile operations the troops requisition their own cattle, so far as the local resources allow.

of new-baked bread. Each of these detachments is capable of supplying 23,000 rations of bread in twenty four hours, working uninterruptedly.

We also visited the courtyard of a private house, where food was served out to a thousand French prisoners three times a day in separate batches. A kitchen on a grand scale with gigantic caldrons has been installed in a shed in the yard. When the hour strikes, the prisoners, drawn up in single file, have to step up and hold out their bowls to a cook, who fills each bowl with a single dip of his ladle. He is incredibly expert and rapid in his movements, and never spills a drop. Probably the condition of the French prisoners will one day disclose the fact that they have not been subjected to a starvation diet.

Here again I sketched a few types: a gilder, an official and a workman, all from Paris, as well as one of their German guards, a strapping Landwehr man. I remember I had half finished the portrait of a young French soldier - of the 113th Infantry Regiment,[13] of aristocratic, melancholy appearance, when the word of command was given that the batch that had been served was to be taken to its quarters and the next lot brought up. At my request, however, my model was allowed to stay behind. He was a bank clerk from Blois, of a highly *sympathique* and amiable nature. Perhaps some day he will remember that sitting at Dun; I shall not forget him.

While I was sketching the soldiers from Paris, I had a dense crowd of onlookers round me, and I threw out to them the following impertinent question:

"What are you really fighting for?"

"We have absolutely nothing to fight for," replied one fellow with a defiant air, and he was seconded with much animation by another man opposite.

"You have your country to fight for, I suppose?" I went on.

"We *have* no country," answered the two malcontents.

I asked a sensible fellow who was standing behind me what sort of persons they were, and was told: "They are notorious anarchists."

13. The 113th regiment of infantry of the line belongs to the 5th Army Corps, and is garrisoned at Blois. Parisians as a rule belong to the 4th Army Corps.

One may be tolerably certain that they would never have dared to answer like that on the other side of the firing lines. And if they had done so, they would have been torn to pieces by their comrades, who, even if they did not know how and why war had broken out just now, nevertheless understood that the future of France was at stake, nay, perhaps her existence as a first-class Power, On the other hand, they were all agreed in regretting the war, and expressions such as these constantly recurred: *"Cette malheureuse guerre - Cette guerre inutile - C'est terrible - C'est très, très malheureux pour tout le monde."* But even to this criticism of the war a reservation must be added. For not a spark of the enthusiasm with which the French soldiers went into the fire is left after they have been taken prisoners. Their hope has then vanished and nothing is left but the regret that they can no longer be of use to their country.

But it was now one o'clock, and I was engaged to dine with Colonel Betz at the officers' mess, where a party of a dozen assembled at a big round table. The mess was installed in a private house, very plain but well preserved, although a few shots or splinters of shell had made their way through its walls. Even the piano had been pierced by a bullet, but its tone was still irreproachable. At this table, again, the German officers spoke with unmixed respect of the French soldiers and their commanders. They are equal and worthy opponents, they are real, fully trained soldiers, not mercenaries who fight for money. They fight for their lives with skill and with the courage of despair.

After dinner I continued my ramble and visited amongst other places a hospital, where trained Red Cross sisters were at work. Finally I halted in the main street and sketched it and the bridge. A sheet was stretched right across the street, and on it was written, in enormous letters that nobody could help seeing, a notice that all empty vehicles returning from the front must be reported at the headquarters of the officer in command, where they would find out whether there were any wounded to be transported home. One constantly sees all kinds of directions, on calico, paper, planks and on whitewashed walls, to drive carefully, to keep to the right, as well as information of the distances in kilometres, the names of villages, where different roads lead, the position of the headquarters and other local offices, especially that of the hospital, and many things besides. Here, as in everything else, an exemplary orderliness prevails. Nobody needs to ask, he has only to follow the painted directions. As regards fingerposts and milestones, however, the French had done a good deal in advance; the notices which had to be added concerned the German lines of communication.

The day was drawing to a close as I walked along the principal street of Dun with Colonels Betz and Fretzdorff. Fresh bands of French prisoners - "Red trousers," as the German soldiers call them - had come in during the day and were now standing with their guards outside headquarters, waiting for orders as to their further destination. The prisoners were patient and calm as usual. Some sat on a bench chatting, others on the kerbstone; but the majority stood with their hands in their trouser-pockets, looking at the movement of the Prussians around them. They had never seen the German Army and its inner life at so close quarters. While fighting, the combatants see very little of each other; and now these Frenchmen had the strange sensation of standing quite close to their enemies without a shot being fired and without there being any question of slaughter. A couple of squadrons of Uhlans, armed with lances, sabres and carbines, were just riding past in close column. Their horses' hoofs clattered on the stone pavement and the rattle of their arms and stirrups echoed in the narrow space between the houses. The prisoners watched the hostile cavalry attentively but calmly: "They are still in the game; we are out of it," they appeared to be thinking, and one would have to have a heart of stone not to feel great pity for them.

Colonel Betz told me how desperate things became sometimes, just at this spot, when columns of different kinds met in the street at night, troops marching through and motor ambulances with severely wounded men anxious to get on. It would be all right if there were any possibility of keeping the street lighted, but the garrison was short of everything in the shape of illuminants, and a street could not very well be lighted with beacons. It was paraffin lamps that were wanted at suitable intervals, and presumably such lamps are now burning at night in the street of

Dun, so that the supply columns no longer need get blocked and delay each other.

It had been arranged that at about half-past six I should look out for the Crown Prince and his staff as they passed through Dun on their way back from Romagne. The time was approaching, and we were on the watch. The traffic had not decreased at all, rather the reverse. For a moment it looked like a block, and it would have been a nice thing if the Crown Prince had arrived just then. We crossed the bridge and were outside the town, when the aristocratic looking cars, bearing the mark, *General Ober Kommando V. Armee*, came tearing along at full speed. Beside the chauffeur of the first one sat the Crown Prince himself in a cloak with a high collar. He made a sign to me to get in and I took my seat behind him. Then he talked for a while to the officers of the lines of communications, and after that we started. But now the pace was slow, as we happened to meet an infantry regiment. The men took hold of their helmets by the spike, raised them aloft and gave a rousing cheer, as if they were charging a French position. But this time the cheer was meant for the Commander of the 5th Army and the heir to the throne, and we drove through a roaring sea of loud hurrahs. Gradually the ranks thinned out and finally came the stragglers - for there are foot -sore men even in the best marching army of all - in small groups of two or three, but they cheered as wildly as the rest. Last of all a solitary man stood by the side of the road. He, too, joined in with all the strength of his lungs. When the Crown Prince had reassumed his motor goggles and turned up the collar of his cloak he was not easily recognised, especially by the men of the transport columns we met, who had their horses to look after. But his Imperial and Royal Highness turned half round to me and said unassumingly that nothing pleased him more than to find that he was supported and understood by the soldiers. He considered it the first duty of a prince to show himself worthy of the confidence of his whole people, and for his own part he could not imagine a greater happiness than to occupy such a position in the minds of the German people.

We reached home in due course and sat down to table. The spirits of the company were as cheerful and unconstrained as usual, though

A bank clerk from Blois. Prisoner at Dun.

one would have expected high-sounding speeches, toasts and cheering. For Varennes had been taken and news had come of Weddigen's exploit at sea.[14] But no speeches were made and there was no cheering at all. The Crown Prince received the news with the same dignified calm as the others; he was glad, but not a muscle of his face moved, only his eyes shone with a moister brightness. The conversation then turned for a while on the question whether the effect of the submarines on the floating forts would be as great as that of the 42-cm. howitzers against the land fortresses. For that matter, subjects of conversation were never wanting at this table, where the spirit of comradeship was always held sacred. The imperturbable calmness of the Germans, especially of the higher ranks, in the face of success aroused my wonder and admiration, as it had done the day before and as it has often done since. And again the thought rose within me of the immense moral strength of the German military power and the conscious will of the German people in its fight for life.

Immediately outside Dun, on the north side of the road to Romagne, lies a solitary grave, covered with wreaths round its cross. In it reposes a captain, who held out with his little band in the thick of the fire when the French were shelling their own town, and who fell at last at his post. His memory lives among the Genüan soldiers at Dun, fresh as the flowers which are constantly renewed on his grave. And he is only one among millions. Life is the least they can give to the fatherland. The virtue of bravery is not a rare one; history has often borne witness to its existence; but the inflexible fulfilment of duty, which distinguishes the Germans in their hour of destiny, has few parallels. Such a nation *cannot* be conquered.

Dinner had been going on for some time when Professor Widenmann, the body physician, came in and took his place. He had been at a hospital, looking after our friend. Baron von Maltzahn, who had been the victim of a motor accident in the course of the day. The car, while going at a terrific pace, had skidded at a corner of the wet road and turned over.

14. This refers to the sinking of the *Cressy*, *Aboukir* and *Hogue* by torpedoes. - Tr.

Road across the bridge at Dun.

Landweir soldier, gaoler at Dun.

Von Maltzahn lay underneath and had the whole weight of the car on his chest. He had a couple of ribs broken, a broken leg, concussion of the brain and general shock. His condition was rather alarming, but the professor had good hopes of his recovery.

That professor is a man one would never forget. We took to each other, more especially as he had travelled all over the world. He had seen a great deal of Africa, and had been very near the summit of Kilimanjaro when he was forced to turn back by wind and weather. We had mutual friends far and near, and long after the others had gone to their rooms we sat up chatting - on that evening, which was my last with the German Crown Prince, the Crown Prince of Prussia.

On the following day, September 24, we made a very early breakfast, after which the cars of the Chief Command of the Army again drove up to the château. I thanked his Imperial and Royal Highness the Crown Prince with all my heart for the great hospitality which had been shown me and for all the memorable things I had had the opportunity of seeing while with his proud army. After a vigorous shake of the hand and a friendly *Auf Wiedersehen!* the energetic young Imperial Prince got into his car and went off to his duty.

As for myself, I was not to leave till twelve o'clock, as there was no convenient car going direct to Main Headquarters before then. Sitting by myself in Madame du Vernier's château was far too slow, and I preferred a walk to the great base hospital, where the chief staff surgeon. Professor Sick of Leipzig, showed and explained everything to me in the most obliging way. We went from ward to ward and spoke to many of the patients, both German and French. The largest ward had room for forty beds. Over the head of each was a paper giving the wounded man's number, name and regiment. On a folding table by the side of the bed stood a number of medicines and a glass of water, and in many cases a little Bible, some field postcards and portraits of relations at home. There was also a chart showing the wounded man's temperature from day to day. Wards, beds and everything were excellent, which was not to be wondered at, since the building was a hospital in peace time. My visit concerned in particular my friend Baron von Maltzahn, who lay wrapped and bandaged in an officers' ward. His condition was better to-day, and I was able to sit chatting with him for a good while. He agreed with me that it was a stupid thing to choose a motor accident, when there were so many other ways of getting killed in war. Not till several weeks later was von Maltzahn sufficiently recovered to be able to stand the journey to his home; but as late as the middle of November, when I saw him again in Berlin, he was still limping and had to use a stick.

I then said good-bye to Madame Desserrey and her charming daughter, and made a hasty portrait of Mademoiselle Blanche, which, however, by no means did her justice. After the conclusion of peace I was to write and remind her of the hours we had spent together during the war.

To conclude with a trifling anecdote: I was standing in the road in front of the château, making a hurried sketch of it. Then up came a sentry and addressed me in a rough tone:

"It is forbidden to draw the Crown Prince's quarters!"

"O-oh?"

"Give me your sketch-book."

"Here you are."

"If you have no permit I shall turn you away."

"You can't turn away the Crown Prince's guests."

"Anybody can say that. Where is your identification?"

I then handed him my *Ausweis*, signed "von Moltke," Chief of the General Staff. He took the paper, read it and gave it back, stood to attention, saluted and begged my pardon. Whereupon I assured him that he had only done his duty, which was always refreshing and pleasant to see.

CHAPTER VI
BACK AT MAIN HEADQUARTERS

IT IS TWELVE o'clock and in the yard stands a covered car with chauffeur and N.C.O., fat and jolly looking. It comes from Cologne and has been to take out *Liebesgaben* to the soldiers at the front. In token hereof it carries on its dash-board the green and white flag of the Rhine Province and the red and white flag of the City of Cologne. I take leave of the château personnel and drive away from Stenay just as two German airmen ascend in humming spirals into the brilliant bright blue sky to reconnoitre the French positions. The little city gate with its arched tunnel disappears behind us and once more we are spinning along the road, which has now recovered from the rain to such an extent that we actually leave a trail of dust behind us.

Now begin the old familiar scenes, these incredible masses of marching troops, supply columns - here made up chiefly of requisitioned vehicles on the way to the intermediate base or the fighting line - and motor-driven ambulance trains with the badly wounded, travelling in our direction soon to return to fetch fresh patients for the hospitals on the lines of communication. Presently we catch up to and pass a convoy of several hundred French prisoners marching three abreast with a German soldier for every twentieth or thirtieth man. The prisoners include a captain, who marches dejectedly with bent head after the heavy blow which fate has dealt him and his men.

Here is the village of Chauvency, and' we pass under the arch of its railway bridge, where the sentry orders us to halt. A supply column of tremendous length is just on the point of crossing by the temporary bridge over La Chiers, resting on the almost dry river-bed close to the permanent bridge which had been blown up by the French. Between the trees on the other bank we catch sight now and again of fresh strings of wagons with their hooped canvas awnings, the white and yellow showing up vividly against the verdant background. Presently they come out on to the bridge, swing up under the archway and pursue their creaking progress westward. On one of the vehicles I catch sight of the lettering *"V. A. C. Etappe Fuhrp. Col. 4 Wagen 48"* (5th Army Corps, 4th Transport column, Wagon No. 48) - but this was by no means the last wagon of the column. It took them a long while to get across, the more so as the notice *Ganz langsam fahren* (Proceed very slowly) was posted in large letters at each end of the bridge. At length the bridge was clear, but we had to look sharp so as to get well on to it before the next column, the creaking of which was already audible from among the trees, had time to arrive. Once we were out on the bridge we could safely obey the notice to drive very slowly, for whilst we were on it no one else had the right to use it.

Soon after we pass a column which has decided to bivouac in a meadow, and presently we see a railway train loaded with Guards troops. At a curve in the line a body of railway engineers are at work. We pause a moment whilst my friend the N.C.O. distributes two boxes of cigars and fifty tins of preserves, the last that he had left of his "love gifts" from Cologne. As we moved away, blue rings were already rising in the air from the happy smokers. Nearly all the houses in the little town of Montmédy have been turned into hospitals, but on a naked piece of wall, all that is left of a wrecked house, some waggish soldier has chalked up the words "first-class waiting-room." Another house had had the misfortune to stand in the way of the new railway built by the Germans, who had adopted the simple expedient of passing right through it. A train-load of Bavarian troops has just passed by and is followed by another full of Saxon Landwehr and engineers belonging to different regiments. It is not enough for the roads to convey gigantic columns to the front - the railways, too, are continually pouring fresh floods of human beings into the fighting zone.

In the market-place of Montmédy we pause a while to fill our petrol tanks. Here we find long strings of cars, most of them Red Cross ambulance wagons, loaded to the roof with medical stores and dressing requisites. Some Catholic sisters are seen to cross the square, attired in dark brown with girdles round their waists, black and white head-dress and wearing crosses suspended by chains round their necks. I take them to belong to the Franciscan Order. The wind sighs sadly in the tops of the leafy chestnut trees. Now and again a police patrol comes riding by.

Once more we drive through Marville, the pretty village with its curious amphitheatrical aspect and red-tiled houses, and its church which rears its tower above them. The fields round about are peopled with bivouacking troops and transport trains. The harvesting machines stand abandoned in the fields, where the German soldiers have brought in the autumn crops. Here and there, however, the corn has been left out to dry after the recent rams.

Although Longuyon has suffered far more from the war, there seem to be more inhabitants left than at Stenay, where only a couple of houses have been damaged by fire, I stood for a moment in the main street to sketch the devastation, the naked walls with their crazy chimneys, the crumpled gutters and broken telephone wires, and the piles of wrecked masonry.

By the roadside are a few soldiers' graves with crosses of untrimmed branches cut from the nearest tree. Next we come to Tellancourt, a terribly battered village in which only a few inhabitants remain, most of them women and children - and cats. Yet a priest comes walking along in his round hat and long black cassock, and behind him some twenty boys - possibly a reorganised school.

A little further on I make a hasty sketch of the remains of a piece of ordnance from St. Étienne, which has been shot to pieces. Several unused shells are still lying in the ammunition box by the side of the gun, and a cross shows that one of the gunners has fallen at his post. Wreckage of the war is everywhere to be seen. Broken rifles, torn knapsacks, scraps of uniforms and helmets - a whole open-air museum. Near by, some French peasants are ploughing their field with two ploughs and four horses.

On the way out I had not had time to visit Longwy, the upper portion of which, within the Vauban fort, has suffered dreadfully through the war, whilst the manufacturing portion of the town down in the valley of the La Chiers has remained undamaged. This time we drove over the two moats up to the picturesquely ornamented gate with its Vauban memorial, over which the German flag was flying. I showed my pass to the sentry at the gate. The galleries are also guarded by sentries. The guard has settled down in a casemate in the counterscarp. Large placards still remained posted on the walls here and there, such as: *Armée de Terre* et *Armée de Mer*. Or again under two crossed tricolors: *Ordre de Mobilisation Générale*, with all particulars, and finally a notice that Sunday, the 2nd August, 1914, was the first day of mobilisation. It is really horrible to read this order, which was destined to cause rivers of France's noblest blood to flow, to ruin all her northern provinces, and reduce the little town inside the fortifications to a mass of wreckage.

From the gates the main street runs through the town of Longwy. In the part we first come to, a number of French workmen are busy emptying the powder out of French hand grenades to render them harmless. No earthquake could have destroyed this street throughout its length more completely than the shells have done. There is not a single house left standing. When the attacking artillery began to bombard Longwy, the inhabitants were ordered to leave the place, and most of them went away. Some, however, preferred to remain, and of them some sixty were buried under the ruins, among them several women. I stopped at the church and walked in. The scene there is one of indescribable devastation. The arches over the aisles had fallen in completely, and elsewhere the shells had made tremendous gaps, the hail of splinters having struck the pillars and cut great scars into them. The force of the explosions had broken practically all the stained-glass windows. All that remained here and there was the lead setting. The pulpit, from which the truths of Christianity had so often been expounded, had curiously enough been spared, and had the priest stood there and read the Mass during the bombardment - as did the Greek patriarch when the Turks stormed into the Hagia Sofia - not a hair of his head would have been touched, and a miracle would doubtless have been proclaimed. The sanctity of the altar, however, had not been proof against the shells, for the floor of the choir was strewn with fragments and débris, covered in turn with a thick layer of limestone dust. The centre aisle was impassable, for the organ with its flattened pipes and the galleries with their benches and rails had been shot down and formed an incredible confusion of débris and rubbish. Heaps of plaster and fragments of ornaments, *prie-dieux* and other church furniture were piled on the floor, all mutilated beyond recognition.

The lower part of the massive temple walls had more or less been spared, together with their oblong panels, in high relief, illustrating the passion of our Lord. I stood in front of one which is quite undamaged, and under which I read the words: *Jésus tombe pour la deuxième fois.* The face of the Redeemer expresses infinite anguish as He totters under the weight of the cross and the sins of man.

Oh, vanity of vanities! Everything seems vain and futile. On a stone tablet I read the following well-preserved inscription: *Hanc ecclesiam Ludovici XIV jussu et pecunia procurante Vauban erectam primar, benedixit lapidem 22 marti 1683… etc.* Now the organ notes are silenced and no words of spiritual comfort fall from the pulpit. The wind sighs through the bared arches and seems plaintively to echo the frailty of human purpose.

Outside the church the scene is one of equal desolation. There lies the skeleton of what was once a motor-car and the remnants of a bicycle amid the wreckage of accoutrements and uniforms, buckled soup-plates of tin, sword sheaths, rifle stocks and barrels, children's toys, colour boxes and Noah's Arks, water pipes, balcony rails and grilles, chairs and tables all entangled in an inextricable confusion of stone, brick and dust. Pompeii could not have been so utterly destroyed as this town, and my old Lou-Ian in the heart of the desert, where the angel of destruction has reaped his harvest for so many centuries, looked less forlorn and desolate than the fortified town of Longwy after a few days' bombardment.

I walk along through the alleys and look round. The silence is ghostlike, except for occasional creaking in walls and joints and the sound of chips of stone falling to the ground. The wind is moaning among the roofless houses, and the gutter pipes, detached from their fastenings, hang nodding into space. Here and there the name of the street is still discernible at the corner, such as Rué des Écoles, or Rue Stanislas. Postcards, frayed and worn away by sun and rain, are lying about amongst the rubbish. I take one up and read the address: *Monsieur Crombez, Subsistant au 164 de Ligne,*[15] *Longwy-haut.* The text is as follows: "Le Mans, 22nd August. Dear Comrade, I have arrived safely at Mans, and have sent my certificate direct to the chief. I hope I shall soon have the pleasure of seeing you again. H…" Has this Crombez, I wonder, ever received the greeting of his comrade and been able to enjoy the pretty picture of the landscape where the tranquil waters of the Huisne and Sarthe flow together? Or has his name gone to make up the list of dead or of those who are missing, never to be found?

The little square in front of the church is planted with trees. Many of them have been cut down and lie piled into logs for fuel, and the leaves are yellow and shrivelled. In a line with the church and looking on to this open space, stands the riddled and shapeless frontage of a house over whose portals I fancy I can read the words *Hôtel de Ville*, and the year 1731. Its entrance hall, leading to the *Bureau de Police*, is one big rubbish heap of rags, broken furniture and paper. The archives of the police station lie scattered about. Here we find the whole edition of a little pamphlet: *Traité pour l'Éclairage au Gaz de la Ville de Longwy du Janvier 1912 au 23 Décembre 1961*, that is to say, covering a period of fifty years. They little thought in printing it that the gas would go out in 1914. I hear a rustling sound among the scraps of paper as the wind passes through the bleak ruins.

The lower part of the town, at the other end, reveals no other signs of war than the none too numerous German uniforms. The German soldiers wander calmly through the streets of the conquered town, in the central parts of which the civil population is quite well represented.

A moment later we are driving over the frontier into Luxemburg, and as the sun sets gorgeously we reach the little Grand Ducal capital, where once more I take up my quarters at the *Hotel Staar*. That very evening I

---

15. A battalion of the 164th regiment of infantry was garrisoned at Longwy in peace time.

had the good fortune to meet Prince Waldemar of Prussia, Admiral von Müller and Major Nicolai of the General Staff. The Chief of the General Staff, von Moltke, was absent from the town.

As regards my immediate plans, I decided to proceed on the following morning, the 26th September, at 9 A.M. by a Landsturm train to Sédan, partly in order to see what sort of accommodation the troops had on the railways. The rest of the day was taken up by various tasks. My purse needed replenishing and accordingly I withdrew a thousand marks on the strength of my Swedish letter of credit. The payment was made less ½ per cent, which after all was not to be wondered at in war time. I was glad enough to get any money at all. The great hall of the Banque Internationale looked empty and deserted.

I had not brought a camera from Stockholm, as I had assumed that I should never be allowed to use it. But at the 5th Army I was told that it was not so very serious a matter - provided I kept within certain bounds and tolerated a certain amount of supervision. I was now fortunate enough to obtain at Luxemburg from a German photographer a perfectly new and excellent Eastman Kodak, thanks to which I have been able to adorn this book with pictures of my own selection.

Through Chamberlain Baron von Reischach I was once more honoured with an invitation to dine at the Emperor's table at one o'clock. Those present, apart from the Chamberlain, included Herren von Plessen, von Gontard and von Busch, the latter being the German Minister at Luxemburg, also the Emperor's Field Chaplain and a couple of adjutants. In the forenoon news had been received of the illness of Prince Oskar. He had contracted some sort of heart complaint through over-exertion. I expected therefore to find the Emperor a bit depressed, but there was no sign of it. He walked in with youthful and military bearing, honoured me once more with a hearty handshake and bade me welcome back from the 5th Army. Thereupon he took a letter out of his pocket and asked me to read it through carefully. Whilst His Majesty was talking to his suite, I read the letter. It was addressed to the Emperor personally and was written by a sergeant who had been at Prince Joachim's side when he was wounded. Now the sergeant wanted to tell his august master how gallantly the Prince had borne himself and what an example he had been to the soldiers. The letter was simply and ingenuously written and showed how deep and strong is the loyalty which binds the German Army to its supreme Chief and Emperor, The loyalty and unity between Emperor and people, between Commander and Army, form the firm and immovable rock on which the German Empire has been built up. When the Emperor turned to me again and asked what I thought of the letter, I merely answered: "It must be a pleasure to your Majesty to receive such messages from the rank and file."

"Yes," he replied. "There is nothing that gives me so much pleasure as these proofs of the faithful loyalty of my people and the close bonds which bind me to my entire army. Such a letter as this I treasure amongst my most valued possessions."

Then we talked about Prince Oskar's illness, and whilst on this topic the Emperor said: "So you see, now Hohenzollern blood, too, has flowed. I have six sons and a nephew with me in the war and among the many German Princes who are fighting at the front several have already given their lives for Germany's sake."

The rest of the conversation was about my experiences with the 5th Army and the wonderful incidents of war.

In the afternoon the great flag of the Red Cross tempted me to visit the Convent of St. Zita, where the sisters are Carmelite nuns of the second and third degrees. Amongst them are some of the very strictest order.

The day was brought to an end with supper at the quarters of the Imperial Chancellor, von Bethmann Hollweg, to which several charming and eminent gentlemen of his entourage had also been invited.

CHAPTER VII
TO SÉDAN

SEPTEMBER 26th. I had been told that if I were at the railway station just before 9 A.M. I could go by the train which was to carry the Weimar Landsturm Battalion to Charleville. I arrived in time, but only to be informed that an alteration had been made in the train timetable and that this battalion would not leave until later, but that an ammunition train for Sédan, of about twenty-two "N" wagons, covered in with tarpaulins, was on the point of starting; if I liked to go by that, a first-class compartment would be placed at my disposal. A few passenger coaches were attached to the train, and I seated myself in one of these. My future travelling companions were the ten or twelve *Ersatz* Reservists, belonging to an Ammunition Park Depot established in Mayence, who were in charge of the train. The latter had been on the road for eight days and the men had slept eight nights on the train. Our carriage had strayed here from the north-eastern regions of Germany, as appeared from its mark: "Prussian-Hessian State Railways, North-East." On the wall of my compartment there was a little map of the railway line from Berlin to Memel.

I had been advised by a friendly soul at the *Hotel Staar* to take with me a supply of provisions, as it was more than doubtful whether any eatables could be found on the way. Four substantial cheese and ham sandwiches, three eggs and two bottles of mineral water had therefore been stowed away amongst my luggage in the compartment.

And so we started. We glided smoothly out of Luxemburg Station, and passed a train shunted into a siding and crowded with soldiers who sat and talked and laughed and seemed to be in the best of spirits. The town disappears behind us. We are out in the open country. We pass by flourishing villages, farms and woods, meadows and pasture lands with grazing cattle, fields with ploughs at work, country roads and metalled high roads lined by two long rows of trees vanishing in the distance. In the Grand Duchy of Luxemburg one sees no houses wrecked by shells, no people rendered homeless. It is true that the billeting of German troops has caused some inconvenience, but the inhabitants have received full compensation for all that has been taken.

On the roads one sees no marching troops, no toiling columns. And why - so near to the front? It is because, as far as the railways are worked in conjunction with the German railway system, they carry out almost the whole of the transport. It is only when railway traffic comes to a stop that recourse must be had to lines of communication by road. Hence the country on both sides of the railway looks quite flourishing, often idyllic. The only thing that reminds us of war are the sights which meet us at the railway stations, and the guards posted along the line. These guards are frequently stationed at such short intervals as to be actually in sight of each other. German railway corps troops are responsible for the traffic. The Landsturm attends to the guarding of the line. There you may see men of over forty, clothed in the dark-blue tunic with red collar and light-blue shoulders traps, black trousers with a narrow red stripe, and peakless blue caps with red band. All are armed with rifles. It is especially at bridges and other important points of the line that one is sure to see these loyal trusty fellows, pacing to and fro, - just as they are doing in every other part of the German Empire. They are always there, always vigilant. *Lieb Vaterland, magst ruhig sein…*

Our route takes us via Mamer and Kapellen. The country is rather flat; gently undulating, sunlit fields extend in every direction. Between two stations the train pulls up - we wonder why. At last we see a long train of empty carriages, nothing but goods-trucks, running up by our side on the up line. There does not seem to be a soul in it and one can hear how empty it is by its hollow ring as it rumbles by. It has carried a body of fresh troops as a reinforcement for one of the armies, and is now hurrying back through Luxemburg to fetch another. When the train has passed by, we run on to Kleinbettingen, where not a single civilian is to be seen, only some twenty of the usual trusty blue Landsturm men.

Sterpenich! So we are now on Belgian soil. There is no change in the landscape. Here, too, German soldiers are on guard, and here and there, as in Luxemburg, a field is being ploughed. But one is not reminded by customs officers that one is entering another country as in peace time; war breaks down all barriers.

We stop for a while in Arlon. We feel tempted to take a stroll through the town, but as I did not consider my ammunition train dependable, I contented myself with having a peep at the church with its grey tower and louvre-turret, and looking at the handsome station building. To the south-west, the dull but distinct thunder of guns was audible, but my fellow travellers could not say whether it came from Verdun or from the Argonne. The distance would be some sixty kilometres or over.

Meanwhile the train moves on at normal speed, but soon repents this effort and runs dead slow as if the murderous load which it is carrying, in the shape of heavy projectiles, will not bear shaking. We are now running on a high embankment and cross a country road by an arched stone bridge. At its foot a solitary sentry, alone with his rifle, looks up at us as we pass.

Here is a village wrecked by shells and burnt. All that is left standing is some bare walls staring at us from between the trees. Part of an avenue has been cut down, as also the trees on the fringe of woods near the railway. At first I thought this had been done to facilitate watching the line and preventing attempts at wrecking it. But further on we found the felled trees stacked in piles, and a goods train on a siding, loaded with hewn timber, suggested that the wood was to be used for sleepers. Large notice-boards *Langsam fahren!* (slacken speed) mark the spots where the straight line changes into sharp curves and where the German engine drivers have not yet become familiar with the ground. Traffic is not particularly brisk, and one does not pass many trains on this line, though it is a double track.

Lavaux, Cousteumont and Hamipre' are small stations. The soldiers of the guard-pickets are sitting peacefully on the platforms smoking and reading the latest newspapers that have come through. Longlier and Neufchäteau are larger stations, where some wrecked houses are to be seen from the carriage window. This is a memento of the fights of a month ago, when the Army of Duke Albrecht of Württemberg beat back the opposing forces. We run into Libramont station alongside a huge troop train which, like ours, is bound for Sédan. All carriages are decorated with green branches, as if on the way to a midsummer fete. Sentences chalked on the sides of the carriages testify to the high spirits of the passengers: - "To dinner in Paris, - now waiting"; "Every shot a Russian, - every thrust a Frenchman, - the Serbs must die," - and such like jokes. Amidst the jovial song and merry talk of the soldiers the train then rolls away to an unknown fate.

After an hour's halt it is our turn to follow in its track. We run through fields in which fragrant stacks of oats are standing in rows like soldiers. A road-bridge of stonework crossing the line has been blown up by the enemy before they retired, clearly in order to block the railway line passing beneath. The Engineers are now busy repairing it. Otherwise there are not many traces of warfare to be seen from the railway in Belgian Luxemburg.

From Libramont our course lies to the south-west. At a small station we stop once more immediately abreast of a troop train, and glide slowly past it. It consists of third-class carriages, the interiors of which are exposed to our view, one by one, through the open doors. On every imaginable projection the soldiers have suspended their knapsacks, rifles, tunics and cartridge-belts, all in picturesque and almost impressive disorder. Some are lying stretched full length on the seats, with their noses in the air, fast asleep; others sit with crossed legs, smoking, chatting or looking out on the scene outside. Officers and non-commissioned officers occupy the first and second class compartments. They are cavalry. The train also comprises "H.Gr." carriages filled with horses. There are eight in each carriage, four on each side, with their heads turned towards each other and they are separated from the central doorway, with sliding doors, by bars suspended on short chains. The halters are fastened to the bars. Between the bars - that is in the middle of the carriage - is a table on trestles, and two benches. On these some men are seated at their midday meal - cold coffee and savoury sausage sandwiches.

Bertrix! Another stop of one hour. Through the window one overhears involuntarily a few scraps of the soldiers' conversation. "Have you heard that the Belgians are said to have a secret wireless station near Arlon, which it is impossible to lay hands on?" - "That was a neat piece of work of Weddigen's."[16] - "But the losses on land are far greater than at sea - a submarine means twenty men, but a bayonet charge on land ten or a hundred times as many." - "Is it true that Rheims has been taken?" - "It is said that the right wing has fallen back a good way." - What rumours one hears in the rear of the fighting line!

The station-master of Bertrix comes up to my compartment and engages me in conversation. He tells me that the stone bridge which we have just passed was destroyed by the Belgians on the 19th of August during the fierce engagements which were fought in this region. "But we railway men," he confessed, "had to sit tight and listen to the guns in the distance. We cannot go into the firing line and fight with the rest." - "Yes, but your work is just as important, after all! How would the fighting troops fare, as to supplies and reserves, if the railway traffic were not kept going?" - "That is true, but at any rate it is terribly trying to one's patience."

He further told me that from Bertrix, for thirty-six kilometres onwards, the railway had been continued by German railway troops to establish connection with the French railway system. All blasting work, cuttings and embankments had been almost finished when the war broke out, but the line in question was not to open for traffic until 1916, as probably a war before then, in these regions, had not been thought of. The new line is a single track and is of the type of a "field railway." Its section is narrow and will not bear too heavy a load. Its traffic capacity would therefore necessarily be very small. This was the reason for our long stop at Bertrix.

At last the train which had been holding up the line arrives and we can go on. To the south-east a boundless view opens towards far-off regions wreathed in a dim blue haze, where, beyond the boundaries of Belgian Luxemburg, Montmédy and Longuyon are situated. One feels

---

16. See footnote on page 126.

glad to see the oat stacks in the fields; many mouths will need feeding here during the coming winter. And for the same reason I was glad to observe the well-fed cattle, of which I caught a glimpse in copses and pastures.

"Have you any recent newspapers?" This from the Landsturm sentries and railway workers as our train slowly rolls by. "I have already given away those I had," I answer. But as I lift up a coat I discover yet another copy of the "Treves Gazette," and next time I see a group of soldiers I throw it out and observe how eagerly they devour the news - one of them reading aloud and the others listening.

Here stands a curious-looking train, belonging to some fatigue party or railway corps. Some of the carriages have been fitted up as repair workshops, with carpenter's benches and grindstones, and saws, chisels, axes and hammers are lying about. Other carriages are crammed with bicycles, wheelbarrows, spades, crow-bars, hatchets, pickaxes and other tools - entrenching tools, such as used by the sappers.

As we issue from a long tunnel, a beautiful landscape presents itself to our view - more hilly than before. Below us several high roads meet, in a vale clad with verdant trees. Towards the nearest road the embankment slopes down steeply. Near by is a guard-hut, with a small detachment of Landsturm men close by, resting from their labours and waiting for their comrades to come out on the line to relieve them. A number of grey-clothed workers with spades on their backs come up to the railway line. "Any newspapers left?" asks one. "All gone," I reply. "That is very unfortunate," he answers, without looking up. Had I only anticipated such avidity for news, I should have bought up the whole edition of the Luxemburg German newspaper. At a small halting-place we see some forty blue and grey soldiers near their piled rifles. Is there no end of all these men in arms? To think of the numbers which the railways alone absorb!

The sun is setting; it is nearly six. After we have passed another tunnel, the panorama of the meandering water-course of the Semois unfolds itself in the valley beneath us. More groups of railway workers returning to their billets. "You have twenty kilometres to the French frontier," one

Wooded height between Sédan and Doncherry.

Houses wrecked by shells at Donchery.

of them informs me, and another points to a wrecked village on the slope of a hill. We are told that whole piles of corpses lie buried there.

The sun has now set, but there is still sufficient light to enable us to see, from a high bridge across the Semois, the main road, deep down below to the right of us, crossing the river on a handsome stone bridge with three spans. The banks are thickly covered with foliage, and we pass through a dusky belt of trees.

The twilight deepens and the shades of night begin to fall. It is a pity to be robbed of the view over this beautiful country. The line winds in manifold curves, now rising, now descending.

On we travel, desperately slow; the train groans and the timbers of the carriages creak under the burden of their load. Ahead of us appears another tunnel. At its entrance a little hut has been erected, where a patrol of Landsturm soldiers are just engaged in preparing their supper. We are travelling very slowly and are able to exchange a few words with the blueclad men. Slowly and steadily we glide into the dark mouth of the tunnel. The engine pants and snorts, the tunnel is filled with smoke, and we quickly close the windows. We advance more slowly still, and the steam makes a horrible roar in front. Now the engine breaks down, and we come to a standstill! One of my fellow-travellers comes into the pitchdark compartment, carrying a little lamp, which makes us feel more cheerful. The smoke becomes thicker and fills the compartment - if this goes on much longer we shall be asphyxiated. I open the window for a moment and peep out - nothing but darkness and smoke! But through the cloud one can see the sparks flying from the engine, which seems to be gathering strength. This train is loaded with powder and shot, and if it should explode just here in the tunnel - well, the railway corps will have their work cut out!

The engine gives another snort, making the walls of the tunnel re-echo. We begin to move again. A light appears ahead - probably the mouth of the tunnel. But no, it is only a lantern dimmed by the smoke. A little later it is the reflection of the engine-fire that looks like the dawning of daylight. Will this eternal tunnel never end? We have been in it for more than half an hour, when at last it gets clearer and we can

151

breathe fresh air again. But there is now little daylight left; the dusk obliterates the outlines of the landscape and the moon, yellow and mocking, floats over the troubled earth.

By about eight the satellite has whitened, and is perched in the tree-tops. It is clear and cold. How easy it would be for snipers to send their bullets from some lurking-place in the woods through the faintly lighted windows of the train! But no shots echo through the night; all is hushed and silent outside. There is nothing to remind one of war - one travels as in times of profoundest peace.

We have left behind to the west of us Bouillon, once the dukedom of Godfrey the Crusader, and are now at Messempré Messincourt, the first station on the French side. One of my fellow-travellers has met an acquaintance from Darmstadt, and gives him messages for his home just as the train moves out into the darkness. A sheaf of flame issues from the funnel of the engine, tinging the steam red. Probably the fire and the powder on board are used to each other by now, after having kept company for a whole week. Over the flat French meadows floats a film like the whitest hoar-frost, but it is only a very thin stratum of mist, lit up by the moon...

About midnight I fell asleep for the rest of the journey, and at 3 o'clock on Sunday morning, the 27th of September, I was awakened by one of my fellow-passengers who told me that we were in Sédan. We had been travelling for eighteen hours. The Commandant of the station. Major von Plato, is already up at this early hour, cheerful and sprightly; he receives me with a hearty welcome and places a room in the station building at my disposal. But before I take possession of my new quarters I must have a cup of tea with the Major and a few other officers, as wide-awake and lively as he. Our early breakfast is served in a strange-looking dining-room belonging to the commissariat station established here, where sixteen lady volunteers provide for up to four thousand wounded daily. In their kitchen huge caldrons are always boiling, filled with nourishing soup. Immediately after the occupation of Sédan, a wooden shed was erected in two days in the station yard, where troops and wounded passing through are now fed at long tables. This morning, too, several seats were occupied, whilst outside a detachment of Landwehr were waiting for their morning coffee and roll. Each man was also to receive dry rations for the day - bread and ham - to take with him on his journey to the front. All were merry and cheerful, no one would guess that these men would shortly stand in the fighting line, to conquer or to die. It was said that, on an average, five thousand men a day had been passing through Sédan, on their way south, during the last five weeks. Meat and vegetables for the maintenance of these troops are supplied by the Sédan "Line of Communication Depot Commandant's District," - a French district the boundaries of which have been defined within the sphere of the Chief Command of one of the German Armies. The provisions are supplied, on requisition, by the French local civil authorities, - such is the custom in war time. The invader lives on the invaded. It will be readily seen how advantageous it is to be able to carry on warfare beyond one's own frontiers. Woe to the vanquished! The invaded country must feed, not only its own army, but also that of the invader. As long as grain was to be had, it was simply requisitioned, but now, towards the end of September, flour had been procured from Germany to supply the requirements of the troops. In the coffee kitchen a dozen large caldrons were bubbling away, and an old Frenchwoman, garrulous but cheerful, was busying herself among them.

The room which was now to be mine had been set apart for Major von Plato and his Adjutant. They were to use it in turn to rest in, but they had never had occasion to do so, as they were working day and night and only snatched a short rest, often without undressing, in the refreshment-room of the station, which did duty as Station Commandant's Office. The detachment told off for guarding the railway station had its quarters in the third-class dining-room. The men were lying on the floor, and were just about to get ready for the morning roll-call.

Our round also brought us to the waiting-rooms and storeroom, where the Base Hospital wards had been established. In one of them none but badly wounded French soldiers were lying, nursed by the Red Cross staff. One ward contained Germans awaiting the day when they could bear being conveyed eastward. I was once more impressed with the importance of being able, even in an intermediate base, to clear the hospital wards immediately. A notice had just been received that a train with wounded was on its way to Sédan, and that five hundred ambulance carriages had been requisitioned by the Commander of the Army - which suggested fierce fighting and bloody engagements. When the train arrived, there was much bustle on the platforms. The sisters of mercy and volunteer civilian workers hurried from carriage to carriage with pails and cans of steaming coffee and large round baskets filled with bread. Bearers stood ready with their stretchers to carry those of the wounded whose condition was critical out to the motor ambulances which were to take them to the hospital in the town. All goes like clockwork - everybody works with zeal and zest in this labour of charity. However many may come, there is always sufficient food for all, stretchers and bedding are never lacking, and the helping hands never tire. The wounded Frenchmen are treated with the same kindness as their own wounded, perhaps even better, as nearly all have a feeling of compassion for those who have fallen into an enemy's hands and who, apart from their wounds, must suffer at the thought that their native country is bleeding under the hostile invasion. Sédan station is like a swarming beehive. Ambulance trains are not the only ones to be seen; frequent trains loaded with fresh troops also run into the station. There is also a considerable number of prisoners. Most frequent of all are the supply and ammunition trains from the north, and trains with captured or worn-out war matériel from the south. Now night is hovering, cold and starry, over Sédan, rich in memories of the past. But to those who are working here for the sake of tending the wounded and providing food, there is no difference between night and day. It is a puzzle to me how the officers, doctors, nurses and working staff can stand it. The force which impels them and prevents their breaking down with fatigue, is the love of their fatherland, which is now fighting its greatest and most fateful war.

During our hurried round the Major narrates some episodes of the locality. The bridge across the Meuse was blown up by the French, and after the street-lighting some civilians fired from the windows. A fine of two hundred thousand francs was therefore levied on the town. A few days later, shots were fired again from houses in the town, and the war contribution was increased by half a million francs, to be paid within forty-eight hours. The Maire was given the somewhat unpleasant task of raising this sum. It was paid after fruitless representations as to the difficulties. If we try, in an entirely objective manner, to enter into the psychological currents which in such cases stir the minds of the French and of the Germans, we come to the following result: The Germans consider that, when a town has been conquered by them in honest and open fight, they are its masters, and the fight is therefore ended. The French citizens who are armed and have seen that their own troops are unable to defend the town, nevertheless nourish a mad hope that they can check the invasion and prevent the enemy from taking up his quarters there. They fire in frenzy and hatred, forgetting that a few fatal shots signify nothing in the serried ranks of disciplined soldiers. Nor do they realise that they are doing an evil service to their fellow-citizens, and that the war levy will become much heavier. An open honest fight is *one* thing, but shots by civilians, after a decisive issue of the fight, are looked upon as murder, and must be punished, according to usage of war, by shooting or hanging, bombardment or imposition of a war contribution. No rules of civilised warfare recognise sparing the lives of sniping *franctireurs* or civilians firing from an ambush.

The sufferings which war brings in its train for the populace visited by it are severe enough without being intensified by cowardice and stupidity. It is best, while there is yet time, to create for oneself an efficient army - *that* will always command respect. Characteristically enough, such attempts as described here are defended and approved by individuals who, in times of peace, oppose the regular military training of their people. When the day of retribution comes they shout themselves hoarse at "right being trampled under foot." But it is futile to disguise the betrayal of one's own country. It is then too late. Jurisprudential sophistries are silenced when the guns talk in their voice of thunder.

When Major von Plato came to Sédan, in the early part of September, the railway station looked more than wretched. Dead horses were lying about everywhere at and on the line. The fallen soldiers had been buried in very shallow graves, contributing to some extent to the unbearable stench which filled the air. The Maire was requested to call out French labourers, whose task was to scour the whole neighbourhood and bury the bodies properly. Now the ground around the station looked well and properly kept.

In the afternoon I went with Major Heyn and a couple of other officers - one of whom was ordinarily a judge at Frankfort-on-Main, and had now become *Kriegsgerichtsrat* or "Court-Martial Councillor" - for a motor drive to the historically famous spots outside Sédan, the very name of which evokes, in the breast of every Frenchman, memories of grief and sorrow.

We drive through the town. The citizens who have remained or returned are not few in number, but the well-to-do have gone away and taken up their abode elsewhere. Some shops are open, and those in which articles of food, preserves, or tobacco are sold, are emptied of stock, the owners having done a brisk business. But the tradesmen on whose shopsigns one reads *Teinturerie* (dyer), *Imprimerie* (printer), *Bijouterie* (jeweller), and the like, might just as well have put up their shutters. A school has been converted into an intermediate base hospital, and the Place d'Alsace is the "motor-vehicle hospital," or open-air workshop. This may not be photographed, as the sentry informs me when I approach with my camera. On one of the "patients" undergoing treatment here, the inscription "Mannheim Brewery No. 6" indicates its avocation in peace time. Even such motor-lorries, then, are mobilised for service in war time! All is arranged and regulated beforehand with the utmost forethought and exactitude. But, for this very reason, everything goes like clockwork when the hour has come. The honest brewer in Mannheim had no need to enquire what he had to do when the mobilisation order was issued. He knew it, and sent his motor-lorries to the prearranged spot.

Impavidus numer o victus 1870 is the inscription engraved on a memorial near a street still showing traces of the fighting, to which indeed the marks of bullets on its houses bear witness. Two bridges across the Meuse, one of stone, the other of iron, have been blown up by the French and replaced by the Germans.

We are now out in the open country and pass over the scene of the hotly contested sanguinary fights of the 25th and 26th of August. The entrenchments have not been filled in, and the parapets and trenches are still in the same state, though they have crumbled here and there. I was told that many of them had been thrown up by the local population, whose assistance thus gave the defenders an advantage over the attack.

Near the village of Frénois we run up to the little château of Bellevue, where after the great battle of the 1st of September, 1870, the capitulation of the French Army was signed on the morning of September 2nd, and where King William I. of Prussia had his historic meeting with the Emperor of the French, Napoleon III. The two monarchs met on the small glass veranda on the ground floor, which forms a porch or vestibule to the château.

The furniture which was there at the time has all disappeared and there is no relic of those days remaining. Yet there is one! The aristocratic and venerable lady - who owns Bellevue, is still there, bowed with age and grief, and is now witnessing for the second time all the phases of a Franco-German war. Her hair was snow-white and she was bent with age, but it seemed nevertheless that she held her head high, and her carriage was proud and commanded respect. We asked whether we might see the interior of the château, but she asked us to excuse her - a wish which, of course, we respected.

It is not to be wondered at that the soldiers, whose way lies past Bellevue, like to look at the famous veranda. But the old lady asked that these visits should cease; she wished to be left in peace, alone with her sorrow. "*c'est bien malheureux; c'est très, très triste!*" she repeated again and again, and she, like her words, evoked the deepest sympathy. Bellevue with its round tower stands like a rock lashed by the tempestuous waves of the two greatest wars of modern history.

Our next objective is Donchery, the little town which now inspires, in a twofold measure, such mournful impressions. It was here that General von Moltke, Chief of the German General Staff, and General

Wimpffen, the French Commander-in-Chief, discussed the terms of the capitulation late at night on the 1st of September, 1870. Count Bismarck, the Prussian Prime Minister, was also present, as well as several officers of both sides. The house where the negotiations took place has been destroyed in the present war. But Werner's picture remains. This has a most stirring effect on the beholder. To the right, the Germanic iron strength and resolution, which will admit of no compromise; to the left the beaten Frenchmen in their dire misfortune. Moltke especially attracts our eyes, as he stands there with his hand thrust upon the table, categorically demanding the surrender of the whole French army, and we may well look with emotion on the picture of the "Iron Chancellor," sitting with his hand on his swordhilt; - these two men, the great strategist and the great statesman, are just about to lay the foundations of the mightiest empire of modem times; - but the central figure of the painting is Wimpffen, for he stands there as the impersonation of the deepest tragedy and the most terrible misfortune that could befall man. He has just been struck by the blow which the terms of capitulation involve for him and all France. He can bear no more - he has risen to go; but he totters, and has to support himself on the table and a chair. The light of the lamp falls upon his face, which betrays the deepest anguish and grief. His name will now be coupled for ever with this calamitous day! A picture of the Corsican hangs on the wall, and the great Emperor seems to cast a reproving look on the unfortunate general. The countenances of his companions express sorrow and dejection for which language has no words. No less grave is the expression of the Prussians standing on the other side. Their features betray admiration for the heroism of the French army and its dauntless courage, which should have deserved a better fate. The artist has created a scene which suggests to us that all those present were conscious of the fact that this day would live in memory as one of the greatest in Prussia's history and one of the most tragic in that of France.

Some parts of Donchery have been destroyed by the shells of the present war, but the Church of St. Onesimus still remains standing amid the desolation and has not suffered any damage to speak of. The chancel with the high altar dates from the twelfth century, the nave from the fifteenth. In front of the altar-piece stands a crucifix of ivory, and filtering in through the beautiful stained-glass windows, a multicoloured light plays upon the pillars. The priest who accompanies us, assures us that not a single shot has been fired from the windows of Donchery and that the punishment which was inflicted on the town was therefore unmerited. But the German documents tell a different tale. A careful investigation in France and in Belgium will reveal, in due course, where the root and origin of the participation of the civilian population in the warfare is to be found. Until the result of this investigation lies before us, it will be wise to abstain from pronouncing judgment.

On the return journey to Sédan we also stopped for a while at the little house by the roadside where Napoleon and Bismarck had an interview on the morning of the 2nd of September. Accompanied by his suite of a few horsemen, the Emperor drove over from Sédan in a landau. He had alighted and stood, broken and prematurely aged, leaning on his stick, when Bismarck came up alone on horseback. This incident, too, has been immortalised by Werner in one of his pictures. The victor and the vanquished then entered the house together, ascended the steep and narrow stairs and seated themselves in the inner of the two larger rooms. The host, the weaver Fournaise, withdrew; his wife, twenty-seven years of age, stayed in the outer room. And Madame Fournaise is still alive - a worthy and kindly woman, with a cheerful and philosophical view of life, in spite of the harrowing scenes which she has witnessed around her abode. The only thing that annoyed her was that two rifle bullets had gone through her windows and lodged in the ceiling. But she gave us a regular lecture on that momentous day, forty-four years ago, and recalled each detail. The Emperor had been friendly and condescending, Bismarck cheerful and jocular, when they had talked to her. And when the interview was over, and both of them went their way, the Emperor had given her four 20 franc pieces, which she still kept, set in a frame under glass, with the following inscription: *Donné par sa Majesté l'Empereur Napoleon III à Mme. Fournaise le 2 Septembre, 1870.*

As a memento of our visit we shall keep the stamp which she imprinted on our note-books: *Maison de la Ire entrevue, Donchery*. And the house itself is known as *Maison du Tisserand*, or "The weaver's house."

At last we return by another road to Sédan, in order to cast a brief glance over the site of the forts which have been razed since 1870, and to enjoy the fine view over the unfortunate town from the surrounding heights. One cannot feel cheerful in Sédan; one feels as if one's breast were oppressed by a leaden weight. Here is a people, generous and yet thrifty, which has suffered and is now suffering - which, in the leading strings of the republican democracy, has been led to an abyss of misfortunes - a people which has deserved a better fate than to bleed to death for the sake of its allies - a people whose children vainly repeat those high-sounding, but in reality empty and hollow words: *Liberté, Égalité, Fraternité*. What brotherhood is it that never thinks of anything but revenge; what equality is it that for political aims sacrifices the fruits of the people's thrift; what liberty is it that drives these same people into the arms of the world's most despotically governed power?

And yet one cannot but love the French, above all on account of their fascinating and attractive qualities, their unbounded patriotism, their brilliant bravery, their ever youthful enthusiasm, their bright wit and their high level of art. And one deplores the desolation which is spreading over their glorious country and which might so easily have been avoided.

Late in the day we drive back into the town, past Place Turenne, where a statue, nearly one hundred years old, has been erected in memory of the great victorious marshal, himself a native of Sédan. In the market-place is the office of the Sédan Intermediate Base Commandant, located in a better-class café, in which busy clerks have taken the places formerly occupied by the habitues of the place. Here we happened to come across a most unusual sight, - a couple of civilians from Germany, who have come to see about the body of a killed relative. The dead man had been traced, and if they could identify his body they would have a zinc coffin made and take him home.

From there I proceeded to the Hôtel Croix d'Or to call on General

Baron von Seckendorff, who is Inspector of the Lines of Communication of the Fourth Army. The "Inspectorate" comprises, besides its Staff - the Chief of which is Colonel von Kemnitz - a variety of administrative branches, with subordinate organisations and establishments. One may truly say that whole armies and endless processions of transport columns of various kinds pass through General von Seckendorff's hands. The task of the lines of communication organisation in general is, on the one hand, to arrange for bringing up to the army reserve troops and matérial of all kinds, and, on the other hand, to relieve the fighting troops of the wounded, prisoners, booty of war, and all worn-out matérial. As already hinted, each class of requirements has its own representative in the Line of Communication Inspectorate. There are supervisors for the provisioning and for the hospitals, for ammunition supply and store maintenance, for the railway traffic, for the telegraph, post-office, and road and hydraulic construction departments, for administration of justice and maintenance of law and order, and for civil administration. It is an immense burden of labour that rests on the shoulders of an inspector of the line of communication. There must be no hitch anywhere. The troop trains must not come too late; the ammunition and commissariat supply trains must arrive at stated times and places. Nothing must go wrong. The inspector must know how to find ways and means in all emergencies, must think of and foresee everything, - else incalculable calamities may arise.

It might not be out of place here to give a short outline of the manner in which the lines of communication between the fighting troops and the home base are arranged.

I reproduce a diagram showing the arrangement of the lines of communication of a German Army. The reader will see how the railway lines coming from the home bases of the respective army corps are made to converge towards the main line of transport which leads to the district of the lines of communication of an army - in a hostile country to a principal line of communication depot or "intermediate base," and how, from this point, a new system of lines of communication of all kinds - railways, field railways, roads, water-ways - diverges towards the operating units at the front. The whole reminds one vividly of a tree with its roots and branches. As far as possible, the functions in connection herewith must be planned in peace time. Of course, instructions and regulations are drawn up, not only for the transport system as a whole, but also for each and every detail thereof, as one can never elucidate with sufficient clearness the various administrative branches of war: the commissariat, the medical service, the veterinary department, the field post-office, the field telegraph department, the field railway service, the war matériel and the army pay departments, etc.

The supreme direction of the organisations of the lines of communication is exercised by an Inspector-General, who is subordinated to the Chief of the General Staff. The various armies each have their "Lines of Communication Inspectorate" subordinated to the Chief Command of the army, organised internally as indicated above. It controls the respective principal Lines of Communication Depot or "Intermediate Base," and has under it the "Lines of Communication Depot Commandants" who in their turn are in charge of one or several Lines of Communication Depots with their surrounding districts.

Now what principles are followed, in their work, by these different controlling authorities of the lines of communication? Well, they have, in continual *collaboration* with the commanders of the troops, to supply to these the requisite information as regards depot, hospital, and other arrangements on the lines of communication, - such as store depots of different kinds of war matériel - and to give timely notice of the arrival of men, horses, matériel and requisites.

Generally speaking, it is the duty of the Lines of Communication Depot Commandant to look after all the requirements of the system of the lines of communication itself, and to provide for the detachments of troops, and transport of remounts and animals intended for food, which may happen to be stationed in, or pass through their district of the lines of communication, while the "Inspectorate of the Lines of Communication," through organisations and establishments directly subordinated to it, requisitions what is needed for the fighting troops from within the whole of its district of the lines of communication, or from the home bases. In order that the organisation of the lines of communication may work quickly in the event of urgent requirements - more especially in case of a battle - it establishes, as we have seen, store depots of matériel and requisites. Books are kept as to all that is stored within the respective district. The "Inspectorate" always enters into close relations with the civil administration, and in a hostile country may often - if the safety of the army requires this - take over this administration into its own hands. Both the "Inspectorate of the Lines of Communication" and the "Intermediate Depot Commandant's Office" frequently requisition, for instance, from the Maire, labour for certain purposes. Some ten labourers or other civilians may for instance be required to bury dead horses or to clear a road. The soldiers of the invading army do not do this themselves.

Frequently, the working of hospital departments attracts, more especially, the attention of the layman; at least such was the case with me. One marvels at the enormous sphere of duties that fall solely to the share of the intermediate base surgeons, subordinated to the "Inspectorate." The Chief Surgeon-General at the "Inspectorate of the Lines of Communication zone of the 4th Army" had under him hospitals at twenty-eight different intermediate depots, apart from the transports of sick and wounded passing through this zone of the lines of communication.

The reader will form some idea of the amount of work which devolves on the officers in charge on the lines of communication, when I mention that the Lines of Communication Depot Commandant's Office in Vouziers alone, usually received every day six hundred requisitions and enquiries which all had to be attended to immediately. This needed men of ready and well-trained skill and energy, who could accomplish the task of ensuring that the fighting troops always had what they needed at the right time and in the right place. Dawdling routine work will never do in war!

If we had before us a large-scale map, faithfully representing the army and its connection with the home base, the lines of communication would appear to form a veritable cobweb, or network, the knots of which

German infantry.

would be formed by the intermediate base depots. But the aspect shown by this network would only hold good for a certain period, perhaps only for one day. For, especially in the extreme ramifications of this network, changes are of course incessantly occurring, owing to the advance of the positions, or transfers of troops. The whole is like a system of blood-vessels in the body of the army or of the nation. The transport columns going west are the fresh blood of the arteries, maintaining combustion and life in the organism of the army; the trains returning east, empty, or loaded with wounded, represent the spent blood flowing back to the heart and lungs to be renovated. You cannot form any clear idea of this complicated apparatus until you have seen and felt, on the lines of communication, the throbbing of the pulses of the army.

The army thus rests on the home country, and draws its food and sustenance from every nook and corner of the whole German empire - just as the roots of a tree, with their ramifications of fibres, suck up from the earth the nutritious juices. Every town and village, every farmstead in Germany feels that it contributes, in its measure, to the vitality of the army. The whole nation takes part in the war, and the soldier out at the front, in the trenches, cannot fight with any prospect of success, unless the peasant at home does his duty. But the German peasants and the whole German nation are doing their duty, not as if it were a hard necessity, but gladly and with pride and devotion.

And now let us return to the "Inspectorate of the Lines of Communication zone of the Fourth Army!"

General von Seckendorff has, - to use a common expression - plenty to do, and he works like a galley slave, I must say! He maintains faultless discipline on his lines and inspects them daily in person. During the campaign he has already covered twelve thousand kilometres in his elegant covered car. On the roads he rules with an iron hand and can, if necessary, roar like a lion at men and officers. But towards me he was kind, and gentle as a zephyr.

He received me with open arms and invited me to stay to supper in the large restaurant of the hotel. Here, some forty of the three hundred officers now in Sédan were assembled - among them a Prince Hohenlohe who had something to do with the Red Cross. At the moment when we entered, the gentlemen were already standing by their seats around the long table and the small side-tables, and the General introduced me, once for all, with a few forceful yet kindly words. The food served was the same as for the rank and file - boiled rice, mutton with beans and potatoes, and pancakes with jam, the last being a luxury in honour of the Sunday.

After a pleasant evening, in the course of which the General invited me to accompany him next day to Vouziers, I walked at midnight through the silent and empty streets of Sédan. The way from Place Turenne to the railway station, where I was staying, was rather long, and it was made no shorter by the six sentries who in turn stepped out from the gloom and challenged me - a suspicious-looking night-bird, perhaps out on some unlawful errand. Each of them read the "pass" issued to me by General von Moltke, and then left me to my fate - and to the next sentry. All were quiet and civil, and they were doing their duty. When I came to the last, quite close to the railway station, I stepped up to him and asked whether he had any objection to reading my *Ausweis*. He replied with a smile: "I suppose it has already been read often enough; and besides, I have seen you in the company of the Chief of the *Kommandantur*."

But this Chief had gone to sleep when I came "home." He certainly needed rest after all the trains he had cleared through the course of the day. And as for myself, I will not deny that I was half-asleep before I lay down on my bed.

CHAPTER VIII
IN THE REAR OF THE FOURTH ARMY

EARLY ON SEPTEMBER 28th I proceeded to the Hôtel Croix d'Or and a moment later I was once more on the way towards the front with General von Seckendorff and his Adjutant. Our way lay in a south-south-westerly direction and followed roughly the Ardenne Canal, which we crossed two or three times. Our first goal was the town of Vouziers. Railway communication exists up to this point, but numerous transport columns, nevertheless, make use of the paved high road. A road on the lines of communication is always animated. The roads in the rear of the 4th Army resemble in all respects those I had seen before in the rear of the 5th. In fact, it was only the setting of the picture that seemed different. We passed a number of inviting-looking bivouacs, in some of which smoke was still curling from the cooking trench, by the fire of which the men of the transport columns were preparing their breakfast. In the avenue of chestnut and maple trees lining the road, which were already turning yellow, marching troops and transport columns of all kinds, supply and ammunition wagons, motor ambulances and long rows of old-fashioned yellow mail-vans, filled with field-post mails intended for Germany, via Treves - where the first sorting takes place - succeed each other in motley procession. The indispensable "Field Gendarmes" (Military Police Patrols) in their green uniforms, with helmets and bright badges, ride backwards and forwards on their road sections to see that all is in order. There lies a horse which has broken down, worn out! A merciful bullet has just put an end to his suffering, and he is being dragged aside; a stream of blood is trickling from his nostrils, staining the road-dust red.

It is a very pretty landscape that unrolls its undulating outlines on either side of the colonnade of ancient trees. Fields and meadows, pastures, groves and orchards - all slashed in different directions by the dark shaded lines of the roads. Now and then one sees cattle browsing peacefully - sheep among the goats. And the peasants who have returned to their land are busying themselves in their yards and fields. We pass through several villages, among others Tannay and Le Chesne on the Ardenne Canal. This country is full of memories. One can without much effort imagine oneself back in the last days of August, 1870, when Marshal MacMahon's army marched in long columns along these very roads - towards Beaumont and Sédan. There, close by, in the wood to the south-west, and south of Le Chesne, the first German cavalry pickets were peering out, on August 29th, on the road to the north. These were horsemen, no doubt, who less than a fortnight previously had gained glory on the blood-drenched fields of Vionville and Mars-la-Tour. - Hark! The bugles are sounding at the head of von Bredow's brigade! - The stranger from the land of Charles XII. feels a twinge in his heart, as his fancy calls up kindred memories of past ages. From remote regions far, far away, other sounds, yet strangely similar, seem to ring in his ears - an echo from the days of long ago, when his people were fighting for the Germanic cause in the east, - Around him is seething the vital energy of the German army, of the German people. He feels something he has felt before. He now comprehends the true significance of the words in which the poor Swedish petty officer Wessling replied to the Generals of Tsar Peter, who asked him how the Swedes could fight so valiantly, two against a hundred: "We were bound to do so for the sake of our most gracious king and the oath we have sworn." This spirit shines from the eyes of every German soldier. - At length we arrive in Vouziers on the western bank of the Aisne.

We do not stop long. The General only remains long enough to hear the reports of a couple of officers of the Intermediate Base Command there, as to what has occurred since yesterday. When he has gathered that all is in the best order he gives the word to drive on, and we soon continue southward on the high road to Séchault and Cernay - the road taken by the 11th Army Corps to Sédan in 1870. At Cernay we are

Infantry reservists on the fringe of a wood at Rouvroy.

A dressing wagon had halted behind a few dark pines.

twenty kilometres west of Varennes. But between these two localities lies the Argonne, where obstinate fighting is still proceeding. From Cernay issues, to the west, the great highway to Rheims. On the first sixteen kilometres of this road, or right up to the village of Sommc Py, I was afforded the opportunity of visiting some highly interesting spots. At the end of September this was the most advanced road to the south then held by the Germans in this region.

The first village west of Cernay is Rouvroy. We did not intend to drive any further this day. We made a short stop to take our plain, soldier-like early meal - long narrow slices of army bread with butter and ham, and a glass of claret.

The General had with him an extra car, filled with bottles of wine, which he distributed among the soldiers. There was no need to be sparing with wine in these regions, where even the peasants have their cellars well stocked. But nothing is taken away off-hand. All will be made good to the owners after the war. The terms of peace will contain a provision to the effect that the defeated side shall pay the amount of every receipt or voucher (*bon*) representing the value of the things requisitioned during the military occupation. The individual is not to suffer direct, but only as a participant in the misfortune which falls on the country as a whole. It is the duty of the State to make good the people's personal losses when the State is incapable of protecting the property of the individual against the enemy. And if the invading power is defeated in the war, its just punishment is that it must make good the losses of the sufferers.

Perhaps someone may object that it is improper to let the soldiers drink wine - seeing that, in the east, the Russians have made the experiment of introducing total prohibition, and are satisfied with the result. No doubt this demonstration of moral strength, *per se*, deserves admiration, though it does not appear to have been fully carried through at home. Nevertheless I think that a draught of red or white wine, now and then, cannot but be beneficial to the soldier if it is distributed at the right time and in the right place, after strenuous exertions. To preach total abstinence is easy enough for those who are not called upon to lie freezing all night in cold, wet trenches where it is not permitted to light the smallest fire.

At Rouvroy we left our cars and proceeded on foot up gently ascending ground, along fields and ditches, through hedges and brushwood. Here the ground was much pitted by shell fire and no one could tell when the rain of shells might recommence. Numerous projectiles were lying scattered about and I took with me a so-called *Ausbläser*, i.e. a shell "burnt out" without bursting.

Higher up the slope we came across some reserves waiting to be called upon to relieve their comrades in the trenches. They lay concealed in a wood, with small bodies advanced to the very edge of the wood, which was protected by all sorts of entrenchments, with semi-subterranean "dug-outs" at the back - excavations covered with branches, twigs and green boughs, and serving not only as shelters for the men but also to screen them from aviators. As is natural, these bodies of reserves always locate themselves on the northern side of the points of vantage which they occupy. They must be concealed out of sight of the French lines. But in this war reconnoitring by aviators has also to be reckoned with. They are therefore compelled, even when on the far side of such cover, such as villages, woodlands and groves, to "dig themselves in" or at least hide as best they can from the buzzing war-hawks which every now and then come spying from the clouds for prey. Hence the most important thing of all is good screening or masking of the position. Exceedingly great care is bestowed on this point. Not the smallest detail is overlooked. The admissibility of lighting fires in these caves depends on the completeness of this masking.

At a spot near the fringe of the wood, a field ambulance was stationed, well screened by some dark pines. It was accompanied by a spare horse, which might be useful in case the pair of horses forming the ordinary team should be shot down. Another vehicle belonging to the medical service corps was fitted with a greyish-yellow folding hood. Grey loin-cloths had been thrown over the horses to approximate their colour as nearly as possible to that of the ground - all as precaution against observation by aviators.

A dressing wagon with hood.

Four doctors breakfasting under cover of a shelter tent.

In a small shelter-hut near by, four surgeons who were in charge of the two medical wagons had taken up their quarters. They had just finished their luncheon, which had been fetched from the nearest kitchen-wagon; I also took the liberty of sampling the food, which seemed as nutritious as it was palatable.

Up on the hill, which afforded a view of the French positions, we found several officers. Close by, under cover of an enormous haystack, was a group of men of various units - presumably orderlies and despatch-riders who had followed their respective superior officers so as to be at hand whenever wanted. All these men seemed to enjoy the opportunity of getting to know more than their comrades. They did not pay heed to the greater danger of their position. Reminders of death were not far to seek. Near by, two soldiers had been buried in the shade of a small copse. Fresh wreaths were hanging on the arms of the cross, suggesting that the brave men resting beneath had but recently fallen victims to the French fire. The solitary, insignificant little mounds were adorned with the helmets of the fallen men.

On our return trip, for which we chose a more easterly route, *via* the villages of Condé, Autry and Grandpré, we passed four companies of Landsturm, headed by a spirited band. It is an unusual thing to hear band music so near the front, where all has to be as silent as possible and where usually the only music is that of guns and rifles. The general drove past the whole detachment and stopped ahead of it by the side of the road. He then alighted, and we followed his example. The whole detachment now marched past. When the first company came up, he called out: "Good morning, first company," greeting the others in the same way and receiving their salute. It was a fine and impressive sight to behold these sturdy men, among whom more than one was nearing the age of fifty.

And what a march-past! It moved me strangely. It vividly recalled to my recollection a troop of old Swedish territorials, whom I saw many, many years ago. They were of a similar stock, faithful in life, faithful in death - without reproach. Their dark blue uniforms stood out in vivid contrast to the rusty foliage of the trees. There was nothing lacking in the equipment of this Landsturm battalion. It was a fine sight, too, to see the General, with his look of determination blended with kindness, his white moustache and his steel-grey hair Erect and tall he stood, in his grey cloak, with his hands behind his back. There had been no need for him to alight and salute them, but it pleased his martial soul to look at these men, who had left hearth and home, wife and children, to bleed and die, but determined also to fight and conquer for their country. "We are comrades," he thought, no doubt, as the last man filed past, and the sound of the music died away in the distance. And so we ran past the Landsturm battalion a second time, and listened once more to the inspiriting strains of the parade march.

On our return to Vouziers the General handed me over to the care of Cavalry Captain von Behr, a brother of the Chamberlain. He was a merry and lively gentleman, and when the General asked him to show me every attention, he promised that I should want for nothing. And he kept his word, for during the period of fully a week which I spent with him and his comrades, I had occasion to see and learn much, and to make the acquaintance of many notable and estimable men, von Behr had retired from the army long ago, but on the outbreak of the war he had re-entered the service in a cuirassier regiment and was now in command of a reserve squadron. His troop was now quartered in the barracks of the 3rd French Cuirassier Regiment. As the day was not yet spent he immediately proposed - like a true cavalryman - a visit to a riding-school which had been fitted up as stables and barracks. There we found the horses well-groomed and well-shod, in their stalls along the walls, while the men had arranged their beds on a litter of unthreshed wheat. The oat sacks were lying piled in large stacks. The bridles, saddles, arms and accoutrements were suspended on brackets and pillars. The interior of this stable, and of another immediately adjoining it, presented an aspect of military order, discipline and precision, which ensured that in case of need the squadron could be in the saddle, fully equipped, in a few minutes.

A third building in the same grounds had been assigned to the French prisoners and their German guard. Thus the strangers were neither

Soldiers under cover of a haystack at Rouvroy.

better nor worse provided for than the cuirassiers. They had arranged their beds in the best possible way along one of the walls. Armed with sketch-book and pen, I paid several visits to them during the following days.

Lastly we also looked in at the barracks, now fitted up as a clearing hospital. We had the best imaginable cicerone, the head surgeon himself. Dr. Zinsser of Cologne. He was famous as a physician and surgeon. As a man he was charming and fascinating. It was always a great pleasure to me to meet him and hear him talk of the experience he had already gained during the war, and which had induced him to introduce many alterations and improvements in the hospital arrangements.

We made a hurried round through some of the hospital wards, where nurses and Catholic friars were passing softly from bed to bed, silent as ghosts. Not all the beds were occupied, but live hundred wounded were expected at night, of whom, however, many would be moved on next day. Here we saw some French prisoners carrying wounded Germans on stretchers to the railway station for further transport - a strange sight! Among the German patients I noticed the same spirit that animates, with infectious ardour, the whole of this wonderful and firmly knit army - no home-sickness, only an irresistible desire to get back to the front. If one ever came across a soldier who said that he wished himself back home, it was sure to be one of the badly wounded, prostrate on a sick-bed and at best doomed to be a cripple for life. We saw an instance of this in the operating theatre of the hospital. A man had his leg so badly shattered by a shell, that he had to undergo amputation. The bandages were skillfully and quickly put round the stump of the leg, and the man came to. But he had forgotten where he was, and it appeared from his confused talk that he was still imagining himself to be lying in the trenches.

One ward contained patients who had recently undergone operations; another was occupied by men who had been wounded in the head. In the case of one, the bullet still remained lodged in the skull. It was horrible to see him lying there staring intently at one spot, and making restless but futile efforts to raise himself. One of those next to him had been rendered blind by a shot, and a third had lost his memory; he readily answered questions relating to the present, but was quite oblivious of all concerning the past.

The wounded officers had a ward to themselves, and seemed pleased to have an opportunity to chat awhile. "What news from the front - any fresh victories?" was the invariable question. The most singular case here was that of a Captain who had been shot right through the neck, the bullet having entered on the right and issued on the left side, without causing serious injury to the arteries, trachea, pharynx, or cervical vertebrae. The Captain sat up in his bed, his whole head swathed in bandages. He followed our conversation attentively, but did not, and could not, utter a word himself. Professor Zinsser said that it would certainly take him half an hour if he tried to pass a probe in the same way through a human neck without inflicting injury. But this bullet had found its way through in the minutest fraction of a second.

Some distance apart from the rest lay the patients suffering from tetanus. It is only in rare cases that their lives can be saved. One-half

Officers' car at Grandpré.

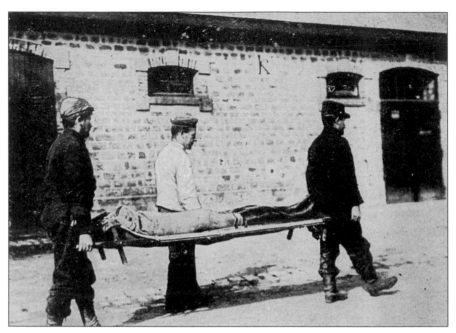

French prisoners carried wounded Germans to the railway station.

of those who died in hospital had succumbed to tetanus. It is a terrible affliction. A surgeon who had been at the front in Alsace and whom I met on a subsequent occasion, thought he had noticed that this disease first appeared when they had crossed the French frontier. It is generated by the so-called tetanus bacillus, a bacillar microbe to be found in the soil, chiefly mould. If such infected earth comes into contact with a wound, say through a ricochet bullet, the latter may carry the bacilli with it and by their poisonous secretions induce this form of muscular catalepsy. We saw a few tetanus patients, and the professor talked to them. A young German had tetanus in the muscles of the mouth, and his face became distorted as he attempted almost inaudibly to speak. I was told that his life might possibly be saved.

About the middle of September Professor Zinsser and his colleagues had had a tryng time at the hospital. It was at the time when, for strategical reasons, the army retired from the Mame to the Aisne. The badly wounded men who could not bear hasty removal involving discomfort, had to be left in the care of surgeons, who thus voluntarily went into captivity - surely one of the greatest sacrifices that could be made in war.

The rest, who could bear being removed, were conveyed in large numbers to these barracks, the floors of which had been covered with straw. Professor Zinsser arrived there late one night, in darkness and pouring rain, and at once proceeded to the improvised hospital. No lights were to be had. But wagon after wagon brought fresh wounded - would the stream never end? They were crammed in anywhere, anyhow, in terrible confusion. Some died during the night. Others grew worse. All were soaked with rain, their bandages were torn to shreds and undone. There they lay, fifteen hundred, light and grave cases, pell-mell. Here and there, among the living, lay a body growing cold in death. A terrible smell pervaded the atmosphere. Of course, none of the patients were able to go outside. Their strength was utterly gone. It was a pitch-dark night - the rain was pelting down! But the professor was powerless to relieve their distress; he had no alternative but to wait till the morning.

In the morning five doctors and twenty men of the Army Medical Corps arrived. A dreadful sight met their eyes in these overcrowded rooms, foul with the stench of purulent wounds and excrements. But they set to work at once and soon received assistance from a field hospital. They were then thirty all told. They worked day and night. But new hosts of wounded kept on arriving. It seemed utterly hopeless! The wounded stretched out their hands to the surgeon as soon as they caught sight of him and cried: "Help us! Help us!" Extra motor-cars were procured to carry away those who could bear removal. Many of the wounded even crept down to the bottom of the steps to find a place in some ambulance wagon - to get away from this inferno. But in the end, the superhuman energy of the medical staff triumphed. A kitchen was fitted up, cattle were slaughtered and meatbroth was made. Soldiers who had been starving for days could at last stay their hunger. All dressings were changed, - those of the graver cases first, the others afterwards. In a few days the medical staff were masters of the situation. But if such is the state of things on the lines of communication of an army which has only fallen back momentarily for some distance, what must happen after a crushing defeat? Of one thing I am certain, none but an army permeated with boundless confidence in its leaders and its chief command, can stand the strain of such phases of war without going to pieces.

In the foregoing I have often stopped to speak of the wounded and shall do so again. It might therefore be opportune to give a brief outline of the system and the organisation which prevails in the hospital service in the field. All is arranged beforehand so as to be ready when war breaks out.

Of course the hospital service assumes a different aspect according to the distance from the actual fighting line. At the front they have Medical Service Corps and establishments to meet the first needs of the wounded. There we find surgeons with military training But all these dressing stations and field hospitals are cleared as speedily as possible to make room for fresh wounded. They pass their patients on, step by step, along the lines of communication, on which their further care, or transport to the home base, is provided for. Here most of the medical staff are not on the normal war establishment, but civilian medical men liable to military service or who have volunteered - though appointed already in peace time for certain duties.

Each field force has its medical service staff whose task is to look after its well-being, to supervise its hygiene, to watch over the daily food supplies, to analyse the drinking water, etc. It is therefore the first duty of the Army Medical Staff to regulate the general hygienic care so as to prevent such epidemics as might otherwise easily spread. Men who have fallen sick among the troops are cared for in "local sickrooms" until they can be handed over to the care of the Army Medical Service.

At the fighting line the army surgeons establish regimental dressing stations. Some surgeons accompany the bearer patrols on to the battlefield, but without, save in exceptional cases, entering the actual fire zone.

Each infantry division has at least one medical service company. The latter establishes, in a suitable spot at the rear of the troops, one or more principal dressing stations, sending its ambulance wagons to an advanced halting-place, so as to get the dangerously wounded as quickly as possible back to the rear. Each medical service company comprises nine surgeons and a large number of bearers, sick attendants, apothecaries, etc. The company, further, has eight two horsed ambulance wagons, two medical-store wagons, equipped with medicaments, stretchers and dressing matérials, two baggage wagons and one food-supply wagon.

For each Army Corps there are twelve field hospitals. These are established in suitable towns, villages and mansions, behind the front. They have to be located in sheltered situations where they may remain

A Chef De Musique of the 11th Infantry Regiment, 17th Army Corps, taken prisoner on Sept 26th, South of Vouziers. Sligly wounded in the head.

even if the fighting line advances. The field hospitals receive the patients from the auxiliary and principal dressing stations, with the exception of such as are sent to a "collecting station for slightly wounded," to proceed thence direct to the nearest line of communication depot.

The field hospital has its own regulation medical wagons and carries with it a complete hospital equipment, such as mattresses, or empty covers to be filled with straw, pillows, blankets and sheets, shirts and other necessary clothing for the patients, china vessels for the convenience of the wounded, and many other things. The first surgical operations are carried out in the field hospital building unless, in quite exceptional cases, these have to be performed at once in the open, for instance, to staunch the flow of blood from gaping wounds. The field hospital staff is military throughout. No nursing sisters, nor, generally speaking, any volunteer nurses are to be found here.

The head of the medical service organisation of the Army Corps is the Chief Medical Officer" of the Army Corps. He is assisted by a consulting surgeon who in civil life is generally a University professor or lecturer and who also inspects the field hospitals.

We will now proceed to the zone of the lines of communication. The field hospital is replaced after a time - as soon as possible when the field operations advance - by a clearing hospital section. This consists solely of a staff - medical men, military nursing attendants and volunteer assistants. Each Army Corps has one such section of nineteen surgeons and a corresponding number of subordinates.

The field hospital is thus converted, on the advance of the troops, into a clearing hospital, or, in other words, when the field hospital with its matériel thus set free or replaced, follows the troops forward, its place is taken by the clearing hospital, which retains all that its predecessor has left behind. When, as at the time of my visit, the advance is slow, no change takes place and the clearing hospital staff has *comparatively* little to do.

Clearing hospitals are found wherever the fighting has given occasion for the establishment of a field hospital, and therefore also at considerable distances from the main lines of communication. In the event of hard fighting, clearing hospital sections with temporary equipment establish their hospitals side by side with the field hospital. The task of these hospitals is ultimately to remove by degrees their patients to the Line of Communication (stationary) hospitals, and to places, such as Sédan in the case of the 4th Army, from which a regular railway connection exists with the home country. The transport of the wounded is effected not only on foot and in empty transport wagons, but also by the motor-ambulance vehicles, of the Sick and Wounded Transport Department, among which one sees ordinary omnibuses from Berlin and other towns and motor-lorries bearing the names of well-known factories and business concerns. These may carry up to seven or ten beds. If slightly wounded are in question, one single large motor-vehicle can take up to fifty men, but then they will sit tightly packed and even on the roof. Thus the wounded are conveyed to the principal intermediate base on the lines of communication, from which they proceed by rail or by canal or river to the home base. I have previously discussed the organisation of the hospital service within the zone of the lines of communication. I will only remark here that just as the Principal Medical Officer of the Army Corps has a Consulting Surgeon, so the Principal Medical Officer at the Lines of Communication Hospital has a Consulting Sanitary Officer who is likewise, in peace time, a University professor. The latter has to examine all suspicious cases of infection and to prescribe all necessary measures of precaution to prevent any outbreak of infectious diseases. The Sanitary Officer is provided with a bacteriological laboratory and is expected to investigate carefully every individual case of typhoid fever, dysentery and similar diseases, to ascertain whence the patient has come, to isolate him and to try to eradicate the cause and source of infection. In certain cases he may find that by way of precaution, the establishment of an infectious diseases hospital in the zone of the lines of communication is advisable. Such a hospital has been established, for instance, in Attigny near Vouziers.

Within the zone of the lines of communication to which the clearing hospitals - which are in charge of a "Director" - form the link of transition, there is first of all a Lines of Communication Hospital

Supply Depot which replenishes the stores of the hospital units and organisations, both at the front and on the lines of communication, the Lines of Communication Hospital, with which we have already become acquainted, the sections for non-dangerous cases of disease, and for convalescents-from which the patients can frequently be sent back to the front after so short a time that their transport to the home country would be needless - the infectious diseases hospital, the ambulance trains - hospitals on wheels - and any incidental trains for the transport of wounded. I have already acquainted the reader with such hospital organisations at intermediate base stations, where we have seen doctors, nurses and medical service men go from carriage to carriage of the ambulance train to examine the patients and pick out those who cannot bear further transport.

In the home country the arriving wounded are sent to home base hospitals - either ordinary hospitals or private houses which have been fitted up as hospitals during the war. Many, too, are sent direct to their homes. The main governing principle all the way from the front to the home country is: make room, make room, make room! Therefore every effort is made to get rid of the wounded as speedily as possible to make room for new arrivals.

Every first-aid medical wagon is carefully divided into compartments and boxes so that each requisite has its proper place and can be found in an instant. The hospital trains are organised and equipped with equally exemplary care and forethought, everything being planned beforehand in peace time. The iron framework supporting the berth for the wounded is always kept ready, all that is required is to remove from third-class carriages the seats and racks, and screw fast in their place the framework for the berths. It is known beforehand how many mattresses, pillows and blankets are required for each carriage. In the medical and apothecaries' store wagons all is arranged with such precision as to enable the doctor to find, blindfolded, the tincture of iodine or quinine he requires, or a piece of sticking plaster, or a safety pin. Everything is arranged on a uniformly fixed system; if a newcomer cannot at once find his way he need only refer to the printed key which applies for

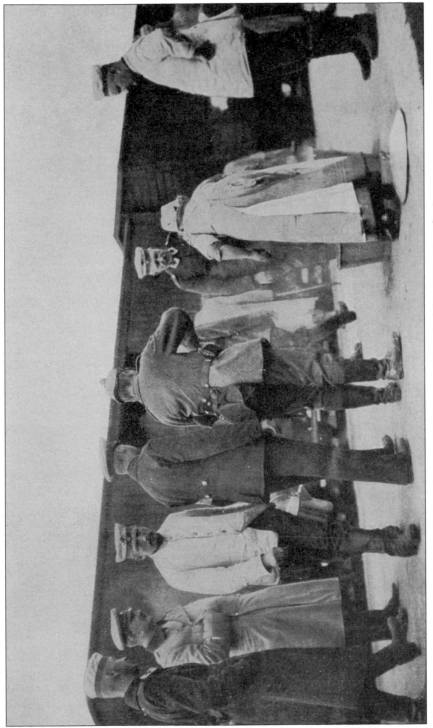

Feeding the wounded (the second from the left is Major Von Plato).

all German ambulance trains. The punctilious thoroughness of the Germans has been ridiculed and called pedantry. But it now appears why this pedantry was useful. All goes like clockwork and no one has any need to search or enquire. And the same order, regulated by strict rules laid down in peace time, reigns everywhere; therefore the Germans do not behave like half-dazed dreamers startled out of their slumber, when they are faced with war in earnest. They are well prepared and trained in everything, whether the duties assigned to them are on the lines of communication or at the operating table.

I have been told in German quarters that the French Army surgeons are better equipped than the German, that is to say that in the French Army there are on hand larger supplies of pharmaceutical and surgical stores. It is said that the French field hospitals are more numerous than the German and are not replaced subsequently by the clearing hospital. This last mentioned circumstance is, of course, quite natural and arises from the situation of the war itself. The Germans have been advancing on French soil; their lines of communication have lengthened. The field hospitals had to be shifted forward step by step. They had to be hurriedly replaced by the clearing hospitals. This is the result of

The Uhlans proceed on their way.

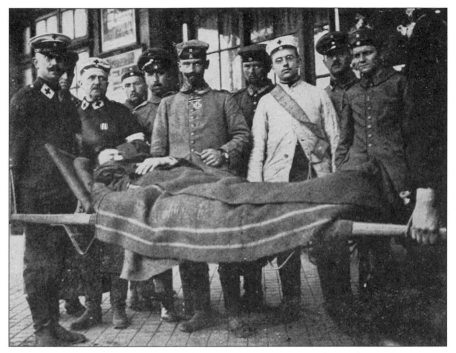

A seriously wounded man carried from the train to the hospital at Sédan.

the spirit favouring the offensive, which is peculiar to the German Army. Hitherto the French have not more than once had any need of corresponding arrangements. They were compelled from the first to keep on the defensive. Although it is a misfortune for them to have hostile armies on their soil, they have at least the advantage that the railways everywhere reach up to their front, whereby all transport of troops, wounded, supplies and ammunition is simplified and shortened. But this advantage is infinitesimal as compared with the misfortune of not being masters throughout their territory. And it also vanishes as soon as the operations assume such an overwhelming character as was the case in the latter part of August. In the present period of stagnation of the war the conditions are naturally different.

The German soldiers have a perfect horror of falling into the hands of French doctors - they would rather die. When prisoners and wounded are exchanged some day after the close of the war, impartial critics in the medical world will be able to judge on what side the wounded prisoners have been treated most tenderly and humanely. In more than one respect this war has demonstrated the impotence and futility of all conferences and conventions of Geneva, The Hague, and other places, bearing names which now have an empty and illusory sound.

But we cannot detain any longer the excellent Captain von Behr who has been waiting with angelic patience while we strayed into the subject of hospital organisation. He now takes me by the arm and we enter the little town.

We enter the house in which von Behr, together with Count von Eichstedt, Baron von Tschammer, and a few other officers have taken up their quarters. Soon the supper bell rang, and we afterwards assembled for coffee in the drawingroom on the ground floor. The scene which met my eyes here and which I afterwards saw repeatedly, reminded me vividly of one of Anton von Werner's war paintings, showing a brightly lighted room and an officer seated at the piano accompanying a singing comrade while the others listen.

Forty-four years have since elapsed, but the picture represented by soldiers billeted in France is still the same. Von Behr sang Schumann, Wagner, and Richard Strauss to von Eichstedt's accompaniment, and the rest of us sat silent like statues and listened. And while the soft sounds of the music were lulling my senses, my thoughts began to wander and I wondered what kind of man it was who, only a month ago, lived in this house and had so lovingly adorned the walls of his drawing-room with portraits of his wife and children. Then came a day when he had to leave his home in haste, to join the army himself and to carry his family into safety. And now his house has become the home of others.

It is usually considered bad taste to examine too closely another man's furniture. But the war sweeps away all conventions, and I cannot take my eyes off the objects surrounding me, not on their own account, but because one has a feeling as if the owner and his family were haunting the room and as if one heard their voices in the sharp tick of the clock on the mantelpiece. Their eyes have fallen daily on the expensive bureau between the windows, their feet have trod the carpet, and they have sat at that very writing-table and entrusted their fears and hopes to note-

A squadron of Uhlans halt outside Capt. Von Rehr's house to await their baggage train.

Protracted halt of an infantry ammunition column. Shelter-tents have been pitched.

paper and envelope, whilst the chandelier had shed its light upon them until the last night before they departed in hurried flight. Why did this unfortunate war come to disturb their peaceful life? Was it necessary for the welfare of France?

Above the writing-table hangs a war painting by Détaille, and from its shelf stares, gloomy and dark, a bronze bust of Bonaparte - not the Emperor, but the victorious General of the Italian war of 1796. A legendary glamour hovers around this image, whose look seems to be strangely penetrating into every corner of the room. However attentively I listened to the song and music and whatever else might attract my attention, my eyes always travelled back to the bronze figure on the writing-table. If it were alive and could talk! What would the Emperor say to the French? "The Prussians hated me; they had a right to do so as my hand had been heavy upon them. But England was my enemy as she was that of France. And Russia assisted her with forces the strength of which I did not realise until it was too late."

Who is host and who is guest in this house? I feel that I am the guest of my German friends as far as we are not all guests - I in a double measure - in the Frenchman's house. For I presume it is, after all, the owner who is the host. Yet, no, war upsets all values. In war everything is settled by force of arms. By right of war, which is the highest instance of appeal, the Germans are at present owners of north-eastern France. And who will insist that Tsingtau is still German, only momentarily occupied by Japanese? No one knows how it will be after the war. But what we do know at present is that in those parts of France which are occupied by the Germans, they are also masters and hosts. Ask the civil population in our little town; they consist, it is true, solely of old people, women and children. They are treated with the greatest consideration and kindness, yet they know who is master here. To have invading troops quartered in one's place is a terrible thing. And yet they are gentle here; inhabitants as well as property are spared as far as possible, and one sees everywhere, in streets and market-places, German soldiers in friendly intercourse with the natives.

Colonel Fischer at his tripod telescope.

CHAPTER IX
WITH THE FOURTH ARMY

O N THE 29th September I made a trip in the company of Count von Eichstedt to the little village of Séchault, chiefly with the object of quietly taking a few photographs of the daily life of the soldiers, such as I found it on a comparatively peaceful day immediately behind the front. We proceeded along a familiar road past marching columns of all kinds, and villages and woods. Our road took us past many fields where there was nobody to bring in the over-ripe corn, whilst in others the sugar-beet was simply rotting away. On reaching the above village we put up the car in a yard and went off to look for some tempting subjects.

Of these there was no dearth and I will simply say a few words by way of explanation. In a field of white beet we came across the encampment of an infantry ammunition column, the men having already put up their shelter-tents. The foreground was littered with beet pulled up and thrown aside. By the side of the road an artillery ammunition column was resting, and its magnificent team of six horses was being regaled with hay, whilst to complete the picture a *Fussart. Mun. Kol. Abteilung (s. F.H.)*[17] comes creaking past. From a side-road there suddenly issues a *Fuhrparkkolonne*, or food column made up of farmers' carts. A mounted military policeman presides over the crossing. He is making notes on the column which is marching past. A little further on another ammunition column has halted by the side of a barn which looks very picturesque with its' decrepit patched-up walls eaten and worn away by wind and weather. We also catch a glimpse of one of those blessed institutions, a

17. Foot artillery ammunition column detachment for heavy field howitzers.

dressing wagon, which I have already spoken of. It is probably not the only one. It looks as if we had chanced upon a spot where what we call in Sweden the first *échelon* of the great train belonging to the army corps in front was about to assemble.

In all yards and alleys in the village we see groups of these strong and cheerful German soldiers, always happy and contented, busy extricating their gear from the baggage wagons or cooking their dinners or patching their clothes. The infantrymen - of whom there are many in the village - are concentrating their attention on their kitchen wagons, which stand steaming and appetising as usual, ranged up at sheltered spots. The others, who had no such luxuries, did their cooking in cooking-trenches in the old familiar way. Around the large awnings stretched over and in front of the wagons, the crews of the transport columns often form really idyllic little picnic groups.

Out in the field a bridging train has halted. Its vehicles, drawn by four horses, have been dispersed. Why? It is because yesterday a French airman flew over the column and dropped a bomb which mauled several horses horribly and seriously injured four men. One of the pontoons was pierced by several shell splinters, but was quickly and most effectively repaired. It is best to be careful - one does at least what one can to minimise the effects of these little visitations. Presently a few infantry soldiers come along, driving a flock of about a dozen sheep before them; we presume they have come across them wandering about in the open. Next day there will probably be Irish stew for at least a couple of companies.

Before a barn stands a steam-engine, busy driving a threshing machine. Soldiers have brought in the wheat, and soldiers are driving the engine. So it seems at any rate that a part of the crop is being gathered. In the copse close by a company of Landwehr have halted by the side of their piled arms. What they are doing I cannot tell, but they seem ready for anything that may turn up.

In the village we come across the 38th reserve field hospital. Accommodation is scanty, and the primitive farmhouses have had to be requisitioned. The wounded are lying on straw on the bare floor. I

A field-kitchen or 'Erbsenkanone' ('Pea-shooter').

'A hero's death'.

cannot resist the temptation of looking in, and step into a little hovel which has once been a kitchen. It is now occupied by six men. They are lying comfortably and softly on their backs and are all fast asleep. They must be terribly tired since they are sleeping so soundly, although it is eleven o'clock. I try to step as lightly as possible on the creaking floor boards so as not to wake them. "Up, ye warriors, arise and hie ye to the fight! "Had I exhorted them thus, they would have lain there just the same, sound asleep with peaceful placid faces and a smile playing about their lips. Why is their sleep so deep, I wonder? They are all shot through the head, and in most of them the bullet is still there.

Here is a reservist. What a tremendous figure of a man. What can Latins, Slavs, Celts, Japs, Negroes, Hindoos, Ghurkas, Turcos, and whatever they are called, do against such strapping giants of the true Germanic type? His features are superbly noble, and he seems pleased with his day's work. He does not regret that he has offered his life for Germany's just cause. I cannot leave him, he holds me back, and I ask for a chair to make if but an imperfect sketch of the dying hero and his neighbours. But yesterday he had sung himself hoarse with the proud refrain: *"Lieb Vaterland magst ruhig sein!"* But yesterday he lay in the cold, narrow trench, and when he and his comrades dashed forward to charge, he was struck in the head by a bullet which lodged in the lower part of the temple. From the first collecting-place he was now on his way to the field hospital.

The doctor comes in accompanied by two assistants. They support and lift him into a sitting posture, whilst the doctor carefully undoes the bandage and lays bare his skull. A large lump of cerebral matter has been squeezed out of the wound and still lies exposed. The doctor does not remove it, merely dries the edges after the hair round the wound has been cut away. The edges of the lump are painted with tincture of iodine, and a fresh, spotlessly white bandage is wound round his head. "But why don't you remove the exposed cerebral substance? "I ask the doctor. "Because one wants to disturb his poor head as little as possible, and cerebral inflammation must be avoided."

"Can his life be saved?"

"There is little or no hope for any of those lying in this room."

The wounded man half opens his eyes. The doctor taps him gently on the shoulder and asks: "What regiment do you belong to? "He mumbles a few unintelligible words which we take to mean "Reserve Regiment 87." The braincentre controlling his organs of speech has been injured. He lapses once more into unconsciousness, his thoughts no longer wander. Shortly they will cease altogether and the soldier will rest, as now beside his comrades, in the little churchyard in the village.

The doctor passes on to the next man and rearranges his bandages. "What regiment?" he asks once more. "Ninetynine," is the reply. "Where are you from?" "Ninetynine." "Are you married?" "Ninety-nine." He gave the same answer to all the questions put to him. "Anyhow, I suppose he really belongs to the ninety-ninth regiment of reserves?" "No, his regiment has quite a different number."

But why this persistent answer to everything? Had there been ninety-nine men in his trench or had he estimated his opponents at this number? Had his battalion or company at some time or other lost ninety-nine men? Or had he thought that he would reach the French trenches with his bayonet before counting to one hundred and had just got to ninety-nine when struck by a bullet in the forehead? Why had this figure, or its counterpart in the mechanism of his brain, imprinted itself on his mind like the image on the photographic plate? Who knows? The dying soldier was about to sink into his last sleep, in which there would be no counting to one hundred to disturb him. And when his immortal soul awakens beyond the churchyard, other sights than bayonets and trenches will meet his gaze.

Right opposite the doorway lay some ten seriously wounded soldiers in a living-room. Near the door lay a man who had had one leg torn away from the hip joint by a shell. A few ragged muscle fibres were all that held it to his body. His face was whiter than the bolster, his big eyes were wide open; I noticed vaguely that he had a good nose and a dark beard. No doubt he had already been drained of blood. But as we stood opposite him, he turned his head and asked for a glass of water. It was brought at once, he drank eagerly and thanked us. We made a

Ammunition column halting beside a barn.

Camp scene on a farm at Séchault.

hasty round amongst the others and in five minutes we were back at the soldier by the door. He was now dead and his vacant eyes were gazing into the unknown. The doctor stooped down and firmly closed his eyelids. He patted him affectionately on the forehead and said in a tender voice, "Sleep well, my poor boy." Later on, the hero, dressed in his uniform and greatcoat, was carried out to the little churchyard outside the village.

Of course it was a depressing and melancholy experience to stand beside so many death-beds. Every day numberless men in the hey-day of youth were thus being gathered to the eternal rest, in hospitals and trenches. But one gets accustomed to such sights, as do the soldiers themselves, for it does not seem to depress or frighten them in the least to see their comrades die.

When a soldier sees his nearest neighbours fall, he does not think: Next time it is my turn. On the contrary his train of reflection seems to be like this: Yes, there they are, poor chaps, but I am still on my feet and the gaps will soon be filled. No need to lament over men who are dying for their country and for the liberty and honour of their people.

Before we left the hospital, we had a look at some of the identification discs carried by the German soldiers round the neck, by the French round the wrist. One of the former read: "*Res. i. R. 17. 6. K. No. 220,*" and one of the latter: "*Seine, 6, Bau (Bureau) 601,*" A third bore the somewhat incomplete inscription: "Leclerc, Alfred, 1902."

The party at dinner, which was served in the open air, included the Commander of the Army, Duke Albrecht of Württemberg, his three sons and his staff, and a young Lieutenant von Hindenburg, son of the famous Field-marshal.

On the return via Cernay, Condé and Challerange I had a further opportunity of adding to my collection of photographs. In the first-named village I took a couple of pictures of an ammunition column, a few soldiers cooking their dinner in a yard, and a company on the point of starting out and receiving their marching instructions. In the next village we came across a fine-looking body of Landsturm, likewise formed up to receive instructions regarding the work in hand, and a parked food column with covered wagons and horses. The most amusing sight was an ammunition column, the wagons of which had been pulled right under the overhanging trees on the fringe of the wood and were in addition covered over with leafy branches, all to conceal them from observation by French aviators. A field hospital had, if possible, masked its vehicles still more skillfully, and had likewise established itself under the trees by the roadside. The horses were not to be seen anywhere. They had disappeared amongst the hazel shrub. A little further on a dressing station had been rigged up in the middle of the wood. The white flags with the red cross could just be seen through the foliage. Similar precautions had been taken for the protection of a number of kitchen wagons.

The French aviators were out daily between 5 and 6 P.M. They - like the corresponding German air scouts - have a double mission, consisting partly in damaging in a military sense, by means of bombs, the more delicate parts of the opposing mechanism, and partly in observing the transfer and grouping of troops, but especially of artillery positions, on the part of the enemy. The bridge across La Dormoise at Autry had been the victim of a bomb attack a couple of days previously, resulting in injuries to a couple of men, but leaving the bridge undamaged. At another point in our vicinity a soldier was struck by one of those horrible steel arrows which the airmen let fall from a height of 2500 metres and which pass right through a horse or bury themselves in the ground after having struck a man on the head. They travel at the speed of a rifle bullet, but weigh more. At Grandpré, a captain was killed a few days ago by one of these arrows, and twenty seven men were injured by a bomb from the same aeroplane. The previous week the Germans were just in the act of putting the last touches to a repaired railway line running through a little town in the neighbourhood, which was to become the rail-head. The French were at once informed through their aviators of what was going on. Three bombs were thrown, which burst close to the station building, but no damage was done. The airman was immediately fired on from an anti-aircraft gun, also without effect. The incident showed however how well prepared one must be for everything. At some points

An ammunition column at Cernay.

A company ready to start out, receiving its marching instructions.

in Germany there is a constant watch for enemy aviators. If one comes soaring along over a fortified town at night-time, several searchlights are concentrated on him, he is blinded by the light and loses his bearings altogether, whilst from the nearest church tower he is pelted by the fire from machine guns, which pour a rain of bullets on him.

The aviator uses various methods of keeping in touch with his own side. This presumably is partly effected by direct signals, such as flags or electric torches, the light from which can be discerned from the ground through field-glasses. If an airman has seen, or thinks he has reason to suspect the presence of troops or transport trains on the fringe of a coppice or wood, he describes by the direction of his flight the outhne of the area in question, and this is promptly followed by a rain of shells. One of the chief duties of the aviator is thus to guide the direction of the artillery fire. If one or several French batteries make it their business to bombard, and if possible to destroy, a German battery the approximate position of which is known by the airman, the latter ascends in the neighbourhood of the target and makes his observations, which are immediately conveyed to the artillery commander concerned. In case of "minus" hits - that is to say if the shells fall short of the object - the airman describes a circle of small diameter. In case of "plus" hits - if the shells burst beyond the object - the airman describes a circle of large diameter. If the shells fall to the left of the object, he makes an abrupt turn to the right, and if they fall subsequently to the right of the object he swings to the left. In this way the airman by his movements in the air brings the fire gradually closer to the target. It goes without saying that all these tricks are countered by the Germans with equal skill. If a German battery notices aerial observations on the part of the enemy, and that the enemy shells are coming nearer, it ceases fire and the battery is moved during the night. One advantage which the French possess, owing to the otherwise unfortunate circumstance that their own country is the theatre of war, is that they can gather much valuable information from the civil population. Amongst the latter it is of course easy here and there to conceal someone who by certain signs or by light signals at night is able to give information about the movements of the Germans. If the chief command of an army corps or other staff has taken up its quarters in a certain village, the French observers are informed thereof by prearranged signals, and it is soon revealed by the artillery fire whether they have been correctly interpreted. Signals can also be given in day-time, for instance, through a peasant driving his cattle to a certain spot when an airman is aloft and can see him.

Constant shifting of ground is the most effective means of overcoming the effects of spying and of direct observation. These changes are made at night. In daylight care is taken to remain quiet and concealed under such cover as the ground affords. The Germans are past-masters in the art of moving troops. The great mobility of the German Army, the rapidity with which its various units can be thrown backwards and forwards, according to requirements, the scientifically developed marching powers of the infantry - there we have a few of the reasons which contribute to make this army the finest in the world.

On our way eastward we just skim the zone which may at any moment be reached by the French fire. But we get past safely and all that we see is a column of yellow smoke ascending from the burning village of Sevron, set alight by German shells. Thenceforward we are on familiar ground and are soon home again after a thoroughly successful trip.

At half-past seven I was invited to supper with the Commander of the 4th Army, Duke Albrecht of Württemberg. The guests included the Minister of War, Lieutenant-General von Falkenhayn, the Chief of Staff, General Use and the Duke's three sons, all fine-looking and talented young men, the eldest twenty-one, the second eighteen and the third seventeen years old. They performed their duties with their units like any other officer and had already on numerous occasions shown commendable ability and courage. We Swedes remember what the Württemberg Princes are like from the time of Charles XII., when Prince Max, not yet fourteen, arrived in the King's camp at Okuniev east of Warsaw and subsequently shared our hard and scanty bread as well as the plentiful fare of more prosperous days, until he died at twenty as Colonel and Chief of the Scanian regiment of Dragoons.

At the end of the meal the son of seventeen rose to go. His duties took him to another part of the front and he had to return. He now walked round the table and said good-bye to all, and last of all to his father. The Duke took his head between both hands and kissed him, but said nothing. No scenes, no tears, no exhortations not to expose himself needlessly to the fire and other dangers. It was like an ordinary, "Good night, I shall see you to-morrow." And yet, how many officers and soldiers are there not in this war for whom there is no such thing as "to-morrow"? How many families on parting from their dear ones do not see them for the last time? How many bonds have not been severed for ever? One of the Red Cross nurses had twenty-four relations in the war, and I was told about a father who had eight sons in the field and a ninth of sixteen who longed to follow their example. The whole German nation has during the past months displayed a fortitude and greatness the like of which has not been seen in our or any other time.

On my return "home" my friends Behr, Eichstedt and Tschammer were still sitting up talking. I settled down beside them. We were just discussing the events and news of the day, when a cavalry captain entered and told us that the inhabitants of two villages about twelve kilometres away had fired on the soldiers, although the village had been in German hands for six weeks. The order had therefore been given that all the men of one village and all men, women and children of the other should be arrested and taken to Vouziers. The distinction made was probably due to the shots in the first village having been aimed at aviators and in the second at troops. Half a company of Landsturm infantry, accompanied by a squadron, likewise of Landsturm, were therefore at 1 A.M. to proceed to the spot. The latter were to occupy all street exits and prevent any attempt at flight. Meanwhile every house was to be searched by the infantry and all inhabitants arrested. On arrival in the town they were to be court-martialled and the guilty ones shot. Such is the severe rule of war. There is no quarter, no salvation. Of course pity is felt for the wretched people, for what could they gain by firing a few paltry shots against a whole army? Is it possible that they believed in the mad rumours that the bridges of the German engineers had been built to assure the German retreat, and that the fortune of war had lately turned completely round? Whence could such news come? Obviously only from the civil population itself. Those who spread such rumours incur a heavy responsibility towards their countrymen for the lives they have risked, and gain nothing in return.

I wondered what would happen to the wretched creatures. The very next day I had an opportunity of seeing them in the dock. They were all old people, peasants and their women folk. The latter wept and looked surprised, the men showed an indifferent demeanour. The war had already taken from them everything, life had no longer any charms. During the few days that the trial lasted they wanted for nothing - once I saw the prisoners sitting round large tables in a yard, eating their dinner. My heart urged me to intercede for them and to appeal to charity and pity, but my reason told me that one cannot and must not interfere in the decisions of military authorities, who are guided by law. I could but harden my heart and let it grow as cold as ice. It may be asked what happened to them in the end, whether they were tied to trees and shot. I lost trace of them for the moment. But a couple of days later I asked one of my friends about their fate.

"They were all released through lack of evidence," he said. "Those who had fired from the villages had clearly fled when our Landsturm arrived. The suspects have all returned to their homes."

It must not be thought that the German court-martials treat such cases lightly or hastily, as if human life in a conquered country had no value. No, the court is utterly incorruptible and carries out its task with the most scrupulous thoroughness. Just as mitigating circumstances are when possible adduced in favour of a German soldier who - which is very rare - has assaulted a woman and therefore been condemned to death, it is sought in the same way to save the country's own children when they are accused of crime. The court-martials of the German "barbarians" are in the highest degree conscientious and humane.

The last day in September was set aside for rest, that is to say, for short walks and excursions. One of the latter was made to the churchyard, where eighteen German soldiers had been buried the previous day in a common grave, which was still open. Dressed in uniforms, greatcoats and caps, the dead are laid in rows alongside one another, with thin layers of earth in between. The reason why this grave has not been filled in is probably that there is still room for more dead. The German warriors who have been resting since 1871 amongst the French crosses have now indeed got company from their own land. On a new grave I read the inscription: "*Hier rum in Gott Ltnt. Hans Greiner, Inf. Reg. 29. Schlaf wohl, tapfrer Kamerad.*" (Here rests in God Lieut. Hans Greiner, Inf. Reg. 29. Sleep in peace, brave comrade.) And on another: "*Hier ruht in Gott Hauptmann Parsohen, Res. Feld Art. 16. Er starb für König und Vaterland.*" (Here rests in God Capt. Parsohen, Res. Field Art. 16. He died for King and Country.) A third grave bore underneath the name and regiment the words, "*Auf Wiedersehen!*" To one of the German graves a French rosary had found its way and hung on the cross over the dead soldier's helmet and two bunches of flowers. An obelisk bore the inscription, "*A la mémoire des soldats morts pour la Patric. Armée Françaisc 1870-71,*" together with a string of names.

Next von Behr and I drove to the flying station at, - where six *Gotha Tauben* with Mércèdes motors were housed in large yellow tents. One of the "doves" had a wing perforated with bullets. The holes had been covered over with little patches. These patches are regarded almost as medals for valour in the field. The more scars an airman has on his machine, the more exposed he has been and the greater has been his daring when above the enemy positions. I do not know which is the more unpleasant feeling, to know that one has an enemy aviator right above one's head or to know that an anti-aircraft gun is planted right underneath and taking aim!

Whilst we were at the station, two "doves" spread their wings for flight. It is beautiful to watch their graceful, easy movements. Before one can quite realise it, the slender wheels have left the ground and the machine is slowly rising from the field and describes a little circle over the tree-tops round about. It gradually rises in a circling motion higher and higher and the two enormous iron crosses under its wings gradually dwindle in size. It reminds one of the carrier pigeon which first rises to a certain height to get a view of the surrounding country and then darts

Bivouacking food column with horses and covered wagons.

off as straight as a die towards its goal. For when our first Gotha "dove" had reached a sufficient height, she went off at a tangent from her last spiral and flew straight south to the French positions and to the rear of them. Once there, it was the duty of the "observer," who sits in front with map, notebook and glasses, to make his observations and then to come back and report them - that is assuming that he does not happen to be shot down on his journey. When over the enemy lines, it is necessary to ascend to a height of 2000-2500 metres so as to be moderately safe from the shrapnel fire from below. But even at 1600 metres the airman and his companion begin to have a feeling of security. After a short while, the second Taube ascended and followed the invisible track of its predecessor through space.

On my return I looked in to see the French prisoners. Five of them, from Bordeaux and Narbonne,[18] were seated round a tub peeling potatoes for their own dinner. Whilst I was sketching them, we had a chat on general topics. They were surprised at the kindly treatment they received in German captivity. They had expected something quite different. "One can't expect more than a roof over one's head, straw to lie on and sufficient food to eat, and all that we get here. We are on friendly terms with our German guards. They often offer us cigars or chocolate. We should quite well be able to live on good neighbourly terms with the Germans." The Frenchmen further told me that they all had wives and children at home who of course were anxious about their fate. They wondered whether the war would last long, whether they would be taken to the interior of Germany, and whether they would be allowed to associate with their own countrymen in captivity so as not to feel too lonely. I was able to give them comforting answers to their questions. One of them said that he had seen quite fifty of his comrades being killed at the spot where he was taken prisoner. Another had lost an old school-fellow by his side, after they had long been together in the trenches. The five prisoners from southern France were calm, self-possessed and sensible men, whose views on the war had sobered down

18. From the 18th and 16th Army Corps or their reserves.

213

considerably since the day they first heard the reveille in Bordeaux and Narbonne. The glamour and the gloss had disappeared, and the triumphant chant of the victory which they had dreamt of, had died down to be succeeded by the naked, bleak reality. Now they saw the tricolor but dimly, as through a haze, and the music of the Marseillaise no longer sounded in their ears.

We spent the evening in the mess together with about thirty officers. The discussion was of course about the events of the day and the hopes of the morrow, and about the news brought by the latest newspapers from all parts of the front. One of those present told us that 270 military trains a day had passed through Kirn (between Kreuznach and Birkenfeld) during the first days of mobilisation, whilst another mentioned that when a regiment at Eiffel was told by its colonel that Britain had declared war, they broke into frenzied cheering. These war pictures were accompanied by the peaceful tones of a gramophone - which not long ago must have had very different listeners! The mess was housed at the residence of a French officer, and I had a look at

A field hospital at Condé effectively screened from observation.

Kitchen wagons 'at work' near Condé.

the pleasing and attractive family portraits in an album, with groups of cavalry officers, amongst them a couple of Swedes, Counts Lewenhaupt and Cronstedt, lieutenants respectively of the Dragoons and Hussars of the Regiment of Life Guards.

On the 1st of October we made an excursion to the troops, and had the company of the delightful and plucky chief of the flying corps, stationed just then at Vouziers, Captain H. von Chamier-Glisczinski. He called for us in his car and we drove at a wild pace through the avenue south-westward to Somme Py. Before however getting so far, we stopped a moment at the flying station, where the Captain had some business to attend to. Whilst we halted a Taube came swooping down in a glorious vol-plane. It descended at what appeared a terrific speed, with its light graceful wings sharply silhouetted against the glorious blue sky. It came to the ground quite close to us and I thought I should have to step aside a bit not to be struck by one of the planes. When near the ground, the machine made a slight movement as if intending to rise again. But it was merely to lessen the shock on landing. Then it rolled along a little way on its wheels and came quietly to a standstill.

The airman and his companion accompanied us a little distance on our way. Once more the many phases of the active life in the rear of the fighting troops unfolded themselves before our eyes. It was not so difficult to advance as I expected, for nowadays it is the custom to keep still and under cover during daylight. Here and there little fires were burning in the shadow of trees. Cooking was going on, and the soldiers were contentedly drinking their coffee, smoking their pipes or taking sun-baths on overthrown wheat-sheaves. The food wagons with their white and yellow arched awnings were as usual covered with leafy branches in order not to attract more than necessary the attention of the French airmen.

Somme Py was not much of a place to stop for, nearly the whole village is burnt and destroyed, leaving nothing but naked walls with sides blackened by the soot of flames. We proceeded on our way. Now and again we catch a glimpse of an ambulance section with doctors and stretcher bearers and vehicles, or of the fighting train of some infantry regiment. We recognise our old friends the foliage-shrouded kitchen wagons, the yellow ambulance wagons, surrounded by stretcher bearers with their white bands round the arm, and rows of grey ammunition wagons, all harnessed up with a team of two horses.

At length we reach a point in the road where four light field howitzers are posted in a strong position by the wayside. Captain Chamier tells the chauffeur to stop and to hide the car well in the shadow of a tree. It is not considered advisable to proceed further, as the car may attract the attention of the French observers. We therefore alight and take a little turn round the battery, which happens to be at work. A salvo has just been fired, and the reloading is proceeding. I seize the opportunity of taking a couple of pictures. The guns, like the ammunition wagons, were well masked and were either dug in or surrounded by a rampart consisting of stone and sand-bags covered over with earth. The target for the day was the village of Souain, 4050 metres distant. I was told it was

*Perot Julien, a 54 year old peasant charged with plotting,
but released through insufficient evidence.*

Saisac of Toulouse, 11th Infantry Regiment (3rd Inf. Div. 17th Army Corps).
Prisoner at Vouziers.

practically in ruins and that what remained was in flames. The firing of the battery was directed from the *Beobachtungsstand* or observation post which we visited later on, and from which the effect of the shells could be discerned through good field-glasses.

When a shell strikes a house or other object, a dark column of smoke composed of gases, dust and earth, rises from the spot, and flames mingling with the smoke soon reveal the fact that combustible substances have been ignited. When unaccustomed to these weapons, one cannot but regard them with a certain amount of awe. This awe is no doubt still further increased with experience. The officers themselves appear perfectly unmoved, but I think this is mostly due to the exercise of self-control. A commander must not betray emotion before his men. He must be perfectly calm. But it *must* nevertheless tell upon the strongest nerves to remain for long under fire. This battery had occupied the same spot for eighteen days without being discovered by the French aviators.

From the battery we proceeded on foot in open order through an avenue of trees, taking care to keep in the shade. Of course our security was not absolute, for here and there the trees had been cut in two by the French fire. We walked some five hundred metres southward to the observation post referred to, from which the fire was directed by telephone, and from which the foremost French positions could be kept under observation. The first thing that attracted our attention on approaching this very interesting point was something resembling a tree, rising above the young growth of the wood. On further inspection we found it to be a mast of the thickness and height of a telegraph pole, provided with a ladder, a little platform and a seat for an observer. A pair of glasses were left there permanently, and the observer was masked by leafy branches.

On reaching the spot we were received by not less than three colonels, of whom, however, two were accidental guests, and by a couple of other officers. Colonel Fischer, Brigade Commander of the Field Artillery, a most genial and amusing man, was full of talk about Asia and more especially India, where he had travelled very extensively. We had thus many memories and friends in common, and I am afraid that on this occasion Asia took precedence over the Franco-German war.

However, I could not go away without seeing the underground abode of these officers, for they live there day and night, and as the spot is exposed to the French fire, they have to take certain precautions. A stairway, the steps of which had been cut out of the soil, leads to a cave dwelling of two rooms, small and dark, faintly lighted by a paraffin lamp and heated by a little tin stove, now burning brightly. A table, let into the wall, made of half a plank, is laden with toilet articles, glasses, maps, instruments and pistols in delightful confusion. In the sleeping apartment the beds are laid on the floor close together. I could not suppress a pious wish that the inmates would be preserved from death by asphyxiation in this subterranean cavern. One must not suffer from a horror of confined spaces if one is to sleep comfortably in these holes. But nevertheless it must be a great comfort to have this haven of refuge if and when the spot is bombarded. I was told that the cave was not quite proof against common shells, but that there was no danger from shrapnel. The officers' meals are usually taken in the cave, so that they may at least eat in peace.

A few steps further on we visited a telephone station installed in the masonried cellar of a wrecked house. This cellar was thus a subterranean chamber, to the walls of which a number of telephone appliances had been fastened. Below them several officers and privates were seated on benches let into the walls. Whilst I was there several telephones kept ringing simultaneously. Constant attention was therefore indispensable. Besides being in permanent communication with its own division, this station was in touch with the whole of the 4th Army through its Chief Command, and with Main Headquarters. There was, in fact, nothing to prevent its occupants from ringing up Germany, except of course that private conversations are forbidden. Two airmen, Lieutenants Count Rambaldi and Bürger, had just arrived at the observation post after a reconnaissance over the French positions. It was wonderful to hear how clearly and concisely they reported what they had seen. Rambaldi stood for a long while with the telephone receiver in one hand and in

Olive, 30 years old, Infantrie Coloniale, 24 eme (2nd Colonial Inf. Div.)
Native of Perpignan, Eastern Pyrenees. Prisoner at Vouziers.

Five reservists from Bordeaux and Narbonne who fought in Alsace and Champagne and were captured the 26th and 27th September south of Vouziers. They are busy peeling potatoes. At Vouziers the French prisoners were allowed to cook their soup themselves in order to get the proportion of meat and vegetables that they liked best.

the other the map on which he had traced his observations. He was speaking to some member of the General Staff of his Army, with the same map before him and doubtless also with a pencil and notebook. The Lieutenant would, for instance, report something like this: 550 metres north-west of the village of X I observed artillery in position, but probably only 2 guns. On the road leading from the west to the village Y I saw a stationary column of eight vehicles. I could not make out whether it was an ammunition or food train. The battery which yesterday was posted in the hollow south of the village Z has to-day been removed, but it is impossible to tell at present where it has gone.

Information thus gained - especially if it is of the kind indicated in the above example - assists in the first place the direction of the artillery fire. But that is not all. The air scouting - as I have made clear above - is primarily at the disposal of the Chief Command in order to discover in time the grouping and shifting of the opposing forces. Movements of troops, in order to avoid observation from above, therefore now take place during the night. This is why between four and five in the morning one always encounters troops of every description on the march, whilst in daylight they are seldom to be seen- at least not the infantry - barring an occasional body of Landwehr or Landsturm.

From this observation post it was about two kilometres to the foremost German infantry positions, which in turn were from three hundred to five hundred metres from the French trenches. Sometimes, when the country is very open and affords no cover whatever, it may not be possible to get closer to the enemy than one thousand metres. In these advanced positions there is never any relaxation of tension. A moment of quiet can never be relied upon. Of course the occupants of a trench need not all be on the alert at the same time. If this were so, exhaustion would soon set in. But in every unit a certain number of men are always told off to watch the enemy whilst the others are "resting." Glasses are always in use as long as daylight lasts. When it is dark, patrols are pushed forward to signal immediately in some way or other if there is any sign of approach on the part of the enemy. It is a dog's life. If one pokes one's nose over the edge, one becomes immediately the target of unwelcome attentions, and bullets start whizzing round one's ears. The previous morning at ten o'clock it had been discovered that the French were proceeding to an attack on a part of the German position in front of us (north of Souain). One could see how, from a little wood at —, they tried to creep forward under cover of the folds and creases of the ground. Two volleys of shrapnel were at once poured over them, 150 men fell and the others retired. But the French pay back in the same coin whenever they have an opportunity, and they fire with great skill from their excellent field artillery. Their ammunition, on the other hand, is said to be less good. Yesterday, for instance, only seven shells had burst out of thirty-six.

The German soldiers retain their good humour in the face of great danger. Sometimes, for the fun of the thing, they place a helmet which has lost its owner on a stick and move it with a nodding motion along the edge of the trench. In a trice the French bullets begin to rain around it and the soldiers bet as to the number of hits.

I am told there is no exaggerated cleanliness in these trenches, although one does what one can to remove anything that does not belong there. In these parts, I am told, the opposing troops have come to a mutual understanding, according to which, on certain solemn occasions, they are allowed to climb out of their trenches and walk one at a time and unarmed in the direction of the enemy. A soldier leaving some project of that kind need only raise his spade over the parapet and swing it three times backwards and forwards. After the signal he may confidently proceed on his errand and when completed return to his trench.

On one occasion two grazing cows happened to find their way to the space between two infantry positions facing one another at a short distance. How it came about it is difficult to tell, but by the mysterious code of soldierly freemasonry it was agreed that a French soldier should milk one cow and a German soldier the other. When the job was done, they returned quite placidly to their trenches. All this shows that the French soldiers also are not wanting in humour and high spirits, even though day and night death is like the breath in their nostrils.

The different infantry forces, large and small, are also in telephone

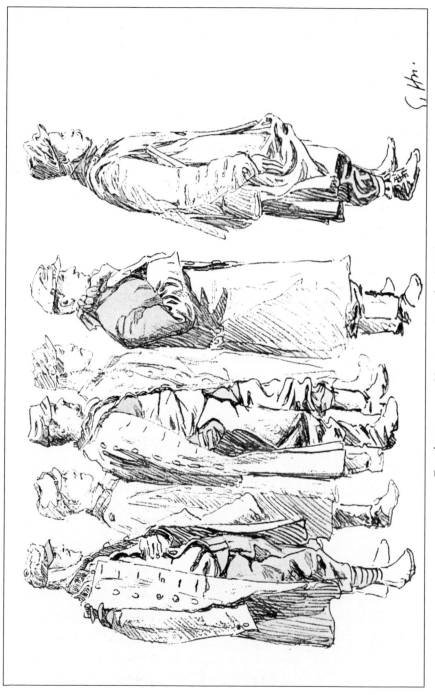

French prisoners at Vouziers waiting for their dinner.

German airmen: Captain Chamier, Lieutenants Count Rambaldi and Burger, and a fourth. The iron cross can be seen on the underside of the left plane.

communication with our observation post. One of my hosts asked if I would like to hear how the battalion in the most advanced position of all was getting on. Why of course I should, I said. I was handed one receiver and was at once ceremoniously introduced to the commanding officer of the battalion, who himself answered the call.

"How are things going, Major?"

"Thank you, very well."

"Have you anything special to report?"

"Yes, there was some firing in the night, but no losses."

"In what sort of spirits are the men?"

"Excellent, as usual."

"Have you received the eight machine guns that were to be sent you last night?"

"Yes, they have arrived and are already in position, but one of them has no shield. However, we will manage with an earth parapet for the present."

"Have you any other wishes?"

"No, thanks, everything else is all right."

The Major's voice sounded calm and confident, but I could detect an undercurrent of solemnity in his answers.

That part of the observation post which lay above ground had been transformed into a pleasant little arbour or enclosure among the young trees, visited now and again by cycle and other orderlies. A telescope, well protected and concealed, stood ready on its tripod. Another had been mounted in the road outside the arbour. With these glasses one can see almost everything, right away to the horizon. Thanks to the vertical position of the tubes, the observer's head can be protected altogether by an armoured shield or a wall. From our commanding position we had an excellent view of the nearest infantry positions. Colonel Fischer explained everything to me. He focussed the horizontal cross line on a German trench. I saw it very clearly, it appeared like a somewhat uneven dark line. I could even see a man getting up out of the trench, probably after having waved his spade backwards and forwards the regulation number of times.

Thereupon the telescope was focussed on one of the French infantry lines. This was not quite plainly discernible, but yet fairly clear.

Still further to the south, about 3550 metres from the point where we were standing, we saw the burning village of Souain and a few clumps of trees, behind which we had reason to suspect the presence of cleverly masked artillery positions.

In the east-south-east, between Souain and Perthes, we could clearly see a French battery of four field guns and a little nearer towards us a few abandoned gun ramparts.

Suddenly the Colonel shouts, *"Deckung!"* A French aeroplane, a Blériot, is approaching. We hurry under the trees so as not to attract its attention, A few orderly mounts, tethered in a hollow, are likewise moved to a place offering better concealment. The airman comes nearer. We hear faintly but distinctly the drone of his motor. He is sailing along right over our heads. Is he going to drop bombs or smother us in a shower of arrows? It would be a useful day's work for him to destroy an observation post from which the fire is directed and where the telephone wires of the neighbourhood run together. Some civilian spy may have conveyed a signal. But the alarm seems needless, the aviator flies past and there are no explosions. With a feeling of satisfaction we see the great bird disappear. He is seeking some other target for his bombs.

Although it was combined with a certain risk, we walked a couple of hundred metres closer to the infantry positions. The ground sloped slightly downward in this direction. We follow the road in open order, keeping to the shadow of the trees, and where there are shrubs we keep close to them. If we are caught sight of from some French observation post, the enemy guns will immediately be trained upon us. However, we safely reach an infantry reserve unit. In this war, where one lies for weeks and months at practically the same spot, the former open fighting has gradually given place to a sort of siege war, with its attendant methods and customs. I here found that every infantry unit was divided into a number of shifts. The "changing of the guard" usually took place at about six every morning. A battalion which for twenty-four hours has occupied the area entrusted to the defence of its regiment, may then

A battery of light howitzers in position.

A salvo has just been fired. The guns are now being reloaded.

return to the rear after a fresh battalion has moved up into the position in question.

But even at the point where the reserves are posted it is necessary to dig oneself in, and above all to be well screened from observation. These shelters usually take the form of niches or "dug-outs" in the soil. The openings are covered over with a slender roof of sticks, twigs and hay. We looked into one or two of these "caves" and saw the soldiers fast asleep and apparently not lacking anything. I noticed that all the men were wrapped up in their canvas tent sections. In this case we had happened to come across a detachment which had arrived from the firing line in the morning and was now to sleep till midday. Afterwards there was to be exercise - *drill*. As darkness comes on, the kitchen wagons are brought up with their comforting hot food. Such was the life in the German reserve positions on the north side of the wooded country north of Souain. Nobody cared to advise us to continue from this point, as in that case we should certainly have been visible from the French observation posts and should have been exposed to a murderous fire. Even a kitchen wagon, which does not travel far except under cover of darkness, was hit the other day by a shell and had four men killed. Some light or other had probably been seen by the enemy, and as he had the range to a nicety, he fired a volley. But now it was daytime and we had open ground before us. I was told on this occasion - in connection with the advice not to proceed further - a story of an attack made from the German side a few days previously in order to capture an advanced French position in the neighbourhood of Souain. The attack was launched at dusk, but failed. Several Germans remained on the ground. The lightly wounded were taken prisoners by the French, but three men had been so badly hurt that they were not considered worth taking, and were left on the ground. The nearest French soldiers took pity on them and went out each night in the dark to take them food and water, and even cigarettes. One line day a plucky German doctor with a few stretcher bearers came forward from the German line. They had brought a Red Cross flag, carried high on its pole. At first a few shots were heard from the French lines, but as soon as the

Frenchmen realised what was up, they ceased fire, as nobody wanted to interfere with the rescue work. Thus the doctor was able to carry his charges into safety.

At another reserve position we chatted awhile with the grey-coats, who had recently lost a Lieutenant Johannes. The mound which covered his remains was surrounded by a perfect battery of shells, standing like a set of nine-pins with the cross for its centre. Young pines had also been planted as sentries round his grave.

After a couple of hours with these friendly, merry, brave and manly fellows, we started out on the return journey to the flying station, where the guard delivered his report to Captain Chamier, adding: "It was lucky

Observer masked by twigs and branches.

Scene on the road in front of the observation post.

you did not arrive a quarter of an hour ago, for just then an aviator passed over the station and dropped a bomb which burst close by here but without doing any damage." As a memento I was given a splinter of the bomb, which it was pleasanter to have in one's pocket than in one's body.

From Somme Py we proceeded south-east to Tahure and passed on the way an ammunition column perched on the fringe of the wood by the side of its little cooking pits. Inside the wood we caught sight of numberless items making up a transport train, such as infantry ammunition wagons, ambulance wagons, kitchen wagons and spare horses.

In the yards and alleys of the little village there was an incessant bustle, and it took us some time to thread our way through. A little way beyond Tahure we left the car once more and proceeded on foot to another observation post, a little less important than the previous one, but otherwise on the same lines. We had hardly got there before shrapnel began to burst around and over us. An officer advised us to seek cover in a little trench, which, however, had no roof. For my part I was quite willing to follow his suggestion, and was glad to stop in the hole until the fire had died away. A few moments later another of those winged monsters of the air, known by the name of war aeroplanes, passed over us, without however showing signs of wanting to harm us.

CHAPTER X
QUIET DAYS

O N OCTOBER 2nd I made an excursion to Sédan to replenish a few items of my equipment. I was offered a seat in Lieutenant Kollmann's covered car, which made this journey daily, and we tore along northward through the thin veil of mist which floated over fields and meadows.

As we reached the bridge at Le Chesnes, a Landsturm man stepped into the road, swinging a white flag. We stopped, and an officer stepped forward, saluted courteously and asked to see our pass. This is curious, I thought, this car ought to be pretty well known, and is manned besides by an officer and two chauffeurs, all in uniform. However, when our papers had been examined, he explained that the watch had been made stricter, as it had been found that there were so many spies about, who were even bold enough to dress up in German uniforms, so that one could not be too careful.

The railway to Vouziers was clearly not yet equipped with sufficient rolling-stock to meet the demands made upon it, for the great road on the lines of communication to the 4th Army were still encumbered with endless transport trains.

"What do the letters E.K.K. mean, that I see on all these cars?" I asked my travelling companion.

"*Etappen Kraftwagen Kolonne*" (Mechanical transport trains for lines of communication), he replied. "They carry food and ammunition like all the others."

Thereupon we chatted awhile about this wonderful life which goes on behind the front, about all these threads by which an army hangs in an occupied country, and about the many types of armed wayfarers on foot, on horseback, and in wagons. We talked about the villages, crops, herds of cattle, and the wretched humans wandering about like strangers and prisoners in their own land. They are utterly cut off from the outside world, for there are no paths so secret and so subtle that news from France can reach them. How the war is progressing, they have no idea. They have not had a newspaper, not a letter, for close on two months. All they hear is an occasional rumour spread by some freelance and intended to make them put difficulties in the way of the invading army.

"But what on earth do they live on?" "Oh, there are plenty of potatoes and poultry, besides the corn still ungathered in the fields. And there are still plenty of cattle, for you can see them yourself grazing by the roadside. Sheep and pigs are equally plentiful, but the one thing there is not much left of is wine. For when the French Army passed through it did not stint itself, and then we came and took the rest. But we pay for everything and nobody will be the loser by what we take. Matches and paraffin disappeared long ago, and so there is nothing left for the inhabitants but to go to bed, like the chickens, with the sun."

Presently we arrived, drove across Place Turenne, attended to our business and met again at the Croix d'Or for lunch. Here every room was still taken up and the restaurant was well filled as usual. The proprietor was very contented and admitted that he was doing a roaring trade, provided that his "*bons*" were redeemed after the war. The town now wears a Prussian air, uniforms, soldiers and patrols wherever one looks. We were glad to sit for a while by the window and look out upon the square. Officers are busily walking hither and thither on the business of the lines of communication of the 4th Army, from the Base Commander's Office to the *Palais de Justice*, where the Base Inspectorate is located, and from the *Palais de Justice* to some other public building where some German authority has taken up its quarters. As they pass the greyclad sentries with their gleaming bayonets, they are always greeted with a smart military salute.

I cannot take my eyes from this window, the warlike, active scene outside fascinates me, and yet everything is done quietly and deliberately, and the greatest order reigns everywhere. Here is a row of cars ranged up in single file with carbines fastened to the screen in front of the driver's seat, ready for use when wanted. Several of the cars are provided with a sort of superstructure of two iron hoops carrying a sharp narrow iron rod which starts from the front of the car and slopes upward over the heads of the occupants, coming to an end just in front of the hood. One might think it was the framework of a tent in case it became necessary to spend the night in the car. But this was not the case. The object of the contrivance is to cut or at least deflect telephone wires which might have been maliciously stretched across the road to injure travelling officers. When driving at high speed in the dark and coming up against one of these wires, one has every prospect of being decapitated.

But the most interesting part of it all was to watch the civil population, the natives of Sédan. Here come two bareheaded girls accompanied by a boy in a cap and cloak. Walking backwards and forwards between the hospitals are nurses in white or black headdress, but always with the Red Cross band round the arm. A couple of them are following a stretcher carried by ambulance men, on which lies a seriously wounded soldier taken from a train. On the other side of the square a couple of elderly women come plodding along with enormous bundles - doubtless washing for officers, who pay them well to look after their wants. I always feel the deepest compassion for these poor creatures. They have lost their country and their liberty, and the war has deprived them of their husbands and sons and ruined their homes. It is the poor who suffer most, the rich and well-to-do have fled in time and taken their valuables with them, leaving nothing but their empty and deserted houses. Yet here and there a wealthy citizen has elected to stop, or perhaps left his servants to guard his house and home. Such families will find their possessions absolutely untouched. In the house where officers have lived, not a pin will be out of place. But during the repeated advances of an army, after the officers have departed from their quarters and left them absolutely intact, it no doubt happens now and again that soldiers subsequently billeted there m.ay not treat the effects with the same respect.

Here come a couple of ladies of the higher bourgeoisie, perhaps mother and daughter, dressed in black and with long black veils. Are they in mourning for fallen relatives, or perhaps for the fate of France? As a matter of fact, the more well-to-do women always wear black. They *cannot* but mourn. They understand better than the common people the position of unhappy France and how unfortunate the policy has been which brought them into this great, sanguinary war. If one lives for a few days at the same spot and passes the same houses several times, and maybe greets the old women standing alone or with their children in the doorways, one of them may occasionally nod pleasantly and answer "*Bonjour, monsieur*," but the next one hardly takes any notice. The first may be well off and hope to see her menfolk once more, the other is probably brooding over her grief and sorrow, for she knows nothing, has nothing, and has lost all hope. Those who cook, bake, wash, mangle and "do" for the Germans are always contented, at least on the surface. The storm has already travelled past them. Whatever they do, they cannot change their fate and must make the best of what is left.

One would have to be of stone, were one not to feel pity also for the old men. Here come a couple slowly walking across the square. Look at their wrinkled faces, their careworn features, their sharp profiles, black eyes and great grey moustaches. They are very plainly dressed and wear felt hats on their heads. They walk bent after their day's work, if they have had any. Look at the corners of their eyes in profile, with all their lines showing, and watch the moist glance and forlorn expression of the eye. These eyes have ceased to cry and see no light ahead. But ask for once the old people if *they* wanted the war and if they think it is for France's good. No, they, the old men and the women of all ages, bear no blame for the nameless misery that is now spreading over France.

I cannot tear myself away from the window. The bizarre life outside is running its even course. In the centre of the square, inside the lamp-posts and the iron railing stands the great Turenne on his stone plinth, scarred and green with age. He stands there like a ghost and an anachronism, and looks down with imperturbable calm on those dim distant ages whose blood-drenched waves are lapping round his feet.

Everything that has been destroyed by the French in order to render the German advance more difficult, and everything that has been laid waste by the ravages of war itself has long since been mended by the German Army and its organisation. The railways are running, new bridges replace the wrecked ones, telegraph and telephone lines have been laid down, watersystems have been repaired and the electric light is now burning as brightly as ever in times of peace. Times of peace! It seems as if an eternity had flown since those days. The clocks in the houses have stopped, there are no French hands to set them going. The great clocks in the church towers alone denote the flight of time. It is German time that they show, and it is important that they should be working, not so that the priests may know their hours of duty, for they need no clocks, but in order that the transport trains, the soldiers, the sentries and the green-clad military police posted round Turenne's statue and at other points may know when they shall relieve or be relieved- and last, but not least, in order that the civil population may know how long it is to nightfall. Anyone found loitering in the dark is shot if his papers are not in perfect order and if he cannot show that he is out on a lawful and proper errand.

But the clock tower strikes its five deliberate strokes and it is time for us to return to Vouziers, if we mean to arrive before it is quite dark. I cast a final glance at the houses opposite, where some windows are open and give me little snapshots into the interior - not of domestic French life, but of German billeting scenes; other windows are closed and further protected by green and white shutters. I have reached this stage in my reflections, when a tall gentleman comes up to me and introduces himself as Baron Bleichröder of Dresden. He is wearing a uniform which I cannot quite place within the somewhat narrow limits of my military knowledge, and I therefore hit upon the simple question, "What are you doing here, Baron?" "I have brought with me twenty-nine motorlorries of *Liebesgaben* for the troops," he answers. "The lorries are filled to the roof with little parcels of cigars, cigarettes, pipe-tobacco, underclothing, socks, handkerchiefs, newspapers, chocolate and other things the soldiers like."

At last we took our leave and proceeded in a south-westerly direction, with the rapidly setting sun before us on our right. There was something remarkable about the sunsets at this time. To-night it was a glowing, burning red, and the sky around was tinted in the same gorgeous colouring. But it made me think of the long, bloody trail now stretching from Belfort to the sea in the north-west, a distance of about four hundred miles. Here the soldiers lie in an unbroken row of trenches, so closely together that a word of command or a piece of news can be repeated from ear to ear from Middelkerke to Altkirch; allowing only one man for every metre, this makes a total of six hundred thousand men. But the density is in reality far greater, and one is almost stunned at the thought that Germany, which in the east, too, has an enormous front to protect and stands in arms at many other points, is yet always able to fill the gaps with fresh, perfectly trained men. It is true that, numerically, the Allies are three times stronger than Germany and Austria-Hungary and that they - the self conscious British, and the French, so rightly proud of their cultured refinement - have instituted a regular import of black and brown human matériel from distant continents. But in real soldiers the Germans are superior. Practically speaking their country is clear of enemies - with the exception of six hundred thousand prisoners - and they are fighting out their fight on enemy territory.

Saturday, the 3rd of October, passed very quietly.

It is pleasant to be able to rest now and again, when otherwise one is always on the move. I dined at one o'clock with Professor Zinsser and the doctors under him. The table was laid in the garden. Over our heads we heard the buzz of German biplanes and *Gotha Tauben*. A cheery and willing Franciscan friar waited at table and joined animatedly in the conversation. After dinner the distinguished old pater Müller came to call. Now and again a batch of French prisoners marched past. A couple of them were carrying a sick German to the railway station, whilst others were carting coal to the hospitals in barrows. I photographed a band of eighteen men on their way to dinner. One can see even in the picture that they are in the best of spirits, well cared for and sheltered against cold and rain. Some scenes I witnessed between prisoners and their guards were inordinately comical. On one such occasion I saw a German gaoler pat his French prisoner on the shoulder and say in a fatherly, patronising voice, *"Hier hast du eine Cigarrette, mein Bursch"* (Here is a cigarette for you, my lad), whereupon the Frenchman gave a friendly nod, accepted the cigarette with a smile and a merci, and lit it from the German's pipe. Among the soldiers one sees no signs of national hatred. But in the French press it glows like a consuming fire. Not to speak of the venom of the English newspapers!

In the evening I spent a few moments with some Jesuits employed in the service of the Red Cross. They had some sanguinary tales to tell of places they had recently visited, particularly Rossignol. I might fill whole books with these horrible stories about streets drenched in blood, fallen soldiers and hand-to-hand fighting in towns and villages, where every house has to be stormed whilst death is being rained upon the attackers from the windows. But this is not part of my task, and I have made it my duty to speak in the main only of what I myself have seen and experienced.

In the Argonne forest much blood has flown, as I myself have seen in its northern part, both from the east and west, when with the 5th and the 4th Army respectively. Although the whole of the front has developed more or less into a siege war with trenches, communicating trenches, barbed-wire entanglements and *trous-de-loup*, this applies even in a larger measure to this forest region. Here the engineer troops have had much work to do, and it is the generals of the Engineers who lead the advance. To progress quickly is *impossible*. The forest, so badly kept that it would horrify a northern sylviculturist, is very difficult to advance in. In certain places one has to cut one's way step by step through shrub and undergrowth. This sort of country is easy to defend, and the French understand their business well. At night or in a fog, the Germans push forward a thin line of infantry about fifteen paces distant from one another. After having advanced as far as the conditions allow, the men dig themselves in. This gives rise to a chain of pits which afterwards, by continued digging longitudinally, are united into a continuous trench. When the men have made themselves at home in this new position and extended it, a further area in front of the one occupied is cleared by fire, whereupon the fresh advance is made. In this way the forest is swept clean. It must be taken step by step, tree by tree, for - as I have already pointed out - the defenders have organised even the tree-tops for defence, and have mounted machine guns there. In the gloom of the undergrowth it is not always easy to distinguish friend from foe. On the occasion of my visit it was not advisable for anyone to come too close to the Argonne forest unless his duties called him there. In certain cases the risk seemed even greater for those behind the firing lines than for those in the advanced positions, for the French usually fired too high. Their shots mostly passed over the heads of their nearest opponents, who, by the way, were remarkably well concealed. This is not to be wondered at, for when the enemy is almost upon one, accurate shooting becomes difficult. The parts of the forest which have already been taken by the Germans look very strange. The ground is streaked with trenches and communicating trenches joining the former together, and the trees are often charred and stripped by the lire.

The French are cleverer at artillery than infantry shooting. One of the doctors here told me that of the 2500 patients he had had to attend to, not quite ten per cent had been hit by rifle bullets; a few had been wounded by sword cuts or bayonet thrusts, but all the rest had been struck by shell splinters and shrapnel bullets. If the ammunition were better, the effect of the French artillery fire would be appalling.

On Sunday morning, the 4th of October, at 5 o'clock, the kindly Franciscan friar came to call me. I dressed hurriedly, and accompanied by a Catholic soldier on orderly duty in von Behr's house I wandered off to the "Home for the Aged," in the chapel of which the birthday of St. Francis was to be celebrated with mass and song. No daylight, no moonlight; the heavy hand of night still grips the earth. A damp mist floats over Vouziers and the stone paving is wet. Here and there an electric lamp is engaged in an unequal struggle against the darkness. Now and then a few hurried steps are heard - monks on the way to mass. In front of a house used for some military purpose tramps a sentry - otherwise the street is still and silent.

On reaching our goal we step into a tiny garden, and are presently in the chapel. It is already filled with worshippers Here sit the Elizabeth

Pater Muller, Professor Zinsser and a Franciscan Friar.

French prisoners at Vouziers.

sisters from Essen in their white veils, and the St Vincent sisters from Hildesheim in black veils; the Franciscan friars have already taken their places. Several Catholic soldiers occupy the galleries, where presently I join them.

At the alter the statues of saints are illuminated by tall candles, just being lit, but the two candelabras are not yet brought into use. It is still so dark outside that the stained-glass windows shut out all light and are illuminated only from the inside. The features and dress of the Virgin Mary and St. Helena in their leaden setting are scarcely discernible.

A friar in a vestment embroidered in white and gold, surrounded by four other friars equally gorgeously attired, steps up to the altar. They carry censers with glowing charcoal, on which one of them sprinkles an aromatic powder. Light blue clouds of smoke ascend to me in the gallery and instantly recall to my memory similar scenes from the Uspenskij Sobor in Moscow and Taschi-lunpo in desolate Tibet.

Now begins the Latin altar service. One of the priests chants, and the congregation responds with the constantly recurring refrain: *"Per omnia secula seculorum. Amen."* *"Oremus"* comes from the altar, and again *"Per omnia secula seculorum. Amen"* from the congregation.

Next comes the sermon. The preacher chooses for the subject of his discourse the life of St. Francis. Prayers coupled with his name are this day being offered up throughout the world. The congregation cannot better celebrate his memory than by fulfilling their duties on behalf of human love and charitableness, and by doing their part towards the relief of the sufferings of wounded soldiers.

The stained-glass windows begin to brighten. Day is breaking outside. The congregation sings a German song in honour of St. Francis. A friar once more steps up to the altar and rings a little bell. I cannot take my eyes off these friars and sisters, who have come straight from the battlefields and hospitals, and whose thoughts are now so peacefully centred round the name of the great patriarch. How moved they seem, how eagerly they make the sign of the cross to betoken their piety! In a picture opposite the choir the crucified Christ looks down from the height of His agony on to the kneeling figures. *"Per omnia secula seculorum, Dominus vobiscum. Gratias agimus Domino Deo nostro. Unus est Deus, unus est Dominus."* The bell rings once more, the censers are swung on their chains, and it almost seems as if the Virgin Mary and Saint Helena had stepped out of the gloom around the altar and had approached us.

The attendant friars greet one another by placing their hands on one another's shoulders and head. Holy Communion is administered to the congregation, and once more the eternal refrain is chanted: *"Per omnia secula seculorum."* It makes one think of all the brave ones dying out in the trenches and of the flower of the male youth of two noble nations which is being sacrificed on the altar of shell fire. Maybe the thoughts of the nuns and monks, too, are more taken up with the strife now shaking the world to its foundations, than with the peace surrounding the name of the Holy Francis. Perhaps the thought of all the soldiers who have died before their eyes is clouding their mental vision. It cannot be easy to die when one is young and strong, and has all one's life before one. But the honour of the country demands that its men be sacrificed. Their memory shall live *"per omnia secula seculorum." Coronas dccoris mernerunt.*

The candelabra on the communion table are now lighted. But they are no longer needed, daylight once more reigns outside and Saint Helena's features now look down clearly on all beholders. Round her lips plays a smile full of gentleness and goodness. She, the friend of the helpless and suffering, seems to rejoice to see so many brethren and sisters devoting their best energies to the relief and care of wounded and dying soldiers.

But now the devotions are over and my Franciscan friar leads me to the colonnade, where the sisters give us coffee with beautiful white wheaten bread and marmalade. Here we spend an agreeable hour together before parting.

The Protestant field service was held at half-past nine. The worship took place at a quiet street corner under the open sky, a safer place than the fields outside the town, where a large gathering of people would make a welcome target for a French airman's bombs. A few hundred soldiers and some fifty officers forgathered here. An octette from the regimental band began playing a psalm - we Swedes know it well - it has been sung before the blue and yellow standards of Gustavus Adolphus, before the Carolins at Narva, on the banks of Vabitj, on the plains of Ukraine, and has brought solace and comfort to the poor forgotten prisoners in Siberian thraldom: *Ein feste Burg ist Unser Gott.* The soldiers joined in with their strong clear voices. Perhaps one ought to have seen and heard this sort of thing to realise what Swedes and Germans have in common. At one time we gave each other the noblest and the best that we possessed. The Lutheran faith preserved by the sword of Gustavus Adolphus was the seed and life germ which has given birth to that Germanic culture which to-day is fighting for its existence. None of us can escape the responsibility for the inviolable preservation of the common heritage. Our German brethren are now shedding their hearts' blood in a cause which in equal measure concerns ourselves, and for which Sweden's greatest Kings gave their all and their lives.

Pastor Marguth of Hessen conducted the service from some stone steps. He was attired in a black gown and, like all other chaplains of the Field Army, he wore round the arm a white and violet band. Taking the Epistle to the Romans as his subject, he spoke on the strength which the Gospel gives. From that he passed to the stirring world conflict which now filled everyone's thoughts. He spoke of the irresistible power sometimes imparted to a people with the knowledge that it has a ruler who likewise is a real leader. The Emperor had done all within human power to avert the war, he said. The Emperor wanted peace, but when he was forced into the war he knew what his position was and understood what the people asked of him, and trusting in his people he did not hesitate to strike a blow for Germany's existence and future.

He spoke of the nation's sense of duty, which is the first prerequisite of victory. The people know what they must do when duty calls. "We must thank God for His infinite grace in thus making us united and strong in our time of trial, in our direst but also our greatest hour." Then he touched upon the spirit of the soldiers and their firm resolve to fight to the last drop of blood and not to give way until the last man and the last horse has fallen. He spoke with simple eloquence, no flowers and no phrases. He spoke manfully with cheerful confidence and an unshakable faith in victory, and the German words roused a ringing echo from the old French houses opposite. *"Vater miser, der du hist im Himmel... Der Herr segne Euch und behüte Euch."* In conclusion another psalm was intoned. It was sung in swelling, rousing tones, as if they were on the eve of the triumphal entry through the Brandenburger Tor in Berlin. Here they stood, these broad shouldered, sturdy Teutons, in the hey-day of youth and strength, with eyes flashing beneath their helmets - eyes whose vision would perhaps be dimmed for ever to-morrow in the trenches. I thrilled with emotion as I heard the ringing song, and thought: These men may know the art of dying, but their nation can never die. And this thought led to the reflection: I am sorry for the Powers who have combined to destroy it; what rivers of blood will flow before they learn to understand that their aim, the destruction of Germany, is unattainable!

> *"Und wenn die Welt voll Teufel wär*
> *Und woll'n uns gar verschlingen,*
> *So fürchten wir uns nicht so sehr,*
> *Es soll uns doch gelingen.*
> *Der Fürst dicscr Welt,*
> *Wie saur er sich stellt,*
> *Tut er uns doch nichts,*
> *Das macht, er ist gericht,*
> *Ein Wörtlein kann ihn fallen."*[19]

Army chaplains almost form a race of their own. They are always cheerful, always wideawake, self-sacrificing and dauntless. They are the

---

19. *And if the world with devils teemed,*
     All watching to devour us,
     Yet are our hearts from fear redeemed,
     Not they can overpower us!
     And let the Prince of ill
     Look grim as e'er he will,
     He harms us not one whit —
     For why? His doom is writ;
     A Word shall quickly slay him.
     (*Congregational Hymn Book* version, slightly modified.)

soldiers' priests, they preach for the living and comfort and console the dying. Creed no longer plays a part, the Protestant and Catholic chaplains arc like brothers together. There is no rivalry between them, they have all *one* God and *one* aim, the welfare of their country. One often sees chaplains hurrying along on horseback, a cross round their neck, the black felt hat on their heads and the white and violet band round the left arm of the field tunic. They not infrequently wear the Iron Cross. This no doubt means that they have stood up in the midst of the shell fire and spoken of the Resurrection and the Life, or that with immovable calm they have remained at their post and addressed the congregation when enemy aviators were flying overhead. Or maybe that they have this very night in cold and rain crept between shrubs and bushes to reach the trenches and celebrate High Mass on Sunday for their occupants.

Once more my thoughts fly away to our own immortal times of greatness. Pictures of solemn Carolin chaplains in boots and spurs seem to rise up before me, men who in strength and fortitude of soul were an example to the soldiers to be resolute and loyal unto death. I seemed to see as through a mist the regimental chalice placed upon the altar built up of silver tymbals, round which kneeling men and haughty officers throng to listen humbly to the Lutheran confession of faith, and to vow in ringing tones that in life and death alike they believe in the forgiveness of sins, the resurrection of the body and life everlasting. The battlefields are a sterile soil for atheism. Man is then too near his Maker and to the threshold of eternity.

Our service ended quietly; no airmen came to disturb us, even the guns seemed to respect the day of rest. We took a walk round the town. The Town Hall, which looks on to an open space, has been turned into quarters for the LandSturm Guard, which is changed at midday. Officers also come in and out to receive their orders. Close by the Chief Command has been accommodated in the *Palais de Justice*, whilst another house has been chosen for the headquarters for the Commandant of the Lines of Communication. One sees no new or handsome houses. The streets look dull, with their monotonous, old-fashioned frontages, not old enough to bear the picturesque impress of antiquity. The only really attractive structure is the Church of Saint Morille; it looks old enough, in fact I was told by a native that it dates from the thirteenth century. Its facade is richly ornamented, but also bears the marks of bullets from 1792, so I was told. The interior of the church is gloomy and typically Catholic with its mighty pillars, its figures of the Virgin, its altar ornaments, memorial tablets and votive tablets to the Virgin.

Facing the church is a statue of Taine on a pedestal, the front of which illustrates his genius reclining against a pile of bronze folios. Over the doorway of a house close by I read the words: *"Hippolyte Adolphe Taine de l'Académie Française est né dans cette maison le 21 avril 1828."*

By the side of Taine's statue stood three elderly citizens, busily chatting together. What they were talking of I do not know, but perhaps it was not hard to guess. I greeted them and they returned my greeting. I asked for some information about the church and about Taine, and from this we passed on to more practical subjects. It seemed that in common with many others they had decided to stop at Vouziers. Those who had left the town, about three thousand, had in their opinion acted unwisely, for they would find their houses and furniture ruined, whilst those who remained behind were able to safeguard their interests and property. Of the coming winter they hardly dared to think. It would be terrible, and would bring famine and destitution in its wake. "But the Prussians will have to provide us with our daily bread." Their political views practically amounted to this: France cannot gain anything by this war, but can lose much; but France will fight nevertheless as long as there is a soldier left. To my question whether they ever received any news, they replied: *"Non, monsieur, nous sommes des zéros."* One feels the deepest compassion for these unhappy people whom God and the world seem to have deserted.

On October 5th I had an opportunity of witnessing the sitting of a court martial of the Chief Command of the Army. It had to deal with five cases of offences. This is not much for a whole army, when one knows that the slightest theft from a house is punished with the utmost severity. A more refreshing intermezzo is furnished by pay-day, which occurs three times a month. Both officers and men receive in wartime nearly double their peace pay. Pay-day happened to come on one of the days I spent at Vouziers. The money is paid in notes, but also in coin. The day after, the field post had plenty to do, as from this single place alone the soldiers sent 250,000 marks by registered letter to their homes. A very large percentage of the enormous sums swallowed up by the army thus returns to Germany.

CHAPTER XI
TO BELGIUM

I HAD NOW camped long enough among the splendid officers of Duke Albrecht's army, and began to long for fresh adventures. General von Seckendorff passed through Vouziers daily, and had courteously asked me just to tell him when I wanted to accompany him back to Sédan. But he always travelled northward at a late hour, and it so happened that one fine morning I suddenly felt inclined to start off. I went round and took a few groups at the railway station, such as French prisoners at work, a few doctors and nurses, an artillery transport train and a company of railway reserves. The station commander, Lieut. -Col. Böhlau, accompanied me. At first I thought I should like to take a military train to Sédan, but abandoned this plan on discovering that the next train would not start for several hours. The Colonel then made another suggestion. Since no officer's car was leaving during the day I might accompany one of the large motor-wagons which carry the field post to the postal station at Sédan. An excellent idea! It was sure to be interesting to see how the field post was managed. The mail was not starting for a little while, and I even had time to lunch with my old set: von Behr, von Eichstedt and von Tschammer. I thanked these gentlemen, took leave with the customary *auf Wiedersehen* and hurried away. Two young artillery lieutenants, Müller and Fuchs, had also been allowed to make use of the mail car. They had been so long under incessant fire that they needed a rest. One of them had been in many hard fights and wore his Iron Cross. They were both jolly and pleasant, and we were all three seated, with none too much room to spare, behind the mail-bags, which otherwise filled the entire vehicle up to the roof. We thus had a view to the rear over and on each side of an orderly standing on the platform. What was happening on the road ahead of us we could not see, but I had by

French prisoners at Vouziers.

Arms and knapsacks of dead and wounded - Vouziers.

now become familiar with its varied life. So off we went, rattling and jolting, towards Sédan.

These wondrous bags, what tales did they not have to tell of the life at the front! One almost seemed to hear the old refrain: *"Lieb Vaterland, magst ruhig sein!"* How often had I not seen the soldiers sitting over their letters home - at the Cuirassier barracks in Vouziers at tables rigged up with planks and trestles, in streets and yards, using the mudguards of the cars or baggage-wagon cases as desks, or in subterranean caves behind the trenches, where they lay on their stomachs and wrote with their notebooks as backing for the paper. If one were to take out a mail-bag haphazard and make it into a big, thick volume, and then read this volume from cover to cover, one could not fail to be impressed with the merry and cheerful outlook of the German soldiers, their faith in victory and their national vigour. One would look in vain for a single word, a single suggestion of complaint over long marches, excessive burdens, intolerable discipline, unnecessary drill at odd moments in between the lighting, insufficient or bad food. One would find that those who talk of marches, say that had they been double as long they would yet have managed them. As to weight of equipment, it is simply not mentioned. Discipline! If anybody mentioned it, he would say something like this: "Thank goodness we have officers who know what they want and take out of us what we can give, who punish if there is anything to be punished and who dare maintain that absolute discipline amongst the troops without which no army can win," "These qualities," they would add, "are possessed by our officers, and that is why we obey them, love them, trust them blindly, and gladly follow them into the fire." Germans understand that silk gloves are out of place in a military education. They demand from their officers that inflexible, iron severity which is necessary for the proper moulding of an army into a whole, into an ever-ready instrument, and they do not permit antimilitary agitation to foment that passive resistance against the leaders which is often discernible elsewhere. The German knows his power. He knows that it is the military discipline which pervades every fibre of the country's body that has given them their strength. But they are not slaves, they are masters primarily of their own will and of their own actions.

Does anyone think that this imaginary volume would contain a single word of fussy and squeamish complaints about food? No, one would read nothing but humorous and almost affectionate jests about the *Erbsenkanone* ("pea-shooter"), the field kitchen, which is always there at the right moment when the soldier's belly is empty. Doubtless there are many who have not touched food for forty-eight hours, if they have been lying under heavy fire in a trench. But to complain would never occur to them. They would only say what a wonderful sensation it was to get the hot pea-soup with its lumps of fat into their stomachs. Besides, they would probably have forgotten all about their misfortune by the time they wrote.

This is the way they talk in their letters. And probably they write about the shell fire and the bayonet charges as if they were part of the routine of daily life. Every letter in the big book would contain affectionate but never sentimental greetings to father and mother, to wife and children, to sweethearts and sisters. So we were in excellent company, Müller, Fuchs and I, as we sat there and shook and jolted among the mail-bags on the twenty-eight mile journey to Sédan. That mail wagon carried a few days' war history, disintegrated into atoms. I could not help time and again casting a glance at the bags and wondering what they had to say. I thought of the many farewell greetings they contained from soldiers for whom the fatal bullet had been cast and who would write no more field postcards, of the greetings from the wounded who would soon lose consciousness for ever, to be carried out to the great common grave in the local churchyard.

My companions had much to tell about these things. But everything moved so swiftly and the wagon rattled so noisily that I forgot the greater part as fresh impressions came crowding into my mind. One of my new friends, after some fight was over, had gone up to a French soldier who lay on the ground with a nasty wound in the abdomen. He had stopped to see if he could help the wounded man before the ambulance arrived. The Frenchman wept bitterly and pulled out of his breast pocket the portrait of his sweetheart, which he showed the German officer. After he had looked at it eagerly for a couple of minutes, it slipped out of his benumbed hand and he sank back and died. Frenchmen also know how to die, and there are no words to express their bravery and heroic contempt of death.

For three weeks Müller and Fuchs had shared the rough and the smooth together in their entrenched artillery position. At first they had suffered great hardships from rain and wet, but once they and their men had had time to dig themselves in properly, like moles under the earth, all had been well - especially when they had found some small stoves in neighbouring villages and installed them in their burrows. They soon became so accustomed to the shell fire that they slept like logs even when the air was filled with thunder and the impact caused the ground to tremble around them - that is, of course, if it was their turn to sleep! On Sunday, the 4th October, the day we heard Pastor Marguth preach, divine service had been held in the church at Cernay. Müller and Fuchs were there, and they told me that it was one of the most moving scenes they had ever witnessed. Too much light was not allowed, and on the altar alone a couple of candles were burning. But it was full moon and clear weather. The moonlight streamed in through the windows and illuminated the aisle and pillars and the weather-beaten faces of the soldiers who had come in from their trenches or transport wagons. Meanwhile French shells were falling in the village, and there was a horrible rending and roaring from the explosions and the collapsing houses. But the chaplain did not permit himself to be disturbed. He seemed not to notice the pandemonium outside. He spoke without a quiver in his voice of the peace in God and the duty to one's country. The soldiers listened immovable, and when the strains of the last hymn had died away and the lights had been put out they dispersed down the little streets and alleys, weirdly illumined by the moonlight and the fire from the burning houses.

Thus the journey to Sédan was greatly shortened, and for my part I should have liked it to be double as long. But the mail van pulled up at the railway station, and there I had to say good-bye to my two interesting companions. On the platform stood Major von Plato at his post, jolly and cheerful as usual.

"Tell me, my dear Major, is there any decent means of getting to Namur without having to encumber an officer's car?"

"There are no direct trains to Namur, but in twenty minutes there will be an ambulance train which can take you some distance into Belgium, and once you get so far, no doubt you can get along some other way. Of course, you must first have permission from the surgeon in charge of the train."

Whilst I was waiting for the doctor I went to have a look at a troop train - an infantry battalion, or something like it, crowded into third-class carriages. These travellers had come from Königsberg, and had swept East Prussia clear of the enemy, so they said, and now they were on the way to Verdun. Every compartment, with normally six seats, now also carried six men. But instead of sitting they were lying down, two on the floor, two on the seats, and two in the luggage racks. They were in the most exuberant spirits, and the din was fearful.

Presently a messenger came to tell me that my surgeon had arrived and I went to see him. Judge of my surprise when I found it was Chief Staff Surgeon Dr. Fröhlich, whom I had met at Sédan and Vouziers!

"May I come by your train?" I asked.

"Why, of course, to Breslau, if you like."

"But, of course, you are going through Belgium?"

"Yes, as far as Libramont, then we turn eastward and in four days we are at Breslau."

Dr. Fröhlich had now been travelling for some time between that city and Vouziers with wounded officers and men. Now he had upwards of three hundred patients on board, whom he was to drop here and there on the way until only a few remained to the journey's end, where they would be taken charge of at some home hospital. That done, he would return as rapidly as possible with an empty hospital train to fetch a fresh batch of wounded. He is therefore constantly on the move with his staff of doctors and assistants, and he was very pleased to have company for a while.

Time is up and the train starts with military punctuality, after we have taken a hearty farewell of the cheery Major von Plato, Presently we settled down in Dr. Frohlich's compartment, which almost resembled a little study. One wall was taken up by a sofa, the other by a couple of chairs, and a writing-table decorated with flowers in empty cartridge cases and still fresh, having been sent from the doctor's home. Other tokens of his domestic ties were portraits of his wife and children and of a son and nephew fighting at Rheims. Here also lay an open diary, in which the doctor notes the incidents of his good work and enters such observations and discoveries as he may make in the course of his practice, together with various suggestions for improvements in hygienic arrangements in the held, which may be found of use in future wars - if any!

We speed past a wrecked road bridge and a railway bridge which has been treated in the same way, and watch an airman ascending from earth in elegant circles, his wings tinted red by the evening sky. Here is another troop train - there is seemingly no end to all these soldiers. Wherever one goes and whatever time it is, everywhere one finds myriads of soldiers as in a gigantic ant-heap. By degrees twilight descends upon us, and the pretty scenery through which we pass evades my gaze.

It is now dark. We sit still and chat whilst the train speeds on and the hours pass. The hours are short in Dr. Frohlich's company, but the train is interminably long - it consists of forty-two coaches. At Carignan, where the line swings round towards the Belgian frontier, and where the ground begins to rise, the train is divided into two sections, each drawn by two locomotives. We felt a tremendous pulling and tugging in our half. We are now on the "war road," whose acquaintance I had made on the journey to Sédan. The wounded, dreaming about battlefields, bombs, and shells, must think that they have suddenly been overtaken by an earthquake, to put a finishing touch to their adventures. The cartridge cases with their flowers came hopping down from the table and we ourselves get a terrible shaking. But we are just as cheerful, and there are no pauses in our talk except when Dr. Fröhlich goes his round among the wounded.

After a plain but excellent supper we retired to rest. At Bertrix the two halves of the train were put together once more, and the poor wounded soldiers are brought a stage nearer to the homeland.

It was four o'clock when Dr. Fröhlich came in to call me, and a moment later we stopped at Libramont. Here our ways parted. But before saying good-bye we paid a visit to the kindly, cheerful sisters, who had steaming coffee ready at the station for the many travellers. Then we asked the station commander whether he could help me to get to Namur.

"No, not the whole way, but as far as Jemelle. Once you get there, you will have no difficulty in finding somebody to take you the rest of the distance."

"Good; when does the train start?"

"Now, immediately. But it isn't exactly a train, only four coupled locomotives ordered from Jemelle."

I have indulged in many modes of locomotion, from the camels of Takla-makan to the rickshaws of Kioto, but it is a solemn fact that I had never yet travelled on a locomotive, and I therefore accepted the offer with the greatest alacrity. So I took farewell of the excellent Dr. Fröhlich, and was conducted with my baggage by a lantern-bearing Landsturm man across a few railway tracks to the four locomotives. The leading engine, which I climbed on to, had the tender in front. I thus had a clear view of the line and of the landscape which by degrees unfolded itself before me. But it was a cold and draughty journey. A thin coating of hoar-frost lay over the ground and its whiteness was emphasised by the moon, which cold and solemn floated above the tormented earth.

The driver and fireman were sturdily built fellows, deliberate and imperturbable. Their sooty faces betrayed no emotion, no anxiety, but they kept their eyes glued on to the line ahead, ready to stop the engine on the slightest suspicion. They were not exactly overworked, for lately their duties had been reduced considerably; but a little while previously they assured me that they had had to work forty eight hours without a break. The firing of *franctireurs* along the line had ceased. They could now travel with a certain sense of security, but had nevertheless to be careful.

The night is calm and still. We meet long military trains, looking weird and fantastic in the unaccustomed perspective, and the stations, at Hatrival, at Merwart, are encumbered with endless goods trains, now empty. Day gradually begins to dawn. Gardens and woods begin to take shape, and the leafy crowns of trees become more plainly outlined against the sky and the white ground. We pass over a wrecked bridge which has been repaired by German *pioniers*. Here comes Grupont with its arched bridge. It grows lighter and lighter. I begin to long for the sun and its warmth. The landscape is exceedingly pretty, with its wavy undulations and its little coppices and meadows dotted about. The driver offers me a little three-legged stool, and as the fireman opens the furnace door to throw in a few shovelfuls of coal, he smiles at me when I take the opportunity of warming my hands a moment.

Forriéres! Now the sun rises like a glittering golden ball, and gives colour to trees, fields and pastures, houses, gardens, and Landsturm men, now able once more to turn down their coat-collars.

We arrive at Jemelle and step down. I thank my friends for their excellent company, but a tip is not accepted. On the platform comes a N.C.O. and asks what my business is. I show him my *Ausweis*, and he asks me to wait in the station commandant's office until his arrival - it is now only 6.30 A.M. Inside a friendly stove is burning, in front of which I settle in an arm-chair and soon fall asleep.

After a while Captain Haaf, the commandant, comes marching in and rouses me, mildly surprised at finding a total stranger in possession of his own office. But we are soon friends.

"When is there a train to Namur?" I ask.

"At 11.30 we have a supply train going through, and if you like to travel by that I shall be pleased to put on a passenger coach."

"Good, that will suit me excellently." The Captain then took me to a Belgian restaurant close by, where a couple of breezy and talkative women soon served up a first-class breakfast. The Captain told me that they did not yet feel quite safe from the attentions of *franctireurs*. A few days previously a rifle bullet had been aimed at the station-house in Jemelle. The culprit was seized and court-martialled, but his fate had not yet been settled. In the neighbourhood of Houyet a band of Frenchmen had recently attacked some Germans, and a punitive expedition of 130 men had been sent out after them.

Time is now up and the train steams away through the hilly country, its little villages and its cattle grazing in the pastures. As yet there is nothing to remind one of war but the Landsturm men on guard along the line, the railway troops at work here and there, and the troop trains halting at the stations. At Marloie one was standing in the station and we pulled up alongside of it. One of the carriages was taken up by Red Cross nurses, and as chance would have it, my window stopped right opposite one of theirs, A couple of the nurses were propped up against each other fast asleep, another couple were reading, the rest were knitting. One of them looked out through the open window. She looked very sweet in her light dress and the Red Cross on the arm.

"Where have you come from and where are you oft to?" I asked.

"We come from Berlin and are going to Sédan," she answered.

"But surely there are hardly any wounded left in Sédan now; most of them have been taken into Germany."

"Yes, we have heard that is so, but no doubt plenty more will be coming down from the front. Where have you come from yourself?"

"From the country south of Sédan."

"Are you a German?"

"No, I am a Swede." In the end I could not help introducing myself to the young lady and her companions. Conversation was soon in full swing and we had just got to know each other nicely when my train slowly glided out of the station. I just had time to wish them success in their charitable work, and in reply was greeted with friendly wavings from their window - and so that little idyll came to an end.

On the way between Aye and Hogne some men belonging to a fatigue party made signs that they wanted to come on board. The train slowed down so that they could jump on to the step and get a free ride with their picks, spades, and rifles.

To the left the country falls away in enormous flat wooded waves which die away on the horizon in a haze of dark green, light green, greenish blue, and bluish grey. Our train takes us through little woods and shrubs, coppices, clumps of fir and oak, and tunnels blasted through the solid rock. Now and then we come across a crowd of Belgian workmen at work on the embankment. The little signal-boxes along the line are guarded by Landsturm soldiers in pickets of ten to twelve men.

The little town of Ciney boasts an unusually handsome station building, round which things seem livelier than elsewhere. Sometimes we meet colossal empty trains with straw in the goods trucks and benches piled up topsy-turvy. One wonders whether they have been to carry reinforcements to the besieging army outside Antwerp. Often one sees attractive and well kept kitchen gardens at the stations or between the fine looking stone houses in the villages. At some distance from the railway we sight at length the fort of Naninnes, flying the German flag. Soon after we cross the Meuse by a *Kriegs-Eisenbahnbrücke* (war railway bridge), where we get a view of the remains of the old permanent bridges which were blown up during the first days of the war, and presently we enter the delightful and prettily situated little town of Namur.

In order to get the information I needed, I applied to a Captain, a tall man with snow-white hair and beard, no less a person than professor emeritus Doctor B. Lepsius, who in spite of his age has gone out to the war. He is a great friend of Professor Svante Arrhenius, and looked after me like a father during my short stay in Namur.

After my baggage had been stowed away at an hotel by the railway station, we paid a short visit to the Governor, General von Hirschberg, who had no objection to letting me see one of the forts of the fortress. As companion I had, besides Professor Lepsius, Major Hans Friederich, of the General Staff.

We drove to the northern fortifications and soon arrived at Fort Marchovelette, now called fort No. 1. Namur is, or rather was, surrounded by nine forts. In the Belgian days they were known by definite names, now they are merely numbered. The first impression that one gets of No. 1 is that the destruction has been less complete than in the Port

A doctor, Prof. Capt. Lepsius and a few Sœurs de la Providence in the convent grounds.

Arthur fort where General Kondratenko was killed during the Japanese siege in 1904. I had an opportunity to visit that "eagle's nest" exactly six years ago. It looked like a huge pile of broken stones and rubbish. But on closer examination of No. I, one is astounded at the appalling effect of the fire from the German heavy artillery. The fort is triangular with one apex towards the north-east. Its glacis is covered with barbed wire-netting stretched out to a height of one metre between the iron posts driven vertically into the clay-bound soil. The netting is close, and covers a belt of thirty or forty metres. Inside is the moat, commanded by the fire from galleries in the counterscarp. At length we reach the heart of the fort with casemates for the garrison, armoured turrets for artillery, searchlights and fire control, and an infantry rampart like a belt round the grey cupolas on the summit.

Ten to fifteen metres away, outside the barbed-wire zone, I noticed in the ground the crater of a 42-cm. shell, 30 metres in circumference and about 8 metres deep. On the almost vertical concrete walls of the scarp and counterscarp I saw the marks of shells of more normal dimensions - streaky scars radiating from the point of impact. Splinters of shells of various dimensions were still lying about. One queer-looking fragment of a 42-cm. shell was so heavy that I had to exert myself to as much as shift it. But then one of these coalboxes" weighs when whole hundreds of kilos. A little splinter which I took away with me showed that the metal had been expanded to about one-fourth of its original thickness.

Everything regarding the giant mortars is kept secret. But this much I was told, that their range is enormous. The vertex of the trajectory is several kilometres above ground. The ranging is done with great precision, but of course one must be prepared for not hitting the target with the first shot or two. "Misses" are, however, very rare. The most exhaustive calculations and observations are made before the shots are fired. Observers are posted at suitable points as near the objective as possible; they are in communication with the gunners and report the point of impact. When a 42-cm. shell comes pounding down from a height of several kilometres, there is nothing built by human hands which can resist it.

In fort No. 1 we saw a good instance of the effect of these gigantic projectiles. One shot had struck the annular armour round the cupola of the largest armoured turret, had passed through the half-metre of metal as if it had been butter and had then continued through a bed of concrete five metres thick. This shell was also provided with a *Zünder mit Verzögerung*.[20] If the fuse is set for retarded ignition the explosion only takes place a couple of seconds after the impact. If one cannot make sure that the projectile has first penetrated the matérial to be destroyed, its effect, at least on armoured concrete, would not be very disastrous.

The engineers from Krupp's were now busy repairing the forts both at Namur and Liège, and a large number of men were engaged in this work. By repairing the occupied fortresses the Germans are strengthening their strategical position and can release considerable forces for the actual fighting line.

The effect of the heavy artillery on the defending garrison will be realised when it is stated that at one fort seventy per cent of the complement were killed, whilst the remaining thirty per cent were severely injured. As we all know, the brave Commander of Liège, General Leman, was wounded in this way. In another fort were found forty bodies, which showed no trace of injury. It was evident that these men had succumbed to the gases of the projectiles or had been choked by the concrete dust which is said to whirl up in the most appalling manner and to penetrate everywhere. The air pressure had also flung many soldiers against the walls of the casemates, and they were subsequently found with broken skulls.

One of the lessons which may be said to have been learnt in the present war is that even the most modern fortifications equipped with the most superb armoured turrets are useless when opposed by artillery of the calibre of the great German mortars. The circumstance that the projectile does not burst until it has penetrated into or even through the concrete bed gives rise to a havoc which challenges all attempt at description. Everything within the "bomb-proof arch" thus struck is

20. Fuse timed for retarded ignition.

rent asunder and destroyed without leaving a trace. The projectile first operates from above downward, and then from below upward through the explosion.

The 42-cm. mortars are brought up to their emplacements on rails laid down especially for their conveyance.

From fort No. 1 we returned to the town, which is at its prettiest at the point where the Sambre falls into the Meuse. South of the Sambre an exceedingly picturesque road winds its way up to the crest of the Citadelle height, on the slope of which the Stadion is also situated. Of the magnificent Grand Hotel Namur-Citadelle, which looked down from the top of the hill, there is nothing left but a skeleton of iron girders and brick walls. The proprietor was a German, and the Belgians suspected that on the approach of the Germans from the northeast he signalled to his countrymen. The building was therefore burnt down. But the view is left, and it is nothing short of superb, especially up the Meuse valley with its innumerable villas and châteaux lining the banks in the direction of Dinant, which are, or rather were, inhabited by wealthy Belgians, for most of them have gone away on account of the German occupation.

The town of Namur itself has only suffered slightly from the ravages of war. The *Hôtel de Ville* has become a ruin, like many houses in its neighbourhood. But it is estimated that only about twenty houses in all have been wrecked by shell fire. The Germans have been blamed for the destruction they have wrought among human habitations, churches, public buildings and objects of artistic and historic value. Such losses are, of course, exceedingly regrettable. But neither attacker nor defender can pay any attention to such considerations when the fate of his country is at stake. If it is noticed by an armed force advancing to seize a place serving as a *point d'appui* to the enemy, that the church tower is being used as an observation post, the church tower is shot down. When the Belgians suspected that Marche-les-Dames, the château of the Duchess of Ahrenberg, near Namur, famous for its priceless art treasures, was used for signalling purposes, they burnt it down. When it is a question of rendering the position of an invading army more difficult or of delaying its advance or cutting its lines of communication, the defender seems to shun no matérial sacrifices, even though he himself is the principal sufferer. Of the numberless bridges blown up by the Belgians in their own country, all in order to delay their enemy, there must be many which were of no importance whatever to the Germans. By so doing, the defenders brought upon themselves a treble loss, namely, the loss of the bridge itself, the cost of removal of débris, and the building of a new bridge after the end of the war - all this caused by a single blasting charge. But the defending army, which is always inferior, is nevertheless compelled, in a far greater measure than the attacking army, to effect wholesale destruction, more especially of buildings of architectural or historic value, whilst as often as not it lies in the interest of the attacker to preserve them. The blowing up of bridges is in itself a vandalism, but is fully justified if it is thought that strategic advantages can be obtained thereby. The destruction wrought by the Germans in their advance has partly been involuntary, and has partly had its cause in the conduct of the civilian population. But the Germans have never destroyed simply for the love of destruction. Assertions to the contrary are intended to create false notions, and it may be assumed with tolerable certainty that if the enemy armies had the opportunity of penetrating into Germany, they would, to say the least, bring about as much destruction as has been wrought in the countries now occupied by German armies.

During the first period after the capture of Namur all windows facing the street had to be kept alight after dark, whilst the streets themselves were not lighted. The consequence was that people out of doors were not clearly discernible, but that if anyone were to fire from a window, he would be discovered immediately. At first all doors facing the street had to be left unlocked. But after a time the inhabitants, out of fear of the soldiers, asked to be allowed to close their doors, and this request was granted. At the time of my visit, that is to say on October 8th, Namur wore a very animated aspect. As late as half-past seven in the evening most shops were still open and the streets were well filled. Even the young ladies, who at first did not dare to go out, began to show themselves on the pavements. But the prohibition against being out-of-doors after 9 P.M. without special permit was still in force. On account of the many uniforms, military motor-cars and transport trains Namur looked more like a German garrison town than anything else. And yet this appearance was belied by the many white flags floating from the windows, especially in the principal streets, which indicated that the inhabitants of those particular houses had agreed to accept the new order of things. When one travels through Belgium one must harden one's heart, for at every step one is reminded of the misfortune of having lost one's liberty in one's own country. And one thinks with horror of how it would feel to be placed in the same situation. A moral judgment is now being passed over Europe. Woe to the people which has not in time put its house in order, or which relies on paper treaties and declarations when force sits in the judgment seat and when none but the strong and wakeful inspire respect in *all* directions.

In the evening there was some sort of festivity at the officers' mess of the 87th Landwehr Regiment. It was attended by the officers of the Higher Command who happened to be in the town. I also had the honour to be present, and spent a couple of very agreeable hours between Generals von Hirschberg and Rathgen.

On the 9th October I made an excursion by motor-car to the magnificent and wealthy convent of Champion, founded in 1834 and now the home of 180 *Sœurs de la Providence*. Its great hall was gorgeously decorated in white and gold, and had stained-glass windows. Many wounded warriors had been housed here, and we paused more especially before two Belgian soldiers from fort No. 1, who had been badly burnt on face and hands, but were now on the road to recovery. After some considerable hesitation I was at last allowed to photograph a few of the charming and hospitable nuns in the convent garden.

We thereupon looked in for a while at the really magnificent *Hôpital Militaire* with its one hundred and fifty wards and rooms, its seven hundred wounded, its twenty-three doctors and one hundred and forty male and female 'sick' attendants. Right from the beginning there have only been eighteen cases of tetanus, most of them attended with fatal results. All possible nationalities were represented amongst the patients.

But from England there was only one patient, a handsome youth, badly wounded by several bullets. He seemed to be in a deep sleep and his face was pale and drawn with suffering. A couple of days before he had lost a chum, and one of the nurses told us that he had felt dreadfully lonely after his friend's bed had stood empty. He seemed indeed terribly alone amongst all these strangers. I could not take my eyes off him, and it was touching to see how he lay there waiting - for what, I wonder? He seemed to lie there as the innocent incarnation of a policy which is doomed to die, and for which he himself had laid down his life.

A band was beating an old Hessian tattoo in the square between the cathedral and the Government building when at half-past two, after dining with the Governor, I stepped into the car which he had kindly placed at my disposal. I was going to Brussels *via* Waterloo, and was to arrive before dusk. Of Major Friederich I obtained an excellent map of Belgium, and after saying good-bye to the venerable but still youthful Professor Lepsius and my other new friends, I soon left the town behind me. I had with me a chauffeur and an orderly, both armed with carbines. The car was a little grey monster with flag and streamer. As regards speed, there seemed to be no limits to its powers. We drove, nay, we flew, at over fifty English miles an hour when travelling at our fastest. I wondered whether the object was to make the aim of *franctireurs* more difficult by presenting them with a more swiftly moving target.

Villages, gardens and fields tore past, and the pace was too great for careful observations and notes. But it is a delightful and exhilarating sensation; one becomes intoxicated with the sensation of speed, and any feeling of danger vanishes with the desire to drive on faster, and still faster!

On the left we first pass fort No. 4, the repairs to which have now been practically completed. The high road is in excellent condition, and there is a little traffic in the shady avenues. Life seems slowly to be returning to its old grooves. In front of farms and houses by the roadside we notice German soldiers engaged in more or less laborious but always friendly and often jocular conversation with Belgian women, or playing with their children after the fashion of uncles. The country is flat, with hardly noticeable undulations. In the fields, which make a pleasing picture with the farm hands busily at work, the crop has been piled up in enormous cylindrical stacks crowned with shallow conical hoods intended to keep the water off the corn. At Gembloux - with its memories of 1815 - a Red Cross flag almost fills the entire street, with the armed Landsturm men keeping watch below in their shining helmets.

The stone houses in the villages look very substantial, but are far less picturesque and pretty than our own red cottages with the dark pine forest as background. At Wawre a house has been wrecked here and there. By the roadside is the lonely grave of a dead soldier. In front of it, on the road, an old woman is driving a barrow drawn by a dog. And so one impression succeeds the other.

After Overyssche the road turns off sharp to the left and runs through La Hulpe and a number of other villages, until at last we reach the famous battlefield of Belle Alliance.[21] This spot is one of the sights for those who visit Brussels. In peace time there are on an average 450 visitors a day to the great hall erected outside Waterloo, in which a gigantic panorama, measuring 110 metres in circumference, gives an excellent idea of one of the most dramatic moments of the battle. Attention is especially directed to the group representing Marshal Ney's furious onslaught with the French Guards against Wellington's artillery and infantry positions south-west of Mont St. Jean. The foreground is strewn with soldiers and horses lying dead amongst the grass and lumber, and the whole has been carried out in natural size, with detached life-size figures gradually merging with bewilderingly telling effect into the painted canvas and its excellent perspective. Some way off one sees Napoleon on his white charger, attended by his Staff, and in the far distance the old Hussar General Blücher with his Prussians, who on that day saved England from perdition. One sees the burning villages around, the roads with their avenues of trees and the shady groves at Ohain and Château de Goumont.

21. The German name for the Battle of Waterloo (Translator).

But reality itself is after all more interesting. I walk up to the crest of the hill, some sixty metres high, on which stands a lion of colossal dimensions, unveiled ten years after the battle by the Netherlands Government. The lion is cast from captured French guns, and its base merely bears the inscription: XVIII June MDCCCXV. It is not the conquered Titan who is symbolised by this pompous lion, but the united powers who made an end of his career. The wounded bronze eagle on his piece of rock, recently put up by the French in memory of the battle, illustrates in a dignified manner the glorious but unhappy struggle of Napoleon and the French arms. But the lion remains at his post and looks out defiantly upon the historic landscape.

Around us we now see the actual panorama with its shaded roads, its villages and church towers, its gardens and fields. Some of these are green - where clover or sugar-beet is grown; others blend in brown and grey - where the crops have been brought in and the plough has furrowed the soil afresh, and harvesters, ploughmen, grazing cattle, and other rural scenes form a picture which seems to speak only of peace and tranquillity.

Dusk is descending over the tormented, blood-drenched earth and the wind sweeps dismally over fields and hills where the echo of the ancient guns and the rattle of harness and stirrups, crossed lances, and doughty sword-thrusts died away just on a hundred years ago. A feeling akin to reverence steals over the wanderer on this battlefield, still marked with the monuments put up by those who wished to honour their dead. Everything recalls his name, that great name still living as vivid and as fresh as ever, and undimmed by the dark nights which for well nigh a hundred years have clothed in their shadows the country between Mont St. Jean and Planchenois.

Now German soldiers are on guard at the battlefield of Waterloo and its historic monuments. Once more the Prussians have taken charge of the spot where the bravery and loyalty of their ancestors under the iron will of Blücher broke Napoleon's strength and gave the British general a victory which he alone would never have been able to achieve. Wellington's country followed the policy which had been its lodestar ever

A group of fugitives.

273

On the way to Ghent and the Channel.

since the time of William of Orange. All that can jeopardise England's supremacy on the high seas must be crushed - if possible by foreign arms. When the powers of the Continent have weakened one another with war, England has stepped in and reaped the harvest. Her position in the world has been gained more through felicitous combinations of circumstances than through any efforts and sacrifices of her own. It is only when Belgium has seemed near to falling into the hands of some strong continental power that England has felt obliged to put her hand to the plough, for her own skin has then been threatened. But the intervention has then been effected under the cloak of the plea of defending the minor states against the enemy's violation of the rights of nations. At the beginning of the nineteenth century France was too great and powerful for England. Its Emperor must therefore be crushed for all time. Hence the vanquished monarch was placed in a cage on a crag in the ocean, and his gaoler obeyed but too promptly the orders he received from London. Now the centenary is to be celebrated with the crushing of Germany. But the success of a hundred years ago is not being repeated.

Hush, is not that the thunder of the guns of Antwerp? We listen. No, all is still. My chauffeurs, still with the poor captive lion, cannot understand what has happened. Daily for the past two weeks they assure me they have heard the guns, and now all is suddenly still. We do not even see the glare of burning houses northward. Perhaps it is the wind and fog. My companions have been told that during the previous night 1500 shells had been flung into the unhappy city, where the destruction must have been appalling. However, I say to myself, even the German artillery will need some time to take a place like Antwerp, which, according to English and French sources, is the world's strongest fortress and absolutely impregnable.

We jumped into the car once more and quickly covered the remaining eleven English miles to Brussels. The road is paved with stone, and seems one long street lined with continuous rows of houses. The electric tramways are running and entire trains pass us filled with Germans and Belgians. Villages and suburbs here follow one another in endless succession, and the traffic becomes livelier. Grey-clad sentries with fixed bayonets are everywhere to be seen, but all is quiet and peaceful. Yet we almost feel the covert hatred in the glances directed on our military car and its German flag. We meet proud women with heads held high and faces set, old ladies in mourning and frowning elderly men with fists clenched in their pockets.

The shadows of night were falling when we reached the capital of the German Governor-General of Belgium. But the streets were well lighted, as were the windows of shops and restaurants. There were plenty of people about, but we saw no vehicles which were not occupied by German officers and men.

We drive up to the corner of *rue de la Loi*, where we are stopped by a double sentry. I show my paper, they step aside, and we drive up to the Palace of Ministers. "Where does the Governor-General live?" I ask my chauffeur, and he answers that we shall be there in a minute. He stops outside the *Ministère des Sciences et des Arts*. In the gateway stands a strong guard. I am taken across a courtyard and into a long corridor with German name-plates on the doors. On one I see the name of Lieutenant Massebus, and it is him I want to see, for he is one of the adjutants. He told me that the Governor-General had spent the day outside the beleaguered city of Antwerp, but that he was certain to return by nine, if I would renew my visit then.

I accordingly proceeded to the *Palace Hotel*, the 400 rooms of which were nearly all occupied by German officers. At the appointed time I was back in the vestibule leading to the reception rooms of the Governor General. Several officers were waiting there. Amongst them I made the acquaintance of a man whose name I had already heard, namely. Captain Dreger, engineer at Krupps' and joint designer of the 42-cm. mortars. This subject was, of course, taboo, but instead, Captain Dreger told me that he had arrived in Bombay in October, 1908, a week after I had left that city, and that he had literally pursued me via Colombo, Penang, Singapore, Hongkong, and Shanghai - with hardly a week's interval.

"Who is in there just now?" I asked.

"It is Frau Martha Koch, of Aleppo," an adjutant tells me; "she and her husband and children have lived there for thirty years. The Governor-General is an old friend of the family from the time he lived in Turkey. Now she has come to offer her services for the Red Cross."

An officer who had spent the day with the Governor General shook his head as he said: "It's a wonder that we still have him with us. Every day he exposes himself to the most appalling risks. The other day a shell came sweeping along a few metres over his head, but he only smiled." "Yes," declared another officer, "he seems to delight in danger. He always picks out the most dangerous spots - one is almost tempted to think that he wants to be shot. It would be a nice ending to a brilliant career. But whilst the bullets avoid him, they are not so kind to those in his vicinity. He even goes as far as to walk up to the firing line, where he lies down and jokes with the soldiers. Of course, his presence is in the highest degree encouraging to them. One day, accompanied by a soldier, he walked up to one of the enemy's trenches, and although it had been quiet for some time there was no knowing whether it was empty. Fortunately it proved to be so. When his Excellency returned, we reproached him for his daring. 'But there was no one there,' he answered innocently. 'No, but it might quite well have been occupied by enemy soldiers.' 'True, but in that case I should probably not have gone.' Just as we were standing there and talking about him, who should come out into the vestibule but his Excellency himself, who kindly asked me to walk in. I knew him from the *Deutsch-asiatische Gesellschaft* in Berlin, where under his chairmanship I had lectured about my last journey. He, too, greeted me as an old friend, and wanted me to begin with to meet Frau Koch.

The Governor-General of Belgium, Field-marshal General Baron Colmar von der Goltz, formerly in Turkish service, and now once more sent by the Emperor to the Sultan's side, is a man of seventy-one years of age, but he retains his vigour and energy undiminished. He was now thoroughly in his element. He is a powerfully built man, thick-set, and rather below the medium height; he looks out from under his spectacles in a friendly and jovial way and seems to me more like a professor than a general. As a matter of fact he is a very learned man, who has published many books on military history which are ranked very high, especially about the Franco-German war of 1870-71, in which he took part.

When we were alone, he told me the great news of the fall of Antwerp on the same day and of the entry of the German troops at three o'clock in the afternoon. So it was not to be wondered at that we had heard no sound of cannonading from Waterloo. I seized the opportunity of asking at once whether I should be permitted to visit Antwerp, the sooner the better, as it might be interesting as well as instructive to know what a large city which had just capitulated looked like. Why, of course I might! I should be allowed to see practically all I wanted, and if I liked I could return the next morning directly after seven o'clock and would then be told whether I could proceed at once without undue risk.

After we had discussed the situation a few minutes longer I went home. It was then ten o'clock, German time, which, by the way, had been made the standard time after the occupation and was an hour ahead of Belgian time. At nine o'clock all shops and restaurants were closed and the streets were silent and still. Across the square outside the *Palace Hotel* and *Gare du Nord* I was not allowed to go, in fact anyone attempting to do so was politely stopped by a Belgian policeman or even Belgian civilians. The reason was probably that the square must be kept free for military cars, of which there were always a great number lined up outside those buildings.

The tramways cease running at ten o'clock. After that the city is empty and deserted, its population having gone to bed.

CHAPTER XII
ANTWERP THE DAY
AFTER ITS FALL

FOR MANIFOLD AND obvious reasons I will refrain from any attempt to describe the progress of the German army's advance on Antwerp and of the operations which culminated in the conquest of the city on the 9th of October. Still less does it become me to pronounce judgment on the manner in which the Belgians and the English defended this city which the allies thought impregnable, especially since certain parts of the country south of Antwerp had been placed under water. All this will, in due course, be described in the minutest detail by the German General Staff, and also in a more popular form by Germans who took part. For me it is sufficient to say a few words by way of preface to what I saw myself.

To a layman it would appear a hopeless proposition to capture an "impregnable" fortress whose environs have been inundated and whose forts and interior area are defended by considerably over one hundred thousand men, but when that layman learns that the Germans not only achieved the conquest but completed it in thirteen days with almost insignificant losses, he is constrained to admit that the German army evidently possesses qualities which make it greatly superior to the allied armies and which mark it as the most consummate instrument of war of our time. German generals of fortifications themselves admit that Antwerp, if not *the* strongest of the world's fortresses, may nevertheless be said to be one of the three strongest, the other two being Metz and Paris. But before the new heavy artillery even this bulwark of Belgium's and Britain's hope was doomed. Nevertheless, after the officers of the German General Staff, Artillery and Engineers had thoroughly examined the equipment and resources for defence, they were emphatic in asserting that had it been *their* task to defend Antwerp, the city would not have capitulated in thirteen days.

On its two lines of defence, the outer and the inner, Antwerp possessed forty-nine forts and redoubts, all equipped with the latest appliances and devices of modern technological science. The outer line had a circumference of ninety kilometres, and for complete investment would have compelled the attacking army to operate on a front of 120 kilometres. But for a regular siege, carried out according to the accepted rules and canons of warfare, the Germans had no time - they had better use for their troops in other quarters. It is always endeavoured to shorten the attack as much as possible. From the artillery positions in a line with the village Heyst op den Berg the Germans proceeded to bombard the great southern forts - with what effect I will show later. Their resistance was entirely broken. But in order to reach the inner girdle of defence as well as the city itself, it was necessary to force the passage of the Nethe and silence the British artillery on the northern bank of the river. The new line was marked by the towns of Malines, Duffel and Lierre. The Nethe was crossed by soldiers swimming through the ice-cold water with ropes between their teeth in order subsequently to be able to haul the pontoons across. When once this was achieved, Antwerp's fate was sealed. At eleven in the evening of the 7th of October the bombardment of the city itself began. By an express order of the Emperor all buildings of great historic and art value, such as the cathedral, the other churches, the town hall, museums, etc., were to be spared. The zoological gardens were also on the list of items which were not to be bombarded.

The bombardment continued the whole of the 8th of October and fire broke out at several points. In the evening and in the night these vast conflagrations were visible from a great distance and threw their ruddy light against the vapours rising from the sea and the whirling smoke clouds. During the night preceding the 9th October the bombardment increased in violence and continued until the forenoon. Then suddenly, at eleven o'clock, the firing ceased. At three the victorious German troops entered the city with bands playing and colours flying. There was no fighting in the streets and no shooting from windows by civilians. Antwerp suffered no damage beyond that sustained by the bombardment.

This, as I have said, happened at three o'clock on the (9th of October. It was now seven in the morning of the loth, and I was on the way to the *Palais* of the Governor-General in the *Rue de la Loi*, opposite the Park. At the entrance I was met by three cheerful young officers, who greeted me as if we had been boys together. They had been instructed by the Field-marshal to accompany me to Antwerp. "If it pleases you, we will start at once, the car is ready." "Excellent." The chauffeur immediately started the engine and took his place at the wheel. At his side sat a soldier and inside the open car were the three officers and myself. All the Germans carried revolvers. We had also three carbines conveniently at hand. It was plain that the road was considered unsafe, and that the visit to the conquered city was not altogether without danger. As yet we had received no information to show the mood of the inhabitants of the captured city during the night and early morning. To me it is quite the same whether I am shot now or later, one has to die in any case," said Lieut. Classen, who was a great philosopher and full of comical fancies and stories. My other two travelling companions were Lieut. Dr. Hütten of Stettin and Lieut. Dr. Walter Kes of Steglitz. The latter was on the active list even in peace time, and yet a doctor of philosophy, a combination which I am told is very rare.

The moment we were ready we started off. The pace from the first was terrific. The journey was exciting and remarkable in every way. It must not be wondered at that my notes were few and scanty - the blame must be put on the speed at which we were travelling. We sat in a state of tense excitement. To my travelling companions the northern portion, at all events, of this road was unknown, as was the city itself, and a road over which an army has just passed is obviously full of tracks and ruts. Merely to take in what one sees under such circumstances is no bad achievement, and demands, from a layman at least, a certain quickness of perception. Before one had heard the end of the explanation of one phenomenon, something fresh has to be noted, which in a trice cuts off the previous train of thought. The whole becomes a chaos of fragments which leave a confused and dazed general impression. But to follow certain threads from their inception to their logical conclusion is impossible. I will, therefore, give the fragments as they were impressed on my mind, leaving it to the description of subsequent visits to Antwerp to dwell more fully on the most interesting points.

Before we knew where we were, the great city of Brussels, whose streets at this early hour were silent and empty, had been left behind and we were out in the open country; here and there a house or a village, a clump of trees or a haystack, would peep out of the fog still struggling against the morning sunlight. Through a glorious old gateway between two round turrets we tear at the same reckless pace into Malines, or, in German, Mecheln, the seat of the Archbishop and famous for its magnificent cathedral, which traces its history to the latter part of the thirteenth century and whose mighty towers, dating from 1452, had been intended originally to surpass in height all other cathedral towers of Christendom. Yet the height of ninety-seven metres, at which the builders stopped, suffices to impress the beholder. On misty days such as this the cathedral is not visible until one is upon it, but when the air is clear it becomes a landmark for miles around. The tower clock, with its face measuring thirteen and a half metres in diameter, has ceased to mark the fleeting hour. The Germans had found that this point of vantage had been used for observing their artillery positions and the effect of the defenders' fire, hence the tower was bombarded, an adventure which did not suit the sober habits of the clock.

Presently we come to the south portal beneath the giant windows, through the lower part of which a shell has made its way into the church. A couple of projectiles have struck between the window and the pillars of the south aisle. From the north the cathedral has also been fired upon, but this damage was done by the retreating Belgian troops, who were anxious to prevent the Germans from reaping the desired benefits of the capture of the city.

From the outside the damage does not seem to be extensive, as my photograph shows. It can easily be repaired. But we have now no time to give to the interior of the cathedral, we merely cast a hasty glance at the

Malines Cathedral, south aspect.

A house of Malines 'laid open' by shell fire.

destruction which the shells have wrought. Blocks and chips of fallen stone lie everywhere. A layer of limestone dust covers the archiepiscopal tombs. But the statues of the Apostles, which adorn the columns between the aisles, are untouched, and the precious pictures of van Dyck, Verhaghen and other masters had been saved before the bombardment began. Wondrous silvery tones descend to us from above, caressing the mighty arches. No doubt a bellringer or watchman is testing the carillon - a welcome music - perhaps a thank-offering that the cathedral has not been more severely visited by the havoc of war.

The little town lies still and empty, and its streets are lifeless except for the troops and transport trains marching through, and the number of stray dogs, half wild, who are sniffing for their lost masters among the ruins. The main street leading to the cathedral recalls in a horrible manner the ravages of war, the relentless destroyer of peaceful homes. On the left we pass a house the interior of which has been laid completely bare by a shell, reminding one of the geological section of a piece of rock blasted for railway work. The ground floor is a pile of wreckage and lumber. From the first floor a tangle of draperies, curtains or mats is dangling down towards the street, like shreds of red flags, and the joists and girders between the first and second floors have collapsed, creating a perfect scrap-heap of wrecked furniture. On the second floor, however, a part of a room has been left intact, revealing a cupboard, a child's cot, and, strange to say, a looking-glass which still hangs perfectly uninjured on its hook.

Leaving on our right the *Grand' Place* with the town hall and other old-world buildings, and the pretty statue of Margaret of Austria, we cross another canal and debouch on the main road to Antwerp. Here we proceed between the important forts of Waelhem and St. Catherine, surrounded by their evil-looking belts of barbed-wire entanglements and *trous-de-loup*, and tack cautiously between the immense craters formed in the middle of the road by shell explosions. Some of these shells had dealt very roughly with the electric tramway lines running into Antwerp from this point. One projectile, which had struck close to the track, had merely succeeded in twisting the rails slightly upward, leaving them suspended over the pit by their sleepers. There was room for Dr. Hütten to stand upright under them, an experiment which we made later on when we could better afford the time.

Onwards we fly through this country, levelled by the alluvial mud of rivers almost to the flatness of the sea outside. It is fertile soil and every inch almost is cultivated, and we were almost startled to see a puny little clump of pines standing lost and forlorn by the roadside. Otherwise there is nothing but parks and ploughed fields, kitchen gardens and nurseries. But many of the farms, châteaux and villas dotted about the country have been wrecked by German shells, whilst others have been levelled to the ground by the defenders themselves in order to clear the line of fire. On both sides of the road we observed some excellent field fortifications, which the Belgians had thrown up on retiring northward, and we noticed that bowl-shaped recesses have been excavated at the sides of the ditches for protection against the rain of shrapnel bullets. On the left, great tracts of country are still under water. Rafts made of barrels, used by the Germans to cross certain waterways, are still floating about.

The population seems to have vanished into space. It is but rarely that one sees a forlorn-looking peasant or other mortal who had chosen to face the hurricane of battle. Yet the life on this great highway almost beggars description and the traffic increases the further north we get. It is the same familiar transport trains in the same endless columns, looking exactly as they did on the southern roads and travelling in the same exemplary order. Again we see the same old Landwehr troops, halting beside roads and trees, with rifles piled and coats, life-belts and cartridge-pouches slung over the bayonet. And here we have entire regiments of Landsturm, with men well into the forties in the ranks, plodding on their way towards Ghent. There is no lack of cheery humour and everyone is in good spirits; the men march along with the lighthearted step of young soldiers and sing as if they were going to a harvest festival, with flowers tied to the rifle barrel and more flowers in wreaths round their necks. After five days' uninterrupted railway journey they are now marching the last forty-five kilometres to reach their post, where they are to guard the German lines of communication in western Belgium, an important and hazardous task, for even here the Fatherland may claim the sacrifice of their lives. That is why they sing so gaily. Yet wives and children have been left behind. It is for *their* liberty and happiness that they fight and fall at their post. They *know* what is at stake. The greater the progeny they have given their country, the more they have to defend and the more important it is for them that Germany's liberty and future greatness shall be assured.

At some of the aristocratic villas and châteaux lining the road we take the liberty of paying a visit. A few of them are guarded by some faithful old retainer, others are empty and deserted. In none of them the owner seems to have remained behind, which perhaps is not to be wondered at. The houses which we visited were quite untouched and bore no trace of burglary or despoilment. We were among the very first to proceed along this road after the occupation, and may therefore be accepted as trustworthy witnesses. As I have already had occasion to mention, the soldiers are punished very severely for theft or wanton destruction. But as such crimes are exceedingly rare, there are but few occasions for such punishment. No doubt an army of a million men must comprise a few undesirable characters. However strict the discipline, a commander cannot be held answerable for all that his men may do when he is not personally present, especially so when both he and his troops are worn out from violent exertions. It must also be remembered that a seaport town like Antwerp, one of the centres of international trade, must contain a certain proportion of cosmopolitan riff-raff who at such times are let loose upon society and steal and pilfer where they can. It is therefore not to be wondered at if private property is found to have been pillaged at the end of the war. But up to now, as far as I could see, no such excesses had been committed. The wealthy homes which we visited were, as I have said, in the state in which their owners had left them. One house had, judging from a military cap which had been left behind, been occupied by a Belgian colonel. Outside the library on the first floor was a balcony looking on to a well-kept park, where the trees were now turning yellow. In another house we found a bedroom which had not long since been occupied by its master and mistress, but now they had abandoned their house and home and fled. Over the beds hung pictures of Christ, the Virgin Mary and Pope Pius X. I was touched on catching sight of the portrait of a beautiful boy in his coffin, with a wreath on his brow. Evidently many tears had been shed and much sorrow had dwelt in this still, deserted home.

As we drive on we pass more ruins and naked, jagged walls. We cross the Nethe by a temporary wooden bridge guarded by an ordinary Landsturm patrol, the permanent bridge having been blown up by the Belgians. In a village, I don't remember which, the church had been badly battered by the bombardment, and in the square fronting it stood a statue of St. Kilian - headless. Along the edge of a tomato field a venerable couple toiled along with their pitiful odds and ends on a wheelbarrow and two goats on a lead. They had clearly, to escape the fighting armies, retired to some quiet spot in the neighbourhood and were now returning to see whether there was anything left of their cottage. The population here is Flemish, as are most of the inhabitants of Antwerp.

The trenches now become more numerous and have been constructed with admirable care. The underground passages have in many cases been enlarged into rooms, with walls of match-boarding. At one point in the town we found traces of barricades across the road. They had been built in the form of stone walls, but seemed harmless enough and easy both to destroy and to outflank. Here and there we come across dead horses lying on the road and in the ditches.

Presently we pass a troop of Uhlans, fine men of superb bearing on big horses and looking splendid in their complete and yet handy and smart field kit, with their long slender lances surmounted by streamers. Near the inner girdle of forts with their belts of wire entanglements we meet a couple of heavy mortar batteries, now no longer needed here. They are evidently on their way to Ghent and to western Flanders. On the other hand a bridging detachment with upturned pontoons resting on long, narrow carriages is travelling in our direction, evidently for use on the Scheldt.

Marché aux Souliers a few days after Antwerp's fall.

Belgian prisoners at Malines.

The town itself is encircled by a wall broken by several gates and by a moat crossed by bridges. German flags are now flying over the gateways. Through the *Porte de Malines* we enter the Berchem quarter and then follow the *Chaussée de Malines* north-westward. The whole street is crowded with transport trains and resting troops. They are evidently on the point of starting off for fresh adventures. Now and again we pass a house which has been struck by shells, and in some places the stone paving has been torn up by the same agency. The broad and aristocratic *Avenue des Arts* here and there has had a tree trunk severed by fragments of shell. The *Place de Meir*, a large and handsome street in the very centre of the town, is likewise crowded with ammunition columns and troops, looking bright and cheerful in the sunlight, but with a bearing and an air as if it were the simplest thing in the world to contribute to the conquest of Antwerp.

There are no women and children about, and the men out looking at the troops might be counted on the fingers of both hands. Most of the population has fled to Holland, the wealthy to England or the Riviera. All shops are closed. The banks are guarded by German soldiers. Yet the town, conquered but a few hours ago by the iron force of arms, is decorated as for a triumphal march. The whole of Antwerp is beflagged - and the flags are Belgian! How is it possible that they can have been allowed to remain? The reason is evident, the town fell yesterday and it was for the Belgian army and the British auxiliaries that the bunting had been hung out. But during the next few days the black, yellow and red emblems gradually disappeared.

Over the houses at the western end of the *Place de Meir* we notice brownish-black pillars of smoke whirling upward towards the sky. On arrival at the *Marché aux Souliers* we find that a whole block is burning brightly, but now the fire spreads no weird glare around it, for the city is bathed in sunlight. The tongues of fire issue from the windows like as many yellow flags agitated by the breeze, and we can see from the street the furnace within. Several houses have been levelled to the ground. From the timber and the lumber of the ruins the smoke rises in dense, dark clouds. There are no curious crowds thronging to watch the terrible spectacle. One fire more or less means little in a time so filled with fearful happenings. German soldiers are on guard at the entrances to the street in the *Place Verte* and *Place de Meir*, but there are few people to keep in order in a city all but emptied of its entire population. "Why is nothing done to quench the fire?" we ask. "The waterworks at Waelhem have been destroyed," we are told, "and all that can be done is to watch the fire and to see that it does not spread. If necessary the adjoining houses must be pulled down, but it looks as if the fire had worn itself out."

No part of the interior of Antwerp has been so gutted as the *Marché aux Souliers* - and yet only the houses on the north side of the street have been touched. Without a doubt the damage was originally done by only a shell or two. The shells usually ignite on bursting, and the flames had then no doubt spread to the adjoining houses. But the block in question is surrounded by open spaces and trees, and thus it has been possible to limit the spread of the fire. Yet the streets are very narrow. In the *Marché aux Souliers* a protracted squabble had been going on between the private individuals who owned the houses, the commune which owned the pavement and the city which owned the street, and the fight had been about the widening of the latter, for it was too narrow for this busy neighbourhood. But nobody would give way. In the end no doubt the house-owners would have lost the fight. But then came the German heavy artillery and solved the difficulty, as King Solomon might have done, at one mighty stroke. Now the street is broad enough for anybody.

We fly through the *Avenue du Sud*, yellowed by the falling leaves, but here we hardly see any trace of the bombardment, barring possibly a very occasional shell hole. At the south harbour we pass the interminable rows of sheds, warehouses and offices, whose brass plates bear the familiar inscriptions: Hamburg-Amerika-Linie, Norddeutscher Lloyd, Compagnie Maritime Beige du Congo, Nippon Yusen Kaisha, Red Star Line, Peninsular and Oriental and others. But now the harbour, usually so teeming with life and filled with a roar and bustle unequalled by almost any other seaport town, lies still and silent. Huge sheds were filled with railway wagons, with or without valuable loads. A whole trainful of petrol in tanks was a find which particularly gratified the German officers. Another train had brought in colossal piles of compressed hay, covered over with tarpaulins. A warehouse had been found to contain considerable stocks of colonial produce, oats, flour, coffee and other supplies, which in due course would be examined and made use of. Some sheds were filled with about a thousand motor vehicles of all kinds, mostly lorries and taxicabs. We made a tour of inspection and soon found that they had all without exception been destroyed with axes, hammers and other implements, and were now perfectly useless. They must have represented a value of about £450,000.

As yet there had been no time to post sentries. The entire harbour lay absolutely at the mercy of robbers, yet there were none to be seen. The silence among the deserted warehouses was almost uncanny. A couple of steamship offices and the offices at the South Railway Station had been left in excellent condition. Everything of value had been removed, nothing but receipts and accounts were left. The coats of clerks and officials were still hanging on their hooks as if the owners had just gone out to lunch.

What attracted more than anything the attention of the visitor to the harbour was the colossal petroleum tanks, which now formed a perfect sea of lire and smoke. The AngloBelgian army had not forgotten to set fire to these supplies before retiring. If the enemy cannot be prevented from entering, then the next best thing to do is to deprive him as far as possible of the fruits of his conquest. That was why the motor vehicles had been destroyed and the petroleum supplies had been given over to the flames. They were a wonderful sight, these jet-black, weltering, rolling clouds with their rims of grey and brown, writhing and whirling up into the sky. We could hear the hissing and seething inside, and now and again the blood-red flames succeeded in forcing their way through the smoke. Occasionally there was an explosion. It was clearly not advisable to go too near this inferno. At one or two points, wreathed in smoke, we caught sight of the American flag still flying on its pole, soon to be reached and devoured by the flames. The only signs of life seemed to be ownerless cows and dogs roaming about in a dazed, bewildered way.

On the river, opposite the *Fort de la Tête de Flandre*, a couple of large lighters were burning briskly. They were clearly anchored and had served as pontoons for an emergency bridge used by the allied armies when retiring across the Scheldt and continuing their retreat to Ghent. Certain defensive preparations at the harbour on the way to this bridge showed that the Anglo-Belgian army had intended to defend itself to the utmost. In some places barricades of thick iron-plate had been constructed beneath the gigantic sheds, and by the side of one of these stood three guns with shields, the fire from which was intended to cover the more open portion of the harbour. Here and there barbed wire had been put up. Judging from their arrangement, it seemed that it had been intended to electrify the wires, but this scheme had never matured.

In the course of a walk round the town we came upon the *Rue Karel Ooms*. Within an iron railing lay a large villa, and in the grounds we found an old lady walking about, supported on the arm of a younger woman. As it was unusual to see any of the wealthier inhabitants who had decided to remain in the town during the past fateful weeks, we walked in and greeted the old lady, who told us in simple and dignified words that she could not bring herself to leave Antwerp in its hour of trial, and that at her age - she was now seventy - she had not cared to venture upon the vicissitudes of a journey. Her garden had been struck by five shells, but the house had been left untouched. Yet, as may be imagined, she had lived in mortal terror. Now she was out for the first time to take the air after the anxiety and strain of the last few days. Her nearest neighbours had been less fortunate, for of their houses nothing but the naked walls was left. No doubt they were away, but she believed that they had left servants behind, for she thought that she had heard cries of anguish from that direction when the shells were falling. Before parting, we learnt that the venerable lady was no less a person than the widow of the celebrated Belgian historical painter, Karel Ooms, and that she had lived in the villa since her husband's death in 1900. The street had, in fact, been named after him.

Food column on the way to the ferry with the Cathedral tower in the background, flying the German flag over the cross.

Food column crossing the Grand' Place.

After a plain luncheon we paid a visit to the northern parts of the harbour, and had a hasty look at the steamers still lying in basins and docks. We went on board one of them. It was a German steamer, the *Celadon,* and the fore-part of the deck showed signs of an explosion having taken place. We learnt later that the boilers of all the vessels in the harbour had been destroyed, so as to make the ships useless to the Germans.

In the afternoon we came across the long bridging train which we had passed on the way to the city; it was now marching past the cathedral on its way to the nearest part of the harbour quay used for crossing over to *Tête de Flandre.* No doubt a bridge was to be thrown across in place of the one which had been blown up.

It was interesting to notice that the inhabitants were already showing signs of returning to their city. There were not many of them, but here and there we saw men and women with bundles on their backs opening the doors from the street. One man was pulling two old women along on a barrow which, besides, was crowded with packages and odds and ends. A couple of cafés and hotels were likewise on the point of opening, and a few shops, especially provision shops, soon followed their example.

It was now time to break up and we turned back towards Brussels. We had not got very far before we met three reserve battalions with colours flying and headed by a band playing cheerful military music. In accordance with their pleasant custom, the soldiers had adorned their rifles with little sprays of flowers, and their faces shone as usual with cheerful determination and high spirits.

Once more we looked in at a château by the roadside. I shall never forget the impressions which thronged into my mind as I wandered through its dim, desolate rooms. In the bedrooms and guest-rooms on the first floor the beds were still in the state in which the masters of the house and their guests had left them. Quilts and sheets had been pulled aside, towels carelessly slung across the backs of chairs and basins were still half-full of dirty water with the pieces of soap beside them, stuck to their dishes. On the ground floor was the large, lordly-looking dining-room. The table was laid. A large dish still contained the remnants of the

297

course last served, an omelette. Some ten persons evidently had partaken of the meal. Some plates were empty, others still contained scraps of omelette. Knives and forks lay pell-mell among the bits of bread by the side of the covers. A couple of empty champagne bottles stood on the table, whilst a third still contained a few drops of the joyous wine, which had now lost its sparkling freshness. A few serviettes lay crumpled on the table, others on the chairs and a couple had dropped on to the floor. Everything testified to a hasty and panic-stricken departure. Perhaps the thunderous music of the guns had come unpleasantly near, or maybe a shell had dropped close by? Or perhaps a messenger had dashed in to report that the Germans had punctured the outer girdle of forts and were now rushing in through the opening? Who were the guests, I wondered, whose meal had been so unceremoniously disturbed? Was it the people of the house themselves, who had waited until the last moment, or was it officers spending the night there on their retreat?

The château was dead and deserted. One heard no sounds but the hollow echo of one's steps and now and then the creaking of the furniture. Yet in the hall, on the ground floor, we found a living being - a white dove - it sat alone and frozen on a table. The white dove is the symbol of innocence and purity, of divine sanctity, but here it seemed curiously out of place. Yet the open window did not tempt it to seek the liberty of the château grounds.

At another villa the grounds had been occupied by a column of open ammunition carts containing Belgian shells with the fuse screwed off. The projectiles had not been used, and had been allowed to fall into German hands in this mutilated state. It now became impossible to drive quickly. The road was filled to overflowing with transport columns and Uhlans. They were on their way to Antwerp and were later bound for Ghent. In the west we heard the roar of cannon in the distance. The Germans were giving themselves no peace. Impregnable Antwerp had fallen in the course of a few days, yet the conquerors were swiftly hurrying westward, ever onward towards the sea. England had wanted war, and England was to have her fill and was to get more than she had bargained for since the days of Wellington. Entire companies of marines came marching

Marines with a "field kitchen" and a couple of calves.

Fugitives returning to Malines from the South.

on, magnificent specimens, all of the true Germanic type. Here and there they halted in villages, where they dragged out chairs and placed them along the house walls to get a good and convenient view of the ever-changing, never-ceasing life on the open road. At a corner in the badly ravaged village of Waelhem stood a clownish figure, beating a cracked drum. He wore a crazy-looking top-hat on his head and had drawn sooty lines on his face to represent moustache, imperial and eyebrows. He sang a Flemish song, twisted his body into extraordinary shapes and looked indescribably comical and jovial. The soldiers were beside themselves with laughter, and we could not help sharing their merriment as the performer broke off his song for a moment to greet us with a whimsical salute.

As we again swung round the cathedral at Malines, where we stayed in the morning, Kes dropped the remark that it seemed to him as if several days had since elapsed. And he was right, for we had indeed seen and experienced much on this remarkable journey. We had come armed as if for battle, but everything had passed off peacefully, and a rumour that what was left of the Belgian army intended to attack the western bank of the Scheldt, had not yet been borne out by events. We had seen none but German soldiers amid the quaint old-fashioned and lavish architecture of the streets and market-places surrounding Antwerp's venerable cathedral. The few people remaining out of Antwerp's civil population were very peaceable citizens and seemed resolved to accept their fate. But in Brussels, whither we returned in the gloaming, we found nobody who would believe in Antwerp's fall, for had not the allied leaders nourished the belief that this city could never be taken? So when the Germans posted up proclamations in French and Flemish announcing the fall of the city and how it had come to pass, people gathered in little knots in front of them and read them, but all were fully convinced that the whole story was an invention.[22]

22. In his recent book, "War and Culture" - a work which I warmly recommend to all and sundry who wish to sound the depths of the sociopsychological labyrinths of the world-war - Professor Gustaf F. Steffen gives the following quotation from the Swedish newspaper *Göteborgs Handels och Sjöfartstidning* of the 9th October, the day on which Antwerp fell:-

"In its first leading article in the number published the 1st inst., *The Times* states that it seems as if the

In the evening, at nine o'clock, some thirty officers were assembled round the Field-marshal's table. Here I met once more Prince Waldemar and Captain Dreger, and made the acquaintance of the Governor-General's Chief of Staff, Lieutenant-Colonel Scheerenberg, and Surgeon-General Doctor Stecho, who spoke Swedish and who has many friends in Sweden. Afterwards we had a Bierabend[23] in the upper apartments, which was honoured with the presence of the Minister of War, Lieutenant-General von Falkenhayn. The talkative old Field-marshal von der Goltz saw to it that there was no lack of animation and favoured us with many interesting items about the fall of Antwerp and its past history, besides being inexhaustible in anecdotes and tales of the incidents of the last few days.

---

noise made by the German batteries outside Antwerp were not commensurate with the importance of the operations. *The Times* goes on to say that they appear, in fact, not to be doing very much damage and it is very unlikely that the German Landwehr troops still in Belgium can achieve anything against the outer fortifications, seeing that the Belgian field army is so strong. Even if all the forts were destroyed, it was still doubtful whether the Germans would be able to take Antwerp, for the important factor in the defence of the city was not so much the forts as the field entrenchments.

"The Belgians were said to hold one of the strongest fortresses in Europe, they had at least 120,000 troops at their disposal and an open harbour, whilst opposed to them were only second line troops; their outer works were the newest and most formidable of all, and they knew that the French and British armies in the north of France were on the verge of victory and must come to their rescue.

"We do not therefore think that there is any need to worry about Antwerp,' writes the paper in question (*The Times*). 'Doubtless the graceful spires of the Antwerp churches will make the mouths of the Huns water; the city presents incomparable opportunities for the destructive side of German "Culture." We can imagine the pretexts which will be gleefully invented for pumping petrol into the "Plantain" Museum. Every German regiment in Belgium seems to possess a special machine for squirting petrol into buildings and to include a squad of methodical incendiaries trained in the specific arts of the higher civilisation, as taught at the University of Berlin. Apparently, too, every German column has attached to it a number of mobilised cinematograph actors, who upon suitable occasions impersonate civilians firing on the soldiers.' "

This is a sample of *British* culture and of the "specific arts of the higher civilisation." This is the sort of fare put before the neutral countries, especially America, by the English newspapers.

23. "Beer evening," that is to say, a social evening enlivened by the consumption of beer (Translator.).

CHAPTER XIII
MORE DAYS IN ANTWERP

IT MIGHT BE thought that the war had dealt Antwerp and its commerce their death blow. But the city is merely asleep and there is no one who can tell how long its torpor will last. Just as the fall of the city was an event in the world's history which brought German power within striking distance of Great Britain, so the city itself will in coming times of peace acquire a status of world-wide importance and become perhaps still greater than ever before. Both from a strategical and commercial point of view Antwerp is bound always to remain one of the nerve-centres of Europe. It was therefore interesting to have seen this great mercantile metropolis at the inception of its fateful crisis, and it is obvious that I could not have been content with my first short reconnaissance. Hence I obtained permission from the Governor General's office to return, and, if I wished to do so, to remain in the city for several days.

I accordingly planned another trip with Lieut. Dr. Hütten, to take place on the 11th of October. Just as I was starting out from my hotel, I met an old friend. Professor Georg Wegener, one of my chums from the time I was cramming with Richthofen at the University of Berlin. We had not many minutes to spare, but exchanged nevertheless a few impressions of the war.

Hütten drove the car himself and I sat at his side. It had been my intention to take a few photographs of the military life on the road and in the town, for the sights which were now to unfold themselves to our vision would soon vanish and make room for more tranquil scenes. The further we travelled northward, the slower we had to go, for the road was encumbered by an unceasing stream of marching troops and transport columns. Uhlans and Hussars, guns and ammunition wagons. Little contingents of marines were interspersed here and there amongst the other troops. They had their own amusing little train,

303

consisting of a barrow drawn by a donkey and laden with an odd-looking contrivance of sheet-iron which might simply have been a stove with its pipes. "What are you going to do with that thing there?" we asked. "It's going to be a field kitchen," replied a stout, jovial fellow who was driving a couple of calves behind the donkey-barow

Farther on we passed a bivouac with its shelter-tents still up and the breakfast boiling in its caldrons. Another war picture, or perhaps I should call it a picture from the boundary line of peace and war, was furnished by an entire caravan of carts piled high with trunks, bags, bundles, bedclothes and what not, accompanied by a group of men, women and children. They were fugitives returning to Malines. But if it was their misfortune to live just south of the cathedral, they were doomed never to see their homes again.

Near Eppeghem we saw on an unpretentious wooden cross by the roadside the following inscription: *"Hier ruht ein tapferer Belgier von seinen deutschen Kameraden bcgraben."* (Here lies a brave Belgian buried by his German comrades.) The fallen hero has stuck to his post up to the last, and by his courage had evoked the admiration of his opponents.[24] Now we drive once more through the ruined street in Malines and stop outside the cathedral. Here are a couple of hundred Belgian prisoners guarded by a few marines. They wear little black caps with a red stripe and tassel, short tunics or greatcoats; some of them have water-bottles, bundles or bags carried on the shoulder by a strap. A herd of cattle is just being driven past by some German soldiers. "Quick march!" orders a German N.C.O., and the prisoners quickly disappear down one of the narrow alleys.

We continue northward past the outer fortifications, with the German naval ensign floating on the crest, and meet fresh groups of returning fugitives, fresh marching columns, amongst them a field telegraph detachment, and fresh swarms of horsemen. And so at length we come once more to the long *Chaussée de Malines*, which in a car takes but a couple of minutes from end to end.

24. Dr. Fr. Klefberg, when in the same neighbourhood, had come across the following inscription: "A brave Belgian soldier buried by German comrades. 4th Company, 26th Regiment of Field Artillery."

In front of the town hall at Antwerp.

Infantry halting in front of Antwerp town hall.

But it was chiefly to take photographs that I had planned this day's excursion to Antwerp, and what could after all be more attractive for the camera than the *Grand' Place*, the noble little square by the Townhall with its quaint gable facades? In the middle of the square stands a piece of sculpture not long since erected, illustrating the legend about the boy who throws the giant's hand: *"Hand werfen, Antwerpen."* A house close by is the birthplace of one of the greatest painters of all time, as is shown by a plate over the door, *"Geboortehuis von Antoon van Dyck, Kunstschilder 1599-1641."* Van Dyck's models and their progeny have disappeared, and the setting of the *Grand' Place* now consists of German troops. It is marines we see marching in with their knapsacks on their backs, rifles on the shoulder, cartridge pouches on the bandolier and bayonet and water-bottle by the side. A dog faithfully plods along beside a private in the ranks - one constantly sees German soldiers who have adopted ownerless dogs. Next come a few batteries of 6-cm. naval guns, pulled by their respective crews. One wonders whether horse teams have not been procured for marine artillery used on shore. In front of the Townhall itself a company has piled arms and is resting. Some soldiers are content to take a nap on the stone paving and use their knapsacks for pillows. Here we see food columns with canvas awnings over the carts and wisps of hay in front of the horses. Marine cyclists are moving about everywhere on their silent wheels. By the side of a car stands the great engineer. Captain Dreger, looking at a map of the road to Ghent, which Lieut. Dr. Hütten has just shown him. But the scene is kaleidoscopic in its variety and there is a coming and going, a rushing to and fro of animal and motor traffic, a tramping of horses' hoofs and a rattle of artillery wagons which baffles all description. We had some singing, too, for as the marine troops crossed the square they broke into the swelling tones of *Die Wacht am Rhein.*

We drive on and reach the land of ferries below the cathedral. Here the scene is still more changing, and there is a literal crush. The car is left in charge of our orderly and we thread our way between horses, carts and closely packed columns of troops. The street leading down to the harbour is thronged with double marching columns. They mark time, move on and mark time again. Belgian (Flemish-speaking) policemen in black coats with silver buttons and black helmets help to keep order in the thoroughfare. "Where are all these troops and vehicles off to?" I asked. "They are going to be ferried across the Scheldt to *Tête de Flandre*; that is, where the road to Ghent begins. They are off to the coast to throw a glance across to England."

It is difficult to get along. Everything seems in such a jumble. I am just on the point of snapping some kitchen wagons when a Uhlan perched on a baggage wagon shouts to me: "Neighbour, it is forbidden to photograph the field kitchen!" "Good," I answer. "I have no need to, I have pictures of them already." The salutation "neighbour" was, I thought, an excellent touch.

At the quay and bridges, built to allow for the considerable differences in level between high and low water, the ferries are in full swing. The bridging train we saw yesterday has not yet had time to throw a bridge across. Instead it has devoted its energies to building a species of ferry, consisting of a platform mounted on three pontoons. A tug took two of these contrivances in tow and three river steamers were busy conveying a double ferry of this kind across with troops, ammunition, ambulance and food wagons, field kitchens, field telegraph equipment and horses. Among the troops I noticed an Austrian artillery train belonging to the 30.5-cm. mortar batteries now stationed in Belgium.

"Drive up," orders an officer. Immediately a column of vehicles moves forward and halts on the brink of the quay. The horses are taken out and the vehicles are pushed on to the ferry by the marines. Then the horses are led across the gangway. They stamp, snort and rear, for evidently they dislike the look of this queer-looking craft. But all to no purpose, on board they have to go. When two ferries are full, the steamer casts off and tows them in a twinkling across the Scheldt to *Tête de Flandre*. Here another gangway is thrown out, the vehicles are pulled on to the quay by hand, the horses are put to and the column proceeds on its way to Ghent.

As soon as the first load had left the east bank, another river steamer with its two ferries came alongside and took another contingent on

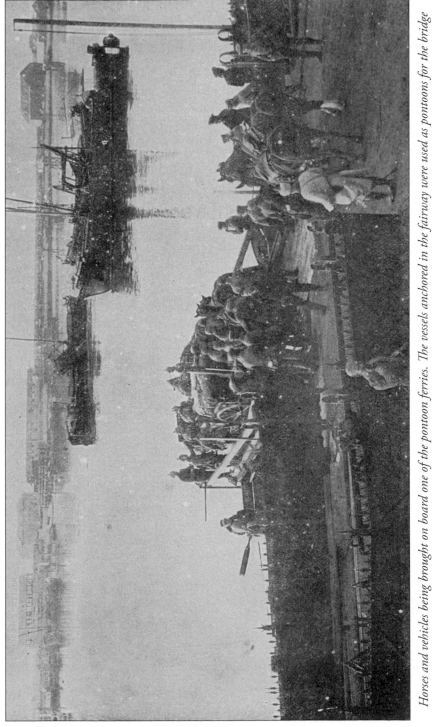

Horses and vehicles being brought on board one of the pontoon ferries. The vessels anchored in the fairway were used as pontoons for the bridge which the Anglo-Belgian army threw across for its retreat. When the last man had crossed, the bridge was blown up.

board. So it went on all day and so it was to continue throughout the night by the light of electric lamps. The same programme would be repeated the next day, and so on as long as there were any troops, horses or vehicles left to ferry across the Scheldt; everything is done with the rapidity, efficiency, order and discipline which distinguish the doings of the German army down to the minutest detail.

The ferries do not return empty from *Tête de Flandre*, for enormous groups of returning fugitives, men, women and children with their carts, bicycles and barrows, bundles and packages are now gathering on the opposite bank. They form a picturesque and motley crowd, such as one is accustomed to see by the side of emigrant ships on the way to America. Most of them are Flemings. A remarkable order seems to reign amongst them. They do not squabble, do not shout, and do not push to get past one another on to the ferries, but wait quietly and obediently until the soldiers show them the way. The military and civilians seem to be on the best of terms. We saw the former, to the accompaniment of jest and laughter, exert themselves to the utmost to make themselves understood, and the result was a bewildering medley of German, French and Flemish.

When the Germans entered Antwerp, they found on the eastern quay in question enormous piles of Belgian uniforms, caps, helmets and knapsacks. None of these had yet been touched. Presumably all this kit had been intended for recruits recently called out.

In the course of our wanderings we also visited the northern parts of the harbour. Here one almost loses oneself in a gigantic maze of docks, piers, quays, basins, warehouses and sheds, and enormous stacks of timber and stores of ironware and colonial produce. Here is a profusion of customs sheds, office buildings, loading gear, cranes, railway wagons, wheelless motor-cars, packing cases and sacks containing I don't know what. *"Verboten te rooken"* (Smoking prohibited) is posted up everywhere in gigantic letters. As I saw it I could not help thinking that *"Verboten te bombardeeren"* would have been, if anything, a more fitting injunction. Without a guide it would have been impossible to find one's way, and we were glad to get hold of a queer-looking fish sniffing round amongst the merchandise, who subsequently took us in hand. To-day there were a few more people about, amongst them Germans who were making the round of the harbour precincts to note the names of all the vessels lying there. I asked them if they had seen any Swedish boats, but the answer was in the negative. Barges, lighters and fishing boats were lying closely packed together in certain parts of the harbour. Here also we came across barricades of iron girders and barbed-wire entanglements, and behind a parapet close by stood a Belgian gun with the breech-block missing.

Comte de Smets de Naeyer was the name of a fine-looking Belgian training-ship with light grey hull, white masts and spick and span rigging, but there was nothing on board to arouse our interest. We also paid a little visit to the great Australian liner, *Tasmania*. In the officers' cabins all drawers had been pulled out and everything of value taken away. Nothing but books, papers and a quantity of accounts and other objects of no value remained. But on a writing-table in the captain's own cabin stood a portrait of a woman and a photograph of a group of bonny children. In the dining saloon a table stood laid with a silver coffee-pot, half-full, cups and a box of cigars which had more or less

The transport across the Scheldt.

311

A Belgian gun in the harbour.

been ransacked of its contents. All the passenger staterooms were empty and deserted. As we wandered through the endless corridors our steps gave off a hollow and eerie echo, and we actually stopped once or twice to discover whether it was really the echo of our own steps we heard, or whether someone was following us. One might believe almost anything in such times as these. Fugitives might for instance have hidden themselves on board. We shouted, but the sound of our voices died away in the abandoned ship and there was no answer. We looked into the forecastle, but nobody now slept in these bunks, so often rocked by the ocean swell. The same grave-like silence everywhere. It was quite uncanny to walk about this ghost-ship, this "flying Dutchman" with its crew of invisible spirits who seemed to eye us from every nook and cranny.

At half-past six we returned to the capital and it was pitchdark before we arrived ninety minutes later. At first the road was fairly clear, but later on we drove past incessant columns marching on their way to Ghent. As so many times before, a kaleidoscope of horses, riders and wagons were brought into successive relief by the light of our lamps. The men, otherwise singing and joking, were now still and sat as if moulded in the saddle. Once again we heard this eternal clatter of iron-shod hoofs against the stone paving, this endless tramp, tramp, tramp which is the music of the marching columns. The rattle of the wagons, the creaking of the iron tyred wheels, the jingling of the chains, the chafing of the leather and the tramping of the horses' hoofs, these sounds seem still to haunt my ears as I write. Like a slow and irresistible tidal wave, like an implacable necessity, this train is rolling towards its goal. It is Germany's train of victory. On hundreds of other roads similar streams are flowing to and from the greatest battle lines maintained by a single country ever since Noah left the ark to people the earth with human beings, for, as everyone knows, the continuous fighting line from Nieuport on the North Sea *via* Rheims and round Verdun to the Vosges is an accomplished fact.

We see eyes gleaming at us through the darkness. It is the light from cars we meet, but what can their business be on the road to Antwerp at this late hour? From under the shadow of the trees fresh packs of horsemen, square-set, sturdy men on well-fed powerful mounts constantly emerge into the circle of light from our lamps. Later on comes a gun team, no longer needed here, on its way to other places where the guns will resume their music for the benefit of the *entente* legions, and here and there among the trees the figures of soldiers preparing their evening meal are silhouetted against the ruddy glow of the bivouac fires. Their pipes are glowing in the darkness and one can see the gleam of their teeth as they break into a peal of laughter at some comical remark.

*　*　*　*　*

At the Banque de Paris and a couple of other banks they shook their heads over my Swedish letter of credit: *"Toutes les lettres de crédit sont annulées."* I should certainly have had no difficulty in getting money by appealing to the Governor General, but when I explained my unsound economic position at the Swedish Legation, Herr Pousette, who was *chargé d'affaires*, said that he would be very glad to lend me a thousand francs against the despatch of a telegram to *Skandinaviska Kreditaktiebolaget*. When this difficulty had been overcome, I took a trip to Löwen, which is German for Louvain. My friend, Lieut. Dr. Hütten, still acted as my guide. We had under our charge the energetic and charming Frau Koch, henceforth to be named Sister Martha, clad in cap and spotless white dress with a red cross on the left arm. The 12th of October turned out a brilliantly fine day. We passed out of the city under the triumphal arch between mirror-like ponds and yellowing trees. The *Chaussée de Louvain* soon developed into a stone-paved road lined with a close beech wood, where hardly a ray of the sun penetrated to the ground and where cool shadows reigned over a bed of fallen leaves. We saw no German soldiers in this direction, nothing but the hand of autumn over this unhappy land which had lost its independence. There were no transport columns to be seen. The only vehicles on the road were civilian carts. The aristocratic carriages of the *grand monde* had disappeared without a trace, after their owners had removed to other climes.

We have eighteen kilometres to go. Ruins do not meet the eye until we have travelled some distance into the precincts of Louvain. The whole city is not wrecked by shells as one had been led to believe. Hardly a fifth has been destroyed. But that fifth contained many precious and irreplaceable buildings, and the loss of the library with its collection of manuscripts, unless by some happy chance some remnants are still intact under the ruins, is regrettable in the extreme. But in the midst of the desolation, like a lonely crag in mid ocean, stands the Townhall, that proud monument from the middle of the fifteenth century with its six slender fretwork turrets. I walked round the whole building, and with the best will in the world I was unable to detect a single scratch in its gorgeously decorated walls. There may, of course, be an occasional scar from a shell, but if so it escaped my attention. The German artillery had given a magnificent proof of its unerring accuracy of aim. It had hit everything round this building but without injuring as much as a cornice of any of the six turrets.

Louvain town hall.

Some of the houses only have the walls left standing.

The reason of the German bombardment of Louvain is well known. On entering the town the German troops were fired on from windows by the civil population, and as there was no other means of checking this outrageous proceeding, a few houses were set fire to. When afterwards the German soldiers used every means in their power to extinguish the fire in the buildings nearest the Townhall, the *franctireurs* lay once more in wait from their ambush. Then things grew serious. Any other army in the world would have acted in the same way, and the Germans themselves greatly regretted that they were compelled against their will to adopt such measures. From Louvain we proceeded to Malines, a lengthy trip along the canal joining the two cities, where we were startled to see the masts of fishing smacks bob up amongst the trees of parks and alleys. We arrived just in time to witness the burial of a marine who had fallen at his post. The body of the dead man was carried to the grave on a Belgian hearse with a silver cross on the roof and drawn by one horse. Behind the hearse followed some hundred soldiers from the army and navy. After the funeral three rifle volleys were fired over the grave, which was then filled in. There were several German graves in the little churchyard, decorated with wreaths and helmets, and also two common graves containing the men who had fallen in some light.

On a country road near by a battery of Austrian 30.5-cm. mortars stood posted. A single one of these batteries of two guns requires a train of forty-two vehicles. The barrel requires a lorry to itself, likewise the gun carriage. Then there are wagons for the men, the ammunition, accessories, tools, provisions, kitchen gear, etc.

In conclusion, we paid a visit to the great military hospital at Malines, where the surgeon-in-chief and another staff surgeon showed us round everywhere. The operating theatres more especially of this Belgian hospital seemed to meet all aseptic requirements. At the present moment there were only 140 wounded on the premises. Over every bed hung a metal frame to which an arm could be bandaged when it needed stretching, and other contrivances with weights and pulleys had been installed for stretching injured legs. Several interesting cases were explained to us. A soldier had received a bullet through the back of the neck, but the spinal medulla was uninjured and the patient could walk about although it was only six days since he was wounded. Another had been struck on the left side of the lower jaw, which had been crushed, the bullet having found its way out on the right side. By an ingenious arrangement of gilt brass wire fastened to the teeth, the doctors had succeeded in giving the necessary support to the lacerated jawbone. The patient could even move his lower jaw and speak. A third man had been struck by a bullet in the head and had lost the power of speech, but understood what was said to him and nodded yes and no. A Belgian soldier had received a nasty wound in the head. He seemed unbalanced, was delirious and spoke of his wife and children. If anyone asked whether he had heard from them or knew where they were, he merely answered: "Look there on the right," and turned his head in that direction. In his delirium he described confusedly the fierce struggle at the Nethe, where he was wounded. Later we stood beside the bed of a little Belgian boy of twelve, who had happened to get too close to the firing lines and whose left arm had been cut off by a shell. Yet he was in good spirits and was looking at a book with coloured plates; he smiled pleasantly when the German doctor patted him on the head. They had succeeded in tracing his mother and she was to visit him daily for a little while.

The corridors were lined with solid-looking iron-hooped wooden cases inscribed: *Nicht stürzen* (Not to be upset). They contained photographic apparatus and plates. There were separate rooms for X-ray photography and some photos shown to us clearly revealed where the projectile had lodged and what damage it had done on its passage. As a rule wounds from rifle bullets are far less malignant than those occasioned by shrapnel or shell splinters.

Soon we were on our way back again along the familiar road to Brussels and we were just in time to get ready for the Field-marshal's supper-table. There were several interesting guests present. Grand Admiral von Tirpitz, regally tall and straight, was there. It is he who, after the Emperor, has worked hardest for the creation of the German Navy. Lofty forehead, frank and merry eyes, fair beard, resolute and manly bearing, in fact a real Teuton. It was like a draught of sparkling wine to speak to him. To such men nothing is impossible, and with them there is no trace of anxiety about the final issue of the war.

I also met here Herr K. F. von Siemens, head of the firm of Siemens and Halske, also a very robust-looking man of the Teutonic type and of a temperament in which humour and gravity are agreeably blended. Talking about the German losses, he estimated them at 250,000, of which, however, the great majority were slightly wounded and had already returned or would soon return to the front, and would then possess the advantage over the new-comers that they had already been under fire and had personal experience behind them. We discovered that we possessed a common friend in the charming Sir Walter Lawrence, one-time private secretary to Lord Curzon when he was Viceroy of India. Probably he was now lost to us as a friend, as this war has proved capable of sundering the closest bonds of friendship.

Another guest was Privy Councillor Kreidel, head of the commissariat department of the Governor-General of Belgium, and seventy-five years old. He had recently been subject to attacks of dizziness through overwork and was now on the point of returning to Germany to get strong again. The new Governor of Antwerp, Infantry-General Baron von Hoiningen, whom I had met in Karlsruhe, was also present. General of Fortifications Bailer, gentle and charming lecturer on aesthetics, was one of my special friends. He was in very good spirits to-day because he had seen his son of whom he had not heard for a long time and who served with one of the armies in France. Lieutenant Bailer had made the long journey through the air and was just on the point of returning in his aeroplane. We also talked about Ghent, which had fallen the same day after severe fighting in the open country. The General was now proceeding thither to study the Belgian field fortifications; the town itself is not fortified. From Ghent the German army was to continue to Bruges and Ostend. Finally we talked about the 300,000 volunteers who had just arrived at the front, where the youthful undergraduates with their merry pranks had greatly enlivened the older Landsturm men, who in turn had taught them their very best drill.

The next two days I rested, wrote, visited the Swedish Legation and spent my evenings with the Governor-General. The weather was by no means suitable for excursions. The rain poured down and heavy clouds from the Atlantic floated over the town. As a lady whom I overheard in a shop rightly observed, life was quite dark and sad enough without the heavens adding their share. But to the soldiers there is no difference between fine and foul weather, and the troops and transport trains passing through the city seem no fewer than usual. But for the German uniforms and military cars, one would scarcely have known what was going on. Apart from these phenomena, a stranger arriving in Brussels would have noticed nothing, unless it be the absence of Belgian motor-cars and the rarity of horse-drawn vehicles; for both cars and horses had been requisitioned by the Belgian army. He might perhaps also have wondered where all the *beau monde* and all the rich and well-to-do citizens had got to, for those who could afford it had preferred to betake themselves elsewhere, rather than to remain under the foreign yoke. It is only the poor and the less well-to-do bourgeoisie who have to remain.

As regards the town itself, it is true that the stranger would notice that the theatres were closed and that a German sentry was posted outside the *Palais de Justice* and other public buildings. But he would have seen no signs of destruction, no smoking ruins, no naked walls black with soot and smoke. The population of Brussels remained perfectly quiet when the Germans entered. There were no ambushes and there was no firing from windows. Therefore all the houses remain untouched and the town has been spared the fate which overtook Louvain and Dinant. And the population acted wisely. They would never have been able to inflict an appreciable check on the Germans, but would, on the contrary, have suffered enormous economic losses. The war requisition of fifty million francs imposed upon the town would in case of resistance have been multiplied over and over again.

I could not refrain from making another inspection of Antwerp, more thorough than the preceding ones.

Antwerp! The city of the dead! Loulan, the desert city, given over to destruction and oblivion when the sea of Lopnor wandered southward, was not harder hit than Antwerp. For have not the oceans retired and

The interior of Malines Cathedral before the removal of the débris.

Destruction wrought by 'fat bertha' in Fort St Catherine.

left high and dry this great hub of commerce which not many days ago was in close contact with all the earth's continents and islands! These gigantic harbour installations now lay dead and idle, and there was not even an apprentice to be found in all the twenty-two ships which lay forgotten by the quayside when the blow fell. The whole city was paralysed. One of the things I wanted to see was whether in the course of the next few days there would be any signs of an awakening from this torpor. Of course, one realised that life in the harbour would remain dead as long as the sea outside was full of mines, and would not perhaps reawaken until the end of the war. But I thought it possible nevertheless that the city itself might rouse itself and that many of the unhappy fugitives who had fled across the Dutch frontier would return.

So on the 15th October I started out for the third time for Antwerp. I had been invited to join in an excursion, and we drove out in five cars. I was with my friend General Bailer and a couple of other officers. The participants included no less a person than the Imperial Chancellor, Herr von Bethmann-Hollweg, as well as His Excellency von Treutler. We quickly reached Malines and stopped as usual outside the cathedral. In view of the Chancellor's visit the interior had been cleaned up. All blocks of stone, dust and lumber had been removed. St. Rombaut's fane now looked quite neat and tidy, and it was evident that it would not cost much, either in time or money, to restore it to its former condition. A tombstone, crushed by blocks of stone which had fallen from an arch between the middle and the north side-aisle, will, however, be difficult to replace. The effect of the shell fire was demonstrated by artillery officers, and it was made clear that the Belgian fire directed from the north had only consisted of shrapnel intended to drive the German observers away from the tower.

From Malines we proceeded north-east to Fort St. Catherine, one of Antwerp's strongest forts, constructed, like the others, by the great Engineer-General Brialmont and equipped with nine modern armoured turrets. Most of these had been horribly knocked about by the heaviest German artillery, *die dicke Bertha una die schwarze Marie* ("fat Bertha" and "black Maria") as the 42-cm. mortars have been playfully dubbed by the soldiers. One of the turrets had been struck plumb by a shell which had Hung its 40-ton cupola some ten metres to one side, where the gigantic structure had alighted on its side and eaten itself into the earth. The cupola having been removed in this somewhat energetic manner, we were able to get an idea of the interior construction of the turret. Another turret had merely been struck at a tangent by a smaller projectile and yet the effect was such that the metal of the cupola had been rent as the soil is torn by the ploughshare. Another shell had penetrated through a bed of concrete several metres thick and upon detonation it wrought the most appalling havoc.

At Antwerp the Chancellor was received by Admiral von Schröder, whom I shall have occasion to mention later on. He was a powerfully built man, with white head and beard, a thorough sea-dog. He also was renowned for his astounding energy.

In the afternoon I drove with General Bailer, Colonel Müller and Major Elert round the grass-clad slopes of the fortifications round the town, the innumerable gates of which were now guarded by German soldiers. It was really an initial tour of inspection that these officers were engaged upon. Among the discoveries made were several searchlights and old guns and a couple of excellently constructed barricades of cobble-stones and sheet-iron. The garrison seemed to have been prepared for street fighting in the town itself, but things had never got thus far. Huts built of boards, tarpaulins and other matérials had been put up for the defenders of the barricades.

We had taken rooms at the Terminus Hotel, close by the Central Railway Station. The German officers paid with *bons* which are redeemed after the war, I in ready cash. The dining-room was filled with officers, naval surgeons and civilian German engineers who had come to repair the waterworks, gas-works, telegraphs and telephones. The shortage of water had made itself felt very disagreeably, but at least one could now get tea and soup, which had been an unobtainable luxury during the first two days, when we had to remain satisfied with wine and beer. No doubt it was distilled Scheldt water, or perhaps well-water which now figured in our soup tureens and waterjugs.

The streets with gas-lighting were pitch-dark at night, whilst the electrically lighted main streets were bathed in their usual brightness. Many shop windows were now also brilliantly lit, especially the tobacconist establishments, which attracted crowds of German customers. In the restaurants we saw the soldiers seated round the tables with their girlfriends, drinking beer or coffee. In the large avenues the traffic was almost animated. As long as daylight lasted we saw little knots of fugitives returning from the Dutch side. Their unkempt appearance, unwashed hands and faces and uncombed hair showed that they had been lying out of doors in the rain and cold and suffered great privations. Now they were returning with their bundles, their children, basket carriages, gramophones and other peculiar furniture, carried on the back or in little barrows drawn by dogs or donkeys. All looked calm and resigned. What else, indeed, could they do? In Holland they had been treated with great kindness and hospitality. In Antwerp they were to find that paralysis had seized upon all industries that gave them their livelihood. Doubtless they have a hard winter before them, but the Germans will, I subsequently heard, do all in their power to lessen the distress, and a special commission has, in fact, been nominated with this object. It may also surely be taken for granted that England, who says that she began the war to save neutral Belgium, and who can now afford to sacrifice £350,000,000 to encompass the destruction of Germany, will be able to offer a thousandth part of this sum to save the destitute in Belgium from that very fate.

CHAPTER XIV
STILL IN ANTWERP

THE 16th OF October - an anniversary! Nine years ago I left Stockholm for Tibet. How quiet and peaceful the world seemed then, how different from the thunders now re-echoing from pole to pole. The RussoJapanese war had just ended. Now the Russians and Japanese are friends. Then Count Benckendorff had frowned on Lord Curzon's Tibetan policy. But when the storm was preparing against Germany, and when it broke loose, Russia and England suddenly became friends - like Pilate and Herod in their day!

The 16th of October broke with a leaden sky, and the German flag hung limp and motionless from the spire of the cathedral, 123 metres above the ground - where it had now been fluttering for a whole week. At the entrance facing the *Place Verte* stood a middle-aged janitor, with an unspeakably sour mien. He scarcely deigned to glance at me when, in my most courteous accents, I asked him whether the cathedral was open. "The cathedral is open," he replied, "but only to German soldiers." "All right, my boy," I thought, and drew forth my *open sesame*, General von Moltke's pass. The janitor read the paper and his face grew longer at every line. When he had finished he removed his cap and said: "Is that really true? If so I may tell you, Doctor, that I am a Swede, a native of Visby, resident in Antwerp for thirty years, and my name is Dahlgren."

Thereupon, the cathedral was open even to me, and honest Dahlgren took me round and explained everything. "Baedeker" does not know one-tenth of what he knew. But I will pass all this over, for this book deals only with the war. All that I will mention is that only one shell, or more likely perhaps a fragment of a shell, had struck the wall near the lower part of the great window above the entrance in *Place Verte*. The damage done is insignificant, and can be repaired in a day. If the shell had been maliciously inclined, and if Kubens's famous pictures, "The Crucifixion" and the "Descent from the Cross," had been in their usual places in the transept facing towards *Place Verte*, where the shell struck, they would have been in a perilous position. But they were removed before the bombardment and stored in a place of safety, like all other valuable pictures and art treasures in Antwerp. The only trace which the shell has left in the interior of the church is a scratch in one of the pillars.

From the chancel one has a splendid view over the seven aisles and the majestic vaulted roof which was lost from view in the deep gloom above. It is a forest of mighty pillars presenting an ever-varying perspective - the nearest columns faintly illuminated from the windows, the more distant ones gradually merging into the sombre tint of the waning twilight. It is dark enough at the best of times in St. Joseph's Chapel and St. Anthony's Chapel, where windows four hundred years old represent the Father, Virgin, and Holy Child, side by side with St. George and the Dragon. *"In hoc signo vinces"* is inscribed on a reliquary, in which a splinter of the Holy Cross is kept.

In the centre of the northern side-aisle, on a portable framework, stands an image of the Holy Virgin, richly arrayed in a long robe, with a golden crown on her head. Each year on the Sunday following the 15th of August she is carried in procession round the town. But this year, when her aid was so badly needed, she was not carried through the streets of Antwerp. This year they contented themselves with lighting tall votive candles before the Queen of Heaven. Yet she seemingly remained deaf to all prayers! But a stained-glass picture in the third window from the left on the northern side shows a portrait of Emperor Charles V. who severed his Netherlands from their connection with the Germanic Holy Roman Empire, leaving the keys of Antwerp in the charge of this very image of the Virgin. The keys of Antwerp! It was "Black Maria" - and not her white namesake - who had the handling of them!

The pulpit was carved by van der Voort in solid oak. It is exactly 200 years old, but perhaps the oaks were 500 years old already when their wood was dedicated to the preaching of the Word of God. One likes to pause before this handsome work of art. The pulpit steps, with their carved crowns of trees and birds, leave us unmoved, but the four female figures which support the pulpit itself are noteworthy. They represent the four continents - Australia being then almost unknown. Three of the figures are light enough, but the one with the thick lips and the flat nose - Dark Africa, the negro continent - is wrapped in deep shadows. Four continents uphold the platform from which the gospel of God's eternal love to mankind is preached throughout the earth - a pretty conception of van der Voort! "Go ye therefore and teach all nations." The artist, no doubt, believed that the world would make progress during the centuries to come after his days. But now there are five continents - supporting the gospel of war and hatred. The two Western powers of the *entente* bear the responsibility for having caused the Dance of Death to involve the whole globe, for they are bringing into the fight masses of men raked together from all parts of the world: Canadians come in their ships from America, Turcos and Senegalese negroes from Africa, and poor Hindus and Ghurkas, bronzed by the sun of India, lie freezing in the trenches - these are the representatives of Asia - and lastly, Australia and New Zealand are sending their contingents, over land and sea, from the Antipodes. And what is the purpose of which the attainment is thought worth such a world-wide levy of warriors? Why, Germanic culture is to be uprooted from the earth. And it is the bearers of this culture, the people of Luther, Goethe, Beethoven, Helmholtz and Röntgen, that are called barbarians and Huns - a danger to the future and civilisation of the white race! It is therefore fit that Ghurkas and Senegalese should come and save us from relapse into the dark ages. The artist who hereafter may be bold enough to immortalise the "levy of all races" of 1914, should not forget that he will find a promising idea for his leading motive in van der Voort's woman - with the thick lips and the flat nose.

On *Place Verte* outside stands a bronze statue of Rubens, bareheaded, with a cloak over his shoulders. Its background is formed by the cathedral which he himself has adorned with some of his choicest masterpieces. There he stands, with extended hands, freely offering to the world the gifts his genius has created! The night before the town fell he stood there illumined by the glare of burning buildings - the *Hôtel d' Europe* and *Taverne Royale*. The picturesque groups of warriors which were seen there five days ago, have disappeared for ever from the *Grand' Place*. Now, only a long queue of civilians stands outside the Townhall, desiring to obtain, from the German military authorities, passports and permits for some purpose or other.

As I sauntered through the old town, I looked at the people returning from their flight - in most cases merely a trip to the Dutch frontier - and who were now opening their doors and rearranging their shop windows. In a side street a group of marines had assembled round a half-starved cat whom they were treating to milk and meat; "the cat will be as fat as a porpoise in a week," they assured me. Then my ears caught the sound of cheerful strains of music floating through the misty streets, and I followed the direction of the alluring sound. It turned out to be the band of one of the marine battalions playing in front of the Townhall - surrounded by a large crowd. At four o'clock every afternoon a band played here, at the Central Railway Station and outside *Hotel Weber*. Order was maintained by Belgian police constables. I addressed one of them and he told me various things of interest.

He knew for certain, he said, that five British marines were taken prisoners yesterday in the town. Then he suddenly passed on to other topics. In the night of August 25th, a Zeppelin had flown over Antwerp, and dropped some bombs, one of which had hit three policemen; two were killed, one was still alive and likely to recover. The police force of Antwerp numbered 800 before the war. Of these, 260 had been called out for active service, 140 had fled when the bombardment commenced, the others had remained and were still doing duty. On account of their small number, even the higher police officers had to do street duty. He computed the strength of the Anglo-Belgian army which had been in Antwerp at 120,000 men, and he expressed himself in very drastic terms as to its mode of defending the town. He did not know where the army had gone to; at any rate it disappeared just when it was most needed. According to his computation, one-tenth, or at most one-eighth, of the population had remained during the bombardment. They had taken refuge in cellars, and stopped up the apertures with sand-bags. Of course, men of his service were obliged to stay out-of-doors. Thus he had seen a cyclist struck by a shell and literally vanish on the spot. On returning home he found that his wife, like all others, had fled and taken their child with her. She had not yet returned, nor had he had any news of her. Further, he had seen the ferries in Antwerp cast loose and allowed to drift downstream towards Flushing, to prevent their falling into the hands of the Germans. He believed that, in a month's time, most of the inhabitants of the town would be back. The young men only hesitated to return for fear of being compelled by the Germans to serve in their army against Russia. And according to rumours which had been spread, the Russians were standing near Berlin with immense armies.

Clearly, the defenders of Antwerp had feared that an attack would also be made from the west, from the region of Termonde, for one day General Bailer and his officers observed entrenchments, several kilometres in length, thrown up at the cost of at least a couple of weeks' hard toil, and with much skill. The matériel was earth and timber, which had been dragged there by the civilian population from the surrounding districts. But even this labour was in vain, and they did not even make an attempt to defend these entrenchments.

On October 17th we commenced with a visit to the Zoological Garden, one of the foremost of its kind in the world. Dr. Hütten, in his capacity as a German officer, was admitted free; I paid the usual admission. The Indian elephants, hippopotami, rhinoceroses and giraffes were just as unconcerned as the chimpanzees and the other simians, about the radical change which had recently taken place in their immediate surroundings. One of the elephants was gravely shaking his head, but otherwise the bombardment did not seem to have made the least impression on the animals; no doubt they mistook the roar of the guns for an approaching thunderstorm.

But the most remarkable circumstance was that all beasts of prey had vanished. This is the only way in which the Zoological Garden has been

The Dutch frontier station at Putten on the way to Bergen-op-zoon.

Fugitives returning to Antwerp from Holland.

affected by the war. The splendid large summer cages were empty, and so were the indoor winter quarters of the animals. An old keeper, who, grave and bent, was raking the paths in the park, explained the cause - shaking his head all the while just like the Indian elephant.

"All beasts of prey were shot," he said. "Four splendid lions, live fine tigers, all the leopards and panthers, all land bears and polar bears were killed. They were driven out into the summer cages and shot - the muzzles of the rifles were thrust through the bars." He sighed, and no doubt he thought that this was the most grievous loss the war had caused, for both he and the other keepers of the wild beasts had become attached to their protégés.

"But why, in the name of common-sense, were the poor beasts shot? Surely they were not suspected of espionage?" asked Lieut. Hütten,

"Indeed not," the keeper replied, "it was simply done by order of a general. They feared lest the cages might be struck by shells, when the beasts might have escaped and created a panic in the streets. That's why they were shot. But now the bombardment is over, and the cages stand empty. Not even a splinter has fallen in the Zoological Garden."

It would be interesting to know what kind of shell it could be that would break a lion's cage without killing the lion!

Lastly I took a snapshot of the combined Asiatic and African landscape, in which my old friends, the Bactrian camels and the Tibetan yaks, were associated with dromedaries from Egypt. One might have imagined oneself far away from the turmoil of the war of nations when standing on the borders of their peaceful retreat!

But before reverting to the war, I will interpolate here a few details gleaned in Antwerp as to what occurred in the town just before and during the bombardment. Most of these I obtained from a gentleman who on my return from the Zoological Garden was awaiting me at the entrance to the *Hôtel Terminus*, and introduced himself as Harald Petri, Swedish Consul in Antwerp. He was an uncommonly amiable, courteous and hospitable man, and as he had stayed in the town during those critical days, he could give me a great deal of perfectly reliable information.

On Wednesday, the 7th of October, the Commanding General had published through the press a proclamation warning the inhabitants that the town might be bombarded at any moment. In consequence of this warning one-half of the population took flight The warning had come none too soon, for the very same night at 11 P.M. the shells began to burst. During the night and on Thursday morning further crowds fled in a continuous stream. They went on foot, as no cars and no horses were to be had. They took with them their valuables and a good many domestic animals - I dare say also provisions. There were weeping women, screaming children and excited men. Many of them, perhaps, had seen shells falling near them. The number of these fugitives might be computed at over 150,000. They made for the Dutch frontier village of Putten, and thence for Bergen-op-Zoom, but many got as far as Esschem and Rosendaal by other roads.

By 10 A.M. on Thursday the town was almost deserted, 10,000 having perhaps remained out of nearly 400,000 inhabitants. Nearly all of these sought refuge in the cellars under the houses which, with very few exceptions, stood empty. Among those remaining were nearly all the Swedes, Norwegians and Danes residing in Antwerp; in fact, many of the Scandinavians who had already taken out their passports, nevertheless remained behind.

The bombardment continued all Thursday, and the town was set on fire by shells in several places. It was a terrific din, what with the roar of the guns and the crash of falling walls. The bombardment increased in intensity during Thursday night, and the fire spread. But at 11 A.M. on Friday, the 9th of October - the day before my visit - all became quiet.

Consul Petri had disdained to seek shelter. In common with other officials, he had been invited to take refuge in the Townhall, but he preferred to stay at home. From time to time he went out into the streets to see the effect of the bombardment. As soon as it had ceased, he went to the Townhall, and then for a long stroll. The streets were deserted and silent; there was scarcely a soul to be seen. But suddenly, he saw a host of people. This was the German vanguard marching in from Berchem, to be followed later in the day by the main body of the besieging army.

The public buildings were taken possession of, the artillery drove up to the quay, and the St, Anne's quarter of the town was bombarded for two hours. Then all was quiet.

Another informant in Antwerp told me that certain prominent persons would have left the town on October 3rd, if the Belgian Government had not ordered them to remain. This was done at the request of the British Government, who had promised to send troops to relieve the town. On the same day, at 2 p.m, Mr, W, Churchill arrived in a motor-car and had a consultation with the civic and military authorities of the city, in the course of which he promised to send 30,000 men to relieve the town, a force which, in conjunction with the Belgian army, should be sufficient for the defence of the city. As a matter of fact, only 15,000 men arrived, of whom 2500 were bluejackets. They had heavy artillery with them and are said to have fought bravely. On October 6th, late at night, Churchill left the town and drove off in a motor-car to the west, no doubt to Ostend.

As the inhabitants during the nights heard, and in daytime saw, troops marching through the streets, they could not but believe that a vigorous resistance would be offered. They were therefore greatly surprised when the town surrendered without a fight and the defenders, at 6 A.M. on October 9th, withdrew over the pontoon bridge, built six weeks before, across the Scheldt, and then blew the bridge up. The British are said to have been the last to cross it.

On October 17th, eight days after the fall of Antwerp, the number of inhabitants was estimated at fifty to sixty thousand. Probably even the young men fit for military service would soon return when they learnt that the Germans were paying well for work done and did not compel them to join their own ranks. Besides, the Governor had issued an order to the effect that all private property should be respected and that no private house should be entered by the soldiers. The three neutral Consuls - of Sweden, Holland and America - had also conferred with the Governor on the measures to be taken to restore normal life. In consequence, the Dutch Consul had advised his countrymen resident in Antwerp, numbering up to 20,000, to return. The German colony was estimated at 18,000, including many wealthy merchants. These also had commenced to return. The neutral Consuls most positively denied that any atrocities had been committed against Germans at the outbreak of the war.

The matérial damage caused to the town itself by the bombardment is very small. Consul Petri calculates that there are 40,000 houses in Antwerp. Out of these, about 300 have been damaged by shells, and 100 burnt down - hence no more than I per cent. He valued the buildings that had been burnt down at something like £500,000, and those damaged by shells at about;£150,000.

Consul Petri's chauffeur had fled, and when we made a tour through the town the Consul drove the car himself. He was familiar with all the spots in the southern parts of Antwerp where shells had struck. The northern part had escaped damage altogether. We saw several yawning rents at the street level, where shells had laid open the cellars, leaving large gaping chasms. The Argentine Consul, who, like most other people, had taken refuge in a cellar, had been killed by one of these shells.

In other places the shells had struck the roof, carrying away the whole garret floor, and leaving here and there nothing but the tattered shreds of girders rattling in the breeze. Frequently a shell had struck in the middle of a housefront without causing any damage visible from the street, beyond tearing a huge hole in the wall and shattering all the panes and window frames. Black streaks on the walls showed that fire had broken out. On closer examination we found, as a rule, that the principal havoc had been wrought on the side away from the street.

We also saw how the shells had struck the roadway and burst, ripping up the stone pavement and throwing large mounds and fragments against adjacent houses, where cavities biting into the brickwork gaped red out of the white plastering. In one place we could see how a shell had carried away a roof and some ten yards of coping, and had then crashed into the opposite house on the other side of the street.

All rubbish and brickwork which had tumbled into the streets and on the pavements had already been piled up in heaps, but had not yet been carted away for want of horses and vehicles. Among the heaps of ruins at the *Marché aux Souliers* the gas was escaping from burst pipes and burning with blue wavering flames, presenting a weird spectacle at night.

Our run also brought us to *St. Jacques*, a magnificent church, rich in works of art representing subjects from sacred history. The candles burning in front of some images of saints were inadequate to dispel the gloom. The features of the Saviour on a Crucifix revealed abysmal depths of pain and sorrow; it seemed as if darkness had descended for ever on the earth and overpowered him. The worshippers were easily counted. Among them I noticed a few young women confessing their sins in the confessional chairs, giving the listening priests an insight into some of the most secret recesses of human life.

St. Paul's can boast if anything a still greater ecclesiastical splendour. The interior was brightly illumined with electric light, but the church itself is jealously hidden in the midst of a dense cluster of houses.

As it was still daylight, we decided to cross over to St. Anne's on the western bank of the Scheldt. The ferries were still plodding steadily to and fro, but were now only bringing refugees back to Antwerp. One of the ferries was just lying to, and a broad gangway was thrown out to bridge the interval of one yard between the ferry and the quay. A restive grey horse shied at the gangway, reared, backed and fell into the river, "He is lost," cried the marines, "he will find no place where he can get ashore." The horse swam out into the Scheldt, but soon turned back. Meanwhile it was caught in the swirling current and disappeared. A boat went out to its aid, and towed it to a steep stairway. The horse was now spent and no longer attempted to swim. Ropes and lines were passed round its body and with united strength they pulled it up to the pavement. Here the horse lay as if dead. They rubbed it with straw. Presumably it revived, for when we returned from the other bank it was gone. It was only a horse! And yet it had caused men's hearts to beat faster for a good half-hour!

Yet, strangely enough, all the dead cavalry and transport horses whose swollen bodies lie on the road between Brussels and Antwerp, failed to move us deeply - not to speak of the graves with the small white crosses which we pass so heedlessly on our road.

A last gleam of daylight was still lingering when we drove up to the imposing *Hôpital Militaire*, where I wished to call on Sister Martha for the last time. She was the only German among a number of Belgian Sisters. The medical staff consists partly of German naval surgeons, partly of Belgians. The surgeon-in-chief, whom I had met in Kobe, had been in Stockholm in July, just before the war broke out. The hospital had 700 beds, most of which were now occupied by Belgian soldiers, a few Germans and seventeen Englishmen. I talked to six of the latter in one of the pavilions. When I asked what they thought of the war they all replied: "Sir, we had got our orders, all we had to do was to obey and do our duty!" One of them admitted: "I suppose we could not well look on idly when the Germans were capturing the world's trade." Another thought it was absurd that men should go out and kill each other, and he declaimed about "this horrible, this terrible war." All were longing for home, and asking whether we thought they would get there by Christmas. I was unable to reassure them on this point. "If at least our relatives knew that we are alive!" they said. They were all serene and dignified, and greatly appreciated the kind and solicitous care they received. What a pity that they should be lying there, counting the lingering hours! Nevertheless one feels greater pity still for the Belgians who have been left in the lurch by their great tempters and "protectors," and who have lost their country and their independence. After all it is best to stand on one's own legs and to follow the watchword of the boy scout: "Be prepared."

We had no time to visit Rubens's house, standing in the street bearing his name. It has been on fire repeatedly since his time, and is entirely changed. But we entered Mrs. Osterith's house. The Governor had taken up his quarters there. He is a refined and humane man, who is doing all he can to infuse new life into the dead town, and wishes to see its industry and prosperity flourishing afresh under the new forms which the inexorable necessities of war have brought forth. Mrs. Osterith herself was an old acquaintance of mine. In 1903 I had been to a great reception at this magnificent house, which might almost be called a palace. The noble lady is seventy-four, and full of humour. She had remained in Antwerp during the bombardment, and together with fifty-eight persons, members of the household and acquaintances, taken refuge in the vast cellars under the house. Her bed had stood between bins of old wine, and she slept there while shells crashed over the burning town. Once the Spanish Minister paid her a visit, and she received him in her "bombardment dress," a peignoir. At last came the hour of release, and she returned with her household from her subterranean captivity to the realms of daylight.

Finally, we made for the *Hôtel Terminus*, where we supped in the company of General Bailer, Colonel Müller, Major Elert, Captain Lamprecht, and a couple of other officers. Our company was also joined by Lieutenant-Colonel Schaubode, who had commanded the siege artillery and had been rewarded for his merits with the Iron Cross of the first class. He was so used to fire that he slept soundly while shells were whizzing around him. He told us various instances of the strange freaks of fate which occur in this connection. During an engagement, a General and a Major stood talking on the high road. A shell fell near them. The Major was sent away on some errand, and had scarcely moved away when there came another shell, which struck the General so effectually that he literally vanished from sight.

On another occasion two officers were living in the same quarters in a town which was being shelled. When the house was struck by a shell, which, however, did no damage to speak of, one of the officers thought that they might consider themselves safe, as surely the same house was not likely to be hit more than once. The other, however, sought new quarters and induced his friend to follow him. As soon as they had left, the house was totally destroyed. It turned out that it was a public office, where the enemy took it for granted that the German commanders would take up their quarters.

Thus, chance often seems to play a great part. To live in a bombarded town is like a game of chance, as no one can tell where the shells will strike. The wisest course is to discard all calculations and to trust one's life to God's hands. We have already seen how the Swedish Consul in Antwerp, who exposed himself to danger, came off scot-free, while his

339

Argentine colleague, who took refuge in an apparently safe cellar, was killed.

During my stay in Antwerp I had an opportunity - though only once - of meeting the Rev. Börjeson, Seamen's Missionary, a son of the great sculptor. Börjeson told me various things about the refugees, and the hardships they suffered. They had camped out in woods and pasture lands, but in Holland they had been well received, and the Dutch had helped them all they could. In this connection I expressed a wish to see one of the high roads leading north, and Consul Petri, with his usual hospitality, placed his car at my disposal; accordingly, on the 18th of October, we started on the road leading to Bergen-op-Zoom.

On our drive through the town we observed, to our pleasant surprise, that some of the railways were already working - a new sign of reawakening life, even if of no great significance. At the bridge across the town moat our papers were carefully examined, whereupon we proceeded through the suburb of Merxem. West of this is the fort of the same name. This had been surrendered without a fight, though surrounded on all sides by barbed-wire entanglements; a number of trees had been felled to clear the range, and houses had been pulled down, all - so it seemed now - needlessly!

The road was stone-paved and shaded by fine oaks and beeches; it passed through the villages of Donck, Eckeren, and Cappellen. Quite close to the frontier we passed between a couple of the extreme fortifications on the northern front. These, too, were surrounded by barbed-wire entanglements and an area of demolition, which had not been caused by the attackers but by the defenders. In one place a barricade had been erected right across the road - all to no purpose.

Dryhoek is the name of one of the northernmost works, where we made a brief inspection, accompanied by a young German lieutenant and a Belgian merchant, a friend of Consul Petri. Dryhoek has been totally demolished, but the destruction was not wrought by German artillery. When the Commander recognised that the fortifications would fall into the hands of the Germans, he decided at least not to leave them to the enemy in undamaged condition, and ordered the garrison of about

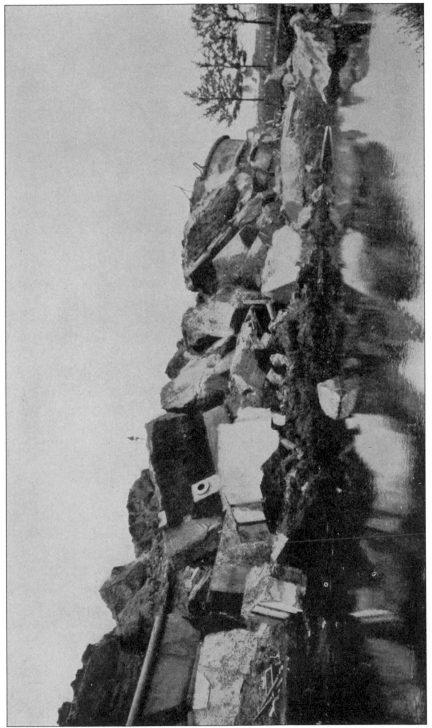

Outworkers at Dryhoek, blown up by their commandant.

A German marine on the pontoon ferry at Antwerp.

two hundred men to march off, whereupon he set fire to the powder magazine and blew himself up together with his fort. The great concrete blocks now lying scattered on the site form a monument over his grave. Even if nothing is won by such an act one cannot but recognise that it requires rare fortitude and resolution.

The German lieutenant told me that several minor after explosions had taken place on the site. Yesterday he had found among the ruins the arm of a man, evidently the Commander's, unless one of the men had remained to die with his chief.

The fort was crescent-shaped, with four turrets for 12 and 15-cm. guns, having a range of 8-10 kilometres, and one turret for 7.5-cm. guns, intended for short-range fighting. This turret faced north, and was the only one which remained intact besides the breastwork of sandbags for the defending infantry.

All along the road we passed returning fugitives. At the village of Putten the frontier post is in the middle of the street, where the Dutch and the German flags float side by side, and where Dutch soldiers guard the frontier. All passports are scrutinised here. As for ourselves, we had no difficulty in being passed through, and we proceeded some distance to the north through a rather sparsely cultivated tract, where young pines were growing on both sides of the road. Scattered paper, rags, empty bottles and other vestiges marked the spots where the fugitives had camped. They had fared very ill in the chilly autumn nights. Some had got separated from their dear ones and were searching for them. They had sped on by night as well as by day on this *via dolorosa*, and it was not surprising that they lost each other in the darkness. The Dutch mounted police patrols could not help them, they could only maintain order. Many a woman gave birth to a child prematurely by the roadside. Indescribable scenes were enacted in this fleeing caravan, distracted with fear and anxiety. But even they, perhaps, could not forbear a smile when for instance they saw a big stout matron laboriously dragging an easy chair on which she sat down to rest at every fiftieth step! And grateful, indeed, they must have felt, when the Dutch regaled them with bread, soup, and other food!

But now they were returning in endless procession, which however, was far more sparse than it had been a few days ago. They came on foot, on bicycles or guiding dog-drawn carts and pushing wheel-barrows. Many were riding in solid vehicles with or without springs. I had scarcely expected to see that so many Belgian horses had got over whole-skinned to Holland. Now they were returning to their old stables.

As one tarries by the roadside awhile to watch this procession of poor half-starved and frozen people deprived of livelihood, home and country, one cannot but ask: *"Whose is the fault?"*

I have on various occasions witnessed scenes of Belgian misery and distress, which nearly broke my heart. I felt glad that there are charitable souls in the world who are collecting means to alleviate this distress.

*　　*　　*　　*　　*

Jesus said to his disciples: "Take heed that no man deceive you... Ye shall hear of wars and rumours of wars: see that ye be not troubled; for all these things must come to pass, but the end is not yet. For nation shall rise against nation, and kingdom against kingdom: and there shall be famine and earthquakes in divers places. But all these are only the beginning of sorrows. Then shall they deliver you up to be afflicted, and shall kill you: and ye shall be hated of all nations for My name's sake. And then shall many be offended and shall betray one another, and shall hate one another. And many false prophets shall rise, and shall deceive many. And because iniquity shall abound, the love of many shall wax cold. But he that shall endure unto the end, the same shall be saved... When ye therefore shall see the abomination of desolation, spoken of by Daniel the prophet, stand in the holy place (whoso readeth, let him understand): then let them which be in Judaea flee into the mountains: let him which is on the housetop come not down to take anything out of his house: neither let him which is in the field return back to take his clothes. And woe unto them that are with child, and to them that give suck in those days! But pray ye that your flight be not in winter, neither on the sabbath day: for then shall be great tribulation, such as was not since the beginning of the world to this time, no, nor ever shall be...

"Watch therefore: for ye know not what hour your Lord doth come. But know this, that if the good man of the house had known in what watch the thief would come, he would have watched, and would not have suffered his house to be broken up. Therefore be ye also ready: for in such an hour as ye think not the Son of man cometh... Heaven and earth shall pass away, but My words shall not pass away."

CHAPTER XV

VIA GHENT AND BRUGES
TO OSTEND

URING THE TIME I stayed at Antwerp news kept reaching us almost daily of the rapidity with which the Germans were approaching the sea. "Ghent is taken," "Bruges is taken," and finally, "To-day our troops have entered Ostend." On my return to Brussels it looked as if the Allies were going to do their utmost to drive the Germans out of Ostend, and a rumour was in circulation that the British had bombarded the town.

Accompanied by the ever-charming and delightful Consul Petri and his Belgian friend, who took charge of the steering wheel, I proceeded on October 20th to Ostend, equipped with a special pass from the Governor-General. The weather was dull and rainy and dark curtains of heavy clouds hung over the bleak landscape. We drove through avenues of elms along a road paved with Swedish granite, so it might be said that we were travelling on Swedish, Belgian and German ground. Every inch of the country is cultivated or built upon, nothing but houses and farms, hop-fields, corn-fields and kitchen gardens. The draught dogs are very busy, since the war has taken all the horses. One sees remarkably few German uniforms, but a good many natives walking along under their umbrellas. As in Malines, the people wear wooden shoes, and we still come across great numbers of returning fugitives.

At Alost we cross the Dendre by a bridge. Here we find numerous marks of shell fire. At Ouaterecht many houses have been destroyed. From Melle the road is lined with an uninterrupted string of nurseries and flower gardens. Horticulture has here reached a high pitch of perfection and potted plants are exported to the United States to the tune of millions.

In Ghent nothing has been destroyed. The town retains its customary appearance. The tramcars are running, all shops are open and there are crowds of people about in spite of the weather. Yet the many German uniforms tell their tale. We stopped to have a look at the magnificent cathedral. We found here an image of the Virgin Mary surrounded by burning candles and by it was a notice that anyone offering up prayers before the image would receive fifty days' absolution. What the many people kneeling on the praying stools were praying for, we could readily guess.

In the palace of the Counts of Flanders we wandered through subterranean crypts and along crenelated walls. From a commanding crest we had a remarkable view over the red-brick roofs and grey church towers of the town, all dripping with rain.

I had been invited for supper by the charming and friendly war historian, Major-General Friederich, where I met several officers belonging to his staff. The General was now in mourning. His only son had fallen on the field of honour for his country. But the General had other sons, to wit: his Landwehr soldiers, sturdy, strong, willing and lusty fellows. The rank and file was composed of workmen, privy councillors, cobblers' apprentices, barristers, brewers' draymen, high court judges, blacksmiths and mayors. Differences in rank, party contentions and class distinctions all disappear in the field without leaving a trace behind them. War levels everything. There is but one rank: that of the warrior who fights for the honour of his country and the freedom of his people.

At nine in the morning of the 21st October we continued our journey. The rain clouds still hung heavy over the narrow streets and the weather did not brighten until we had left the town behind us. At Eclo a company of German cyclists were resting. Bridges span the canals here and there and the latter in turn intersect the country in all directions to carry the many fighters to and fro. There is not much traffic now. Now and again we see large wagons which serve as homes for itinerant families moving from place to place to buy up the tresses of peasant girls, to sharpen knives, to do tinkering and so forth.

Bruges is one of the most celebrated cities of Europe on account of its old-world air, its picturesque houses, its trees and bridges over the canals and its mighty city gates with rounded turrets. I felt I should like to remain to enjoy the repose which seemed to dwell over the many waterways. But now there is no time. We go on through a beech forest and over open fields and reach the village of Ghistelles; a few kilometres further on towards the south-west and we come to a crossing, where we are stopped by an infantry picket. As we halt we hear a violent cannonade within a short distance. Our papers are examined, and we are told that an artillery duel is going on at Middelkerke and that the German positions are on the near side of the long canal connecting Ostend with Nieuport and Dunkerque. A squadron of British warships is said to be lying off the coast and bombarding the German positions, which are also attacked from the land side by Belgian and French troops. But the road to Ostend, which runs first to the north-west and later to the north-north-east, was said to be free. The soldiers thought that we were practically, if not entirely, safe from shells on that road. The most dangerous point was the bend on the other side of the canal, where the road changes its direction. We met coming from Ostend several ammunition columns on the way to the troops at Middelkerke, where numbers of wounded soldiers were returning to the rear.

We got safely past the dangerous corner and arrived safe and sound in the handsome and aristocratic town by the sea, to which Baedeker has given the following testimonial: "Ostend is perhaps at present Europe's most elegant watering place." We drove on to the avenue along the front with its rows of big hotels facing the sea. Most of them are only open during the season, which ends on the 15th September, and during which some 45,000 visitors reside in the town. But Ostend is also the terminus of one of the passenger routes between England and the Continent and this traffic goes on all the year round. Travellers held up by gales or by fatigue can find hotels of a less pretentious kind, but they are situated in the interior of the town.

It was two o'clock when we arrived. I had never been to Ostend and knew none of the German officers, but I had my pass and felt I ought to report myself to the commandant, who was said to be stopping at the *Hôtel Littoral* facing the sea, so we proceeded there and lunched immediately in the restaurant, for Consul Petri's time was nearly up and he had to be back in Antwerp before nightfall. I accompanied him and his Belgian friend to the door, thanked them for their companionship and saw them drive off with a little Swedish flag in front cracking in the breeze.

It looked strange, this grey and dreary sea, as one cast one's glance westward. One seemed to feel the hot breath of war blowing in over the land. The rain had ceased, the weather was clearing, but the sky was still overcast. In the west, at a distance of nine or ten kilometres, we saw plainly and clearly the outlines of thirteen British warships, of which a couple were cruisers and the others large destroyers of the older type. They were firing against the German positions on the Belgian coast and were themselves under fire. One could see them constantly on the move so as to render the German aim and fire more difficult. Yet on the whole they retained their positions and their black hulls were sharply silhouetted against the light horizon. Huge black clouds of smoke rose from their funnels and were blown across the horizon, giving the sky a peculiar streaky appearance.

The swell rolled in, dull and sleepy, over the fine smooth sands of the *plage*. The road facing the sea was open to traffic, but the spacious promenade outside, separated from the sea and *plage* by an iron rail, was reserved for the German troops. At high tide the sea ascends to the foot of the stone wall of the promenade, whilst at low water it recedes some distance, leaving a wide belt of sand high and dry. This was now occupied by German horsemen who rode out into the water to refresh and harden their tired mounts.

I called upon the commandant at Ostend, *Kapitän zur* See (naval captain) Tägert. He was staying on the first floor of the *Hôtel Littoral*, and from his balcony we once again observed the British warships. He told me that he and his brother naval officers had arrived at Ostend early the same day, the 21st October. They had gone first to the *Majestic Hotel*, which was supposed to be the best in the town. The proprietor declared that he had no rooms available, which was not true, as the season was long since over. Possibly the name of the hotel explained why there was no room - for German officers. Instead of availing themselves of their right to insist on accommodation, the Germans, anxious to avoid a fuss, went to the *Hôtel Littoral*, which was placed at their disposal from top to bottom. They subsequently found that they had no cause to repent the change. The army officers and doctors, on the other hand, were less amenable and settled down without further ado at the *Majestic Hotel*, where kitchen service and attendance were quickly working at full pressure.

Captain Tägert, a refined and conscientious man, immediately ordered that a room (by the way, the last available at the *Littoral*) be placed at my disposal forthwith. I took possession at once. The corridor on the second floor led straight into the apartments overlooking the sea, the inner doors being already furnished with the name-plates of the German naval officers occupying them. The outer glass doors led to balconies with comfortable basket chairs. From these balconies we had an uninterrupted view of the sea and could watch the British squadron and its movements.

From my splendid point of vantage I could enjoy at leisure the varying phases of a wonderful sunset. In the west the great ball was shining with a curious pink glow now and then running into yellow. The fleecy clouds near by were fringed with gold reflected in the glittering sea. The rest of the sky was overcast and a thin drizzle fell fitfully, whilst the windows on the front gleamed as if the houses were on fire. The British ships lay in the centre of the patch of sea turned golden by the rays of the setting sun. They had been bombarding the German positions all day and I could see the flashes from the guns, followed a long while after by the roar of the report. Now, at 5.20 P.M., German time, the thunder from the guns was so loud and insistent that the windows of the Kursaal shook and rattled. Half an hour later the firing ceased. We assumed that the squadron had gone north to replenish its ammunition. By this time the beam of light had shrunk and the golden tint had faded from the water. Twilight descended upon the sea and the blinking of a couple of gas buoys began to assert itself. They are there to guide the shipping, but now the fairway was empty and deserted.

During the day I had seen many civilians about, but towards evening they gradually disappeared. Nobody was allowed out after 9 P.M. or before 5 A.M. The streets themselves were not lighted, but several shops were kept with their lights burning until the former hour. On the promenade at the front there was not a single lamp alight - here one wandered in darkness among the German soldiers. Light issued, however, from many windows facing the sea. This was not thought risky, as the enemy vessels well knew their bearings in any case. It was not thought that the British ships would bombard Ostend, as the killing of a hundred or two of Germans and the evacuation of the place would not make up for the loss of the considerable British capital supposed to be invested in the town.

I had been invited to regard myself as a member of the German naval officers' mess for dinner and supper at the *Hôtel Littoral*. When therefore we assembled at eight o'clock in the restaurant for the first time, I made the acquaintance of them all. Among my special friends, apart from the chief, were Captain-Lieutenant Bess, Lieutenant Haak, Staff-Surgeon Schönfelder and Doctor Kübler. We kept together during the next few days and went through many experiences which we shall never forget.

Whilst we were sitting at table a report was handed in that light signals had been made from a church tower, clearly addressed to the British warships. The instructions issued to deal with this matter ordered a very thorough investigation of the circumstances. The day's bombardment from the British ships had done no damage beyond killing a few horses. Apart from this the shells had found an "empty billet."

We sat up late talking, and Captain Bess told us about the sinking of the old "tin box" *Ariadne*, a cruiser of 3000 tons, by the British on August 28th. Bess was navigating officer on board and he assured me that it takes some time before one's nerves recover their equilibrium after the shock of such an experience. The *Ariadne* had been doing patrol duty in Jade Bight when in the morning of August 28th she was ordered to scour the sea north-west of Heligoland. The weather was misty and it was impossible to see far ahead. Suddenly a huge grey hulk loomed up through the fog. It was a British "Dreadnought," and her heavy guns at once began to play. The first "coal box" flew right over the *Ariadne*, so close that several of the crew were flung against the deck by the air pressure. After that the shells kept raining over the doomed little cruiser, which immediately headed for the Jade Bight, her guns returning the fire as best she could. One shot after the other struck the *Ariadne*. After a while her stern was on fire and there was no possibility of bringing the powder magazine under water so as to avert a catastrophe. The fore part of the ship also caught fire, but not in the bows, where the wounded had been taken and where it was still possible to make one's way. Next the steering apparatus was hit and the ship seemed to want to make for the British vessel, but somehow or other it was put right again. Words cannot describe the appalling noise which denoted each hit. A deafening crash resounded through the entire hull when the projectile struck its sides. The fire soon spread. Presently it became impossible to serve the guns. In the end the flames reached the parts of the ship where the ammunition was stored. Now began a terrible crackling and hissing as one projectile after the other exploded and shells and splinters poured out in every direction. Another "Dreadnought" dived through the fog, but did not take part in the light, uneven enough already. The *Ariadne's* commander and Bess were on the bridge, the plating of which was perforated from beneath by the exploding ammunition. The heat was unbearable, everything was wreathed in smoke, the deafening detonations followed closer and closer and the final catastrophe was clearly approaching. When the crew saw that the end might come at any moment they broke into a rousing cheer for the Emperor and another for the *Ariadne's* commander. Then they sang the

> "*Stolz weht die Flagge schwarz-weiss-rot*
> *An unsres Schüfes Mast*
> *Dem Feinde weh, der sie bedroht,*
> *Der diese Farben hasst!*

Sie flattert an dem Heimatstrand
Im winde bin und her,
Und fern vom teuren Vaterland
Auf sturmbewegtem Meer.
Ihr wolln wir treu ergeben sein,
Getreu bis in den Tod,
Ihr wolln wir unser Leben weihn.
Der Flagge schwarz-weiss-rot. Hurra!"[25]

But salvation was near at hand. The two cruisers *Danzig* and *Stralsund* showed up through the mist. The crew jumped overboard from the red-hot, burning ship. The British disappeared. The commander and Bess would have been roasted had they remained longer at their post, and they too dived into the sea. As regards the latter, he did not recover consciousness until he found himself in a comfortable berth on board one of the rescue ships. The *Ariadne* had lost close on seventy men out of her full complement of three hundred.

Thus ended the first day which I spent with the German naval officers at Ostend, that glorious watering-place, at other times the rendezvous of *la haute volée* and "the upper ten," that pleasure-ground of innumerable good-for-nothings, where dissipated diplomats bathe their jaded bodies in the pure salt sea, where namby-pamby dandies flirt with idle, fascinating women. Now German imperial power stood like an impenetrable iron wall on the brink of the sea, with its spear pointed at the heart of England. The first goal had been reached, England -

25. *Black, white and red our noble flag,*
   Up at our masthead flies —
   Woe to the foe who scorns that flag.
   This ensign who defies!
   It gaily flutters in the breeze
   Upon our native strand
   And out on many storm-tossed seas
   Far from our fatherland.
   Beneath it firm and true we'll stand
   Our blood we'll gladly shed
   And to our last breath will defend
   The black and white and red!
   Hurrah!

fearful of her world supremacy on the sea and jealous of the rapid commercial and economic rise of Germany - had made up her mind to join in the fight and had declared war on Germany. Now, if ever, was the opportunity to get at a hated rival - without too great a sacrifice of her own resources. But already German forces had reached the ocean shore. Antwerp had fallen, the city which Mr. Winston Churchill, like the Duke of Wellington of old, had wished to convert into a British base for operations on the Continent, a point from which the Belgians could be put to rights should they perchance become less patient and show less interest in the sacred cause. Yes, Antwerp - the city which was to be saved for Great Britain even if the rest of Belgium went under - had fallen, in spite of Britain's protest and in spite of the showers of abuse which the proud British had poured over their honourable enemy. The greatest drama of the world's history was in full swing. Were the Teutons to go under and the culture of the German "barbarians" to be wiped out? No, never! Such a purpose would require other means for its fulfilment than those hitherto tried by the Allies. The military position of Germany is too strong, and all attempts to crush her people are and must be hopeless. But woe to those who bear the blame for the agony of the vanquished!

It was with a queer feeling that I went to bed in a room where I could look upon a sea from which British warships had only a moment ago been bombarding the coast a few miles away. The fire might easily have been directed on Ostend itself. But this did not come to pass. At least I heard nothing, for I slept like a log. When I awoke war had resumed its thunders in the west.

22nd October. The British bombardment of the coastal zone south of Ostend continued throughout the morning and was still more severe than on the previous day. The window panes in the hotel restaurant shook in their frames. We wondered whether the deeper sounds emanated from newly arrived German heavy artillery or from British naval guns.

Two German infantry detachments were occupying a line running from north-west to south-east of the north-eastern side of the Yser

Canal. On the south-west side of the canal the Belgians and British had entrenched themselves firmly; they also held Nieuport. The immediate German object was to command the crossings of the canal, which in itself formed a very valuable defensive work in the hands of the Allies. The villages of Leffinghe and Slype and the road between them, running south-east of Middelkerke, had been bombarded by the enemy. Leffinghe was only six, Slype nine kilometres from Ostend. The positions of the Germans were enormously strong. They clearly did not intend to let go the advantage they had gained, although encircled by fire from the north, north-west, west, south-west and south, both from the sea and from the land side. The Allies on the other hand realised that every German advance west-south-westward, that is to say towards Nieuport, Dunkerque and Calais, was, to say the least, fatal to themselves. Hence the remnants of the AngloBelgian Army, which had thought fit to leave Antwerp before it was too late, had halted in its retreat after receiving considerable reinforcements both from France and England, and had offered a desperate resistance in fortified positions in the western sector of Belgian Flanders, intersected by canals and waterways. It will readily be understood what important British interests were at stake. As soon as England herself was in danger, the famous phlegm was transformed into unbridled hysteria.

Captain Tägert now suggested an excursion to Middelkerke, situated on the coast, eight kilometres from Ostend. Captain-Lieutenant Bess and his adjutant were to accompany me. We drove in the covered car of the former, following the inner sea-road parallel with the shore, but separated from it by intermittent rows of houses. Towards Middelkerke the life and traffic increased. Long food and ammunition columns were being brought up to the rear of the troops. In a street in the little town the men were busy hiding the light canvas awnings of the provision wagons with twigs and branches, and the vehicles looked like so many leafy bowers. Yet I was unpleasantly impressed by the sight of this kind of leafy bower, for in my mind it was too closely associated with impending danger. As I have said before, this sort of disguise is necessitated by the enemy's air scouting.

We asked a picket where the General-in-Command von Werder had his quarters, and were directed to a modest little house. The General was busy at the moment receiving details of the situation in this part of the theatre of war. A report on the subject had to be sent to Main Headquarters. As soon as this matter was disposed of, we were shown in. The General received us with the greatest kindness. He was in brilliant spirits and possesses in a high degree that immovable equanimity required in difficult situations. Lieutenant-Colonel Wittisch was told to lend us an officer familiar with the field of battle, who would take us to a point of vantage from which we could obtain a view of the situation without too much exposing ourselves to the enemy's fire. The Colonel asked whether he might not undertake this job himself, and so we promptly seated ourselves in his open car and continued on our way along the sea-front under cover of the only row of houses separating us from the sea. These houses are, however, intersected by several narrow streets like the openings in a gallery, through which we caught sight of the sea and two destroyers which had detached themselves from the British squadron and were now two kilometres away. They were clearly out to observe what was passing on shore, but did not fire, at least not at the moment.

On reaching the last of the stone houses at the western end of Middelkerke we alighted from the car and proceeded on foot some distance south to the crest of the highest dune in the neighbourhood. At this point we were only a little over seven kilometres from Nieuport, which was in the hands of the Allies. We had with us a map of the neighbourhood and commanded a wide radius of the blood-drenched country. Below the crest of the dune, to the south-west, stood the nearest German batteries. They were just on the point of hurling their messengers of death into the allied positions. At every shot we heard that peculiar whining, whistling sound of the projectile, and presently a puff of smoke indicated the point of impact at the other end. All life in the vicinity of this target is destroyed. A hit can kill twenty men and wound as many or more. Yesterday British shells had been raining down from Nieuport and they had reached the spot where we now stood. It is difficult to avoid a feeling of excitement, and one's attention is strained to the utmost when witnessing an artillery duel over a large area and hearing the incessant heavy dull booming of cannon.

With the map in his hand and with really impressive calm Colonel Wittisch explained everything that was passing in front of us; now and again we stole a glance at the destroyers outside, wondering whether they would soon begin to shoot. In the south-west we noticed the little white puffs of smoke which denote the bursting of shrapnel shells.

When everything had been fully explained to me, the Colonel thought that it was not advisable to remain any longer. There were four of us, and we were within range of all commanding points in the vicinity. If we were noticed from the south side, it would be assumed that we were directing the German artillery and the enemy's guns would be trained on us. It is a peculiar sensation to know that one may at any moment become a target.

So we walked down from the dunes and back to the car. From the mouth of one of the little streets running down to the sea we observed the two incredibly impudent destroyers, which we were told had been stealing along the coast for the last three days. They had gradually come nearer and nearer, since they noticed no evil intentions from the coast at Middelkerke. Through our glasses we could see the officers on the bridge and the crew moving about on deck. They on their part could see us with equal clearness, but I suppose they did not think us worth powder and shot from a revolving gun. After a while they seemed to make a large sweep, one to the south-west, west, north-west and north-north-west, and the other to the north-east, north and north-north-west, gradually approaching the remainder of the squadron, no doubt to report what they had seen. Of the squadron itself only five ships were discernible through the mist.

Now we could proceed without any risk on our return journey along *La Digue*, the broad, hard road skirting the shore, with its excellent view of the sea. Here all civilian traffic was forbidden and no lights were allowed in the windows. In the evenings and at night the darkness was complete.

After supper, at ten o'clock, I was sitting once more on my balcony, the two gas-buoys were burning and the swell was breaking drowsily upon the shore, drowning the steps of the sentries in the street. But I could see the soldiers by the light from the windows. They moved mostly in pairs, whilst other soldiers stood chatting in little groups, leaning against the iron railing of the promenade and watching the sheaves of fire from the British guns. In the course of ten minutes I counted 141 shots; probably there were more, as several might have coincided. In ten hours this meant 8500 shots, an expensive business.

So I went to bed at Ostend for the second time. I left the balcony doors open - it was too tempting to lie awake awhile to watch the clear sky and listen to the harmonies of the ocean swell and the booming guns. Gradually I drifted into a deep and refreshing sleep.

A Petty Officer with a few Marines at a street corner in Ostend.

Military policemen inspecting the damage outside the 'Majestic' Hotel.

CHAPTER XVI
OSTEND BOMBARDED

O**N FRIDAY THE** 23rd October I was called by Dr. Kübler, who suggested a walk to the lighthouse and to the old fortifications. So we wandered off to the new outer harbour, where a sailor rowed us across the canal, whereupon we continued to the flying station, where we arrived just in time to watch the elegant ascent of a *Taube*, which circled up to a considerable height and then disappeared towards the south-west. The lighthouse rears its white minaret fifty-eight metres above the ground. Tempting as it was, we refrained from climbing up to the light to have a look at Nieuport, Fumes and Dunkerque, which can be seen from the top.

Instead we traced our steps to the ancient fort and its moat, its earth-clad slopes and its five guns dating from 1862. We returned by the electric tramway. The car was filled with soldiers and civilians. The former included an old Landsturm man, who told us that he had three sons in the war, but where they were and whether they were still alive, he had not the faintest notion. "I don't grudge their dying," he said, "one must sacrifice all for the Fatherland."

On returning to the promenade, we settled down on a bench by the Kursaal and examined the British squadron through our glasses. The sky was exceptionally clear, the weather radiant; even the sun came out to have a peep at us.

Just before half-past twelve Captain-Lieutenant Bess came to fetch me. He had just returned from Middelkerke, where he had been with Admiral von Schröder. He told me that the road in which yesterday we had seen the foliage-enshrouded wagons was now anything but safe, and that in fact a couple of shells had been dropped there. Even the soldiers were forbidden to show themselves on the front. Bess dissuaded me, therefore, from attempting a second visit to Middelkerke.

He had another suggestion, combined with less risk, namely to visit a couple of his companies of marines and inspect their quarters. A company and a half had been billeted in the theatre, which was only a few steps away. Outside stood a couple of 6-cm. so-called *Bootskanonen* (boat guns), neat looking little guns of the same grey colour as the armoured ships. Their ammunition wagons were lined up along the pavement.

We stepped into the large, handsome foyer. The men had rigged up their beds along the walls - mattresses and pillows had been requisitioned from the Mayor of Ostend. Their arms and clothes were hanging on chairs and coat-hangers and the tables were littered with their cups and crockery.

The first-tier boxes had also been converted into sleeping berths or armouries. The whole of the corridor was filled with beds. We had a look into one or two boxes where the marines were sitting cleaning their rifles, patching their clothes or polishing their accoutrements. In front of us we had the handsomely decorated well of the theatre. Only three months ago this had been the scene of every conceivable extravagance from Paris, Brussels and London, From the box where we were standing we would have been gazing down on row upon row of elegant ladies intent on displaying their charms and jewellery. Not long ago coquettish, languishing glances had been exchanged across the stalls which now stood bare and empty. Then life was a whirl of dissipation and excitement. The days had been spent in bathing and in lounging in the high-backed basket chairs or basking on the sun-baked sands. Excursions, dinners and festivities had followed close upon one another and the evenings had been spent in the theatre in careless idleness. Then suddenly the curtain was rung down for the last time, and the war broke out.

We could not resist the temptation to pay a visit to the theatre kitchen. Here stood the fat, jovial, naval cooks in their long white coats and caps and sleeves tucked up. The caldrons were on the boil and appetising fumes filled the atmosphere. Needless to say I was made to taste the dishes, and a gigantic portion of *goulash* in a soup plate was put in front of me - stewed meat, potatoes, vegetables and broth. "Excellent! This is even better than the food we get at the hotel," I thought to myself. I ate my dish with great gusto. No wonder that German soldiers are so strong, fresh and contented-looking when they are fed like this. If I were to be put on field diet for a long while and could choose between officers' and men's fare, I would unhesitatingly take the latter. It is wholesome, nourishing, and tasty food, and does not encumber the soldiers' stomachs with unnecessary ballast. That the state of health in the German Army is as good as it is to a great extent due to the excellent and ample hot food.

But it is now five minutes to one and we must not be late for dinner at the officers' mess, for which I, for my part, had thoroughly spoilt my appetite. We walked up the *Rue du Cerf*. At the corner of this street and the *Digue de Mer*, the road fronting the sea, stands the *Hôtel Littoral*. The former street lies a few metres lower than the *Digue de Mer*, which is perched on the dune skirting the sea. The streets are paved with granite slabs. The last bit of the *Rue du Cerf* forms a slight rise. Up at the corner of the *Hôtel Littoral* a group of officers were standing in animated conversation, pointing to the west and busily using their glasses. We went up to them wondering what was up. The British squadron lay in its accustomed place to westward and west-south-westward, perhaps a little closer in than usual - about seven or eight kilometres away.

A destroyer had just detached itself from the rest and was making at full speed for Ostend, parallel with the coast, as close as possible to the shore. Presently another destroyer appeared, following in the wake of the first. What could they want, these ruffians? Strong language was heard - it was a piece of consummate impudence to come steaming right under our noses like this. Evidently they were reconnoitring - but what insolence, they must have known that we had occupied Ostend! Aha! they suspect that there are submarines and destroyers in the inner harbour, and want to see whether they can detect anything from outside!

Well, whatever their intentions are, we may as well go upstairs and get ready for dinner. I stepped on to my balcony, feeling convinced that by this time the destroyers would have turned back or gone out to sea again. But no! They kept on the same tack as before, and at a speed which made the foam break over their bows. My neighbours, Bess, Haak and Kübler, were also out on their balconies with their glasses. "Astounding insolence," I heard them mutter. There will be something doing presently, I thought to myself, and went in to stow away my diaries, sketches and photographs in a handbag. Once more I cast a glance at the bold destroyers outside. Beneath my balcony I heard an officer shouting out orders in a stentorian voice to the effect that the street was to be cleared and that not a man must show himself on the front, except the sentry at the *Littoral*, but a moment later, he, too, was called in for *Deckung*.

My friends had disappeared; I looked into their rooms, they were empty. Then I took my glasses and hurried downstairs. Bess had warned his colleagues against remaining on the balconies, and he thought that I had gone down already.

In the elegant, carpeted vestibule of the hotel, where sofas, tables and chairs stood in little groups between the huge green plants, officers hurried to and fro, and it was plain that something unusual was pending. "Are they going to shoot?" I asked Bess. "Oh yes, they are going to shoot all right," he answered with stoical calm. Through the glass doors of the vestibule I could see clearly what was going on at the end of the *Rue du Cerf*. Admiral von Schröder was in command and I caught sight of Captain Tägert and his men of the naval brigade, hurrying to bring up the two 6-cm. naval guns and their ammunition carts which we had seen a moment ago at the theatre - there was no other artillery available in the town for the moment. The street had been cleared of civilians, and there were no military visible save those required for serving and directing the little battery. I was not allowed outside, of course, but I had time nevertheless to admire the astounding swiftness and precision with which the two guns were unlimbered, loaded and the range found: "Load! Ready! Fire!"

The first shot rang out. The report re-echoed down the street and the window panes in the hotel rattled in their frames. I went into the restaurant, whence I had an uninterrupted view of the sea and the leading destroyer. A moment later came the second shot. The first shell struck the water right in front of the destroyer, but it was impossible to tell whether it did any damage. The second shell also struck quite close to the target.

There were several officers in the restaurant. I was standing with Dr. Algermissen of Colmar, Lieutenant in the First Naval Reserve. The room was very large, with eight windows looking on to the sea and two others on to the *Rue du Cerf*. At the former little tables stood laid, and on the east side of the room stood the large table where we used to take our meals. Along the centre line the restaurant was supported by four solid pillars. Algermissen and I were standing at the second window from the west.

Directly the German shots had been fired, the two destroyers swung round to port and at the same moment opened lire. Their guns seemed to flash out straight at us. *Deckung!* shouted Algermissen, and we retired immediately behind our pillar, forgetting that it would have been blown away like paper if a shell had struck it. Some of those in the room followed our example, but others contemptuously disdained even this measure of precaution, which perhaps they considered insufficient. The leading destroyer was now about 1400 metres away. Its first shell fell short and dropped into the sea just in front of the *Littoral*. Tall columns of white spray showed where it had struck. Immediately we turned our glasses on to the enemy vessel. There is another flash. Once more we take cover, but only for the body, not for the head, for one simply *cannot* take one's eyes off such a spectacle, whatever the cost! But it would be vain to attempt to describe the excitement which we felt between the spurt of flame from the gun and the impact of the shell. We felt, indeed we were conscious that *we* were the target of the sinister monster speeding towards us through the air. It was not fear, for if anyone had offered to take me to a perfectly safe spot in the centre of the town, I should not have stirred. It was a mixture of breathless excitement, intense interest and a fixed determination not to miss the smallest detail of what was passing. That was why we kept our glasses fixed, now on the boat, now on the point of impact. One projectile ricochetted from the surface of the water, sprang aloft and struck the roof coping, fifty-eight paces away from us, as I subsequently measured. Another described a most peculiar path - how it did it I cannot imagine - but in the end it landed on the stone promenade nearest the sea and buried itself beside the iron railing without bursting. There it lay for a couple of days, and the guard saw to it that nobody went up to interfere with the fearsome object. Twice we saw and heard the shells strike the water, dancing like flat stones over the surface, and finally crashing into the quay wall. First we saw the flash from the British gun, then the impact on striking the water - then came the report. A second or so later a horrible crash struck our ears, announcing that some house frontage had been hit, and followed by the clatter of bricks and stones smashing on to the pavement.

The second destroyer, which I could not see from my point of vantage, was blazing away as cheerfully as the first. As we could not even see *when* she fired, the protection of our pillar was still more illusory. The two German guns fired five or six shots each. Whether they did any damage, I do not know. As the street sloped upward towards the front, the recoil was very severe, and the guns had to be pulled up afresh for each round. The laying of them was combined with considerable difficulty. The whole affair was over in twelve minutes. The destroyers turned almost completely round and steamed with all speed back towards the west, firing continuously. According to the German officers they fired about thirty rounds. They also used machine guns. But the distance grew, and after a while the firing ceased altogether.

One can hardly be in a more dangerous situation than the one we had been exposed to. We had been right in the middle of the shell fire, and yet got away unscathed. The shells had struck, some in front of us, some to the east of us, and the machine guns seemed to be trained on the lower floor of the house adjoining the *Littoral* on the left. Several shots had made their way through its windows. We afterwards discussed this remarkable whim of fate.

"How is it that not a single shot hit our hotel?" I asked. "The British ought to have seen that the German fire was directed from our street corner, and the men serving the guns were the only human beings in sight on the whole front."

"Well, it might seem so, but with the rapid movement of the ships it must be difficult to tell where the fire comes from. Possibly they may have had their attention fixed on the harbour, in the belief that we had torpedo-boats lying there. Several shots went in that direction."

"I hear," said another, "that the *Majestic Hotel* was struck several times, and that one or two officers there were killed. The *Majestic* is a large white monumental building, and the British no doubt thought that they were making a good haul."

"It is very significant," added a third, "that they honoured us with their attention just at one o'clock when they knew that all the officers would be at dinner. Probably they thought that they would get past unimpeded after carrying out their reconnaissance before we were ready."

What can have been the intention of the British? It may perhaps have been - apart from the general reconnaissance to discover what the Germans had in the harbour - to tempt the German artillery out of its hiding-place. Their persistent fire, although the German reply was so slight, would hardly have any other explanation. They gained nothing by the affair, and did themselves and their Belgian Allies a certain amount of matérial damage.

When all was quiet again we settled down to our meal, after which Bess, Kübler and I went over to the *Majestic Hotel*. On the way we passed the house where a shell had lodged in the coping. Some men and women were just issuing from its gates with a lusty-looking child in a perambulator. The elders looked frightened and perturbed. "Where are you off to?" we asked.

"Surely you can't expect us to remain in a house which has been shot at," said one of the men, and added with a touch of sardonic humour, "these are strong pills for little children - we are going to move away."

In the 1910 edition of "Baedeker" the *Majestic Hotel* appears under the name of *Grand Hotel des Bains*. Since then it has changed its name and probably its proprietor. Its handsome white frontage had been badly knocked about by the six shells which we had counted, and which had torn great gaping holes in the walls. On the pavement outside lay huge piles of stone, bricks and masonry, and we noticed the fragments of one of the ornamental plaster angels with wings lifted for flight, but which nevertheless, by the irony of fate, had ended its days in millions of fragments on the stone pavement.

We went into the lobby, where cupboards, tables and chairs lay in picturesque disorder. An hour ago the restaurant had been one of the most elegant in Europe. Its floor was laid with rich red Brussels carpets, the walls were decorated in white and gold and mirrors, with magnificent chandeliers hanging from the ceiling. Now the whole room was a picture of the most ghastly devastation. Two shells had entered just by the lower part of the long row of windows. Their splinters had torn gaping holes in walls and ceilings. The plaster ornaments had fallen down and now lay shivered into fragments, and the carpets had almost disappeared beneath the thick white dust. The windows had been smashed to atoms. Mirrors had cracked into all sorts of curious starry shapes which threatened to collapse altogether if touched. All the furniture lay about in little bits. The tablecloths had been torn to shreds. Yet in the corners of the room, more particularly the western corner, the tables were still standing, but glasses and crockery had, of course, been smashed. I noticed the bases of claret and champagne glasses still standing, whilst the bowls had been shivered to pieces, leaving an edge like an irregular saw blade.

When the bombardment began some fifty officers had assembled together for dinner in this room, and some of them had already begun to eat. Most of them had been seated in the western end of the room, and had thus miraculously escaped death. But at a window in the eastern corner of the room a surgeon, Dr. Lippe, had sat down with an Adjutant of the Naval Brigade, and they had already begun their meal when the bombardment commenced. A shell had burst its way through the lower half of this very window. Probably the hotel had already been struck by a couple of shells, and as the two gentlemen had perhaps felt that they were rather too exposed where they were, it seems that Dr. Lippe had got up to go away, but he got no further than the other end of the table when he was literally torn to shreds by the shell, which struck him right in the back. What was left of his body lay flung forward on the floor, the head resting on the arms in a pool of blood. All that was left of the uniform was a few ragged tatters. A piece of one of his legs was found under a table at the other end of the room, and all the rest of him, in the form of blood-stains, organs and bowels and their contents, were spattered about the white walls and ceiling and the tablecloths. Dr. Schönfelder, who had hurried to the spot, could do nothing but order the remains of his colleague to be gathered together in a tablecloth and carried to a mortuary. The Adjutant, who was badly wounded in the head, was taken to the nearest hospital. A fine-looking Landsturm soldier, who was in the restaurant together with his son, told me that all the other diners had got out of it alive, but most of them had been hurled to the ground by the air pressure, and some had been cut and bruised by flying splinters. They were dazed for the moment, but soon recovered.

A Maubeuge gun doing duty at Middelkerke.

The Western end of the dining room at the 'Majestic' seen from the street. One shell had crashed through the upper part of the window.

Fate is indeed inscrutable. Why should he, who saw the danger and was on the point of seeking a safer place, be overtaken by death, whilst we, who stopped to observe the spectacle from another room, were spared? I was told afterwards that our post had been far from safe. In a confined space the risk is always far greater than out in the open. Strictly speaking the gunners at the street corners were far safer than we. So it came to pass that the visitors at the *Littoral* had no reason to complain of the inhospitable treatment they received at the *Majestic*. If the German naval officers had been well received there, some of us might well have shared Dr. Lippe's fate.

A great change suddenly came over Ostend with the altered situation. Counsels were divided as to what to do. Most people seemed to think that the town would be exposed to renewed firing, but others thought it unlikely that the night would bring a fresh bombardment. Orders were issued that nobody, not even the soldiers, was to be allowed on the front

A 'direct hit' on a house near the Hôtel Littoral.

without special permission. All of the frontage looking on to the sea was to be cleared of people, excepting the guards at the street corners. In the evening and at night there must be no light whatever in the windows looking on to the sea. My friends at the *Littoral* therefore decided to move over to the *Hôtel de la Couronne* opposite the railway station, where a room was also prepared for me. Our luggage was thereupon transferred to our new abode in two baggage carts.

We ourselves remained, however, at the *Littoral* until the evening, and some of us sat in the dark to keep Lieut. Haak company, as he had been ordered to take a battery to the zone beyond Middelkerke. He ate his supper, smoked his cigarette, bade us good-bye and started off with his sailors, horses and guns. The rest of us took our supper at the usual time in the dimly lit lobby, whereupon we said good-bye to the amiable proprietor and servants, and brought our memorable visit in the house to an end. From the corner of the *Rue du Cerf* we cast a glance westward, where the sky was lit up by the fire from the British guns. Then we marched off to *La Couronne* through the dim and silent streets in a darkness unbroken but for the light from an occasional lamp invisible from the sea.

CHAPTER XVII
TWO MORE DAYS ON THE CHANNEL COAST

THE NIGHT WAS calm and still, and when in the morning of the 24th October I was called by Dr. Schonfelder's *Bursche* (servant), he assured me that no shells had fallen on Ostend whilst I had been asleep. But the roar of the artillery duel over at Nieuport was nevertheless the first sound that greeted my ears - an incessant hammering at the last remaining little corner of the Kingdom of Belgium. At midday it was reported that a couple of British ships had been hit, whereupon the entire squadron vanished in the fog.

The day was spent in visiting the troops and transports bound for the Yser Canal front, the wounded in hospitals and the Belgian prisoners in the Kursaal. The latter were but a small contingent of some ten men. They, too, had been told that the Russians were only a hundred kilometres from Berlin. What they said *en passant* about the British policy in Belgium and its result, I simply cannot repeat.

The proprietor of the *Littoral*, where I looked in for a moment in passing, gave the following details of recent happenings. When the Germans were pushing forward against Antwerp, numberless bands of fugitives kept swarming into Ostend. The hotels were crammed and there was a life and bustle in the town such as had never been equalled even in the season. One ship after the other carried the fleeing inhabitants to England and France. The great majority went to Folkestone, the better-off to Eastbourne, Brighton and Bournemouth. But at Dunkerque no one was allowed to land. The vessels arriving there had to continue to Havre. Any sort of craft was good enough, even sailing boats, launches and row-boats. The first person who fled to England was a gentleman from Brussels who had already withdrawn to Ostend with his family.

When a German *Taube* on September 24th dropped a couple of bombs over that town, he interpreted this as a message and a warning that the Germans were on the way. And so he fled precipitately across to London with his family.

From about that time the number of fugitives increased daily. They came in ever-increasing throngs from Antwerp, Ghent, Bruges, Termonde and elsewhere. On October 12th the last shipload of fugitives left the town, and after swarming with life like a beehive, it now became empty and deserted. A few members of the Belgian Cabinet remained, but on the 13th they, too, left by a Government steamer, the *Aventi*. They had been staying at the *Majestic* and *Littoral* - the latter had also been the residence of His Excellency Vandervelde.

By the 14th and 15th of October there were no steamers left at Ostend for the fresh bands of fugitives who kept on arriving, and anything in the nature of fishing-smacks was eagerly snapped up. The reports of the advance of the German legions became louder and more insistent, and the civil population which remained was in a state of the tensest excitement, expecting to see them march in at any moment. Two hours before the first Germans appeared the last Belgian lancer, without helmet or sword, flung himself on his horse and galloped down the stone-paved road towards Middelkerke. The German "advance guard" was not formidable - it consisted of two cyclists and a horseman. It was then half -past ten in the morning, Belgian time. The last fishing-smack with sixty passengers had just cast off its moorings, but was compelled to return. The next few days saw the arrival of increasing bands of German troops, and then came the occurrences which I have just described.

Now, on the 24th of October, the situation at Ostend was, to say the least, interesting. Everybody expected with imperturbable calm that something remarkable would happen. The possibility of an attempted landing was not overlooked. The Germans were prepared for it, at any rate. Anyone who had attempted such a step would have met with a warm reception, for large quantities of troops had been massed along the coast. At our hotel they realised, it seems, fairly plainly what was on

Half of Capt.-Lieut. Bess and the whole of the author on the way to Blankenberghe.

A self-igniting mine explodes.

foot. The stairs were thronged at all hours of the day with officers and men, and outside my door I heard late at night hurried conversations about dressings and bandages, ambulances and stretchers, and fresh batches of wounded who had been brought into the town and lodged in deserted empty houses.

On Sunday the 25th of October the weather was brilliantly fine and as warm as a summer's day, but a thin film of vapour lay over the sea like a delicate veil.

Captain Bess suggested a motor trip to Haak's battery among the dunes beyond Mariakerke. So we started off down the *Rue de Tourout*, dodged about awhile in the open country and finally found our friend Haak amongst his guns. His battery, consisting of four *French* 7.5 cm. guns, looked a very motley lot. The guns themselves had been taken at Maubeuge, the horses were Belgian, and the harness and saddlery English.

In order, without being seen from the sea, to reach the position - well concealed behind the crest of the dune - it had been necessary to pass through a communicating trench which led up to it. We were thus fairly safe and did not have to expose ourselves to any objectionable missiles which might be thrown ashore from the English destroyers. The guns with their grey-coloured shields were also practically invisible from outside, as there was nothing but a small embrasure in the dune wall to indicate where they stood.

Officers and men had dug out caves for themselves, some covered with boards, some, for the lack of something better, with sticks and twigs. It looked quite homelike in their abodes. The sand of the dunes was soft to lie upon, albeit a little damp on account of the advanced autumn.

In the ridge of the dune they had contrived a little niche with boarded floor, where an exceptionally powerful battery telescope had been adjusted on its stand in such a way that only the lenses showed above the crest. With the aid of this telescope we were able to scan the mist-enshrouded sea and the sandy, sunlit coast.

We had just settled down on the edge of the communicating trench, where we sat as close together as in a crowded tramcar, when suddenly an officer up at the battery shouted, *"Deckung, Flieger!"* ("Cover, aviator!") We looked up, and right above us soared an aeroplane at a very great height. "An English biplane," somebody said. "No, I think I can see the Iron Cross under the wings," answered another. But a third, lying on his back, with glasses focussed right on the thing, said quietly: "I can see the red English streamer." We were then told to keep absolutely still. Everyone had to remain where he stood and no one was allowed to move. Otherwise the airman might have noticed the movement and bombs might be dropped over the guns. Now and again he disappeared among the little white clouds; the rascal was evidently following the coast to see what the Germans were up to in the neighbourhood of Ostend. When he was at his nearest, we could hear the droning of his engine. As usual, it was with a certain feeling of satisfaction that I saw him diminish in size and gradually vanish.

Once more we took our seat on the edge of the trench and were just being threatened with coffee when Haak, sweeping the misty horizon with his telescope, reported that a destroyer was in sight. We went up to have a look. Quite right; the outline of the boat was quite distinct, though faint. The distance was gauged at three kilometres. Things suddenly became livelier. One could not tell exactly what might happen. The coast batteries had fired on British ships earlier in the day and it was thought that two of them had been hit, seeing that the squadron withdrew. Perhaps it was now returning at full strength. We had reason to think that the ships were receiving heliographic signals from the coast. Yesterday a couple of spies had been caught, who could not give a satisfactory account of themselves and who, if convicted, would land in the churchyard.

So the order rang out to man the guns. The men scuttled off to their posts like as many rats. Ready to fire!" The first shot rang out, and the other three followed at short intervals. We could see where the shells struck from the cascade of spray that formed on striking the water, but could not tell whether any hits had been scored. In any case, the destroyer remained where she was. She seemed to take it very quietly but could not tell where the fire came from, and her crew had long been inured to the rough music.

On the way back we stopped a moment at Mariakerke and peered out from behind the cover of a house. A battery further west had also begun to fire and the little water-spouts were clearly discernible. But the destroyer's guns had not seemed anxious to join in the tune and the boat soon disappeared in the mist.

This had, however, given me an opportunity of seeing how a coast battery is worked and what sort of a time the officers and men have of it. Constant watchfulness day and night! "Ever ready!" That is their motto. The discipline is of the very strictest and the officers expect the most absolute and immediate obedience to their orders. The result is that the understanding between officers and men is always the very best. Such things as sour faces, grudging steps or disinclination to obey an order are absolutely unknown. Anyone showing symptoms of this kind would be regarded with contempt by everybody, and his life would be made unbearable by his own comrades. The German language has a special word, *Drückeberger*, for individuals of that type, but the type itself is extraordinarily rare. It is no secret how disciplinary shortcomings are punished in war time. But it is not in order to avoid punishment that the German forces on land and sea do their duty. It is because they all have a common end in view, Germany's salvation in this terrible crisis, Germany's victory over her enemies in every part of the world, Germany's future and honour.

On the way home we met an ammunition column clattering along at full speed. The drivers were riding at full "manoeuvre trot" and the horses of some wagons had even broken into a gallop. The wagons with their murderous load rattled heavily and noisily over the stone-paved road. It was easy to tell that the men well knew there was no time to lose and that some coast battery was in urgent need of fresh ammunition. These columns, when really and seriously on the move, are a joy and a feast to the eye.

A little further on we passed a contingent of fifty French prisoners who were being taken into safe custody under a German guard. The fighting had shorn their red and blue uniforms of their lustre, and the men themselves looked pale and tired. What a contrast to the marines and gunners we had just seen! But then joyous faces are not to be expected from prisoners of war.

In the afternoon, accompanied by Bess and Schönfelder, I made another excursion along the ideal automobile road which skirts the coast north-eastward, just inside the long line of dunes.

In the magnificent pavilion of the Royal (Knocke) Golf Club we inspected a platoon of marine infantry, who seemed to be having the time of their lives. *Via* Venduyne we went on to Blankenberghe, where the sea promenade resembled that of Ostend, except that the population had remained and in addition had been reinforced by numberless refugees from Brussels and elsewhere. The hotels had been taken possession of by well-to-do people, and the beach was filled with a motley crowd of men, women and young girls; they all seemed more or less to be enjoying themselves. We met a couple of naval officers, among them a cheery and

Dr. Schonfelder and the author on the dunes at Ostend.

A traverse at Dorpfeld.

amusing corvette commander named Mönch. He told us that no British warships had been seen in this direction. The sea had probably been mined in this part. Not far north-east of Blankenberghe lies Zeebrugge, the port of Bruges. The two towns are connected by a canal, which might have been laid out with a ruler.

In the gloaming we drove past the great Belgian hospital on the eastern outskirts of Ostend. A funeral was taking place in its little cemetery. Several officers and a number of men were standing round the grave. The naval chaplain had just finished speaking and the band was playing a funeral march. The funeral was that of Chief-Surgeon Dr. Lippe, whose career had been ended yesterday by the shell from the British destroyer.

In due course we got back once more to *La Couronne* and assembled as usual for supper at eight o'clock. The restaurant is neither as large nor as fine as at the *Littoral*, and we missed above all the drowsy music of the swell breaking on the beach. Our former large company has now been split up into several little groups. Bess, Schönfelder, Kübler and I stick together as before. The clock strikes ten, we dawdle over our coffee and cigars discussing the war, reciting Kipling and exchanging anecdotes. We laugh till our sides ache over Schonfelder's desperate efforts to repeat quickly the words: *"Didon dîna, dit-on, du dos d'un dodu dindon."* But he got his revenge by confronting me with the following awkward problem: What does the following sentence sound like when spelt backward: *"Ein Neger mit Gazelle zagt im Regen nie"?* [26]

Such was the mood at our table, and such is the mood of the fighting men all along the front. Anxiety as to the result, nervousness, overwork, fear, are terms of which they do not know the meaning. Nothing made a deeper impression on me than this wonderful calm, this absolute certainty of victory everywhere, this incredible superabundance of physical energy and of matériel in men, horses and iron. It seemed to me that the German armies on the western front had not yet realised the irresistible strength which they had at their disposal. The

---

26. Spells the same backwards.

apparent pause was a link in a strategic chain. When the moment for the great decision arrived, the army would still be in possession of its full collective strength. As yet everything was running smoothly and easily, as if it had been merely a matter of some well-prepared, gigantic autumn manoeuvre.

As we were sitting there chatting, a petty officer from the Naval Brigade entered and announced to Dr. Schönfelder that fresh transports of wounded had just arrived from the vicinity of the Yser Canal. They had been accommodated temporarily in restaurants and public-houses and any other vacant houses that were available. The two doctors at once rose and said good night. To my question whether I might join them they said "by all means." So we threw our raincoats over us, for it was pouring in torrents, and marched out into the pitch-black night accompanied by the petty officer.

At first he took us to a moderately lighted low-class eating house. The doctors threw off their tunics and put on their white operating coats. A couple of assistants from the naval hospital section were there to help them and had brought dressings, instruments and drugs in bags and cases. A table was brought out into the middle of the floor under the lights with a cushion covered with a towel for a pillow. "Bring in the first man," ordered Dr. Schönfelder. A little, fair-haired, sturdily built man was carried in and placed on the table. "Name?" - "Korte." "Regiment?"- "Eighth company of 35th Infantry Reserve." "Where is your wound? "- "In the left calf." His breeches, fitting tight over his leg, were slit open. The first dressing, saturated with pus and clotted blood and stiffened into a solid lump, was removed with scissors and knife. The wound looked very unpleasant, the flesh hung in shreds, the skin had been torn away and a nasty smell issued from the open sore. "Please look away," said the Doctor as the soldier tried to look at his wound, and I did my best to attract his attention. Powder of iodoform was sprinkled upon the wound, a few little plugs of gauze were pressed in with pincers in order to keep the wound open for the escape of the pus and to induce the growth of fresh skin. Shreds of dead tissue were removed and a fresh dressing was applied. The man had been wounded four days previously at a new bridge over the Yser Canal. It was a splinter from a shrapnel shell that had hit him.

"Next man!" He came in limping, supported by two ambulance men. His bullet had caught him in the head, his skull was cracked, but the brain was evidently uninjured. He was a wonderfully plucky chap. According to himself it was nothing to speak of, and he deferentially asked the doctor to be so kind as to see that he was put right as soon as possible as he wanted to get out again. He seemed a little peculiar, however, and seemed to have had a terrible shock. The hair was cut and shaved away, the wound was washed with sublimate and benzine. Tincture of iodine was painted on with a brush and a piece of gauze with iodoform applied. Thereupon he was bandaged so thoroughly that only mouth, nose and eyes were free.

"Next man!" He was a Fleming in Belgian uniform. He had been shot through the seat, and was treated with the same care as the German soldiers. An ashen paleness lay over his features and he looked tired and done-up, but seemed very grateful for the attention given him as he was carried away from the table.

And so it went on. Every time that "next man" was called, another wounded soldier was brought in for treatment, I had thought of making a note of the cases, but they were too many and were dealt with in double shifts by the two doctors.

When the whole lot had been seen to, we went out guided by a lantern. The rain had formed great puddles in the street. *"Wer da?"* cried a sentry, but let us pass when he saw we were doctors. We were now taken to a house of three stories where every room was occupied. The few beds there were, had been requisitioned, and when they were all gone the wounded men were laid on the floor. Most of them were in a deep and heavy sleep, dead-tired after all they had gone through. Some snored in different keys, it was rest, rest, rest that they wanted above everything. Now and then we heard a deep sigh, but no groaning, no complaining. The French and Belgians are as submissive and as patient as the Germans.

They are too many to be taken down to the emergency operating theatre. The doctors go from bed to bed, and now and then a light is projected to display the wound, which is treated in most cases in the way I have described. The broken victims of war show no fear of the doctor or of his intentions. On the contrary, they are glad that he is willing to help them. Clenched teeth and grimaces alone show what they are going through. Never a sound of complaint, never a word about the pain, never an entreaty to be left in peace. In the eye of some of the badly wounded who will be cripples for life I sometimes seem to read the reflection: shall I ever see father and mother and brothers and sisters again, shall I ever settle down again in our quiet home as of yore, shall I ever go back to the workshop, to the mine, to the dock, to the tram, to the field, or whatever may have been his former occupation. The torn, dirty, soiled and sooty grey uniforms bore eloquent witness to the hardships they had gone through.

We pass from house to house among the victims of war's harvest. We were told it was the Belgians who had been attacking - a hopeless struggle for the last little strip which still remains to them of their country.

Finally we came into a room containing among other wounded a soldier who had been shot through the left hand. "How do you feel?" asks the doctor. "Oh, pretty well, though it hurts a bit." - "Come with me down into the bar; it is lighter there and we shall see what can be done." A chair is brought for the soldier, the dressing is taken off, his hand is blue and swollen. "Will he keep his hand?" I whisper into the doctor's ear. "I hope so, it is not a very serious wound." The bullet has struck him as he was lying down in his trench and only had the left hand exposed. Whilst the wound is being examined, I ask the soldier: "Where are you from?" - "I am a Hamburg man, but live in Berlin." "What is your occupation?" - "Actor," he answers with pathetic humour. "It is a long way from the stage to the trench," I remark, and he nods as he smiles his approval. By the light of the lamp I discerned a handsome, refined, clean-shaven face with Roman nose and solemn blue eyes. One could see that he was thinking of life's great tragedy. Probably he had never played a better part than that which he had just performed out on the battlefield with the lurid glare of the shells for footlights. *"Gute*

Besserung!" we said and patted him on the shoulder. *"Danke vielmals,"* he replied, and went up to his bed again.

Now the round was over and we went out into the night. The rain was pelting down, but the sound of it was drowned by the thunder of the cannonade which after an hour's cessation had now since lo o'clock become more violent than ever. No human beings were to be seen, only here and there a sentry with the rain pouring off his greatcoat. As we passed St. Peter's and St. Paul's the clocks struck twelve slowly and deliberately. It was a terrible night for the soldiers in the open trenches, which must by now have been half full of water. I could not take my thoughts off them as I entered the light and cosy warmth of *La Couronne.* But ask them if they would like to change with you, and the gruffness of the answer will surprise you: "No, thanks, warm beds there will be enough of at home when the fighting is over. Just now we are out on the country's business, and in the trenches we stop even if we are up to the neck in water and if it rains brimstone from the heavens!" Such things as sentimentality and fuss are utterly unknown to the German soldiers. They *know* what they are doing and they want to do nothing but their duty.

October 26th was my last day in Ostend. As nothing startling seemed about to happen in the immediate future, I thought I might as well return to Brussels, but now Bess came with the suggestion that we should take a little trip to the stores and depots in the inner harbour, to which I readily assented - Brussels, after all, was only a couple of hours away and could wait. The stores contained all sorts of spare parts for ships and their engines, plates, propellers, screws, cables, compasses, a surfeit of useful things which might be wanted at any moment. We likewise inspected a training ship now used for accommodating troops.

Just as we were busy over our inspection, we heard four sharp reports from the sea. It was not the usual firing in the west, the sound came from the north and the source of it could not be far distant. Is it the English torpedo boats? we wondered as we hurried into our car and drove down towards the beach past the lighthouse. On the way we met a naval officer who told us that the reports came from mines, which had

Group beside one of the guns of Liet. Haak's battery. (Furthest to the left are Capt. Lieut. Bess and Lieut. Haak).

Gun crew getting to fire on a British destroyer.

detonated on their own account. Some ten such explosions had been heard during the night, and the waterspouts thrown up by the four we heard had been visible from the coast. If we cared and had patience enough to sit and wait among the dunes, the lieutenant had no doubt that we should see some more.

So we went down to the belt of dunes north-west of the lighthouse, where some men of the naval brigade were busy digging in a battery of guns mounted on a temporary plank emplacement. They were also digging trenches in the dunes for themselves and their ammunition boxes. Bess showed the soldiers how to mask the guns in the best possible way with grass and plants.

We had not been there very long before a dark column of water flung itself into the air on the horizon. We estimated its height at thirty metres and the distance, calculated from the interval between sight and sound, at 5.6 kilometres. The column was almost black, as if the water had been mixed with slime from the bottom and resembled a naphtha fountain in the Balakhani. We at once sent a man to fetch chart and compasses. I myself had my kodak ready, but was too late to snap this first explosion.

However, it was not many minutes before the next water column spurted up from the surface of the sea in the same northnorth-westerly direction as the other and accompanied by the same deafening report. This time I was just quick enough to get a picture. A moment later two other mines exploded, this time to the north-north-east and only about 3.3 kilometres away. We waited for two more explosions at 3 and 4.3 kilometres respectively, and had then had enough.

The bearings of the six mines were pricked on the chart and in this way the officers obtained the necessary data for determining the position of the mine-field. Possibly it extended right across the Channel. The mines we had noticed exploded, curiously enough, in couples. They had clearly been laid in double or multiple lines and had been equipped with time fuses. What the time was, we could not tell, perhaps a week, perhaps longer. Mines of this type are employed for the temporary blockade of a harbour, which it is intended to attack on a more suitable occasion. But now, as it happened, the only creatures incommoded were the fishes in the sea. The Germans, on the other hand, were very glad to know where the mine-field lay and that the fairway was now clear.

After dinner I learnt that a motor-car had arrived from Ghent with one of Krupp's engineers, and was to return immediately to that city. Captain Jakobson, one of my friends, arranged for me to avail myself of this opportunity, so I made ready to depart. Good-bye to Tägert, Bess, Jakobson and Kübler and greetings to all the others - these splendid and capable fellows who had been my companions during these never-to-be-forgotten days and with whom I shared the memory of dangers happily survived. Then off I went at the usual break-neck speed.

At Ghistelles I stopped for three-quarters of an hour to see Colonel-General von Beseler, one of my old friends from the *Gesellschaft für Erdkunde* (Geographical Society) in Berlin. We had much to talk about, and he related many episodes from the last few days' fighting on the Yser Canal. Of the result he had as little doubt as anyone else and reiterated time after time: "We *must* win!" von Beseler is one of the finest generals of the German army. It was he who took Antwerp and he was now commanding the extreme right flank nearest the sea. As a man he is congenial and fascinating.

I continue my journey. A convoy of French prisoners is being taken into the interior - marine infantry, my chauffeur tells me. The road hereabouts abounds in inns and public houses, I wonder how many. It would have given me something to do to count the inn signs by the roadside. At Bruges we did not stop; at Ghent we drove up to the Base Commandant's office, in a narrow street, flying the German flag. A couple of obliging officers immediately offered to assist me, but for the moment all I wanted was to get to Brussels; if possible, I added, I should be very grateful for the loan of a car to the capital. Yes, there would be no difficulty about that, they assured me. General Jung would be sure to arrange it for me. So my name was taken in to the General and a minute later he came dashing out and greeted me with the utmost warmth, for he remembered me well from a fete in Posen where I had lectured in February, 1910.

"But there cannot be any question of your starting off just yet," said the General. "You must first sup with us at seven and a car will be ready for you at nine."

I did not need much pressing and spent a couple of delightful hours with these officers. At nine to the minute the car stood ready. It was a covered car, which was thought safer at night, and had a couple of exceptionally powerful head lamps. And, best of all, I had a delightful Austrian lieutenant to keep me company - one of those in charge of the Austrian 30.5-cm. mortars in use on the western front. It was surpassingly interesting to listen to all that he had gone through. The ninety minutes which separated us from Brussels were all too quickly over.

CHAPTER XVIII
TO BAPAUME

MY NOTES DO not contain much concerning the 27th of October. In the first place I had a good long sleep and the rest of the day was mostly taken up by "attending to private business," completing my sketches and plans and writing letters. While I was sitting in the hotel over my late breakfast, a fine-looking officer came straight up to my table. He smiled humorously, wondering whether I would recognise him. Certainly I did! In fact I called out his name before he had time to utter a word: "Duke Adolf Friedrich of Mecklenburg!"

The Duke had been a friend of mine for several years. In the geographical world he bears a great and famous name, thanks to his travels in Africa, which had been conscientiously planned, most skillfully carried out and ably and entertainingly described. He was now Governor of Togoland, but happened to be in Germany on leave when the war broke out. Under these circumstances, in Germany's great hour of destiny, he simply *could not* return to Africa, and since, in his capacity as governor of a colony, he held no military command in the home country, he volunteered for service as intelligence officer, and was appointed to his old army corps.

The Duke seemed glad to see me, and we sat and talked until it was time for him to return to his duties. The upshot was that I faithfully promised to accept his kind offer to come to Bapaume and spend a few days with him. He said I should not want for anything; he himself lived in a small house, but he would find accommodation for me near by. We were to take trips in various directions, as just now he had plenty of spare time; no large operations seemed to be in prospect, I might come whenever it suited me; I should always be welcome. And so we parted for the present.

I had supper with Field-marshal General von der Goltz. The guests included on this occasion Duke Ernst Günther of Schleswig-Holstein, brother of the German Empress, and Duke Georg of Meiningen, who had lost his father and his brother in the war. The Field-marshal proposed that I should accompany him on the 29th of October to the front in the region of Dixmude. As, moreover, General Bailer asked me whether I was disposed to go with him and Councillor von Lumm on a trip to the outer forts of Antwerp on the 28th, my programme was well filled for the next few days.

October 28th broke with a clouded sky, and a thick mist was lying over town and country in the morning. The two gentlemen and the young lieutenant, who sat at the wheel beside the chauffeur, came to fetch me in the morning, and we started out on the familiar road to Malines.

As already mentioned, our purpose was to inspect as many as we could of Antwerp's southern forts and redoubts. I shall not give any actual description of these fortifications. The few words I will say concerning them are merely added in order that the two or three photos which are reproduced here may not be beside the context.

First of all we drove to Fort Waelhem, where a "42-cm." had gone right through the bed of concrete, here, as elsewhere, five or six metres thick, and where an observation tower, resembling a gigantic church-bell, had been thrown over on to its side by the air-pressure. One of the turrets is supposed to have been blown up by the Belgians themselves when they evacuated the fort. A few Belgian 12-cm. guns inside and outside the fort had been deprived of their breech-blocks. Lying near a barrack-wall were heaps of cartridge cases, tin boxes and baskets for carrying the shells. These latter were as finely and slenderly woven as if they had been intended for carrying grapes.

We drove on to the east and north-east, and our next stopping-place was Fort Chemin de Fer, which had been rather severely peppered with smaller shells, while its shattered turret had been blown up from the inside by the defenders themselves. Fort St, Catherine I have already mentioned, and we will therefore pass on, *via* the village of Wavre, with its wrecked church, to the Dorpfeld fortifications. An object of particular interest was the infantry breastwork surrounding this entrenchment. Sandbags, and sometimes gabions, had been plentifully applied here. There were numerous traverses, intended for protection against enfilading or slanting fire, and generally consisting of sandbags in timber-lined trenches. The gabions, I thought, looked like defensive works similar to those used in the seventeenth century. But they were as useful now as then.

We did not stop at the Boersbaek fortification, but went straight on to Fort Koningshoyckt, which had received some nasty hits and where a number of captured 12-cm. guns, all without their breech-blocks, had been ranged up in a row.

Fort Talaert tempted me to take one or two photos, which need no comment. In one of them the reader will observe a huge gaping hole in the concrete. Another will give him an idea of what disarranged wire entanglements look like.

Fort Lierre, in Dutch Lier, is the largest of all the fortifications in the outer girdle of Antwerp. Here several 42-cm. shells had wrought terrible havoc. One had struck through the lower part of the concrete bed of a turret and penetrated into the interior regions, smashing all that was in its path. In the interior of the fort we found extensive quartering accommodation for the garrison. Belgian uniforms left behind were still lying about. Generally speaking the Germans found the barrack-rooms in the fort in great disorder. All scraps and lumber had now been removed and formed regular rubbish heaps outside.

The small town of Lierre has fared terribly ill, but the church stands almost untouched among the ruins. The village of Duffel has also suffered considerably. In its labyrinth of narrow lanes people were busy removing the rubbish.

On our way back we found the market-place of Malines crowded with carts and carriages full of visitors who had come from Brussels to see the scenes of destruction. On the road to the capital, too, we passed quite a procession of sorrowful pilgrims.

At night I saw the Field-marshal for a minute. He said he should be unable to travel the next day, as the King of Saxony was then expected in Antwerp. Remembering that a bird in the hand was worth two in the bush, I thereupon decided to go on to Bapaume. A car was to be placed at my disposal whenever I wanted it.

I accordingly proceeded on the morning of October 29th to the office of the Governor-General, where I was informed that the Field-marshal had instructed von Siemens to take me to Bapaume. I said good-bye to my friends Majors Nethe and von Weller, stowed my luggage away in the car and was ready for starting. I cannot abstain from remarking that I never had a more distinguished chauffeur than on this occasion, as it was the head of the firm of Siemens and Halskc himself who had donned the motor goggles and thick driving-gloves, and with strong skilled hands grasped the wheel. I sat down by his side and was thus conveniently at his elbow. A soldier was seated in the car, armed with rifle and revolver. The weather was fine, but the air was damp, as usual at this season.

It was 10.45 when, with piercing shrieks of the hooter and the warning trills of the pipe-horn, we bowled along the Boulevard du Midi and Rue des Beiges and came out on the Chaussée de Mons - a hybrid between a country road and a paved street and with a canal running by its left side. A whirl of fallen brown leaves rose in the wake of the car as it dashed on to Hal at the rate of seventy-four kilometres an hour. Narrow winding streets lead up to the market square of the little place, where the market was in full swing and where pigs and vegetables were being sold from peasants' carts and stalls. Perfectly peaceful, rustic scenes, bustling life and motion - nothing to remind one of the war.

In Tubize the bells of the village church were tolling, as if for a funeral. The country further on is somewhat hilly. Beyond Braine le Comte the splendid high road was without stone-paving. The autumn wind moaned in the yellow crowns of the trees, and the leaves were falling around us like snow-flakes.

We reached Soignies in a couple of minutes. Our speed was up to eighty-two or eighty-four kilometres per hour, falling off on slight curves to sixty. At all cross-roads, bridges and villages German Landsturm men in spick-and-span helmets and dark-blue uniforms stood posted, trusty and alert as ever. The road to Mons is straight and was in excellent condition, but the traffic was very inconsiderable. About noon a tyre burst, but was replaced in thirteen minutes - one could see that a great engineer was handling the nuts and tools.

In the Mons region we passed through the great coal-mining district. All useless mineral taken out of the pits had to be cleared away so as not to take up any space which might be utilised to better advantage. By means of special tipping arrangements the refuse had thus been piled up into veritable pyramids, or rather huge cones, whose strange-looking summits towered high on either side of the road. To the right we saw a whole row of tall smoking chimneys - one is always glad to observe any signs of resumed activity and reawaking life. The smoke hung like a dark pall over the neighbourhood. It was no longer a country road, it was an unbroken street as far as Boussu - which therefore seemed to be an integral part of Mons. *"Sehr starke Industriegegend"* ("very 'pronounced' industrial region this") shouted von Siemens in my ear; he had been here on business just before the war.

Just on the other side of Quiévrain we crossed the French frontier. Poplars, stately and solemn like cypresses, rose up on both sides of the high road, now once more provided with stone-paving. Here, too, we observed the absence of men in the prime of life. Only old men and boys are to be seen, and now and then a cripple. Women are greatly in the majority - widows and sorrowing sisters and brides who for three months have not heard a word from their men-folk.

Valenciennes, an Intermediate Base Commandant's post - numerous motor-cars and innumerable troops! The country opens up more and becomes flatter. We leave Demain and Bouchain to the right of our road, which runs *via* Douchy. The mist lies over the landscape like a heavy veil, through which we dimly discern the outlines of thickets and orchards. Many of the crops were still standing in the fields, waiting for hands to bring them in. But these are not forthcoming! Only in one little field did we see some old people and children busy gathering beets into baskets. Of horses not a sign. The carts that were at work were drawn by oxen. Lonely women, ever and anon, looked after us with sad, wondering eyes.

Hole made by a 42 cm. shell in Fort Talaert.

At the entrance to Fort Talaert.

One could guess their thoughts, but their demeanour was always calm and demure; now and then one saw, not without pity, a white-bearded old man, with his staff in one hand leading a waif by the other.

At Cambrai von Siemens drew up at the Base Commandant's office to obtain some information. Numbers of cars were passing there, or waiting in the market-place. I noticed here once more the first indications of our proximity to the front. Cambrai is a railhead, and at the station troops were busy transferring the matériel from the railway wagons to the lines of communication transport column, or direct to the Army Service Corps detachments of the troops ahead. Fresh bodies of troops were also detraining to march west.

We next proceed through a landscape characterised by extensive shallow undulations. The road is perfectly straight, stone-paved and lined with autumn-tinted or leaf-bared trees.

We meet several cyclist orderlies and pass a supply column with its wagons covered with green branches.

When finally we reached Bapaume we had been three and a half hours on the road, whereof three-quarters of an hour had been taken up by stops on the way. One could scarcely cover a distance of about one hundred English miles in a shorter time - allowing for the slowing down in passing through towns and villages.

We drove direct to the quarters of Captain Trutz, who had charge of all matters concerning cars, petrol, quartering and the like, and began by taking lunch with him - consisting of bread and butter and ham, hard-boiled eggs and claret. Then my excellent friend von Siemens took leave and sped back to Brussels. Duke Adolf Friedrich was out, but was expected back about five. I was advised in the meantime to take up my quarters in some house near the Duke's. A noncommissioned officer was ordered to conduct me to the Maire and I received from the latter a quartering ticket entitling me to occupy a room just opposite the Duke's quarters. The French Maire was sitting in his office up to his eyes in work and surrounded by big piles of papers. But he was very polite and obliging, and no doubt consoled himself with the trite reflection that "necessity knows no law."

I also had to report myself at the Base Commandant's office, where I was received, as always, with the greatest kindness. But then came the Chief himself, an old Bavarian Colonel who had retired from the service, but on the outbreak of the war had rejoined. And now he began to storm. "Who the thunder is this civilian?" he roared - "what business have you here? - where do you come from? - are you a pressman? I shall want to know what you are here for, and whether you have permission to stay here in Bapaume!" I tried to conciliate the irate Colonel by every imaginable means, but he went on raging like a model drill-sergeant. A few days later I met him again, and he then said: "Can you ever forgive me for being so rude the other day?" "Yes, dear Colonel, I assure you that it was a priceless pleasure to me to see a Bavarian warrior in the full flower of his vigour and forcefulness; I might have been a spy, and you had your orders to obey." Of course we became friends for life, and it would give me pleasure to meet him again some day.

I was then conducted by my non-commissioned officer to the house where I was to stay. A name-board bearing the inscription *Notaire* was over the door. We rang the bell and an elderly servant came and opened it - followed, close at her heels, by an old gentleman of distinguished appearance, tall and with lofty forehead, kindly dark eyes below bushy brows, snow-white hair and white moustache and whiskers. This was the *Notaire*, Maître Emile Cossart, who had not been scared away from house and home by the war, but had quietly remained behind to face the turmoil. He asked me kindly to put up with the only visitors' room he had to offer me, and which was duly shown me by one of his three nieces. Mademoiselle Lengagne, and the servant. The room was plain but neat and cheerful, and its two windows looked out on to a little garden.

As regards terms, I told Monsieur Cossart that I would pay rent for the room for the days I should occupy it. But he would not hear of this. Without going into lengthy details I pleaded my capacity as citizen of a neutral country - a circumstance which forbade me taking quarters without paying for them. But it was all no use. To all my arguments he had but one reply: *"C'est impossible!"* - uttered in an inimitable manner. In the end I had no alternative but to thank him for his great hospitality.

M. Cossart was a typical elderly *rentier* in a French country town - and a most attractive and estimable specimen. Notwithstanding the storm which had burst over his country, his province and his home, he still retained an unquenchable good humour. In the war of 1870-71 he had served in the army and had been taken prisoner in Peronne and interned in Jüterbog, where he remained two and a half months. He had been well treated while a prisoner in German hands, and had never had cause to complain, and I was able to assure him that at the present moment the French prisoners were treated most kindly. We talked together with the greatest frankness. M. Cossart did not believe that the Germans would win. In the former war it was different, but now they had England, too, and great and powerful Russia against them. The fact that Germany, by her astounding offensive power, had been able to swamp Belgium and part of north-eastern France, did not signify so very much after all. The fortune of war would soon turn, and change in favour of France. "We shall see! We shall see!" he said over and over again.

I tried to explain to him the position in the eastern theatre of war and told him of Hindenburg's victories, of the great calmness which reigned in Germany, and of the Russians' "march to Berlin," which General Rennenkampf had promised but of which nothing had been seen so far. It had not been beneficial for France, I said, to invest thousands upon thousands of millions of francs in a country whose aid failed just at the moment when it was most needed. If I did not admire France and love her intelligent, industrious, thrifty and patriotic people I might have rejoiced at a diplomacy which had brought about such calamities as the present; as it was, I was grieved at a policy from which no good could ever come.

"Nous verrons - nous verrons," M. Cossart replied, nodding his head and smiling. But then it occurred to him that perhaps he had said too much, and wondered whether the German officers would take offence and cause him trouble if they got to hear of it.

Certainly not, I assured him, he need not be afraid of that. He might tell the German officers without fear that he blindly trusted in the victory of the French arms and the eventual retreat of the German hosts, without causing a single forehead to frown in anger. Any German officer would honour such speech and show his respect for a man who had fought for his country in his younger days, and who still, in the autumn of life, was cherishing great and glorious ideas concerning his nation. "For you may say what you like of the Germans, and look upon them, if you like, as your sworn enemies, yet it is a fact that the Germans admire in others the qualities which they cherish in their own people. Therefore the German soldiers feel nothing but esteem for their French opponents; as regards General Joffre, the whole German army is unanimous in thinking him a great and talented general." Among the Germanic race, I told him, there is not a vestige of national hatred of the French, nothing but good-will and sympathy.

And when I told him how sorry I was that the whole of his people should suffer in consequence of a mistake which had been made by a few responsible professional politicians, he could but shrug his shoulders and raise his eyebrows and reply: "But please always think and speak well of France!"

We had many a discussion on this topic as I went in or out through his hall. And when I had time to spare before joining the German officers at dinner, I would knock at the door of the French drawing-room - for was I not a neutral? - and was always met with a cheery *"entrez."* There sat M. Cossart in his rocking-chair, and his three amiable nieces were busy with their needlework round the table beneath the lamp, and then we could argue on politics to and fro without either party yielding one jot. Not because he was of the Latin and I of the Germanic race, but because our political views were as irreconcilable as fire and water. If Germany was crushed, I maintained, Russia would push forward to the Atlantic, and this could only be done over Swedish soil - across the Scandinavian peninsula, up there in the north. Therefore, for the sake of my country, I *could not* but wish for Germany's victory - a complete victory. But to M. Cossart Germany's victory meant fearful calamities

The interior of Fort Lierre.

Privy Councillor Von Lumm beside the hole made by a 42cm. shell.

for his own native land. Hence it was, and *could not* but be impossible for us to agree.

Yet we always spoke with dignity and calm. The old lawyer never forgot himself, and I entertained the warmest and sincerest regard for him. I was always glad to have a chat with him, and regretted that, as a rule, time was so short.

How different he was from those hot-heads I met elsewhere, who when confronted with an opinion at variance with their own, are so far from being able to master an opponent that they cannot even master themselves! Or how unlike a newspaper press which - Heaven knows by what means - may be induced to be silent on questions which concern the very life and existence of a nation, but loses all restraint and dignity in the face of a frankly and openly expressed opinion.

M. Cossart was a man of quite another kind. There was no room in his soul for malice or cowardice. He was a gentleman to his finger-tips. His name, his avocation, his address are all stated above, and he is easily found. I have no fear lest my openness of speech might cause him any harm. He runs no risk as far as the Germans are concerned. I would, moreover, entreat my German friends in Bapaume - if this book should ever meet their eyes - to show him if but a fraction of the kindness they have shown to me. And as regards the French, they may - when peace once more reigns on earth - ask M. Cossart whether my statement is true. Nor should they forget to thank him that, in the face of the overwhelming might of the invasion, he always fearlessly stood up for France, with unruffled brow, unflinching eyes and manly speech - speech which made one bow in fancy before the laurel-wreathed tricolor over his head.

CHAPTER XIX

AN EXCURSION TO THE FRONT AT LILLE

THERE CAME A knock at my door. *"Entrez!"* I cried as neutrally as possible, and in stepped Duke Adolf Friedrich of Mecklenburg, young and gay and manly. He held out both hands to me and bade me heartily welcome to Bapaume. He hoped that I would be pleased with the few days I was to spend there. "But this room is too small!" - "Oh no, it is quite big enough." - "Right. We will take all meals together, for I am now free for several days and shall be able to take you round and show you the sights."

Thereupon we sat and chatted until it was time to get ready for supper in the officers' mess. When we entered, they were all assembled. The large table was presided over by Infantry General von Plettenberg, Chief of the Garde-Corps, Adjutant General to H.M. the Emperor and an old friend of our own Chief of Staff General Bildt. He was a tall man, thin and fair, a real soldier and a brave and plucky man who was never more at home than when the bullets were whizzing round him. Like Field-marshals von Haeseler and von der Goltz, he had the incurable habit of always turning up at odd moments where danger loomed largest. He had a way of walking out to the foremost trenches in the middle of the night and drawing the French rifle fire at a range of two hundred metres, and this merely to see how the soldiers were getting on and to make sure that everything was in the best order, A magnificent trait, in my opinion, for a plucky leader braces the soldiers' courage. We Swedes have always demanded this quality from our leaders. General von Plettenberg was a man of quick and impulsive temperament, but he was serious nevertheless, partly perhaps because he had recently lost a son in the war. At table he would sit wrapped in thought for a long while, then

Streets at the Port Douai which have suffered through the bombardmant.

Hereditary Prince Friedrich of Hohenzollern and
Duke Adolph Friedrich of Mecklenburg.

suddenly his eyes would fill with humour and he would break into a jest, as when he said that it was bad for the health to go out to the war, for they shoot so thoughtlessly and lay the guns so carelessly that at times shells will actually drop at the very spot where one is standing.

When the General had retired early to go about his night's work, the Duke asked a dozen merry and entertaining officers to join him at his house. There we gathered in the drawingroom, cigars were lighted and the frothing nectar was poured out. They were all in brilliant spirits. No gloomy faces among these men, many of whom looked death in the face every day from trenches and aircraft and on daring scouting duty.

They represented among them many of Germany's most illustrious families. The talk was loud and frank and gay, but when an officer of the General Staff came in straight from the Chief Command and read out the latest news from the eastern battlefields or from far-away tropical seas, perfect stillness and silence suddenly came upon the room and everybody listened intently. After that a more serious mood came over the assembly and they began to discuss the solemn business of war.

The guests included the young Hereditary Prince Friedrich of Hohenzollern, a beardless Apollo, related to three royal houses. He is a nephew of the King of Roumania, In some way or other, I forget how, he is a kinsman of the unhappy King of Belgium, and the brother-in-law of no less a person than - ex-King Manuel of Portugal. The Prince was an exceedingly pleasant young fellow, brimming over with good spirits and full of jests and pranks, but I never saw him laugh.

Another guest was the amiable Herr Schoelvinck, a director of Benz and Company. He was now serving in the army with the rank of Captain and was one of the four *parlementaires* who were despatched to Rheims to discuss the terms of capitulation. They were taken prisoners and regarded as spies, and would probably have shared their usual fate had not the Emperor appealed to the American Ambassador in Paris, who managed to secure their release. I should say that in time to come they will have something to tell about the reception accorded them in France.

Another of the four *parlementaires* was also present at this evening's sitting, in the person of volunteer Cleving of the Royal Theatre of Berlin, a perfectly fascinating man, full of humour, anecdote and song. An actor with the Iron Cross is probably something out of the ordinary, but what is there that is not striking on this endless German front of warriors! Perhaps Cleving's greatest charm is his genius for accompanying himself on the guitar after the fashion of our own Sven Scholander. The two troubadours were to have started out on a singing tour together this autumn. But Cleving was destined to listen to a very different kind of music - that of the shrapnel shells, and it was a very different kind of theatre that he was about to perform in. He did not grumble at the change. Before he had scattered joy and merriment around him with his acting and his song, now he also bore the glory which surrounds a warrior who has fought with honour and bravery for his country.

Yet the war had not quite been able to part him from his guitar. He had brought it with him and presently he settled down on a chair in our little circle and all became silent. French *chansons*, German soldier ditties of long ago, winter songs from 1530 and *"Die Goldene Kugel"* with music by himself, all succeeded one another but too rapidly. To me he seemed to keep the best to the end, when he surprised me with a selection from our own Swedish lyrical poet Bellman.

But Cleving could sing of Mandalay, too, choosing a far prettier and more inspiriting tune than the English one, and with other words than Kipling's. "But I must have a piano accompaniment for this," he declared. The Duke pressed a button and an orderly entered. "Bring in a piano," he said, *"Ja wohl, Hoheit."* In a quarter of an hour the doors were thrown open and four gigantic soldiers strode in, carrying a piano. "Where have they found that, I wonder?" I asked. "Oh, I suppose they've conjured it forth from some house in the neighbourhood," the Duke answered. And so we got the song about Mandalay, and indescribably wistful and dreamy it sounded with its alluring refrain of *"Bei den alten Tempeltoren"* ("By the old temple gate").

And so our evening passed away. Time crept by imperceptibly, the hour of midnight chimed from the clock-tower and it was nearly two when for the last time we intoned the thundering refrain "Trarallalalala" from one of Cleving's Swedish adaptations.

What did they think of it, I wonder, those wretched people tossing restlessly on their beds, though doubtless they had learnt by now the woes of billeting? Nobody could possibly think that the Germans were on the point of preparing for a retreat, a rumour which had spread mysteriously among the population. No drooping spirits or depression, the precursors of a pending catastrophe, could be discerned among the troops billeted in Bapaume. No, their mood was such as it always is and such as it must be in an army marching with an irresistible iron will to victory and thinking of nothing, speaking of nothing, believing in nothing but victory all along the line - victory even if the whole world were to be ransacked for fresh legions to bring against it on this front where the enemy is either shot down or taken prisoner and carried off to Döberitz or other internment camps in Germany.

It is this *will* to win which permeates the entire German army and makes such a deep impression on the stranger. Enviable, admirable, happy is the people which united marches on under its country's standards when its hour of fate has struck. The dead would cry out from their lonely graves by the roadsides did not thc living carry the fight to a glorious conclusion; but their sleep is untroubled, for they sank into it with the firm knowledge that those coming after would give their lives and all that they held dear with the same steadfast determination for the sake of home and country and future. No era has ever witnessed such national greatness as that attained by the German nation at the present day. It is an uplifting experience to have seen the Germans in their sublime struggle, and one which can never be forgotten by those who have been with them in this time.

The mood and spirit of the German army finds expression in song. The officers sing in their messes, the soldiers on their marches, on their baggage wagons, in their bivouacs. In the trenches alone there must be silence. Perhaps the French soldiers, too, sing, but as to the Russians, their wistful airs have doubtless died away in the soldiers' throats during the long weary marches backwards and forwards across the Polish plains.

After breakfast in the mess on October 30th we entered the Duke's car to proceed to the field of battle between Lille and Armentières. We were four all told, the Duke's chauffeur at the wheel, the Hereditary Prince of Hohenzollern by his side, looking after the hooter, the Duke and I. It had been raining and the by-roads were in a horrible state, whilst the great main roads were slippery and unreliable and a great wet blanket of fog darkened the whole of north-eastern France.

At first we took the great main road to Arras, which we kept to as long as we possibly could without exposing ourselves to shell fire. At Boiry, almost levelled to the ground by fire and shell, we turned off to the right, but lost our way in the tangle of by-roads, until at Croisilles we once more got on to the right track. Here the Red Cross flag was hanging from many houses, and we saw the wounded being carried into the hospitals. A column of light field howitzers rolled away towards Arras. In a field some soldiers were placidly digging potatoes, and near by old men, women and children were gathering in the sugar-beet, which is an important item of cultivation in these parts.

At last we come out on the great main road between Cambrai and Douai. The streets of the latter town are filled with civilians and military. After crossing the *Pont-à-Marcq* we reach the outer girdle of forts at Lille, and in a few minutes we drive in through the *Porte Douai*. The part of the town nearest this gate is in ruins. The Germans, who at this point were advancing seven or eight battalions strong with artillery, wanted to spare the town and tried to induce its authorities to capitulate. The French resisted. Thereupon the Germans unlimbered a battery inside the gate and shelled the nearest houses and streets. The *Mairie* and railway station were also brought under fire, the latter in order to stop all transport facilities. The town fell without having suffered any appreciable damage. The quarters exposed to the bombardment and which I had an opportunity of visiting, have, however, been reduced to ruins and the part round the *Porte Douai* presents a sad picture of desolation. The worst damage had been done by shells which burst after they had penetrated into the lower part of a house. The effect of the detonation spreads to all the storeys and everything collapses utterly. In many cases nothing but skeletons and iron girders remain. Otherwise Lille is quite untouched. One can pass through one street after the

A 15cm. Howitzer battery.

Of some houses there is only the skeleton left.

other from beginning to end without noticing any trace of shell fire. In the central parts of the town the traffic is almost animated and there are plenty of people about. Young women of not even doubtful virtue and dressed in almost the latest fashion flit about like butterflies on the pavements. Many shops and hotels are open, and seem to be carrying on as if nothing has happened. The only reminder of war, apart from the wrecked quarters of the town, are the German infantry, cavalry, guns and transport trains.

Meanwhile we drive through Lille and in passing I throw a glance at the statue of the noble Pasteur, who spent three years of his life in the scientific faculty of the town, and of the brave Joan of Arc, clad in armour and with her standard in her hand, sitting tall and straight and glorious on her gilded steed. Our road now runs along the canals, crammed with lighters, and after swinging off to the west through deserted suburbs we emerge into the smiling countryside slashed in all directions with meandering paths and by-ways. We have now left the village of Lomme behind us and proceed in the direction of Armentières. Little groves and coppices, parks and gardens, farms and villages dot the road on both sides. The road we are travelling by is narrow and badly cut up through the rain. We drive past a skillfully masked battery, working at full pressure. From the enemy's side the booming of cannon comes nearer and nearer, but is still out voiced by the eternal whirring hum of the car. It is only when we slacken down or stop that the thunder sounds alarmingly near. By a farm - or perhaps it is a modest château - we come to a clump of trees as yet unshorn of their leaves by the autumn winds. We drive at full speed past this spot, which can only be about one hundred metres north of the road. Fortunately we espy in time a young lieutenant with his two or three men in the shadow of the trees, making the most frantic signs to us and shouting "halt" as loudly as their lungs permit.

We pull up as sharply as the tearing pace allows and drive over a marshy meadow up to the lieutenant, who is standing at a table littered with maps, compasses, pens, field-glasses and other paraphernalia. He explained that it was a matter of life and death to proceed a step further in that direction. I felt almost inclined to believe him, for it sounded to my ears as if we were surrounded by fire on all sides. The nearest German infantry positions were ahead of us along a line running from north-north-east to south-south-west, and we had German artillery in front of us, beside us and behind us. The battery which we had just driven past was firing salvo after salvo, and we heard the shells whining over the treetops. In front of us the French batteries were pounding away in the north, west and south-west. I felt as if I were enclosed in a ring of fiery throats all spitting out amiable pleasantries at one another.

Near the coppice from which the young lieutenant was making his observations stood a 15-cm. howitzer battery. It was extremely interesting to note the skilful manner in which the guns had been concealed among the trees and bushes. They could not even be seen at a very short distance, and I had to come right up to them to realise where and how they were hidden among the boughs and branches. As an extra safeguard they were partly covered over with leaves so as not to be seen from above. The ammunition stores, huts for the gun crews and provisions were as effectively hidden. For protection against the enemy's fire the gunners had dug the customary underground dwellings. At the present moment they were very busy attending to their guns. "Why don't they shoot?" I asked. In answer the lieutenant pointed to the south-west. "Over there, above those trees, you notice a French airman, and it is probably his business to try to locate this battery. We have been shooting from here and have probably done some damage on the French side. Now they are on the prowl to find us, but so far without success. The enemy shells are bursting just now at only 500 metres to the south-west of us. Up to now they have not reached us, but they are getting nearer and may hit our battery at any moment. If we were to fire now whilst the aviator is in the air, their fire would be on us in no time."

As he spoke the airman described circle after circle above the covert. As long as we remained at the observation post he kept circling over the same spot. It was clear that he was seeking the answer to some question. Perhaps he thought that the projection of his line of flight on the earth's surface would give the confines of a spot which might profitably be shelled by the enemy. Our friends fancied they had seen him signal with flags and with white and red lights. The batteries which the Germans had opposed to them at this part of the front were all said to be British.

The lieutenant and his men at the observation post and battery followed the aviator's movements with the closest attention, and special pickets were posted under the trees to stop anyone from moving in the vicinity when the aviator had his machine turned in such a way that he had a free outlook in our direction. But when he swung slowly round and turned his back on us, we were able for the moment to move more freely. However, the circles he described were small, and it was all that we could do to hurry from the battery to the observation post and vice versa before he swung round again and we ran the risk of detection.

The gun crew were therefore taking it easy. Beside one of the guns the men were eating their breakfast, beside another a man was reading aloud from a newspaper. I took a couple of pictures of them to their great delight.

We then took the opportunity, when the airman's back was turned, to hurry back across the meadow to our car under the shelter of the trees. It was still too early to go home, and we thought we might make another trip in the direction of the firing line to the north-westward; accordingly we turned back to the outskirts of Lille and took the road to St. André, Verlinghem and Quesnoy. At St. André, where a local command was quartered, we halted awhile, the Duke asking the General how far we might proceed in that direction. He thought Quesnoy and a little way beyond it might be quite safe. With a little luck, we might even see the Austrian 30.5-cm. mortars in action.

We drove off in the direction indicated and passed several large supply columns proceeding to the front to provide the troops with fresh food and ammunition. Patrols showed us the way to one of the Austrian batteries. The road was very mediocre; its centre was stone-paved and at each side was a belt about three metres wide without any sign of paving and now converted into a sea of mud. The traffic was lively, and it was *impossible* to drive fast. Presently we reached the ammunition column of the mortar battery. The fighting battery with its two pieces of ordnance was ahead of the column, which had halted, occupying the right half of the road, so we left the car and proceeded on foot.

The road lay a good metre higher than the ground to the right. From the left, or south-west, the enemy shells kept dropping quite close to us. Constantly fresh little white tufts of cloud kept forming in the sky and out of them flashed a spurt of flame. This was a signal that the zone of fire was spreading towards us, and we bent down instinctively to take such cover as the road and battery-lorries afforded. We were right under fire and might be hit at any moment. The *Deckung* we had was altogether insufficient, for the wagons stood at several metres from one another. The further we advanced the denser the little tufts of wool in the sky seemed to be. Then we met an officer who told us that the Austrian battery was not yet working and that it would be more than risky to continue in the direction we had taken. Probably the whereabouts of the ammunition column had been discovered through aviators. Although the enemy could not see it, they had trained the fire from several batteries on the sector where it was bound to be. The uncanny whistling sounds kept piercing the air; and so we thought it wisest to leave this dangerous spot.

Just as we were getting near our car and had reached the road, we were honoured with a salvo from an English battery. The four shots followed at short intervals, and all of them seemed to be seeking our car. The first shrapnel shell burst some ten metres above ground just in front of us and the car, and I had a very distinct sensation of being within its zone of dispersion and wondered that I did not feel a sudden twinge in some part of my body. The other two shells burst a little to the side of the first. Then came the fourth - a devilishly impudent fellow! He came straight at us and the deathwhistle rang in my ears. He arrived from the south-west. The air seemed to hiss and splutter and burn where he tore along. The whistling sound came nearer, passed just over our heads and died away behind us. We all three bent down so to bring our heads a metre nearer to the ground. This movement is entirely instinctive, and even officers who have been many times under fire resort to this device. But in time one gets rid of the habit, realising how little it avails. I have subsequently heard artillery officers say that when the whining sound

Well masked guns

Gunners studying the news.

seems closest and one thinks that the projectile is upon one, it has in reality passed by. We wondered at what height above us this shell had passed. The Duke estimated the distance at eight or ten metres, the Prince at fifteen at the most. To me it seemed so near that I almost expected to see my fur cap singed by the fire. But the most remarkable thing about this amiable greeting from the British was that whilst the three first shells burst, this fourth one never exploded at all. Had it done so we should in all probability have been flung to the ground. The projectile passed by us whole and entered the soft, wet earth some distance behind us.

As a rule there is a moment of quiet after a salvo. With a car, or at the worst with a horse handy, one has time to seek a safer spot, provided that the enemy artillery is aiming at the same point as before or one is so hardened after one's previous baptisms of fire as to take no notice at all. We might now reasonably take it for granted that we should be allowed a respite, and thought it safer to take this chance of withdrawing some distance. The Duke, who struck me as an exceptionally calm and fearless man, remarked that he did not want to have my life and limbs on his conscience, especially as I happened to be his guest.

So we jumped in and drove off to Lille again. To the right of us the shells kept singing in the tree-tops, and one of them gave a wonderful pyrotechnic display as it burst. Presently we met an ammunition column which forced us off the track into the mire. As long as we could drive straight on, things were all right, but when the column had passed and we tried to climb on to the stone-paving again, the wheels skidded and the car got thoroughly stuck in the soup of mud. It almost looked as if we were to have more compliments paid us by the British. In the end there was no alternative but to get out of the car, which thus lightened was able to climb once more on to the firm surface. Thereupon we got to Lille without any further mishap.

After dining we drove back to Bapaume in pelting rain, arriving soon after dark. The Duke had a party in the evening, and the incomparable Cleving was there with his guitar, accompanied by Herr Kummer, one of the four *parlementaires* of Rheims.

CHAPTER XX
TRENCH LIFE

SATURDAY THE 31st of October was spent quietly and peacefully. Duke Adolf Friedrich conducted me in the morning to the château of Vélu east of Bapaume. We followed the great main road to Cambrai a few kilometres and then struck off on to a by-road leading to this handsome château, built in 1719 and taken over in 1883 by a gentleman named Goer. It is still tenanted by a Madame Göer. The magnificent apartments were still haunted by an old French butler, and in the dining-room the table had just been laid for the officers who had been lucky enough to have found this comfortable billet. The house is surrounded by a large park, and we wandered up and down its neglected alleys on the softest of carpets of decaying leaves. Here we strolled and chatted about our travels in Africa and Asia, and about the new colouring that the world's map would certainly be given at the end of this war - when we were disturbed by the rattling of heavy rifle fire in the neighbourhood. We at once made for an open space in the direction of the firing, and espied a French airman who was being hotly attacked by the German infantry, but seemed entirely unperturbed by the interest he was arousing.

On our return to Bapaume we dined at the mess with General von Plettenberg and his usual set. Among the company was the famous surgeon. Professor Hildebrand of Göttingen, a sociable, learned and altogether charming gentleman, and an old friend of the family of the late Professor Gyldén of Stockholm. Professor Hildebrand told me among many other interesting things that the cardinal principle of modern surgery in the field is not to amputate except in cases of the utmost urgency. Formerly arms and legs were amputated in a far larger measure than at present; now the surgeons attempt to save all that there is a possible chance of saving. Hildebrand was one of the inner circle which often foregathered at the Duke's house of an evening.

The excellent light of the early afternoons just at this time tempted me to take several photographs, one or two of which I am reproducing here. All through the day heavy ammunition and supply columns of all kinds kept marching through the town, and the civilian element was almost drowned by the military. In the course of my walks through the town I witnessed many fascinating scenes of soldiers' life.[27] Here are a few Landsturm soldiers sitting in a circle peeling potatoes which are afterwards to be cooked in a bucket over a coal fire. Others have rigged up a temporary awning over benches and tables, where they are writing their *Feldpostkarten* home to parents and sweethearts. Another little coterie is sipping coffee beside a kitchen wagon. In a meadow stands a threshing machine which had just finished work for the day; the grain is being loaded into one cart and the straw into another. Close by an open-air barber has rigged up his shop by the side of a train wagon. An orderly comes leading a couple of officers' horses, and in a field four Bavarian Landsturm men are lazily blowing clouds of smoke out of their enormous pipes.

Presently we come to the little square adorned by Faidherbe's statue, and further honoured by the presence of the Townhall with its handsome facade, supported by a Gothic arcade. Here a notice board has been posted up so that the latest war news may be studied, for a newspaper is now being published at Bapaume composed and printed at the Town *imprimerie*, and called *B(apaumer) Z(eitung) am Mittag*. Herr Cleving is its editor. Its circulation is six hundred copies. The paper is not large, only one page, in large type on thin yellow paper. I reproduce below a text of the number of October 27th, which I have selected because it also refers to the bombardment of Ostend, although with a wrong date:

(1) "The fighting on the Yser - Ypres Canal front is exceedingly violent. In the north we have succeeded in crossing the canal with a strong force. East of Ypres and south-west of Lille our troops have advanced slowly after severe fighting. Ostend was yesterday bombarded by the English ships.

27. One photograph shows a street in which the only civilians are two young ladies.

(2) "In the Argonne our troops have likewise made progress. Several machine guns have been captured. We have taken a number of prisoners and two French aeroplanes have been brought down.

(3) "East and north-east of Arras the enemy has received reinforcements. Nevertheless our troops have succeeded in making progress at several points. About five hundred British, including a Colonel and twenty-eight other officers have been taken prisoners.

(4) "West of Augustovo the Russians have renewed their attacks which have all been repulsed.

(5) "At Ivangorod 1800 Russians have been taken prisoners. South-east of Przemysl the Austrians have scored several successes," and finally: "Copies for distribution among the various units may be obtained from the Commandant of the lines of communication."

That is all. There is nothing else to read in the number of October 27th, 1914. Short and concise sentences, written with military precision, and above all - no lies. The *Bapaumer Zeitung am Mittag* follows the same honourable principles as the rest of the German Press. This Press knows its enormous responsibility towards the nation and towards the fighting armies. For the soldiers, whose duty it is to bear the sweat and labour of the day, and to spill their blood for the Fatherland, nothing but the truth, the pure honest truth, is good enough. In the Entente countries the Press has an extra and exceedingly important duty, which the German Press is spared, namely to fire the soldiers' courage, and to keep burning the flame of hope among the population. As gladdening news is rare just now, its counterfeit is manufactured in the editorial sanctum of the newspapers. The German Press has no need to fire the nation's courage, for it burns with a pure and clear flame. The German people insist that their Press shall tell them the *whole* truth, whether gladdening or not. Good news is not exaggerated, bad news is not minimised. The whole nation insists on being fully enlightened on the progress of events on all fronts, for it will not build its hopes for the future on a tissue of falsehoods which in the end cannot but collapse. If anything goes wrong, it is best to know the full bearing of the disaster, so as to make good the loss and prevent it from occurring again. In

Soldiers reading the latest number of the 'Bapaumer Zeitung am mittag'.

Two young ladies are the only civilians to be seen.

Germany the people rely implicitly on the truthfulness of the Press and its sense of responsibility. There hundreds of thousands of volunteers hurry to the colours without artificial and false inducement. They come, driven by the Germanic spirit, by national pride, by sense of duty and ambition. There is not a single man able to carry arms who hesitates to go out and die, for it is clear to all that if it is God's wish that Germany shall go under, the last German shall have fallen in the last trench before the waves close once for all over the wreck. For these reasons the Press of the Central Powers has in this war a far easier task to fulfil than the Press of the enemy countries, for it has but to register the trend of events and to announce the news from east and west and from faraway tropical seas, but it has no need to resort to the dishonourable makeshift of deceiving its readers and inventing tales of victory so as to drive fresh throngs to the recruiting offices.

To return once more to the Townhall of Bapaume, every day, at the hour that the local newspaper was published, brought fresh groups of eager soldiers to the notice board. It was quite refreshing to stop awhile and observe them. There they stand with their cigarettes or pipes and hands in trouser pockets reading through the news attentively and slowly. Up to the present they have had little news that is not good, but all news is taken with the same calm. At most one notices a passing smile or a momentary gleam in the eye. The same spirit is shown if a piece of bad news is posted, such as the loss of a warship.

Sometimes the soldiers are not content with reading, they must copy the whole of the paper into their diary. And why? Probably because they are on the way to the foremost trenches, where they will impart the contents to their isolated comrades.

Duke Adolf Friedrich and I were invited to supper with Lieut. General von Winckler, the Grenadier *par excellence*, the Chief of all the Grenadiers of the Guard. At seven o'clock we started out on the great main road to Arras, but long before we reached half-way we turned off to the left along a by-road leading *via* Hamelincourt to Boiry. The evening was still, the air was clear, and the moon was brilliantly radiant. We could hear no cannonading, and yet there could be no doubt that we were approaching the line traced in iron, blood and fire across the face of France At every village we were stopped by pickets who stepped out on to the road and cried "Halt!" If you do not stop, you get a bullet through your back. *"Armé-oberkommando"* ("Chief Army Command") calls the Duke, and we continue on our way. The strictest control has to be exercised, especially at night. Not even the German uniforms are a guarantee against spies. I feel that I am once more on the brink of glorious and wild adventure - on the way to the field of battle now lighted by the moon, and where every bush and tree trunk may hide a lurking spy. But the silence is unbroken except for the rhythmic thud of the engine.

At length we stopped at the gate of a farm, where several officers of the General Staff came out to meet us and conducted us into an unpretentious little house. Here we were warmly greeted by General von Winckler himself, a soldierly figure with a fine head, distinguished, weather-beaten, kindly features, steel-grey hair and a dark well-groomed moustache.

We sat down to table almost at once. It would have been wrong to call the mood of the company solemn or heavy. From the first moment lively and interesting conversation was afoot. More cheerful officers it would be hard to find - and yet these men had been at work since daybreak, and might well feel tired, but they showed no traces of fatigue. The company included the Surgeon-General of the Forces, Dr. Reichard, who had much to tell about his experience among the wounded, also a young lieutenant who that night was to have his first experience of trench duty, that strange phenomenon of modern warfare. One might perhaps have expected this youth to sit quiet and thoughtful, but he joked and laughed and chatted with the rest of them. He was delighted that his turn had come at last to be in the forefront of battle. He ate his supper, drank his wine and smoked his cigarettes without giving a thought to the cold and hardships which awaited him later in the night, for an advanced infantry position in close touch with the enemy is in very truth a living grave.

At nightfall the occupants of some trenches immediately west of the village of Monchy-au-Bois, about seven kilometres from Boiry, were to be relieved. At this point it was done every forty-eight hours. Those who had been on duty for this length of time were then allowed to withdraw to the rear to rest, sleep and get some hot food. I had of course passed numberless empty trenches in Belgium, but thought it would be far more interesting to see them with the soldiers in possession. But when I happened to drop a hint to this effect, the General dissuaded me very strongly from visiting his fighting line. It would after all have been a great responsibility for him to let me go there. At Monchy the foremost German trenches were only eighty metres away from the French, with the distance widening to the north and south. The men can only be relieved after dark when the night is at its blackest. But to-night the moon shone brightly and hardly a sound was to be heard. It was eleven o'clock, and there was probably no intention to relieve the men in the trenches for another four or five hours. Even if the Germans had crept along the ground like leopards through the grass, the French would have seen their outlines and shadows. The slightest rustle would reach their ears if they held their breath and listened carefully; for the French do most emphatically *listen* at night. They are exceedingly vigilant and wakeful. If one is discovered before having time to reach one's trench and gain its welcome shelter, the bullets come whizzing round in extra quick time. The greatest danger lies, however, in the French fighting and scouting patrols, who are thoroughly familiar with the ground and begin to prowl about at nightfall.

To-night, the last night of this fateful month of October, it was deemed impossible to relieve in the usual way. Only one or two men were allowed to creep forward at a time. When there is no moonlight or when the countryside is wrapped in fog they can advance close together without danger. But on a night such as this the risk was almost as great as in daylight and the very greatest caution had to be observed. It needs long and systematic training to move troops on moonlight nights.

Even a man with uncommon grit and courage must feel a certain amount of excitement as he crawls through the grass on toes and elbows, particularly as he has his rifle to think about as well. Now and again he has to pause, either because this mode of locomotion is too tiring or because he has to take his bearings and listen. Then he proceeds a little further, holds his breath and listens and peers round like a tiger on the prowl. Everything is still, but at any moment he may hear the rattle of rifle fire and the ping of bullets. At last he sees the trench before him like a long dark line. Will he get there without being discovered by the French? That is the question. He hugs the earth still closer and moves still more slowly and cautiously. Now he only has twenty metres left, now ten. The parapet is clearly defined in the moonlight, it is but a step or two that separates him from his goal, and yet this step seems like a mile, for just here the danger is at its greatest, and it is on this point that the French sharpshooters and pickets have their attention riveted. He knows that the furrow in the ground beneath him is two metres deep and one metre wide and full of alert, wakeful men, but not a sound is heard, no sign of life is seen, not even the faintest flicker from a puny fire. Not even the scent of a cigarette strikes his nostrils, though perhaps there may be other odours that reveal the nearness of human beings. Now he has but a metre left, there is no sign of life from the French, and he slips noiselessly and softly like a cat over the edge and is safe. Thereupon one of his comrades down below rises from his shelter and creeps back with the same caution to the ramparts behind the trenches, where he gets hot soup and sinks into a deep and well-merited sleep.

The new-comer has forty-eight solid hours before him. At night or in a fog he and his comrades must keep wide-awake, for then the danger of assault is greatest. Here and there a man may be allowed to doze off for a moment, but if a man sleeps when on duty his life is not worth much. In daytime most of the men are allowed to rest in their "dug-outs" under the parapet, but even then special look-outs are always posted along the trench. They all have their own little section of the battlefield to answer for. Within that section no life must stir but that they are aware of it. It is chiefly movement along the ground or the outline of some figure silhouetted against an indistinct background that reveals to the look-out the presence of the enemy. Clumsiness in real war is tantamount to a death warrant. The Germans disappear like fieldmice in the inequalities of the ground. But the French, in return, are gifted with keen eyesight.

In the trench wall nearest to the enemy bowl-shaped niches or dug-outs are excavated in the soil, providing effective protection against overhead bursts and not infrequently against direct hits. But it is not impossible for a shell to pitch in the wall, and in that case even the occupants of the dug-outs are doomed. To provide against this the men often dig out a cavern, and these caves are often so elaborate and luxurious that it is thought fit to put up curtains at the entrance. Along the walls of these caves straw is laid out for sleeping berths and the little tent section included in each soldier's packing is often used as a blanket. When the distance between the opposing lines of trenches, as in the case I am describing, is only eighty metres, no light must be lit even in these subterranean caves, still less a fire, and the air in them is therefore cold, damp and raw. But if the nearest enemy is three or four hundred metres away, these rigid rules are sometimes dispensed with. But even then no fire must be lit and no naked light is allowed in the trench proper.

The soldiers bring with them dry rations intended to last for the whole of their shift, but they are sometimes cut off through heavy and incessant fire from all communication and are then obliged to starve for a day or two. But even that misfortune is accepted good-humouredly.

The dangers of trench life may be realised when I say that before Monchy-au-Bois alone the dead and wounded numbered sixty to eighty daily. Neither dead nor wounded can be removed. If you put up as much as a little finger above the edge of the trench the bullets come whizzing round immediately. The dead bodies must therefore be allowed to remain in the trench, that is to say the dead man is got rid of by digging a grave for him in the floor of the trench. A few days ago it happened in the trench which I am describing that a soldier was so badly hit by a shell that he was cut in two, one half remaining locked by a trench prop. He could not be removed without risk to the survivors and was therefore allowed to remain. But presently he began to give rise to a horrible stench and whatever they did the men could not get away from the mutilated, blackened features. Sometimes arms and legs torn away from the body are allowed to lie about at the bottom of the trench until somebody finds time to dig them down. One gets hardened in time. When it is for the sake of the country one does not mind occasional horrors.

In rainy weather the trenches become almost unbearable. I saw for myself in Belgium what they looked like. The rainwater collects in them and they look exactly like the ditches by the side of a field, half-filled with grey and yellow water with a scum of mire and filth. General von Winckler told me that his men had stood in water up to the knees for twentyfour hours without complaining and without anyone collapsing from the effects. When the soldiers got back to the rear they told their comrades with much droll humour of their adventures. One would have thought that it would sour the temper to lie steeped in mud for twenty-four hours on end. I am speaking now of the Grenadiers of the Guard, of whom one expects that they will go through anything. But the same applies to all German troops. You never see any gloomy faces amongst the German soldiers, nothing but good spirits and laughter. To fight against the inundations, the General ordered drainage trenches to be dug, through which the rainwater escaped into cisterns, likewise hollowed out in the soil.

In places communication between the trenches is made easier by real saps which lead in zigzag to the front line from some suitable declivity in the ground. In this way the work of relieving and replacing the returning units is greatly facilitated.

The trenches do not run in straight lines, umless, as in the country south of Antwerp, the ground is absolutely flat. Usually their length and outline depend on the formation of the ground. As a rule they are situated so as to offer an uninterrupted view of the enemy positions opposite and so as to avoid dead angles. A free field of fire is the most important consideration. A trench thus often receives a very irregular shape, resembling a curve with numerous bends and salients.

As I have already had occasion to mention, the trenches are often interrupted by traverses. If the trench runs in a wavy line it is not always possible to prevent parts of it from being flanked and enfiladed by the enemy's artillery fire. The traverses not only prevent such enfilading from becoming effective beyond a certain distance but also limit the effectiveness of an explosive shell. As a rule the distance between the traverses is only ten paces, provided always that there has been time to improve and extend the position occupied. Behind the various sections one often finds - as I have mentioned more than once - deep caverns which afford more or less complete protection against direct hits. These spaces are used as refuges if the artillery fire becomes too unpleasant, but the trench must immediately be manned if the enemy's infantry shows signs of advancing to the charge.

When, as at Monchy-au-Bois, both sides have been stationary for some length of time - in this case since the 6th October - the art of field entrenchment usually reaches a very high pitch of perfection. It must not be thought that these advanced firing lines are always connected and continuous. The formations of the various units are adapted to the conformation of the ground according to its appearance and the possibilities which it affords. Yet there are no unprotected or unguarded places. The intervals between the trenches are always protected by wire entanglements or other obstacles effectively flanked by machine guns or rifle fire. In front of the German lines at Monchy there are numerous wide belts of wire entanglements, alternating with deep *trous-de-loup* with stakes at the bottom. These obstacles, interrupted at certain points by open passages, can only be contrived under cover of darkness or fog, and even under favourable conditions the work is highly dangerous, not least on account of the enemy's pickets who utilise the darkness of night to find out what the enemy is up to.

These pickets are the eyes and feelers of their unit. The men to whom these scouting and guard duties are entrusted need the utmost vigilance, sense of duty and intelligence for the performance of their task; for the risks which they run are enormous and they could not possibly cope with the strain if they had not been trained in peace time to realise that boldness and alertness combined will overcome all obstacles. There are many kinds of patrols, but in a war such as this the outpost pickets have by far the most important task to perform. When the distance between the fighting units is small, they work at night only. The manner in which they discharge their duties is often the deciding factor in the execution of important plans. They are despatched to a certain limited area, with a definite task to perform. If possible, they are to avoid collision with the enemy. Other patrols are sent out to prevent similar scouting duty by the enemy. In the part of the front of which I am speaking, these tasks were often facilitated on moonlit nights by the number of corpses, chiefly French, remaining on the field from earlier outpost skirmishes between the two fighting lines. It is often difficult to tell a living from a dead man. In the dark it happens not infrequently that German and French patrols run against one another, which always gives rise to hand-to-hand fighting and losses. The boldest picket leaders, who in the midst of the most appalling danger think of nothing but the duty they are entrusted to perform, and who are *determined* that this trust shall be carried out, take advantage even of misfortune. Whilst the others are engaged in a struggle of life and death they continue towards the enemy position, find out what they can, and return to their line - and to the Iron Cross. Their comrades are either dead or wounded. The latter crawl back as best they can. If the night is sufficiently dark they get help. The former remain to contribute to the foul stench of the atmosphere. At Monchy-au-Bois such incidents were of nightly occurrence.

From Monchy I also heard told that on one occasion Frenchmen and Germans had installed themselves in one and the same trench. A French scouting unit had lost its way one dark night and had taken refuge in a part of a German trench for the moment unoccupied. When the Frenchmen realised the situation they threw up parapets in both directions in the trench itself, and from behind these walls the opposing soldiers fired at one another at a distance of a few paces. I do not know what happened in the end to the Frenchmen, but they were clearly doomed. Their position was absolutely untenable and their only way out of it was to surrender when their provisions failed them.

Of course the conditions vary greatly according to the situation. When the enemy is relatively far away the communication with the rear is rendered easier and in such circumstances life becomes more bearable in the front line, if only because hygienic measures are in some measure possible. But at Monchy-au-Bois I was told that the state of things in these underground caverns literally defied description. This cannot but increase the admiration one feels on witnessing the cheerful spirit amongst the men, their absolute readiness for any sacrifice. Any man complaining of the cold or of the food below ground would be chaffed to distraction or worse by his fellow-soldiers - but I never heard of a single case of this kind.

In a village in the neighbourhood where we were now stopping, Prince Eitel Friedrich had his quarters. I heard it said of him that he lived in a farm-house more or less shot to pieces by shell fire, and that he slept on the bare ground. Everybody praised his courage and endurance and his great qualities as man and soldier.

As I have already had occasion to remark, the fighting on the western front with its interminable lines of trenches is assuming more and more the character of a siege war. The opposing sides have dug themselves into the ground all along the front behind wire entanglements and *trous-de-loup* . These field entrenchments become more formidable as time goes on. They can really only be destroyed by heavy artillery. Hence this arm is of cardinal importance. The infantry can only sap ahead and stick to what it has gained. Every position must be treated by attackers as if it were a fortress in itself. Every metre of open country, every tree in the Argonne must be captured by what might almost be described as a separate engagement. The French are defending themselves with the most brilliant courage, and even General von Winckler characterised them as worthy opponents to the world's finest soldiers.

In some places ordinary wire entanglements on level ground are not deemed to be sufficient, and they are placed in holes or declivities, the bottom of which is covered by fire.

In conclusion I should like to say a few words about the intelligence service in the field. The French are past masters in the art of using civilian spies. The wounded in a field hospital are safe as long as they have a couple of Frenchmen amongst them, but as soon as they have been removed for transport eastward, even this sanctuary comes under the enemy's fire. How is it that the enemy *knows* that these particular wounded have been removed? In a village a soldier had made the acquaintance of a woman. One fine day she told him that she was going away. Why? he asked. Because to-morrow this village was going to be bombarded. The soldier did not pay much attention to the prophecy, but the woman was right. How did she know it? Of course because she had been warned by a spy. Once a peasant came strolling along from the French side into the German lines, where he was immediately seized. He declared with the most innocent face in the world that he had come to look after his cattle, which unfortunately had been left behind on the German side. Let the poor fellow look after his cows, they thought, and so he was allowed to pass. Of course there could be no question of letting him return to the French lines, for he might be a spy sent out to gather information. An hour later he was seen driving a little herd of cattle before him, but nobody took any notice. This was a daily occurrence. However it so happened that he drove his beasts right up to a German battery which had been so well masked that the French had been unable to detect it. There he left the cattle grazing and vanished completely. Presently a murderous fire descended upon the battery, which had to be moved in the night to another position. The peasant was in the employ of his countrymen, and his movements had been noted by an aviator, who had signalled to the French artillery positions.

The German regulations governing the liberties of the civil population have naturally to be made much more stringent on account of such incidents, and that is why even officers are sometimes stopped at night when travelling within the fighting zone. But even the most vigilant are sometimes outwitted by the French spies. Complete telephone systems have in several instances been discovered below ground, clearly laid down in anticipation of the French retreat. The main cables no doubt existed already in peace time, but on the outbreak of war an additional system of temporary lines had been added, and during the retreat telephone stations were rigged up in all sorts of unsuspected places. It was often palpable that the French fire had been directed with the aid of telephone communication. But where is the underground cable and where is the

436

operator? Usually it is chance that leads to the latter's discovery. It had been noticed several times that within a certain area the French fire had searched and struck the most susceptible points on the German side with such rapidity and accuracy that the direction of the fire could only be explained by the existence of equally rapid and accurate information. It had also been noticed that no airmen had haunted this particular point and the conclusion was not far to seek that telephone communication alone could lie at the root of the skilful operations of the enemy artillery. All houses and cellars in the neighbourhood had been searched with the utmost thoroughness, perhaps with useful results, perhaps not. There might be subterranean vaults anywhere under meadows, gardens or fields; or strange as it may sound there may be telephone stations above ground, which are very difficult to detect.

Anyone travelling through north-west France in the autumn cannot but be struck by the enormous straw stacks dotted here and there about the fields, often reaching a height of six to eight metres, cylindrical in form and capped by a flat cone. In the interior of such stacks the Germans have often discovered telephone operators. When I drove past one of these stacks for the first time I saw that it had been pulled to pieces, with the straw scattered in the greatest confusion. I asked my companion for the reason of this "eccentric treatment" and was told in reply: "It was thought that a man with a telephone apparatus might have concealed himself inside and they wanted to make quite sure." I have since often seen similar stacks in the fields and wondered what it must feel like to sit shut up in one month after month. I had a shrewd suspicion that he must get his information from the civil inhabitants of the neighbourhood. Spies in the guise of vagrant peasants or shepherds no doubt steal up to the stack in the dead of night and creep in through some hidden passage to tell the operator what they have seen.

The following episode was told me by a German officer. The Germans had billeted themselves on a French village and had requisitioned against *bons* what they needed for their reasonable wants. Thereupon an elderly curé turned up at the commandant's office and pleaded in the most beseeching tones to be allowed to keep the modest little stock of wine in his cellar which he said he needed for the sake of his failing health. His request was readily granted and orders were issued that the priest and his wine-cellar should be excluded from all requisitions. After a time the Germans noticed with amazement that the French fire in these parts was directed with almost uncanny precision. A thorough search was instituted, houses, cellars and straw stacks were ransacked, but without success. Nobody thought of the curé, who was old and broken in health, and who with the most innocent air in the world was seen daily tottering along laboriously to and from his little church. But at last things grew so suspicious that even the curé's house had to be searched. There in the wine-cellar stood a large cask and inside it was a telephone apparatus, the wires from which passed through the cellar floor into the earth. It was the old curé himself who at night gave all the information which had proved so fatal to the Germans in the neighbourhood. On the following night the telephone was once more in operation. This time, however, it was a German officer, speaking French without the slightest trace of an accent, who took his seat in the wine cask. And what *he* had to report may be left to the imagination. In any case there were no more direct hits after that night.

When a village within the German sphere of operations continues to be inhabited by the French civil population it is not bombarded by the French, but if the population for any reason leaves the village, the fire is immediately directed against its farms and houses. Information in these respects can only be given through the underground telephone lines or through light signals at night. The latter method is, however, extremely dangerous, for when the Germans notice any suspicious lights their patrols bear down like hawks upon the point from which the light was seen.

The village of Boiry where we now were has in peace time a population of nine hundred, but at present there are only a hundred and fifty left. After a while the population seemed to grow without any migration into the village being noticed. It was then found that the apparent new-comers had simply been hidden in the cellars, where they had tables, chairs, beds and all sorts of supplies. Thus they had lived for weeks, until they realised that the Germans were not such "barbarians" as they had been made out to be. But, nevertheless, the fact that Boiry was inhabited by French people made the German troops quartered there fairly safe from aviators' bombs, whilst they were out of range of the artillery.

On the other hand the French airmen evidently had their eye on a German flying station in the neighbourhood. That very day a *Taube* had been damaged by a bomb, which had, moreover, wounded three men and killed twenty horses belonging to the flying section. But the Germans had revenged themselves amply, for the following day 155 Frenchmen had been captured in the same neighbourhood.

I was told that it costs France tens of thousands of millions of francs to have the German armies in occupation of a part of their country, and this disadvantage is but slightly compensated for by certain benefits which I have briefly touched upon above and which include the greater facility of organising the intelligence service. But it must not be thought that the Germans are entirely deprived of the information they need. They have inexhaustible supplies of ordnance maps of the entire country, together with appertaining military and topographical data; they have, moreover, their incredibly skilful and bold flying corps and other scouts and, besides, the information vouchsafed by prisoners. Opposite Monchy-auBois they had the 69th Regiment of the 20th French Army Corps. In the same way it was known to a nicety how the various enemy units were located along this front of six hundred kilometres. Any movements of troops, and what such movements might portend, were also known immediately.

But it is getting late. We take leave of the most charming General and his Staff and drive home through the moonlit silent night. And I for my part could not help thinking of the young lieutenant about to embark on his first experience of trench life.

CHAPTER XXI
SUNDAY THE FIRST OF NOVEMBER

FOR OVER A thousand years the Catholic Church has kept, on the 2nd or 3rd of November, the solemn festival of "All Souls" in remembrance of the dead and as an admonition to the living to send up prayers to the throne of God for the souls suffering in purgatory. A Mass for the departed is held in the churches, and the graves in the cemeteries are adorned with wreaths and flowers.

In the parish church of Bapaume a German "All Souls" celebration was held on Sunday the 1st of November in remembrance of the fallen soldiers. Duke Adolf Friedrich and I arrived in good time for the service but found the church filled to overcrowding with four thousand soldiers. We succeeded however in getting up to the chancel, where two chairs were placed for us among a group of officers.

The old church makes a truly imposing and magnificent impression. The first thing I felt constrained to do, after taking my seat, was to cast my eye over the fane, with its lofty Gothic arches and handsome windows. On either side of the mighty nave are small side-aisles supported by massive pillars. The transept walls are adorned with large memorial tablets, which however are of doubtful artistic value. The sunlight filters in through the stained-glass windows and falls in all the hues of the rainbow upon the white pillars. One wonders why a town of little more than 3,000 inhabitants should need a church capable of holding 4,000 persons, but at the great festivals this place of worship attracts people from the whole surrounding country.

All pews are overcrowded, soldiers are standing closely packed all down the aisles, with their helmets slung over their arms. There are Catholic Sisters in their black dresses, white coifs and Red Cross armlets.

Both officers and men are unarmed. No rattling of sabres is heard. No one is commanded to Divine Service. The soldiers are at liberty to spend the hour of High Mass as they please. Yet the church is crowded from end to end. These hardened warriors feel the need of approaching God and hearing His word before they go forth to face death.

A Divine Service in the field under the open sky is more impressive in its way. But I cannot imagine anything more beautiful than this High Mass in Bapaume Parish Church. Perhaps they preferred to celebrate All Souls' Day under these lofty arches so as not to be disturbed by airmen. War is inexorable and does not hesitate to kill the children of man, even while performing their devotions, A Field Chaplain told me that on Sunday the 18th of October he was preaching on a hill-slope outside Douchy when a hostile aviator dropped a couple of bombs, intending to interrupt the service in this catastrophic manner. They exploded close to the listening troops. No one stirred, and the preacher calmly continued his sermon.

It is a strangely fascinating sight that meets my eye as it travels over the nave from the raised floor of the chancel, and I feel that my heart beats in unison with those of the four thousand South Germans. Weather-beaten and sunburnt they stand - a picture of manhood, imbued with iron will and humble trust in God. Their field-grey uniforms have assumed a tint now truly at one with the colour of the fields through constant contact with the soil in trenches and "dugouts." But here and there I also observed the dark blue tunics of Bavarian Landsturm men, sturdy and steadfast like the solid rock from which the pillars of the church were hewn.

I hear that the credit of decorating the church so festively for All Souls' Day was due to these Landsturm men. The chancel had been transformed into a solid bank of foliage, and all the pillars were hung with large green wreaths, in remembrance of the fallen. But the most remarkable thing of all was the reverence which the good Bavaüans had shown to a small statue of Joan d'Arc standing on the left of the choir just within the triumphal arch. There was nothing in the least remarkable about this plaster image of the seventeen year-old Maid of

Orleans. She was just as one sees her in many other places. She stood, majestically erect, in her shining armour, holding in her hand the white standard adorned with *fleurs-de-lys*. And yet I could not keep my eyes off her. She seemed to scrutinise the German warriors in the nave, and an ironical smile seemed to hover about her lips.

But how did she get here? It is true that just twenty years ago she was declared blessed by Pope Leo XIII, - perhaps she has meanwhile been actually received into the Canon of Saints.[28] At any rate she is the object of almost divine veneration in this part of France. One could see that her image was not a regular part of the decorations of the church, because it had been placed on an upturned packing-case scantily draped with some cloth. When the war was hanging over France like a dark thunder-cloud she had been carried into the church, and the believers had fallen on their knees before her, imploring her to bestow her spirit and her victorious aid on the French. To propitiate the noble virgin, the citizens of Bapaume had offered her numerous candles which were arranged on a stand in front of the image. And now comes the strangest part, the good Bavarians had glorified her with a background of tall plants and had lit all the candles, those candles whose flames were burning prayers for victory over - the Germans!

The blessed virgin had yet another and greater cause to smile at human folly. In her time, more than half of France was overrun by the English and their allies. It was against them that she had fought - them that she had vanquished - and when, overpowered at last, she fell into the hands of her country's enemies she was delivered by them into the hands of the inquisition. She was derided, locked up with rough soldiers and finally burnt at the stake - all this by those very Englishmen whom she was now invoked, by burning prayers and candles, to assist against the Germans. One may pardon the young lady for making a wry face and feeling somewhat perplexed! The Bavarians might well light the candles without misgivings - she did not heed them, and her helmet prevented her from hearing the presumptuous prayers.

28. She was canonised by Pope Pius X. in May, 1909. - Translator.

The peals of the organ now rise loud and clear towards the roof, and lusty voices from four thousand young warriors' throats sing Bernard de Clairvaux's eight-hundred-year-old Latin hymn *Salve caput cruentatum* in its German version composed in 1659 by Paul Gerhard:

O sacred Head, surrounded
  By crown of piercing thorn!
O bleeding Head, so wounded,
  Reviled and put to scorn!
Death's pallid hue comes o'er Thee,
  The glow of life decays.
Yet angel hosts adore Thee
  And tremble as they gaze!

In mine own hour of passion,
  Good Shepherd, think of me
With Thy most sweet compassion,
  Unworthy though I be.

In Thy sweet arms abiding
  For ever would I rest,
In Thy dear love confiding,
  And with Thy presence blest![29]

When the last note of Cleving's sonorous voice - which, though I could not see the singer from where I sat, could easily be distinguished and rang with the fervour of devotion - had died away, Franz Xaver Münch, Divisional Chaplain of Düsseldorf, ascended the pulpit. He was a tall and powerfully built man. With authoritative dignity he stood and looked down upon his congregation of all grades and all arms, of horny handed soldiers and Sisters of Mercy, of Protestants and Catholics. The service was a joint service for all creeds. The priest himself was a

29. "Ancient and Modern Hymns," version slightly modified. - Translator.

Catholic. But now, in the German nation's greatest hour, all barriers of creed were broken; there was no longer any distinction between Protestants, Catholics or Jews - there were only *Germans*. "We have now all become as *one* man, and we all have *one* God."

But the priest stood in the pulpit and delivered the following sermon:

"Dearly beloved friends and comrades!

"'O Sacred Head surrounded!' This is how the German master Grünewald, the placid, great mystic, saw Him when he pictured that Divine 'Man of Sorrow,' His pain and His wounds, and His bruised and pierced body! This is how Bach beheld Him when in his ' Passion according to St, Matthew 'he prayed and lamented over the dying Son of God: 'Help, ye daughters… help me lament!'

"In this sacred hour, when we mourn our dead heroes, we realise more powerfully than ever before the passion of Our Lord. For are not we Germans ourselves undergoing our Passion, and is not our Empire itself transformed to a suffering Christ? We too have passed through our hour of trial on Mount Olivet when, with our Emperor, we prayed that 'this cup of suffering might pass away' from us, and obeying the unfathomable Divine Will, we began to drain it. We too felt the war weighing upon us like a cross, and we are bearing its burden, trusting in the same aid which comforted our Heavenly Master. We too have been forsaken by those to whom we had only shown what is good and right, and around us too has roared the cry, full of hatred and envy: 'Crucify him!' And like the Master, we too, in this our German Passion, are bearing wounds, among which the noblest and most bloody are our dear dead Germans!

"Standing by the common graves in which we have buried our dead, we lament deeply and sorrowfully. For we Germans too can weep and lament! And with our lamentations mingle the sobs and wailings of the poor German widows and orphans, whose husbands and fathers rest in foreign soil.

"And yet we do not sorrow like the heathen who have nothing to hope for. Even the dead live, and urge us on to the task incumbent on the living. I fancy I can hear, from those trench graves, the imploring, earnestly beseeching cry: *'See to it that our sufferings may not have been in vain!'* The task which the dead lay upon us is, untiringly, and with the utmost exertion of all our powers of mind and body, to accomplish the work of liberation of our threatened empire. From the earliest times it has been a prominent characteristic of German effort in every domain to go about the task in hand thoroughly and perseveringly and to accomplish it accurately in every detail. This purely German talent we shall also employ, with all the energy mercifully bestowed on us, in this fateful hour. Just as in times of peace we were a nation who created new resources, beneficent even to others, so we will not now rest till we have forced upon our enemies a peace which shall not only bring a new spring of prosperity to our land but shall also be a guarantee for the tranquillity and security of all Europe.

"Yet another cry I seem to hear from those trench graves: *'Do not forget our sufferings and our wounds!'* My dear comrades! Those among our people who still retain their moral earnestness will never forget the wounds and the sufferings which this war has brought with it. The price of our liberation and of our victories is the most precious and most noble that a people can pay - the blood of our young manhood! Come and see how we are burying the young! We cannot even give them a plain coffin! We cannot, as the ancient Teutons did, raise them on our shields and carry them over hill and dale to their German home. But, dear brethren, I know of a sarcophagus which is more precious than a coffin - fashioned by the hand of a greater Master - I mean the sarcophagus of the German heart. Deeply enshrined there, let us lay our dear dead to rest and carry them home with us, some day, to the Gennan native land. And if, some day - which God our Protector in our German fight forbid - a time should come when a generation of young men and young women does not know what the peace and the new prosperity of the empire has cost us, when people in laxity and luxury only live to enjoy the fruits, when people abandon themselves to the strange gods of demoralising and pernicious habits - then, my dear brethren, the time will have come for us, who have been standing to-day in sorrow around these tombs, to open the sarcophagus of our hearts and exhibit to a slothful generation our dead, their wounds and their dying moments! Then the spirits of the fallen shall fight another and a harder fight against those of our own people who no longer preserve the memory of the gaping wounds of war in the innermost recesses of their soul!

"Thus this day on which we commemorate our dead is in reality a day of surging life, of new hopes and of urgent tasks. These graves are a gigantic reproach to our enemies, but to us they will be a sacred memorial in the time to come. Those who have sown the storms shall reap the whirlwind! And this whirlwind is now raging over their land! Led astray by petty motives and by small groups of selfish partisans, 'they have sown in the flesh and they shall reap destruction.' We venture to swear before God that we have sown in the spirit of righteousness and peace. To us the war is a momentously spiritual matter, which touches the innermost heart of a nation which has risen in unity, which has been hurt in its most sacred sentiments, and has been forced to defend itself. "And through the Spirit of Righteousness and Peace our people shall reap eternal life. Amen."

"O God, who by Thy holy Apostles hast commanded us to love the Ruler Thou hast given us, pour the richest blessings on our Emperor and all his house! And above all we pray Thee, in these the great days of fateful warlike complications, to bestow Thy grace on our Imperial Lord! In holy trust and deep humility he has committed his people to Thy protection! For the sake of all of us, preserve his health and strength! Enlighten him in his counsels! Comfort him, while with a father's heart he grieves over the wounds of his empire! Reward him with victory for his army, and with an honourable peace! This grant him, God, the Righteous, for the sake of the atoning death of our Divine Lord and Saviour! Amen."

"O Lord of Hosts! Uphold our brave German Army! Thou knowest what a righteous cause it is fighting for, and how it is pressed by enemies on every hand! Grant its leaders wisdom and skill, - grant its soldiers the spirit of constant self-sacrificing courage and ready obedience! Let them all find shelter under the wings of Thy mercy. Thy divinity and Thy grace! Grant us this through Thy son our Heavenly Lord and Saviour! Amen."

"O Lord and Saviour Jesus Christ, who Thyself didst live, with Thy holy parents, a holy family life, have mercy on our families at home! Protect our fair and fertile land, our villages and towns, our fields and vineyards; our trade and handicraft! Protect above all our German youth - Thou the divine friend of children! Let the young be deeply imbued with the import of the times and with love of their native land, in this fateful hour! But especially comfort each wife whose husband is resting in foreign soil, for Thy Father is the God of the widows and the fatherless! Thou Thyself hadst a mother whose heart bled with pain and grief! Console the mothers, give comfort to the children! Have mercy on brothers, sisters and betrothed who are mourning their beloved dead - Thou who livest and reignest from eternity to eternity! Amen."

The bands play a hymn whose magnificently solemn notes re-echo through the church. A quartette strikes up the *Ave verum corpus natum* and finally the congregation sings the doxology:

"Mighty God, we worship Thee,
Lord, we praise Thy glorious name!
Heaven and earth bow down to Thee
And Thy wondrous works proclaim!
As from all eternity,
Thou for evermore shalt be!"

The High Mass was over and the soldiers filed out, past the little maid who, thanks to Schiller's magnificent romantic tragedy, was no stranger to them. The candles might well be lit in front of her - had she not vanquished the English? The French Maid, as she stands there, brings to our minds those proud words which the German bard put into her mouth when, a prisoner in the hands of the English, he makes her boldly exclaim to the ferocious and insolent Queen Isabeau:

"France never shall the Briton's fetters bear.
No, never! For, ere that, it shall become
  One vast engulfing tomb for all your hosts!
The flower of your army's gone - betimes
  Think of a safe retreat - already now.
Your glory's faded and your might is broken!"

Perhaps there were also some in Bapaume Church who thought of those grand words, in which Schiller makes her predict the ultimate triumph over truth:

"Without the Will of God no single hair
Falls from man's head! - See yonder sun
  Descending to the horizon - Yea, as surely
As in the morn he'll rise anew in splendour.
  As surely comes the day when truth prevails!" -

Then the lights were quickly extinguished and the Maid of Orleans remained alone, pensive and still.

Pastor Münch remarked to me how profoundly impressive it was to witness the soldiers' and officers' spiritual cravings during the war. At divine service the churches were always crowded, and hundreds of soldiers were attending the weekday Vespers. The sermons were printed in tens and hundreds of thousands of copies for distribution in the trenches. War was carried on, not only with rifles, bayonets and artillery, but also with the weapons of the fear of God and prayer!

For his own part he thought that Catholics and Protestants, however strictly they each adhered to their own particular tenets, yet well understood each other. The German Catholics had most fervently taken to heart the situation of their common fatherland in the face of the war, and their sentiments were as genuine, sincere and true as those of the Protestants. Perhaps one of the results of the war would be that the two creeds would have learnt to esteem each other and to abstain in future from dwelling on those points in which they were most strongly

Band playing beside Faidherbe's statue.

German soldiers beside the French General's memorial.

at variance. Already it had been realised in German evangelical circles that, although the Roman Catholic Church comprises all nations, yet the German Catholics were fighting with unshakable consistency and conviction for German national interests.

A sanguinary reminiscence of the Franco-German war is connected with Bapaume. On January 3rd, 1871, impelled by the precarious situation of Paris, General Faidherbe attacked, with the French Northern Army, - the 22nd and 23rd Army Corps - General Goeben's forces, collected in and about Bapaume, whose nucleus was the 15th Division of the , 8th Army Corps. The Germans held their main position though outnumbered by more than two to one, but at the end of the day were totally exhausted, and moreover short of ammunition. General Faidherbe, on the other hand, saw his best troops badly spent and the *Gardes Mobiles* demoralised by the fatigues undergone. He would not venture another blow, and fell back on Arras and Douai. The deficient military training and discipline of the French militia rendered it impossible for the General to take advantage of the otherwise favourable situation.

Forty-four years have now passed since then, and Bapaume is once more in German hands. The French have erected, in the centre of the market place, a statue of Faidherbe - a worthy memorial to a brilliant career. Time after time this brave man had been entrusted with the solution of important tasks at home, in Guadeloupe, in Algiers, Senegal and Kabylia, until in the end he was appointed by Gambetta, in November, 1870, to the command of the Northern Army. He was by no means lacking in courage, confidence, initiative, patriotism and fervent zeal, but with his militia troops he was like a general without an army, in the face of the thoroughly and carefully trained Germans.

Faidherbe survived his failure for a good many years. He died in Paris in 1889 after eighteen years' grief at his generalship being wasted uselessly in consequence of the blindness and ignorance of those who represented the nation and who brought that nation to the deepest abyss of national misfortune ever witnessed in our times.

There he stands, in bronze, on his white pedestal - one of the victims of his nation's baneful mistake. And around him stand sons of the people who vanquished him, now following victoriously in the footsteps of their fathers. There he stands, defiant and resolute, with crossed arms, his right hand clasping the hilt of his sword. His whole bearing seems to evince an unflinching resolution not to recede one step but only to push forward! His greatcoat seems to flutter in the wind, and his cap is jauntily cocked to one side. He bears his head high and proudly, his eyes are turned towards the German troops - now as in the days of the past. For now, as then, he has closely serried ranks of German soldiers before him. Many of those who had attended the church service have now assembled in the market place. The German military band forms a semi-circle in front of Faidherbe's statue. Baton in hand, the bandmaster steps forth, and now the "Watch on the Rhine" rings out. Grand, sonorous and stirring, its notes swirl round the hero up there on the pedestal. He seems more defiant than ever, with his bared sword, and an air of deep tragedy seems to hover about his features!

But the German musicians and their comrades stand calm and undismayed; a sentiment of confident expectation of victory pervades all these warriors. Cleving begins to sing and others join in, until a mighty wave of song sweeps over the market place:[30]

"The tocsin rings like thunder peal,
Like roar of waves and clash of steel: -
To th' Rhine - the Rhine, - the German Rhine!
Who will keep guard upon the Rhine?

Chorus:
Be undismayed, dear country mine:
Firm stands and true the watch. - the watch on th' Rhine!
(Rep.)

Through hundred thousands thrills the call
And boldly flash the eyes of all:

30. *"Die Wacht am Rhein."* Having failed, in this and in other instances in this book, to discover an "authorised" version, the translator has been compelled to make literal translations himself.

452

The German, loyal, staunch and true,
Protects that sacred landmark blue!

(Chorus)

He gazes upwards to the sky.
Where valiant fathers dwell on high,
And proudly vows: For evermore
Shall German stay the Rhine's fair shore!

(Chorus)

While yet a drop of blood we hoard,
Have yet an arm to wield the sword -
To pull the trigger yet one hand -
No foeman's foot shall tread this land!

(Chorus)

The vow rings o'er the wave-swept vale-
Proud banners flutter in the gale -
On th' Rhine, - the Rhine, the German Rhine -
We'll all keep guard upon the Rhine!"

(Chorus)

Before we left the market square we looked in at the Base Commander's office, to see the old Bavarian Colonel who had been so ungracious on my arrival in Bapaume. But now, as I have mentioned, we were firm friends.

The brilliant assembly of guests round the Duke's hospitable board included on this occasion the Chief of the Staff, Count von der Schulenburg, a lively and pleasant gentleman, who evoked great merriment by his happy wit.

When the guests had departed, we mounted the Duke's car and drove to Hamelincourt, whither we had been invited for tea by Rittmeister von Hollen. When we passed through the village before, night had fallen; now we inspected more closely the slightly damaged church and a few wrecked houses. Even this little place was swarming with troops and officers; we also met a stout and jovial Catholic priest who had been out that day to the foremost fighting line to preach. He had passed through the most remarkable adventures with his lively little grey cob, and he recounted some of them while we were seated at von Hollen's hospitable table.

On the notice-board of the Townhall we had seen the announcement: "This afternoon at 5 P.M. a short service will be held in Bapaume Cemetery in commemoration of our fallen comrades." When we left Hamelincourt, we therefore made straight for the cemetery. Crowds of officers and men were filtering along the paths between a forest of crosses and tombstones. There was here a common grave, in which Frenchmen and Germans have been resting side by side since 1871, also some fresh graves dating from the present war. A surgeon lay buried here, whose fox-terrier, for three days and nights, could not be induced to leave his master's grave,

A group of nursing sisters come bearing large wreaths wherewith to adorn the graves of the dead soldiers. The band strikes up a slow and solemn funeral march; a preacher delivers an address in remembrance of the dead, and a choir of Bavarian Landsturm men ascend a little mound and pay homage to their fallen comrades in beautiful song. They are good-natured fellows, these powerful and strong Bavarians, but in war they are awkward customers to tackle. Then they no longer think of *"Eine ganz frische Blume"*[31] and can even dispense with their beloved *Hofbräu* beer. Their younger comrades in the trenches are notorious for their eagerness to fight and for their undaunted courage. They never give way. If the word is given to charge with the bayonet, nothing can hold them back. A Bavarian "Hurrah" is something terrifying. But when the enemy throws up his hands and yields himself up as prisoner, these warriors become their old gentle selves. If the situation permits it may happen, however, that they rummage in their opponents' pockets and knapsacks for cigarettes. When, in the former war, the Germans

---

31. Title of one of their songs.

reproached the French with having pressed half-savage and heathen races into their ranks, they are said to have replied: *"Eh bien, vous avez vos Bavarois!"*

On the extreme fringe of the audience stood sixty Landsturm men, who had been ordered to the cemetery to open fire in case a hostile airman should show himself. Aviators are mostly out between five and six, and the air was calm and clear this evening. Just imagine what havoc might be wrought if a bomb or two were dropped among these closely packed crowds! While the priest is speaking, the warning whir is heard overhead. But not a muscle moves on the faces of his audience; the preacher's voice never falters nor does he lose the thread of his discourse for an instant. One little sister alone raises her blue eyes to the sky, but seems quite unconcerned. "It is a German airman," the Duke whispers into my ear, and he told me afterwards that one soon learnt to distinguish French from German aeroplanes - by their sound. The German machines have a duller note.

On returning home I called in as usual to see M. Cossart and Mdlles. Lengagne, and sat and chatted with them for half an hour. They had been greatly upset on hearing that large numbers of the male population of Bapaume had been carried away into captivity in Germany, but on enquiring into the matter I was able to assure them that at most only a hundred were in question, who were considered of military age and had therefore been taken away to be interned; they would return after the war in unimpaired health and strength. Then I told them about the incidents of the day, the High Mass and the music in the market place. They themselves had not been out of doors; they *would not* go out - they *would not* hear the Prussian music in Bapaume! What could I say to console them? How can one console people who see their countryside occupied by hostile armies? It could not cheer them to hear the latest news from the theatres of war - about Hindenburg's fresh advances in Poland, and the doings of the Turkish fleet in the Black Sea! And if I did say anything of the kind they simply would not believe it. I felt very sorry for them - just as I did for Faidherbe, out there in the market place!

But it was now nearly seven o'clock, so I crossed the street to call for the Duke. We were to drive to Douai, where we were invited to take supper at 8 p.m. with the Chief of the 6th Army, Colonel-General Rupprecht, Crown Prince of Bavaria. The distance is nearly thirty-four kilometres and can easily be covered in three-quarters of an hour, but the numerous posts stationed on the road took up much of our time. It was five minutes to eight when we arrived. An adjutant conducted us to a drawing-room, and we had not waited half a minute when the Crown Prince entered.

He is one of those rare men whom all love and admire - all except the English, for I think that even the French cannot help paying him a meed of respect. In the German army he is looked upon as a very eminent general - a born strategist and a thoroughly schooled soldier. As regards appearance, manner and speech, he is fascinating and congenial in the highest degree, neither regal nor humble, but without artifice and modest like an ordinary mortal. When one *knows* that he has recently experienced the greatest private sorrow which could befall him, one fancies, perhaps, that one detects a trace thereof in his features - an air of sadness - but otherwise he does not betray, by a look or a sigh, how deeply he grieves over the death of the little prince of thirteen, the darling of all Bavaria. When the country and the empire are in danger, all private sorrows must be put aside! The Crown Prince has no time to grieve or to think of the void and bereavement which he will feel on his victorious return to Munich. He lives for and with his army, and is like a father to each and all of his soldiers. He devotes all his power of mind, all his physical strength, all his time, to the one great object which dominates all else in the minds of the whole German army.

Crown Prince Rupprecht walks in with brisk and easy stride, stretches out his hands towards us and gives us a truly cordial welcome. And then he adds half-humorously: "I expect some other distinguished guests at my table to-night."

"Who can that be?" asks the Duke.

"The Emperor!" replies the Crown Prince, and claps his hands.

"The Emperor?" we cry, for we had no idea that His Majesty was in this part of the country.

"Yes, the Emperor has visited several units in this neighbourhood to-day, and has promised... Hush, I hear his car!" and with that the Crown Prince hurried out.

Meanwhile the Officers of the General Staff of the Army came to greet us, and presently the Emperor's suite, among whom I knew several, also entered. Before I had time to wonder where the supreme War-Lord himself had gone, we were asked to step into the dining-room. The Emperor was already seated at the table. We all stepped up to our chairs, but no one seated himself. The Emperor sat with bowed head, looking very grave. But suddenly his blue eyes flashed up, and he nodded kindly in all directions. When he caught sight of me, he extended his hand across the table and cried gaily: *Guten Tag, mein lieber Sven Hedin; es scheint Ihnen gut zu gefallen in meiner Armee,*[32] a sentiment which I confirmed with the greatest alacrity.

Perhaps it might amuse the reader to hear who were the ten people seated round Crown Prince Rupprecht's table. Duke Adolf Friedrich of Mecklenburg sat at the Emperor's right, and Prince Löwenstein at his left. Right opposite the Emperor sat the Crown Prince - the host - with Colonel General von Plessen, Adjutant-General, at his right and myself at his left. Next to me on the other side was Lieut. General von Marschall, with Colonel Tappen, of the Crown Prince's staff, on his left. To the left of Prince Löwenstein sat General Falkenhayn, Minister of War, and between him and General von Plessen the chief of the Crown Prince's staff, General Krafft von Dellmensingen. At another table of about the same size, covers had been laid for the other gentlemen of the Emperor's and Crown Prince's staff and suite.

The Emperor was in brilliant spirits. I really do not know whether he *can* be otherwise, for whenever I have had the honour to meet him, he has always been merry, amiable and witty. He can certainly express at times in words of thunder his displeasure at some contemptible act on the part of the enemy, but he is soon sunshine again and bursts into irresistible laughter at some whimsical idea. He has a wonderful gift of

32. "How do you do, my dear Sven Hedin; you seem rather to like being with my Army."

instilling life into a party and keeping the conversation at high pitch - as he did here for over two and a half hours. He told us a great deal of most interesting news, things which had happened in different parts of the field during the last few days and which, at least to me and to the Duke, were news indeed. If one asks the Emperor any question about the conditions in more or less remote countries, as to which sparse or contradictory information has come to one's ears, he will, off-hand, and with a masterly marshalling of facts, deliver a veritable lecture on its internal and external policy, its public sentiments, its resources, and its military strength. I think I have never met a man who can rival Emperor William in this respect.

He also possesses the faculty of grasping with lightning quickness and judging the opinions expressed by others. He listened with the liveliest interest to Crown Prince Rupprecht as the latter gave him various details about his army, and to me when I described the bombardment of Ostend.

It was past half-past ten when the Emperor laid down his cigar and rose to say good-bye with that vigorous hand-shake which leaves its mark on one's knuckles. The Crown Prince alone accompanied him out into the hall, which immediately adjoined the dining-room and from which a few steps led out into the road. A soldier stood ready holding the Emperor's light greyish-blue cloak, with dark fur collar; another handed him the plain Prussian officer's field-cap. After the host and his guest had exchanged a few more words they went out to the car, which drove off rapidly into the night, whereupon the Crown Prince rejoined us.

We then arranged plans for the morrow - another trip northward. Captain Lübke was ordered to accompany us. He was to watch for us when we returned to Douai about ten o'clock.

So we said good-bye to the Crown Prince of Bavaria, Chief of the 6th Army, and left his quarters where we had spent a memorable evening. Our return journey was most tediously delayed by the zeal of the guards posted along the road. Every moment we were stopped, and if we gave the slightest sign of disregarding the challenge, the sentries at once prepared to fire. Any attempt at running away might have cost us our lives. We therefore stopped discreetly. The commander of the picket came forward and turned his lantern upon us. The Duke asked why the guarding of the road was so much stricter now than it was three hours ago. "Well, we have received information that a couple of spies in German uniform accompanied by a woman, are out driving in a car somewhere in this neighbourhood. We have orders to let no one pass, no matter whom, without the closest scrutiny."

"Well, that is right; watch well, lads! Good night!" the Duke exclaims as we drive on - until the next lantern once more compels us to stop.

CHAPTER XXII
ENGLISH PRISONERS FROM YPRES

U P BETIMES FOR early Mass and away across Artois' desolate plains to Douai! At the headquarters of the Chief Command we were met by Captain Lübke with his car, and he introduced us to two other participants in the day's excursion, Councillor Göppert and the Austrian battlescene painter, Professor Hans von Hayek, Thereupon we jumped in and tore away past Pasteur and Joan of Arc, before whom we had no further occasion to stop. We were through the town in a twinkling, and drove out under the *Porte de Roubaix*, following in a north-easterly direction the long unbroken street connecting Lille with Roubaix.

At the latter place we came across 250 English soldiers who had recently been captured, together with a number of officers, all of whom were to be conveyed to Germany in the afternoon. The men were lodged in a large hall, probably a dismantled restaurant. There was no furniture, but large beds of straw had been spread out on the floor, especially along the walls. Here the men could fix themselves up for the night. They certainly had nothing to complain of. One "Tommy," who had a slight wound in the head, was just being treated by an English doctor, who was also a prisoner. An adjoining room with a glass roof contained long rows of tables and chairs, where the prisoners took their meals. Here I photographed a couple of groups, and the reader will be able to see for himself that the English soldiers in German captivity look neither downcast nor ill. In one picture they even have a rather cheeky and lively Frenchwoman, inclined to stoutness, sitting between them, and I must admit to their honour as serious soldiers, that it was she who begged and prayed to be allowed to be photographed with her allies and customers -

Tommy Atkins at Roubaix.

The French waitress and her English customers.

for the noble lady was no less a person than the chief waitress, and it was she who saw to it that the prisoners were amply and well fed.

In the restaurant kitchen the prisoners' fare was being cooked in large caldrons, and here, too, the kitchen staff was predominantly French. Anyone accusing the Germans of stinting the prisoners' food allowance should take a peep at the restaurant in Roubaix. Everything was most ample and excellent. It is true that they got no oysters, truffles, lobster or plum pudding. But they got sound, solid food, and these mercenaries, who perhaps were natives of the east end of London, had probably not for a long time been so well looked after as at Roubaix. Moreover, the French waitress was not a little in love with "Tommy Atkins," and watched over him as the mother eagle watches over her brood, to see that he always had plenty to eat.

A few days previously the catering, both in food and other things, had threatened to assume more liberal proportions than the German authorities thought desirable. The fact was that the citizens of Roubaix had decided to make a collection of *Liebesgaben* for the English prisoners. But then the Germans thought that things were going a little too far, and stepped in and prohibited the intended feast.

In the great hall I found other members of the genus "Tommy Atkins" resting on the straw. They looked well and cheerful, and many had attractive, manly and kindly features. When I stopped in front of a group to talk to them, they made no sign of rising, but answered very politely and with the ineffable calm which distinguishes their race. They said straight out that they were satisfied with the treatment they received and with the food given them. One of them thought that one could not very well expect in war better treatment than they received here. The only thing that worried them was that they were not allowed to smoke in the hall. But the German officer standing by explained that the hall was built of inflammable matérial, not to speak of the dry straw, and that the Germans had no wish to see their English prisoners burnt, A large and pleasant room on the first floor accommodated three English officers, a captain and two lieutenants, and a French captain. Each of them had his own bed, clean and neat-looking, and the room also contained tables and chairs and other useful and necessary furniture. The Frenchman was in mufti, and explained, when I asked how this was, that he lived in Roubaix, and had received permission to fetch fresh clothes from his home. Like the others, he had nothing to complain of, but he was deeply distressed over the misfortunes which had come over France. He wept as he spoke of it, but comforted himself with the thought that the pendulum would soon swing the other way. Germany *could not* in the long run keep her end up against the combined armies and navies of France, Britain, Russia and Japan, no, not even with the assistance she got from Austria-Hungary, but I could tell that his hopes were not very deeply rooted, for tears welled up in his eyes as he spoke. Poor French captain! Think how he must feel, first to be taken prisoner on the field of battle, and then to sit as a prisoner in his own native town, with his wife and family close by. But he admitted that the Germans had treated him kindly.

It is really horrible and distressing to see two of the world's leading cultured nations endeavouring with every conceivable bait to lure the Japanese into sending their armies to the European battlefields to destroy Germanic culture. What would the result have been had this plot against the white race been successful? The whole thing is unthinkable. One obvious effect would have been the weakening of the white races in favour of the yellow. What would the future have had to say to a diplomacy which thus administered its charge? Happily the Land of the Rising Sun has wiser and more farsighted statesmen than the Western powers. The Japanese realise that if the Europeans continue to destroy one another, those areas in the Far East which mean so much to them, will drop like ripe fruit into their hands without a single Japanese soldier having to spill his blood in the land of the white races. And, besides, has not Japan herself immense problems to solve on the coasts of the Pacific Ocean and among its islands? Is it not in Japan's interest that the war should leave Germany's enemies as weak as possible? The more feeble they are after the war, the greater are Japan's prospects of figuring as their heir and successor in the Far East. But even for the solution of these problems, which belong to the near future, Japan requires a considerable display of force. In her own obvious interests she must conserve her forces during this world struggle, and patiently bide her time. Then, far beyond the European battlefields, she has another political problem looming up on the horizon - America.

Whilst I was talking politics with the French captain the Duke stood chatting with the English soldiers. I saw him point to me, and heard them exclaim: "No, really, *that* fellow?" A moment later I had my revenge and told them who the German officer was that they had been talking to, and this surprised them even more. Perhaps they themselves will tell of our visit when the hour of peace has struck.

One of the lieutenants was a well-bred and pleasant young fellow, the son of a prominent merchant in London. His father did business with Germany, and he himself had stayed there - I believe in Hamburg - to learn the language. He said that the war had turned all his plans completely upside down, "but we had no option but to come into the war," he thought.

We took a friendly farewell of the four officers, and drove back to Lille to pay a visit to the citadel, where a body of Indian prisoners were said to be interned. The French citadel is now a German barracks. German soldiers and military cars and a number of captured guns were ranged up in the yard, but there were no Indian prisoners, I am sorry to say. They had been moved east the same morning - for it is necessary to clear as quickly as possible all available space to make room for the fresh batches which pour in from the front in a continuous stream. However, I could do without the Indians. I had seen them before, in their own country, under India's burning sun. There they are in their element. That is where they ought to be now. But I cannot deny that it would after all have been very interesting to meet them here again, and to find out what they thought of life in the foggy autumn of Artois and Flanders. I myself knew what it was like to try to acclimatise Indians in a colder climate. On my last journey in Tibet I had with me two Rajputs from Kashmir. When we got up amongst the mountains, they nearly froze to death, and my caravan leader, Mohammed Isa, declared that they were of no more use than the puppies we had with us. So they were discharged, and sent back to their tepid valleys. The same thing happened with my Hindoo cook from Madras. I realised that I had been guilty of a piece of stupidity in thinking that they could be used outside India. In Tibet one lives on meat, in India on vegetables. How could they possibly stand a sudden change both of climate and diet?

And now I had read in the newspapers that the British had organised a complete importation of Indians into Europe. I had found it very difficult to believe these reports, but at the front I found that they were really true. "How do you treat these Indian soldiers?" I once asked some German officers.

"We arrest them," one answered, and another added:

"It's not necessary, they soon freeze to death in the trenches."

When I admit that I myself had been guilty of stupidity in thinking that the Indians could be employed in Tibet, I think I am entitled to say that Lord Curzon, who really is a man of character, made a mistake seven times greater when he expressed the hope "that he would see the Indian Lancers clear the Berlin streets, and the little brown Ghurkas make themselves at home in the park at *Sans Souci*."[33] But as regards the actual performance of carrying this importation into effect, I consider it more than an act of stupidity - I consider it a crime.

Great Britain has for nearly 150 years superbly acquitted herself of the task of acting as India's guardian, and I doubt whether any other nation would have succeeded in so gigantic an undertaking. Indian troops have fought with honour against many neighbouring peoples, and have helped to maintain order among the three hundred millions. But never before - until the present Liberal Government tried it - had it occurred to a British Government to employ coloured heathens against Christian Europeans. Such an act is a crime against culture, civilisation and Christendom, and if the English missionaries approve it, they are Pharisees and dishonest propagators of the Gospel - what the German missionaries in India think does not now matter, for they are under arrest. India's British masters rightly despise all matrimonial bonds

33. Quotation taken from Professor Steffen's book on "War and Culture."

between the White Man and the Hindoo, and children of such marriages are indeed to be pitied. They are regarded as, and often called, mules; they are neither horse nor donkey, they are "half-castes." In Calcutta they have their own quarters, and must not live in any other part of the town. But when the question arises of crushing the German barbarians, cooperation with the bronze-coloured peoples of India becomes good enough even for the Englishman.

Is it perhaps thought a fitting act of culture and civilisation, worthy of the twentieth century, to convey the unsuspecting Indians thousands of miles over land and sea to throw them into the struggle against the German army on European battlefields? If this question is answered in the affirmative, I for one, with the memories I have of Asia and Europe, nevertheless retain the unshaken conviction that such conduct is the height of cruelty. I do not mean cruelty to the German soldiers, for I know what they think of their Indian opponents - a blend of contempt and compassion. Besides, I do not think that the sweeping clear of the Berlin streets will come to anything, nor do I think that the trees of

They were clothed in neat and practical field uniforms.

Here and there was a slightly wounded soldier.

Sans Souci will ever spread their shadows over the warriors from the Himalayan slopes, for Ghurhas may be ever so useful in a campaign against Tibetans and other frontier tribes, but in Europe they are no good. Therefore I contend it is an act of cruelty to them to force them over to the white man's country - to die all to no purpose.

What opinion will these Indian troops harbour of their white masters? The future will show, and the survivors - if there are any - will return to India and tell what they have gone through. He who has seen something of the land of the Arabian nights - who has ridden across the crests of Himalaya - who has listened to the sighing of the wind through the deodars of Simla - who has dreamed under the moon of Tadj Mahal - who has seen the Holy Ganges slowly glide in ashen ringlets past Benares quays - who has been spellbound by the stately procession of elephants under the mango trees of Dekkan - he, in short, who loves his India and admires the order and security which British rule has brought into this vast country, needs no imagination to understand the thoughts with which the Indian soldiers will return, and the feelings with which their families and countrymen will listen to their recitals round the fireside of the humble little cottages in Himalayan valleys. I think of it all with a feeling akin to horror, for I cannot rid myself of the conviction that here, in the name of civilisation, a crime is being committed against humanity and Christendom,

Kipling has described (in "Mandalay") in glowing, unforgettable lines the longing - one might almost call it the homesickness - which the English soldier feels who has served his time in India or Burmah.

If the English soldiers long so, with what feelings must not the Indians themselves dream of their homeland's sunshine, its palms and tinkly temple bells! But their longing is vain. They have been taken to Flanders' bloody battle-front and trenches to die instead to the music of German shell fire.

One cannot help asking: "Are these Indian contingents really necessary? Do not Great Britain's, Canada's and Australia's white millions suffice, not to speak of Frenchmen, Belgians, Russians, Serbians, Montenegrins, Portuguese, Turcos and Senegalese negroes? No, it almost looks like it. In "The Times" of September 5th I read in the biggest and fattest type the following heading: *"The need for more men."* So already at that time more men were needed to eradicate the "culture "of the German barbarians." In the article following this heading I read the following words: "The educational campaign undertaken by the Prime Minister as to the origin and purpose of the war had a splendid opening in the Guildhall yesterday."[34] So there was to be an educational campaign! So the British nation must by special means be educated up to understand the cause and the object of the war! Otherwise the Englishman will stop at home and play football and cricket. No doubt the education is to be coupled with a lesson in the course of which one learns what use the Hindoos are going to be - in an emergency. The situation should really be judged against the background of G. B. Shaw's very sensible words to the following effect: "What we must bear in mind is that if our side wins, the consequences will be a shifting of the balance of power in favour of Russia, a situation which will be much more dangerous to all the other contending parties than would be the triumph of Germany, a result which we are now by war endeavouring to prevent."[35] In other words, a Russian victory will be much more dangerous to the warring states than a German victory. For an all powerful Russia would threaten the whole of Europe, including England and her mastery in India, but a victorious Germany would entail no menace to Europe. One must forgive the British if they need a specially organised education to understand such a complicated problem!

And what is this new popular education going to turn out like? The answer to this question is given in the English press every day. It consists in a systematic suppression of the truth. The fatal and momentous reality which is slowly bringing England to the brink of a catastrophe must be concealed under an exceedingly severe press and telegraph censorship. Of Hindenburg's victories the English people have not the remotest idea. The realisation of the German operations in Poland is distorted

---

34. Steffen, page 115 et seq. are well worth reading.

35. Steffen, page 97.

The last houses of Kruiseik.

into futile attempts to stop the victorious Russian march towards Berlin. The most shameful lies and malevolent calumnies are disseminated concerning the German Emperor. The Teutons are barbarians who must be crushed, and this laudable enterprise must be shared by the cultured peoples of Serbia, Senegambia, Montenegro and Portugal. The whole war is conducted on the English side on a foundation of distorted information and conscious untruths. The truth is as rare in the English press as lies are in the German. But do the people really believe all that is said in the English papers? They do, blindly and absolutely. Of this I have been convinced by letters received from England.

When one asks English prisoners why they joined in the war they answer more or less logically: "We must obey orders, you know." If one goes further and tries to find out the reasons for England's participation, the answers become less certain: "We must keep abreast of German competition; we must defend Belgium, whose neutrality we have guaranteed; England was bound by treaties and must keep her word."

In the press one finds yet further reasons, such as the necessity for destroying German militarism! An appeal which was sent to me and which is signed by many learned men, including several Nobel prize winners, concludes with the words: "We deeply regret that under the unfortunate influence of a military system and its lawless dreams of conquest, the state which we have once honoured now stands unmasked as Europe's common enemy and as the enemy of all peoples who respect the law of nations. We must carry to an end the war to which we have committed ourselves. To us, as to Belgium, it is a war of self-defence, fought out for liberty and peace."

At the same time as one feels grateful for the information that it was for the sake of liberty and peace that England declared war on Germany on the 4th of August, one cannot help feeling a little surprised that the learned gentlemen who have put their sonorous names to this paper could believe that the neutral Germanic nation of the North could ever be induced to see in the Germanic nation of the South its own and Europe's most dangerous enemy.

A shell crater in the road is being filled by engineers.

472

Hussar patrol. Riding through Kruiseik.

The talk of German militarism recalls the old parable about the mote and the beam. Is not Britain's supremacy of the sea built up on a military system? Can one imagine a more widespread militarism than that which spreads its recruiting nets over five continents, which reaches gratefully after the straw held out by Republican Portugal, and which advertises in every newspaper and at every street corner "the need for more men"?

The warning words of Kipling written after the Boer war now ring with a deeper and more earnest meaning than ever before.

If English culture and English learning accuse German militarism of indulging in dreams of lawless conquest, I ask: How about the Boer war? Is it perhaps an expression of the same humane solicitude for the small States that now induces England to break a lance for the sake of Belgium's independence? It would be a wasted effort to attempt to elucidate now, when it is too late, how the great war would have developed had England kept out of it. But one thing is certain, namely, that had she done so, Belgium would not have lost her independence for longer than the duration of the war. The war would not then have assumed the dimensions of a world war such as it is now - the greatest and most tragic catastrophe that has ever visited the human race. No nation has had a greater and more world-wide responsibility to bear than England.

Before this spectacle and generally before the situation in which Great Britain now finds herself every sincere friend of England must shudder at the meaning of it all as he reads and re-reads Kipling's "Recessional" written for the Sixty Years Jubilee in 1897. The whole British Empire was then in transports of exultation over the history of past years and over the fabulous power and glory of the immense Empire. Kipling alone stood like the guardian of the nation's conscience and his voice was lifted up in words which will re-echo as long as there is a Briton left in the world.

Now that I have unburdened my heart to the English, let us continue our trip after the pause in the Citadel.

We drove out through the *Porte de Gand*, where there is quite a crush of fresh troops marching to the fighting line, wounded soldiers on the way to hospital, motor-lorries, ammunition columns and all that we are accustomed to see on the great war roads. On the left, we leave the *Fort de Bondues* - one of its towers is visible from the road. In the same direction, but far away, we see a captive balloon at a height of 150 metres. In its car sits an officer with a telephone through which he speaks incessantly. He cannot be reached by the enemy fire, and yet his life is in danger all the time. A little while ago one of these balloons was hit by a bomb dropped from a great height by a French aviator.

At Linselles we stopped a moment in the market place whilst Captain Lübke entered a house to find out how far we could travel in the direction of Ypres. Whilst we were waiting. Crown Prince Rupprecht came walking along. It happened to be his dinner-hour. We chatted a couple of minutes, pausing a moment whilst an officer handed in an important report. The Crown Prince was visibly pleased with the news and hurried up to his dinner to return immediately to the fighting line. We met about twenty officers during this short pause. It was impossible to catch and note all the names in the course of the brief introduction. But one thing I do remember, and that is that they were all cheerful, friendly and full of youthful vivacity: *"Nun wie gefällt's Ihnen, Herr Doktor? - Was denken Sie von unseren deutschen Soldaten, famose Kerls, nicht wahr? - Draussen in den Gefechtslinien ist's etwas heiss, aber doch grossartig."*[36] And so on, always in the same light-hearted and jovial tone, as if it were a question of manoeuvres; no difficulties, no unpleasantness, simply "quickmarch and keep your eyes open!" - Forward, that is the main thing. Officers whose duty compels them to remain behind the firing line always long to be where the danger is, but as they always march at the head, the casualties amongst them are proportionately greater than among the men.

We drove on northward to Wervicq and across the La Lys Canal, which forms the frontier between France and Belgium. A large part of the population has remained and makes a curious picture in these quaint old streets where German kitchen wagons stand steaming and

36. Well, Doctor, and how do you like it? What do you think of our German soldiers? Fine fellows, eh? - A trifle hot out in the firing line, but otherwise first-rate."

smoking at quiet street corners. We advance but slowly. The whole road is encumbered with infantry, horsemen and vehicles. Here comes a party of 150 men armed with spades. "Where have you been?" we ask. "We have been to bury the dead," they answer as if they were saying the most commonplace thing in the world. They looked more like conquering heroes than grave-diggers. They were not singing to-day, but they found it quite natural that when all Germany's men are fighting for their country, not all can hope to return home, some must remain behind in the foreign soil, and the sacrifice is one which all are willing to make when it means Germany's salvation.

Here lies a wrecked windmill with broken sails and near it a motor-car which has come to grief. The transport trains which we pass are as usual wreathed in foliage to mislead aviators. The smell of burning strikes our nostrils - it is not to be wondered at, for just to the left of us a whole village is in flames. I became a victim of the same excitement that I had felt each time before as I had approached the danger zone.

Presently we come to a village bearing eloquent testimony to the cruel realities of war. It boasts the peculiar name of America. At the last house in the main street we stop to make sure once more how far we may drive. Colonel von Oldershausen steps out. He is a magnificent type, a thorough soldier, straight as a poker, stiff and gracious at the same time. "Listen," he said in answer to our question, "drive first to Kruiseik, two kilometres from here. From there you may continue one kilometre on foot until you come to the crossing between this road and the Ypres-Menin main road. If you wish to go further in the direction of Ypres I should advise you *not* to take the main road as the whole avenue is covered by the English artillery fire. But if you keep a little way outside the ditches," he went on, "it is not at all unlikely that you will come back with a certain amount of life left in your bodies."

Leaning against the car, the Colonel stood gesticulating with great animation and tried to describe the situation which would have greeted us, had we continued on the main road. He fully meant what he said and assured us that he had tried several times the prescription he now recommended to us - without once being killed! The day before

First came a German soldier with an English Colonel on his left.

Then came the convoy.

yesterday he had made an attack at the head of his regiment in which a third of his men had fallen; of the others, 150 got the Iron Cross. The object was realised. The enemy's position was taken and several prisoners fell into the hands of the regiment. An English officer with whom the Colonel had been conversing had made the following remark: "We don't mind your shells, and don't care a rap about your shrapnel. Your rifle fire doesn't frighten us, and we can put up with your bayonet charges. But when your men commence their infernal noisy hurrahs, it is all up with us. There is nothing in the world so trying to the nerves. One feels entirely paralysed before these confounded jerky hurrahs."

So we took leave of the excellent Colonel and drove on in accordance with his directions. On our left, to the westward, we saw the familiar little puffs of smoke caused by the shrapnel bursting. A little further on a French airman was having a trying time with the German fire. Just as we drove into Kruiseik a shell came whizzing right over us. A large force of infantry reserves was quartered here, and the streets were crowded with officers and men. We pulled up by the side of a house and waited awhile. We were strongly dissuaded from continuing. On the previous day Kruiseik had been exposed to severe shell fire, and at the entrance to the village the road had been destroyed by some nasty holes, which were just being filled in by the engineers. Any moment we might expect a further pounding, as the enemy artillery had not changed its position since yesterday. I was much struck with the immovable calm with which officers and men stand here waiting for the fire and a very good chance of being killed. The same calm and light-hearted indifference also characterised the troops which we met further on towards Ypres. Take for instance that little hussar patrol riding towards the road swept by the English shells.

"*Deckung gegen Flieger!*" ("Take cover against aviator!") roars an officer, and immediately everybody flattens himself against the house walls so as to present as small as possible a target from above. I suspect, however, that the aviator who was just that moment soaring over Kruiseik had something else to think about, for the anti-aircraft guns must have given him a lively time. Anyhow, he dropped no bombs on us. We had thought of returning to Bapaume, when someone came up to us with the news that if we liked to wait a minute we should see a batch of British who had just been captured at Ypres, which was only nine and a half kilometres from Kruiseik. They were 390 men all told and were expected to arrive any moment.

True enough, it was not long before the street was black with human beings. There they came, Albion's proud scions. If you examine closely the five photographs which I took of them whilst they were marching past the outskirts of Kruiseik, you will get a very good idea of what a brand-new convoy of prisoners from the front looks like.

First came a German soldier with an English officer on his left side, a tall man of distinguished appearance. He carried his hands behind him, under his greatcoat; he did not seem to notice us at all, and appeared quite unmoved by the harrowing events which he had doubtless witnessed that very day, and his glance was fixed with an expression of utter indifference on the horizon straight ahead of him.

Then came the convoy, three abreast, the most diverse types one could imagine, dark and fair, handsome and ugly, well set up and slouching, cheerful and downcast. As I lifted my camera at them, a facetious Tommy cried out, "May I have a copy, sir?" The German guards did not love their charges. That, after all, is easy to understand, but I saw no expressions of hatred. Rank after rank drew past. They were dressed in practical and neat uniforms, a little browner in colour than the German. Most of them had nothing to carry, but some wore coats slung over the arm or over the shoulder. Some were smoking. Here and there was a slightly wounded man. When they came inside the village, they were all ordered to halt and here the prisoners were allowed to rest awhile, although they looked by no means tired. A young German lieutenant who was present when they were captured and who now headed the convoy, assured me that this particular English unit had surrendered five minutes after the attack began. But up to then they had obstinately defended their position. All the Germans I spoke to were of the same opinion respecting the individual bravery of the English - it was above all praise. The rear of the convoy was brought up by a row of carts and wagons containing seriously wounded English soldiers. One of them, I think he was a Colonel, lay comfortably on a stretcher which had been placed right across a cart, as shown in the accompanying picture. He was pale, but did not complain and lay with eyes closed without noticing the noise and bustle around him. Perhaps his light was going out, perhaps his heart had already stopped beating. Slowly the cart disappeared from view in the long procession of wounded Britons.

A moment later we, too, were travelling southward and once more drove past the melancholy cortege, "My poor old Tommy," I thought to myself, "you have plenty of time before you to ponder over the problem why you, of all men, have been fighting against the German 'barbarians' and whether your pay was worthy of your doughty deeds between Ypres and Kruiseik! If anyone confronts you with this poser you will always answer: 'I don't know I'm sure, I had to obey orders, I suppose.' But it will never occur to you to reply: 'I had to go over for a while and crush the German militarism, you know,' for such an absurd idea would remind you too forcibly of the parallel argument of putting down the drink by consumption!"

The life at and behind the front is rich in contrast. A few hours after we had seen Tommy's tragic convoy disappear in the distance, we were listening once more to Cleving's inimitable jest and song.

CHAPTER XXIII
FAREWELL TO BAPAUME

THE DAY OF Hubertus falls on November 3rd, and is celebrated throughout Germany with the diligent pursuit of game, for Hubertus is the patron saint of all huntsmen. Nor even at Bapaume was the day allowed to pass by unnoticed. A field of fifty-five officers of all ranks forgathered early in the day at the village of Miraumont, situated nine kilometres west of Bapaume, immediately in the rear of the fighting line. With Captain Schlüter of the cavalry as guide, I drove out with Duke Adolf Friedrich to Miraumont to be present at the day's sport. We took up our posts on a hill by the side of the road, and had an excellent view over the broken country with its natural and artificial obstacles.

We had not been there long before a couple of horsemen hove in sight, and immediately on their heels came the entire field in scattered groups. They took the fences and ditches in fine style and then disappeared up a steep hill like a whirlwind. There was nothing remarkable in this, nor perhaps in the fact that amongst them were many riders who would never see sixty again. But the remarkable thing about this ride was that all the horses were recently requisitioned farm animals, which had not even been trained. The Germans spare their horses no less than their men. When the horses of cavalry and train begin to tire and need rest and care, they are replaced from the farms of Germany and of the conquered countries.

After the sport all the members assembled in a field, where in the shadow of the willows a table stood laid with sandwiches, *kaltes Aufgeschnittenes*[37] and hot punch. Here I made the acquaintance of many of the horsemen, among others Infantry-General von Soden

---

37. Cold collation

The convoy halted just outside the village.

An English Officer on a stretcher placed across a cart.

and Lieut.-Gen. von Pawel, who had been in command in Kamerun. The crisp, clear autumn weather seemed to create the highest of spirits. Nobody could have imagined that we were almost in contact with troops engaged in severe fighting, had not the booming of cannon reminded us of it. Indeed it would have been difficult to gather an impression of anxiety, nervousness, hurry or want of officers as one listened to the animated conversation and contagious laughter of the grey-clad warriors of Miraumont. One would have thought, on the contrary, that war was the simplest thing in the world and that the Germans for the moment at least were not exerting themselves in the slightest. What they gained, they clearly gained without difficulty, albeit that for the time being they are content with merely holding their positions.

Suddenly we got something else to think of, and the familiar cry, *"Deckung!"* rang out across the field. An airman flying the tricolor was seen to be approaching. The main thing was to bring the horses as quickly as possible under the shadow of the willows, but the officers, too, together with their civilian guest, thought it wisest to withdraw to the nearest avenue of trees, for had the airman suspected for |a moment that he could have killed fifty precious birds with one stone, he would certainly have sacrificed all the bombs in his armoury. Gradually he came nearer, glided past immediately above us, but could not have noticed anything, for not a single bomb burst in our vicinity, and soon the hostile aeroplane disappeared in an east -north-easterly direction. It could almost be taken for granted that his goal was a certain flying station, which had recently been favoured with several bombs.

Presently we saw the characteristic little "tufts of wool" forming round the airman. They came from nowhere, grew, and were followed by a flash and a report. They have a peculiar knack of remaining for a long while at the spot where they are formed. Hence, as the Frenchman progressed on his journey and the guns kept firing at him, a little string of white cloudlets gradually formed in his wake, sharply defined against the blue background of the sky and pricking out his track through the air. One of the officers thought that the firing was almost as dangerous as the bombs, seeing that the shrapnel bullets must obviously come down sooner or later, and that when they do, they strike with the velocity and deadly effect of a rifle bullet.

When this little excitement was over, the party of officers grouped themselves with the Duke and the two Generals in the centre, and I took a few groups which would have been the finest and most distinguished in my collection had not this particular roll of films turned out a complete failure on development.

The next item on the programme was Frenchman number two, who came sailing serenely along over our heads and gave rise to the same precautions as before, but he likewise failed to realise the fine catch he might have made.

A German airman told me one or two details from his own experience. He usually required three-quarters of an hour to rise to a height of two thousand metres, and did not proceed towards the French lines until he had reached this altitude. The view is glorious. He has the landscape in which the fighting is raging right underneath him. In fine, clear weather he can see plainly the marching troops, the ammunition columns and their transport trains, even when they are covered with foliage. He spots the artillery positions, unless they are too thoroughly concealed by hedges and bushes. He can even see isolated horsemen and pedestrians on the roads.

But there are many other things that meet his eye in the course of his aerial adventures. He sees the fire and smoke from the German and French guns, and he sees the impacts and the explosions. Beneath him rages a constant turmoil of thunder and lightning. He admits willingly that he is a prey to intense excitement. He has never yet been wounded, but his machine has had its wings perforated by bullets more than once, and the holes are mended with little patches. He hears the rattle of the machine guns and the rifle fire, and knows that all this noise is for his benefit and that he is being observed through field-glasses from every conceivable hiding-place. When he hears this eternal din and knows that at any moment he may be hit and brought to earth, he must indeed summon all his self-control to retain his presence of mind, for a situation such as this may overstrain the strongest nerves.

He is out to do his duty, he *must not* fail. He cannot entirely eliminate the nervous tension, for he is but human, but he never turns back until he has carried out his orders and finds out what he *must* know. His attention is strained to the highest pitch, he sees everything, hears everything, nothing escapes him. He sights far away a French aeroplane steering straight towards him, but he does not change his course. They come nearer and nearer to one another. Neither makes the slightest sign of giving way. The spectator from below cannot but think that they are sailing to an inevitable catastrophe, that they are lost already. But they seem to change their minds before it is too late, for a collision would bring them both to earth and kill them, and this is considered by both parties to be a useless and unpractical sacrifice. Hence one of them gives way before it is too late. The Frenchman is often armed with a machine gun for the benefit of his German colleague. In that case the German by a skilful manoeuvre suddenly dips under his opponent or passes over him. If he passes under, the machine gun becomes useless, as it cannot fire downward. If he passes over, he benefits by the protection of the lightly armoured bottom of the aeroplane. The main thing to avoid is to remain on the same plane with the other machine. Again it may happen that the Frenchman likewise rises, and that a sort of skyward race begins between the two opponents, each trying to get above the other. In such cases the breathless spectator sees the machines circle round each other like a couple of playful may-flies, approach, separate, pursue, fire, but always avoiding collision. It is a tension which simply cannot be described, and whilst this goes on in the air the guns thunder angrily below and the soldiers lie in wait for one another in the trenches.

When everything goes normally, the airman may be up for three hours. When he has completed his task he returns to the German lines, stops the motor and glides to earth in four minutes, although the time seems infinitely longer. He volplanes down and may under certain circumstances alight without restarting the motor. He admits that it is not without some feeling of relief that he sets foot on the ground once more. Yet he is never entirely safe, for the flying stations are always singled out for special attention from the enemy bomb throwers.

French airmen often go up without an observation officer, but his weight is taken up instead by an extra bomb supply. When the machine is burdened by the weight of two men only three bombs can be taken, otherwise six or more are carried. The accuracy of aim depends on the amount of practice. Most bombs do no harm at all. Curiously enough, it seems to be the horses who suffer most. A few days ago an airman passed over a bivouac in the neighbourhood of Bapaume, Five men thought it advisable to seek protection underneath a heavily laden baggage wagon. But as luck would have it the wagon was hit, and nothing but the lacerated remains of the men remained when help arrived.

I have already spoken of the immensely important role which aeroplanes are playing in this war, and how during the few months the war has lasted they have been manoeuvred with continuously increasing skill. My informant thought he was justified in saying that the side possessing the best flying machines and the best pilots would come out the winners in a war of entrenched positions, a literal siege war, such as is now proceeding on the western front. For it depends in a very large measure on aerial observation whether the artillery fire can find its target and score with decisive effect.

On our return to Bapaume we went to call on Divisional Pastor Münch, at whose house we were regaled with coffee, together with quite a crowd of doctors. All the war hospitals of the town together now contained barely five hundred wounded, and the city was therefore more than amply provided for with its 130 nurses.

We looked in at the chief hospital, in the chapel of which some French wounded were being tended. One of them had received a bullet through the base of the nose which had lodged in the brain, where it still remained. He cried all day, *"de l'eau, de l'eau,"* and if one gave him water he drank, but went on calling, *"de l'eau, de l'eau."* Another, who also had a bullet stuck in his head, wandered about with quick, jerky steps, and had to be watched so that he did not tumble on to the beds. Two others had had a leg amputated, and were now out of all danger. The Frenchmen spoke well of the German nurses and doctors, and said they could not have received kindlier treatment in their own country.

One soldier complained because he was separated from his people, but added: *"Nous sommes très bien ici; nos blessures sont très bien soignées."* We also made a hasty round of the German wards and spoke to the wounded warriors. They were all, as usual, in cheerful spirits, and hoped soon to be put right so that they could go back and fight again.

On the way home Pastor Münch told us of a little episode which is rather illuminating. As I have mentioned before, it is strictly forbidden throughout the German army to take anything, whatever it may be, in a house or church in the occupied territory, and any breach of this rule is very severely punished. Now it so happened that a gentleman who served in the army had discovered amongst the vestments of a village church in the neighbourhood a piece of embroidery which he intended to take home as war booty. When his offence came to the knowledge of his superiors, he was discharged and sent home. Had not extenuating circumstances existed, he would have been still more severely punished. To carry away "war souvenirs" is considered in the German army to be equivalent to theft. To be dismissed for such an offence is a terrible disgrace at a time when no one can conceive a greater happiness than to be allowed to serve his country in the field.[38]

After sitting chatting for the last time in the dim lamp-light with Monsieur Cossart and the demoiselles Lengagne, I proceeded with my most gracious friend, Duke Adolf Friedrich, to the officers' mess, where the rest of the day and a good part of the night was passed in a most agreeable atmosphere of gravity blended with humour. Among the guests I met Colonel von Alers, late of the Second Artillery Regiment of the Prussian Guards; he is related to our Swedish Counts Wachtmeister. He had fought in the wars of 1866 and 1870-71, and was no chicken. But he meant to fight for his country once more, and so he turned out as volunteer. Nothing but real men wherever you go in Germany! Age is nothing, whether you are young or old it is all the same, and no one is too old to remember that he is still a man.

---

38. This relentless severity, as actually practised, shoulf be compared with what the champions of truth in *The Times* and *Standard* have to say about the German "Huns", "incendiaries" and "burglars". Steffen, pp.132-133.

In the morning of November 4th the Duke and I were seated at our usual breakfast tête-à-tête. We were quite ready to start off, my luggage had already been stowed away in the car, and I had taken a hearty farewell of my German friends who happened to be about and Monsieur Cossart. Now I was off to Metz, a distance of about two hundred English miles, Duke Adolf Friedrich himself took charge of the steering wheel, and I sat beside him, map in hand. A soldier was seated inside the car.

At 9.20 A.M. we started. It was the fastest journey I have ever experienced, a record in speed. The Duke drove and managed the car with amazing coolness and presence of mind. Where the great main road was straight and clear he spurted up to between ninety and one hundred kilometres an hour. I felt sometimes as if I could hardly breathe, but it was a glorious sensation to fly over the country at this mad, tearing pace.

At 9.52 A.M. we entered Cambrai where the Red Cross flag over the school-house was still wrapped in a thin veil of fog. To the right of the road was a large common grave, richly ornamented with flowers, and in the fields close by French peasants were gathering in the sugar-beet. A whole column of heavy carts loaded with beet drove up into a village we passed, but in this case the drivers were French peasants.

At 10.25 - Le Cateau. From this point we turned off on to some by-roads without stone-paving in the direction of Bergues and Le Nouvion. The civil population here is fairly numerous, and whatever else there may be a shortage of, there is certainly no lack of poultry. Le Nouvion has been hardly dealt with. In the main street there are only a few houses left, all the others are in ruins. At the far end of the village a road runs through a wood where barricades have been thrown up. German troops are only met with in the large places, such as Hirson, where a fort meets the eye to the right of the road.

After a long pause necessitated by a burst tyre we arrived at Mézières at 12.52 and crossed the Meuse. Half an hour later we drove into the market square at Sédan, where Turenne was still looking down on the disquietude of distant generations. Here we sacrificed an hour for dinner, and were soon off again in the direction of Carignan and Montmédy, where we found life was as busy as ever.

Group of Officers at Bapaume- the Duke, the Prince, the Chief of Military police, Clevig, Baron Fleming and others.

An enormous ammunition column had come to a stop at Barbas.

The next place we come to is the grey and solid-looking Marville. Afterwards the country becomes more broken, until we reach the utterly ruined village of Noërs. At one point the road rises, curving slightly. We are tearing forward at a furious pace when just on the crest of the hill we meet another car as much in a hurry as ourselves. We had the narrowest possible escape from colliding at an aggregate speed of about 120 English miles an hour. There could not have been room for a sheet of paper between the two cars and we had the Duke's perfect coolness to thank for having escaped with our lives from that little adventure.

Next we drive into our old friend Longuyon and follow a long straight street which has suffered less than other parts of the town. Outside the wall of a house stands a group of workmen who have finished their day's toil, and on the other side some children are playing in the gutter. Opposite, on the left-hand side of the street, stands a curly-headed little chap of three or four in a blue smock, watching the other children. We come along at full tilt and are some twenty metres away from him when the little fellow takes it into his head to cross the street. I felt how I froze stiff and went quite white in the face. I leant forward to try to get hold of his head to throw him backward from the car. Surely this wretched people had suffered enough as it was! We were now into the bargain to run over its children, its one hope for the future after the war had wrecked and ruined its homes! It would have been my fault, for why had I decided to travel to Metz of all places, through this country where the population drops from year to year even in peace time and where every child is so precious! I can see him now in front of me. He was in the attitude so characteristic of running children, his body leaning slightly forward, head down, arms bent and raised, hands levelled with the ears, slightly curved and with the palm facing forward. He did not see the car, never noticed us and did not realise the danger, simply staring on the pavement and intent on reaching the others. The car came nearer. I seemed to feel the slight jolt as the wheels passed over him and crushed his ribs. It would have been quite impossible to stop. Instead the Duke put on a spurt and in a second we were past. How could we have comforted the wretched sorrowing parents, when there was no comfort to give? We should of course have had to stop in any case. I could see in my mind's eye the pitiable little funeral procession to Longuyon cemetery, and seemed to hear the bells ringing among the ruins. At the same instant as we passed the little group of workmen and playing children, I almost flung myself upright in the car and turned round. There stood the little chap in the middle of the street with hands clasped and looking after us in mild surprise. Not a hair of his head had been touched.

Presently we come to Xivry. The light begins to fail. By the roadside stands a row of pathetic little wooden crosses; some of the graves are adorned with helmets, but when the spring comes doubtless the helmets and crosses will disappear and the little mounds will be levelled by the plough. Darkness descends over the earth. We pass through Briey and cross the German frontier. Seized with a feeling of ease at being once more in Germany, we drive past the memorable St. Privat and through a bewildering chaos of main roads, by-roads, suburbs, tramway lines, bridges and vehicles all lit up in turn by our headlights and vanishing behind us. But by degrees the confusion disappears and we debouch slowly and majestically upon a brilliantly lighted street in Metz. There are enormous crowds of people afoot. They line the pavements in serried ranks. Officers and soldiers everywhere. The police keeps order. At a street corner we come to a halt and have to wait a minute. The Duke asks a policeman what is up. "It is the Emperor, he is due here in a moment; the Empress is here already." We decided to preserve our incognito as much as possible. The whole town was filled with officers. The hotels had not an inch of room to spare, we enquired at six different hotels and at last, at a third-class place, we found a moderately decent room and "cupboard" on the third floor. The Duke would not allow me for a moment to sleep in the latter, his splendid gifts of hospitality would not desert him even here; but I declared that I would sooner lie in the street than in the big room, whilst he lay in the cupboard. Of course we were both equally obstinate - without that quality we should not have got through Africa and Asia. At last we agreed to draw lots and I drew the cupboard and slept excellently when once I got to bed and had finished thinking of the curly-headed little boy.

But it is still far from late. It is only nine o'clock and the Duke's hospitality will not be denied. So we went to the *Europäischer Hof*, where the Duke ordered a sumptuous champagne supper. There we stayed for several hours talking of the wonderful things we had seen together during the last few days, commonplace enough for him who is a soldier, but the more exciting and unforgettable to me.

The witching hour of midnight had already struck when we quite suddenly caught sight of the Deputy-Governor of Metz, General von Pelkmann of the Artillery, a little man with a grey moustache, very eccentric, with very decided views on life, on the universe, and on the whole creation generally. In his company was Baron von Tauchnitz. That the latter was *"Kommandeur der Kraftfahrtruppen des Armeeoberkommando Falkenhausen"* [39] was not to be wondered at, for he was no less a person than the nephew of the head of the great publishing firm known throughout the Continent by its "Collection of British Authors, Tauchnitz Edition." This chance acquaintance, in itself very agreeable, had the result that I could not resist the temptation to accompany Baron Tauchnitz on the following morning to Blamont, where a fight was to take place and where a French position was to be stormed.

It was nearly three o'clock in the morning when the Duke and I returned to our humble establishment. I had arranged to call at 6.30 in the morning for Tauchnitz and the officers whom he was to drive to Blamont. The Duke, on the other hand, was due to return to Bapaume at about nine. Thus we were not to meet again for the present, so I said good-bye and thanked him as heartily as my restricted powers of eloquence allowed. For he had not only given me his time, his hospitality and friendship, he had given me opportunities of visiting some of the most remarkable points in the fighting line and of gathering deep and abiding impressions of this great world war. But the recollection I cherish

---

39. Commander of the Mechanical Transport of the Falkenhausen Army Headquarters.

most of all from that memorable week is that of his own personality, for he is a fine and noble man, a man whose outlook is not dimmed by his exalted birth and the glamour of fame, but who remains ever modest before men and humble before God. We felt quite sure that we should meet once more at some future time. Then we would empty the store of our memories and would recall the shrapnel shells at Quesnoy, which whizzed so close over our heads but forgot to burst and part us for ever from each other.

And now, to conclude, one more hearty handshake and *"Auf Wiedersehen!"*

CHAPTER XXIV
A FINAL DAY ON THE WESTERN FRONT

NEEDLESS TO SAY the human alarums at the hotel forgot to call me in the morning, but happily I awoke without their aid and dressed quietly as a mouse so as not to disturb Duke Adolf Friedrich. Thereupon I wandered off in the pitch-dark night with no other weapons than my Zeiss glasses and my camera to the *Europäischer Hof*, where the others were already assembled. I was asked to join the party in the car driven by Tauchnitz, and already occupied by Captain Kriebel and Lieut. Baron von Peihmann, both attached to the General Command of the Falkenhausen army. Our road took us south-eastward *via* Château-Salins in German Lorraine. We crossed into France further south at Rixingen.

It was 7 o'clock when we started off. Day was just beginning to break, but the sky looked threatening, the weather was most unpleasant, and a thin layer of clayey mud lay over the hard surface, making the road as slippery as soap. My two companions inside were as agreeable and as light-hearted as all other German officers whom I had met. As we were skimming along, the pretty and interesting country we were passing through was being explained to me on the map. We were only a few kilometres from Rixingen when one of the pipes of the engine broke, and the car absolutely refused to move another inch. However, providence has presented us with legs, and so after walking a short distance we came upon a motor-driven hospital wagon, on the roof of which we made ourselves comfortable. We were soon to find that this motor conveyance was not without its dangers, for the wagon skidded about terribly on the slippery road and threatened any moment to dive into the ditch. However we held ourselves ready for any emergency so as at least to fall feet foremost when the catastrophe came. In the end we managed to get to Rixingen and reached the commandant's office just as the wagon began skidding so hopelessly that the back wheels took command and the whole bag-of-tricks was on the point of overturning. Our somewhat eccentric entry into Rixingen aroused violent mirth from all who happened to be about. Here, however, we secured a third car and drove on gaily to Blamont.

On leaving the village to the southward, the road turned up a hill to a slight eminence, the right-hand side of which was wooded. In a field immediately to the north of the little wood and evidently concealed by its trees, stood a battery, which was thundering away for all it was worth. It was really a very impressive sight to watch the guns firing their salvos. The officer in charge gave his orders in a loud voice according to the information received from the observing station. Then followed the usual brief, brisk words of command: "Load! Ready!! Fire!!!" The target for the moment was the village of Ancerviller, situated about 5600 metres south of Blamont. As the gun is discharged a sheaf of fire issues from the muzzle and a white smoke cloud forms several metres in front.

In order not to attract the attention of the enemy, instructions have been given that the battery must only be approached on foot. On the crest of the hill stood the local commanding officer, Lieut.-Gen. von Tettenborn, acting Adjutant-General to the King of Saxony, surrounded by his staff, some twenty officers. He was a powerfully built little man with steel-grey hair and moustache. Hung over his shoulders he carried a light brownish-grey cape with red collar and on his head he wore a helmet with a grey cloth cover. Reports kept pouring in regarding the progress of the action. Now it was a horseman, now a motor-cyclist, now a car that came tearing along at full speed with information, whilst orders were sent out with equal rapidity to the various fighting units.

General von Tettenborn received me with the greatest kindness and we stood chatting awhile on the hill as if there had been no war within a hundred miles. I was also introduced to all the other officers and in two minutes I felt thoroughly at home. The general atmosphere here was exactly the same as I have had occasion to record and admire all along the front, calm, reliant and cheerful in the consciousness of the monstrous strength of the German army.

Two kilometres south of Blamont and about half that distance from the point where we were standing, lies the little village of Barbas in a picturesque hollow, its church tower dominating in a lordly manner the pretty little red-roofed stone houses beneath. One and a half kilometres south of Barbas, sharply outlined against the light rising background, were two little dark clumps of trees. On the north side of these coppices two German batteries were actively shelling the enemy positions. On the western border of the wooded belt to the right infantry fighting was in actual progress. At the moment the Germans were proceeding to the attack of the French positions. Both sides had concealed themselves gingerly behind trees and bushes, but the rattling fire from rifles and machine guns was deafening. One moment the shots would succeed one another in a continuous din, the next minute one heard but isolated reports. Of the actual fighting itself we saw nothing, but it became evident in the course of the day that the centre of activity was shifting southwestward, which meant that the German attack was progressing.

Behind us the battery at which we had just stopped kept pounding away, and once more we heard the horrible, sinister whistle of shells pass overhead. The German artillery was very active, but the French did not reply to the fire. Towards the afternoon the German fire also ceased, the attempted goal having been reached. It was assumed that the French batteries, which had but lately occupied this point, had now been removed to some other place where they would come in more useful. I for my part was quite content to do without their fire, and it was a pleasant and restful experience not to have to be in constant dread of a shell coming on the top of me. The day before the French had sent a couple of shells into Blamont, but without doing any appreciable damage. Neither did we see any aviators on this occasion. I was told that they were less numerous in these parts.

After a short visit to Blamont cemetery and a walk through the pretty village, where we dined, I returned with a couple of officers to the hill, but found it deserted. The General and his Staff had, it appeared, advanced a couple of kilometres to Barbas, where we found all the officers assembled in an open space, a cross between a street and a market-place. This had now become the point from which the operations on the whole front of the division were directed, and horsemen and cycle-orderlies kept dashing backwards and forwards as before on the hill.

I remained at Barbas for another four hours and took the last photographs destined to appear in this book. Wherever I turned, I found picturesque and warlike subjects for my camera. In the open space referred to, officers with maps in hand stood gathered in little groups. Outside a house, several horses stood ready for the orderlies. In the next street, which was part of the great main road, an ammunition column had halted. It extended from one end of the village to the other and a bit beyond as well. The wagons were crowded with artillerymen, full of life and in good spirits as usual, and they usually asked for a photograph when I came along with my camera. On the fore-carriage of a gun sat a man fast asleep. In the outskirts of the village two companies of reserves had halted and were evidently waiting to take their place in the firing line.

"How are you, boys?" I asked.

"Oh, first-rate, but it's a nuisance to have to lie and wait like this."

"What are you waiting for?"

"Why to go ahead and fight, of course."

Here I found a chaplain, a strikingly humorous and amusing man, who knew thoroughly how to get on with the soldiers; but then he had been in war before, in Pekin and German South West Africa. As we stood chatting on the road, we were gradually surrounded by a narrowing circle of grey jackets, who listened intently to what we had to say. In the end they must have numbered fully 150, and there, in the centre, stood the pastor throwing out jests and calling them his grey field-mice, and they all laughed gaily at his whimsical ideas.

"What do they do for a living in peace time, I wonder, all these soldiers?" I asked.

"Oh," said the pastor, "there are all sorts, loafers and county councillors, blacksmiths and professors, all jumbled together."

Kitchen wagons.

On the fore-carriage of a gun sits a soldier fast asleep.

"What is your occupation, my lad? "he asked of one who stood near, as he seized him by the collar.

"Lecturer," he answered.

"What subject?"

"Comparative philology of modern European languages."

"Excellent! There you see, doctor, what use the philology of modern European languages can be put to!"

"And what are you?"

"Metal worker at Siemens and Halske's."

"And you?"

"Village schoolmaster."

"And you?"

"Navvy."

"And you?"

"Professor of zoology."

"There you see the levelling effects of war. No trace of class distinction. They all lie side by side in the trenches, eat the same food and are comrades through thick and thin, and the professor is no better treated than the navvy."

"How many of you are keeping diaries of your war experience?"

"I don't write a line," said one, standing with his hands in his pockets in front of the circle.

"Why not?"

"There are plenty of them who do as it is."

"Nonsense, you are a lazy beggar," says the pastor.

"All who keep diaries, put up their hands," said I, and a perfect forest of hands rose into the air.

"Perhaps it will be simpler if those who *don't* keep diaries put up their hands."

They did so, and there were ten out of fully 150. What a monument of memories and impressions, of wild adventures and heroic deeds told in simple and honest words must they not represent, these diaries, written from day to day between the fights, in the trenches and by the light of the bivouac fires!

To conclude, I asked in a loud voice - although it was a stupid thing to do and I ought to have known better - *infandum jubes renovare dolorem*: "How many of you are social democrats?"

At this there was a shout of laughter, almost of derision, and I suddenly felt exceedingly awkward and wished I were back at Metz again. Even the pastor laughed and shook his head. At last a burly-looking soldier answered for himself and the others:

"There are no social democrats any more. *There are nothing hut German soldiers.*"

I made a desperate attempt to cover my retreat by saying: "Of course, of course, I know; but are there any among you who have *been* social democrats?"

Some shouted no, others shrugged their shoulders and one replied: "Even if there *have been* social democrats among us, all that rot has been washed away by now. It is real and serious business we are dealing with now, and none of that kids' game!"

Presently the men were ordered to form up and the circle melted away, leaving me alone with the divisional pastor and three young officers with whom I chatted for a few moments.

Then I went back to my friends and travelling companions from Metz. The day's work was over. The result of the achievements of the day had been reported to the General in Command, but they had to wait at Barbas until fresh orders arrived, which might not be until midnight. For my part I could return to Metz whenever I wanted to.

The sun had long since set when Captain Kaufmann came up and offered me a seat in his car. He was a fine fellow and had moreover many memorable and interesting things to tell me from his experiences in the war. So I said good-bye to my charming host for the day, General von Tettenborn, and the other officers, jumped up beside Kaufmann and a lieutenant and in a second we were on the way, eating up the ninety kilometres separating us from our destination in the north-west. We had our head-lamps lighted. At least twenty times we were stopped by the patrols guarding the road, who swung their lanterns across the road and shouted "halt!" I consider we were very fortunate to get through with a whole skin, for if one overlooks a single sentry, it is all up and one gets a bullet through the back. There were numerous cavalry patrols about, evidently on their way home after their scouting in the gloaming. They, too, were stopped by the pickets, for otherwise French patrols in German uniforms might easily infest the roads and villages held by the Germans. We were also stopped on entering and leaving every village.

However, at last we got safely back to Metz, and thus ended my last day at the front.

CHAPTER XXV
HOME TO TRÄLLEBORG

IN THE MORNING of the memorable 6th of November I left Metz by the train for Saarbrucken, the town where the first shots were fired in the last Franco-German war. I had some time to spare, and settled down at a table in the restaurant of the *Terminus Hotel* to read some really recent newspapers. Life seemed to go on here just as usual, and one noticed nothing of the war. The regular customers came in for their *Frühschoppen* (early mug of beer) as they always do, and here and there an officer or a civilian was breakfasting.

At Ludwigshafen a conductor came along and shouted into every compartment of the train that the windows were to be kept shut, and that nobody must lean out whilst passing over the Rhine bridge. It was pleasant to see the alacrity with which his order was obeyed - after all one had plenty of time to contemplate the great and mighty river between that town and Mannheim. Just as the train was starting, this same conductor jumped into my compartment. Aha, I thought, he thinks my shabby field clothes look suspicious in a first class compartment, and he sees that I am busy with map, notebook and pencil. However, I met him half-way in my frankest manner, and asked whether the window-closing order was a precaution against bomb attacks on the bridge. He smiled and answered that the orders were that the windows were to be shut. Then I asked what the consequence would be if one disobeyed the order, opened the window and looked out. "In that case," he said, "there are sentries outside who would note the compartment and the window, and the end would be that the guilty party would land in a place where he would find no windows at all."

At Mannheim nothing happened. But at Heidelberg I had hardly stepped on to the platform before two officers came up to me. One said in firm but very polite tones that I must accompany him to the District

A group of soldiers with the divisional pastor in the centre.

The last picture from the Western Front.

Commandant's office. "Of course," I said, "I shall be delighted, but I hope you will be kind enough to let me bring my hand luggage." "Why certainly," was the answer. On the way to the office, which happened to be close to the platform, the officer remarked: "Your passport must be examined by the military authorities." "Why can't you look at it at once?" I asked, and handed him my pass, now soiled and frayed at the edges. "Well, perhaps I might do so," he answered, and we stopped. He read the paper with General von Moltke's name, turned to his companion and whispered my name in his ear, whereupon both saluted and held out their hands, which I pressed almost as heartily as I laughed at the little adventure.

"Aber Herr Doktor, sie müssen uns dock entschuldigen, wir..." ("Really, doctor, you must excuse us, we...")

"Bitte, bitte, das ist ja reizend." ("But please don't mention it, I am delighted.") Thereupon my German eagles also broke into hearty laughter over their prey.

"Your train does not leave for an hour. In place of the examination at the office, won't you come and drink a glass of beer with us at the buffet?"

"Why, of course, I shall be most happy!" And so the time passed all too quickly, and we got a lot of fun out of the little adventure - an adventure which I might have repeated at every station, had I liked to do so. But it would not do, war is too serious a matter for jest. My new friends told me that the conductor had found me very suspicious-looking, especially on account of my maps and notebook, and had telephoned from Mannheim. At Heidelberg he had conducted the officers to my compartment. I assured them that I could find no words to express the admiration which I felt for the alertness and vigilance which pervaded the whole of Germany from frontier to frontier - it seemed like clockwork where every cog drops into its place with automatic precision, and where the hours strike their solemn strokes to the fraction of a second. When it was time to part they saw me into my carriage, and as the train moved out they gave me a final friendly salute and bade me God-speed.[40]

At Karlsruhe, on the following day, I waited on the noble and high-minded mother of our Queen, the Dowager Grand Duchess Luise, as well as on the Grand Duke and his Consort. I was only due to leave for Berlin by the night train, and was therefore very glad to be able to accept the Grand Duchess Luise's most gracious proposal that I should inspect the gigantic and ideally equipped hospital in the Gewerbeschule under her Royal Highness's own august guidance. I met there two distinguished head nurses, the wife of General von Oetinger and Frau Sautier, also Fru Linder from Stockholm who was here to study hospital arrangements in the field and who had met with the greatest hospitality in Karlsruhe.

It was most touching to see the Grand Duchess, in spite of her seventy-six years, walk from bed to bed, from ward to ward, encouraging soldiers and speaking to them in a way that went straight to the heart. In her black dress and her black lace veil over her head, she looked like a pious abbess giving comfort and solace to the wounded warriors, and indeed she made a most welcome break in their long weary hours of suffering. Behind our Queen's mother came several nurses carrying armfuls of flowers and little packets of portraits of the Grand-Ducal pair. Before

40. This little episode, which seemed as harmless as it was amusing to us three "conspirators" whilst we discussed it over our mugs of beer, found its way into the German press, and was received with much mirth. In the French press it appeared under a different guise. Thus, for instance, the "Journal des Débats," in a telegram from Bordeaux, dated November 22nd, publishes the following: -

"Un télégramme de Bâle dit qu'en quittant l'Allemagne, Sven Hedin l'explorateur suédois bien connu, a été arrêté et retenu quelque temps à Heidelberg comme suspect d'espionnage."

The "Figaro" has quite a little article under the heading of *"Vieil Heidelberg."* Other headings are as follows: -

"Le germanophile arrêté pour espionnage. - Ils arrêtent leur meilleur ami! - Arrestation de M. Sven Hedin. - Arrêté comme espion. - Les allemands soupçonnent leurs meilleurs amis," and so on *ad infinitum.* An English newspaper, the "Newcastle Chronicle," of November 24th, managed to improve on these versions: "The adventure at Heidelberg of Sven Hedin, the Swedish explorer now in the pay of the German Official Press Bureau, appears to have been amusing. He delivered a lecture in public at the ancient cradle of German culture, and knowing him to be a foreigner, the Heidelberg police regarded his intense enthusiasm for the greatness of Germany as suspicious. He was accordingly arrested, and detained for several days until his employers of the Press Bureau could be communicated with and establish that he was not a spy. Perhaps this little experience may cool Sven Hedin's ardour. In any case, why was he lecturing in Heidelberg? His services in Holland or Italy, the United States, or any other neutral country requiring enlightenment would seem natural and appropriate, but surely Heidelberg needs no lessons in pan-germanism."

The surprising thing about the English description is not its wealth of detail given with the same readiness as when it is a question of great and serious matters, such as, for instance, Hindenburg's continuous defeats, the uninterrupted German retreat from Flanders, the funeral of the German Crown Prince, which takes place on an average of about once a month, etc. No, the really surprising thing in this article is that the newspaper would find it natural and suitable if I were to plead Germany's cause in neutral countries, such as Holland, Italy or the United States. *A bon entendeur, salut!*

leaving, this guardian angel of the wounded graciously handed a packet and a picture to each soldier as a souvenir of her visit.

The most delightful part of my visit was the witnessing of the homage paid by the convalescent soldiers to the venerable and beloved lady, as they stood assembled in the great hall of the hospital. When the Grand Duchess came out, they spontaneously broke into the stirring and moving tones of the great German National Hjonn here given in translation: -

(Tune: "Praise the Lord, ye heavens adore Him.")

Germany, be thou exalted
Over every other land,
If but in the hour of peril.
True thy sons together stand
From the Meuse unto the Nienien,
From Adige to Baltic strand, Germany,
be thou exalted Over every other land!

German women, German faith, and
German wine and German song
Shall their ancient fame and glory
Still retain through ages long,
And to noble deeds inspire us
All our path through life along -
German women, German faith, and
German wine and German song!

Unity and right and freedom
For our German fatherland -
This let us together strive for,
Brothers all, with heart and hand! -
Unity and right and freedom -
Pledges of a blessed land -

In the glory of such blessing
Flourish, German Fatherland!

"Thank you, thank you, God bless you all," said the Grand Duchess, and disappeared as unpretentiously as she had come.

In Berlin I looked up several old friends and also had the honour and pleasure to be invited to supper with the pretty, charming and altogether delightful Crown Princess. In the evening we sat round an open, flaming hearth, and I recounted my recollections from the front and from the desert, whilst my illustrious hostess and her ladies-in-waiting were listening and knitting socks for the brave soldiers in the trenches. The Crown Princess had another guest whom it was a great pleasure to me to meet again - Baron von Maltzahn, who now, after his unlucky motor drive, had recovered sufficiently to hop about on crutches.

The streets of Berlin looked the same as they had done two months previously. Men and women, motor-cars and buses moved about as busily as they had done before, and the streets were flooded with electric light all night just as in piping times of peace. At the appointed hour the Palace Guard came marching along *Unter den Linden* as it has always done, with its alluring, rapturous military music calling to fresh deeds of valour. Had one not known it, one could not possibly have guessed, but for the shouting of the newsboys, that the country was involved in the most gigantic war of all time. Neither did I notice any thinning of the numbers of able-bodied men in the streets, and yet had I not seen through the carriage window from Metz armies of recruits, reservists and volunteers all drilling in barrack squares and fields along the line?

It has been stated in certain newspapers that the Germans treated their prisoners of war in a cruel and inhuman manner. That this was untrue like everything else which forms part of the educational campaign, I readily understood, but all the same I thought it would be interesting to find out for myself the facts of the case. Accordingly I paid a visit to the acting General Staff. Not only did they give me the usual prompt permission to go out to the prisoners' camp at Döberitz, but I was given as guide a most capable and learned major.

At the entrance to the camp we were received by a colonel and several other officers, who took us round and explained everything. Here were four thousand Russians, four thousand British and a few hundred French, Belgians and Turcos - I am sorry to say there were no other specimens from the ethnological colour-box at Döberitz. The prisoners live in gigantic tents where they have their beds close together on the ground in four enormous rows. I went into one of the tents and found a group of Russians with caps on the back of their heads and coats or blankets over their shoulders, and asked if they were satisfied with the treatment they received. "Oh yes, nitchevo," was the answer. But one of them shouted, "It is too cold to He on the ground in late autumn." "Yes," I answered," of course it was warmer in the firing lines in Poland. How would you like to go back and warm yourselves a bit?" "No, Heaven preserve us!" came as a chorus on every side.

My old friend Tommy Atkins was strolling about inside the barbed-wire fence and looked and felt very bored. But he was not ill-treated, on the contrary, he was very well looked after. I saw him at dinner with his ally Ivan Ivanovitch. The 8500 prisoners were fed in three-quarters of an hour, and the whole thing was despatched with the utmost smoothness. In front of the kitchen building, in which gigantic caldrons were steaming, railings had been put up, permitting the men to advance in files of eight to the window opening, through which the mess cooks with the adroitness, touch and quickness of a virtuoso filled to the brim the bowls held out to them with wholesome, nourishing, steaming soup. When their bowls had been filled, the men went back another way so as to avoid congestion. The system is the same as at the booking offices at busy railway stations.

The British soldier is, under *normal* conditions, a sinewy and well-knit man, who has hardened and trained his body with football, tennis, cricket and other salutary exercises. But in Germany he merely vegetates and swells in bulk and by no means over-exerts himself over the work offered him in confinement, by which he can earn a couple of *pfennigs* a day for tobacco. If therefore on his return home Tommy tries to make out that he has been living "below starvation mark" in Germany, his comfortably rounded form and his *eloquencia corporis* will give him the lie!

It is surprising and peculiar to see Tommy Atkins and Ivan Ivanovitch arm-in-arm - figuratively speaking, of course! For in the concentration camps they hate one another heartily. Tommy regards Ivan as a lousy savage and Ivan looks on Tommy as an impudent upstart whom the modest patron of the *samovar* ought not to associate with. And yet, for all practical purposes, they march arm-in-arm and use all the most hellish infernal machines of modern militarism to destroy the German militarism and free the earth from the Germanic barbarians. Great Britain and Russia! It really staggers the imagination when one thinks that these two countries have neither in Europe nor in Asia, in heaven nor on earth, *a single positive interest* in common.

We need only think of India, the most precious jewel in Great Britain's crown. Of the possibility of a Russian invasion of India Lord Curzon, the greatest and most clear sighted Viceroy India has ever had, has given utterance to the following: "It would involve the most terrible and lingering war that the world has ever seen; and it could only be effected by a loss, most unlikely to occur, and more serious in its effects upon the human race than that of India itself, namely, the loss of the fibre of the British people." Elsewhere, when saying that India's safety is Great Britain's foremost duty, he speaks as follows of a Russian attack on that country: "It can only be prosecuted in the teeth of international morality, in defiance of civilised opinion and with the ultimate certainty of a war with this country that would ring from pole to pole."

The *Novoye Vretnya* writes at about the same time (1st December, 1888): "Our attention has been focussed on the necessity of bringing Khorasan under Russia's exclusive influence, the more so as through Khorasan runs a convenient road in the direction of Herat and in case of military operations against India, Khorasan would therefore serve as a base of supply for our further operations." Then we have Skobeleff's and Kuropatkin's very detailed and minute plans for an invasion of India.[41]

41. Curzon: "Russia in Central Asia," 1889, and "Persia and the Persian Question," 1892, Vol. II.

Many years have elapsed since Lord Curzon thoroughly and exhaustively, as usual, dealt with this question. But is there anyone who believes that the danger is less serious now that the Russians have been checked in the Far East by the Japanese and in the Far West by Germany and Austria-Hungary? It is true that there is one other outlet in the west - a truth which the *Swedes* should bear in mind. But nevertheless the danger to India is far greater now than it was twenty five years ago.

It is therefore not a little peculiar to see Tommy Atkins helping Ivan Ivanovitch with blood and iron, on land and sea, to gain that power and strength which he needs for carrying out an invasion of India. For England this world war is a national calamity, however it may end. "We have forty million reasons for failure but not a single excuse."

We also visited the hospital at Döberitz, where the prisoners receive all the care that human charity can give to the sick. It is not charity alone that demands the greatest sacrifices in this respect, for a concentration camp where thousands of men live huddled together on one spot *may* become a source of contagion, if ill-managed. Hence skilled doctors, sick attendants and nurses are engaged, and the slightest symptom is immediately followed by isolation to prevent the possibility of an epidemic.

In one of the paths I came across a Tommy walking up and down. He looked very pale, but was convalescent.

"How are you getting on?" said I, but received no reply.

"I hope you will soon become a little bit of all right by and by," I tried once more in my very best colloquial English. Tommy only smiled and looked at me.

"Is he deaf or is he mad?" I asked the doctor who accompanied us.

"No, he is Russian," answered the doctor, laughing. But how this Russian had got into Tommy's uniform remains an unsolved riddle.

It is a rather significant fact that whilst the good-natured Russians need only four per cent of guards, the self-conscious English require ten per cent; in other words, four German soldiers look after a hundred Russians, whilst a hundred English need ten guardians. The reason may possibly be found in the inborn servility traceable to generations of serfdom, but the principal reason of the difficulty in handling the English prisoners is probably that they have no national service and have not accustomed themselves to discipline. The cases of insubordination in the prisoners' camps are almost entirely confined to the British prisoners. The punishment for the first offence consisted in letting the culprit stand a couple of hours to guard the guns on a little flat eminence near the camp, where the wind usually blew cold and strong. After a graver offence the delinquent was usually tied to a tree for an hour or two, but this latter punishment had only been resorted to in isolated cases.

My impression of the treatment of prisoners at Döberitz confirmed all that I had witnessed in this connection at the seat of war. But the world *will* be deceived and is deceived. Hence the educators of the British nation spread broadcast the meanest calumnies concerning the "Huns' barbarity" to their unhappy prisoners.

The magnificent drawing-room inside the hall of the *Hotel Kaiserhof* usually formed the rendezvous of a little Swedish colony in the evening. Here I met Cavalry Captain Count Gilbert Hamilton, who had become a German subject and officer in order to strike a blow in the Germanic fight for existence. He was just on his way to his regiment and was looking forward to a very different reveille from that he was accustomed to at our own sleepy horse-guards barracks at home in Stockholm. Here also I met once more my old friend Colonel Gustaf Bouveng, who had spent two and a half months at the front and who, among innumerable other impressions, was also taking home with him the conviction that in a military sense Germany simply *cannot* be defeated by her present opponents. Instead of tiring and becoming decimated, the German army grows in strength and numbers from month to month.

On the 12th of November I took my departure from the *Stettiner Bahnhof* and set out on my journey home to Sweden. As I reached Sassnitz, dusk was descending over the Baltic. The passports and effects of the passengers were subjected to a most careful scrutiny. The same calm, the same sure self possession, the same discipline and order as I had noticed everywhere in Germany and in the firing lines, made themselves felt here, too, on the outermost planks of the harbour pier. At Sassnitz fourteen torpedo boats lay ready for immediate action, and in the roads a gigantic hospital ship was riding at anchor, ready to receive wounded from the sea.

The ferry cast off her moorings. Little by little in the gathering gloom we lose sight of land, that land whose seconds are as long as years, whose people is now writing its *epos* in runes of blood on the pages of the world's history - a united people, a virile people, a people which stood ready in its hour of trial, armed for the defence of its honour, its liberty and its future when the ravenous monster of strife rose up upon its frontiers, a people which has the *will* to win and which therefore in the time to come will march at the head of the ruling race upon our earth.

But the belt of sea between the ferry and the German coast grows wider. The song *"Lieb Vaterland, magst ruhig sein"* has long since died away. The twilight, the transition between day and night, is over. And in the north bides the deep impenetrable darkness.